AMERICA AND WWI

A TRAVELER'S GUIDE

AMERICA AND WWI

A TRAVELER'S GUIDE

Mark D. Van Ells

Interlink Books

An imprint of Interlink Publishing Group, Inc.
Northampton, Massachusetts

First published in 2015 by

INTERLINK BOOKS
An imprint of
Interlink Publishing Group, Inc.
46 Crosby Street
Northampton, Massachusetts 01060
www.interlinkbooks.com

Library of Congress Cataloging-in-Publication Data

Van Ells, Mark D. (Mark David), 1962-
America and World War I : a traveler's guide / Mark D. Van Ells.
    pages cm.
ISBN 978-1-56656-975-0
1.   World War, 1914-1918--United States. 2.   United States.
Army.   American   Expeditionary   Forces.   3.   World   War,
1914-1918--Campaigns--Western Front. I. Title.
D570.V29 2014
940.4'0973--dc23
                                                2014022829

Printed and bound in the United States of America

TABLE OF CONTENTS

ACKNOWLEDGMENTS

I am indebted to many people on two continents. At the risk of omitting anyone, I would like to thank the following people for devoting their time to answer my questions, send me valuable information, locate source materials, and in some cases guide me to fascinating places I would never have seen or fully appreciated on my own: Philippe Abalan, Marianne Anderson, Eugénie Anglès, Eva Assayag, Louis Aulbach, Alexander Barnes, Curtis Bartosik, Jerry Battle, Christian Baujard, David Bedford, Cecilia Bell, Véronique Bernier, Sébastien Bonhomme, Yvan Boukef, Bill Brewster, Ron Bridgemon, Debra Brookhart, Shelia Bumgarner, Ernest Cable, Martin Callahan, W. Charles Campbell, Frédéric Castier, Hervé Chabannes, Jayne Chapman, Hal Chase, Gilles Chauwin, Ariane Chevalier, George W. Contant, Mike Coonce, Colin Cook, Francesca Costapereria, Christian Couty, Gary Cozzens, Margaret Daley, Michael F. Davino, Simon Davis, Jean-Paul de Vries, Nicholas Di Brino, Barry R. Dlouhy, Tony Dowland, Barbara C. Eberhart, Richard S. Faulkner, Mylène Feydieu, Gail Francis-Tiron, Fred Forrest, Linda Fournier, Michel Gautier, Clarita Geoghegan, Timothy F. Green, Linda Gorski, Jeff Gudenkauf, Alessandra Guerra, Marie-Jo Guyot, Steve Hakes, Carl Hale, Jim E. Hall, Mike Hanlon, Luther Hanson, David Harrison, Cindy Hayostek, Shawn B. Heacock, Karel Herbots, Tom Hill, Julie Hiscox, Russell Horton, Claudia Johnson, Robert Johnston, Gary Kempf, Kaye Kernodle, Bob Kerr, Jake Klim, Ric Lambart, Becky Lambert, Christian Laude, Teresa Leal, Anne-Sophie Lens, Ken Maguire, Michel Mahé, William Manthorpe, Michael Martin, Stéphane Martin, Paul Matthews, Agathe Maugis, Suellen R. McDaniel, Conner McGee, Rainey McKenna, Mike McKinney, Laureano Meir, Phoebe Merrick, Neera Mohess, Emilie Moussard, Joseph Murphey, Eric Nelsen, Malcolm Ogilvie, Benoît Odelot, Tony O'Mahony, Amanda Pearson, Melissa A. Peck, Rick Perkins, Oliver Pinzer, Elodie Pioche, Lise Pommois, Paul-Marie Pouliquen, Chuck Preble, Charles Province, Matthew D. Rector, Mary Redman, Brian Rhodes, Cybèle Robichaud, Pepe Rosado, Mindy Rosewitz, Andrew Ryan, Mitch Ryder, Beate Scheffler, Monique Seefried, Margaret Shields, Becky Slayton, Andrew J. Stevenson, Michael E. Telzrow, David Trojan, Jess Tucker, Ross Turle, Martine Vallon, Tom Vasti,

Katrien Verwinnen, Franck Viltart, Sarah Voiles, Bill Wehner, Mary Whisenand, Ben Whittaker, Giles Williams, Gary Wilson, David Wood, and Andrew Woods.

I would also like to thank my family for their love and endless patience. For them, the only thing more difficult than my absences on research trips was my inattentiveness while I was at home writing. This book is in many ways a family production. One of my daughters, Annika—an employee at our local public library—helped me get my hands on scores of books, while the other, Sarah, provided valued clerical assistance. My notoriously bad French may well have caused some international incidents had it not been for the translation talents of my wife, Paula. *Merci, mein Schatz.* Interlink Books was marvelous. In particular, I must single out Pam Fontes-May, Moira Megargee, Paul Olchváry, Jen Staltare, Pam Thompson, and, of course, Michel Moushabeck. Finally, I would like to thank Edward M. "Mac" Coffman, the dean of America's World War I historians, who gave me much helpful advice and encouragement. For decades, Mac has been trying to convince Americans about the significance of World War I and their nation's place in it. With the Great War centennial at hand, perhaps they will finally listen. This book is dedicated to him.

INTRODUCTION

The Great War. The World War. The War to End All Wars. The conflict we know today as World War I was so bloody, horrifying, and destructive that when it was over no superlative seemed to do it justice. It raged from 1914 to 1918 and left ten million people dead, twenty million wounded, and the stage set for another, even more ghastly world war. It left Europe shattered and the whole world shaken. The First World War was also an immensely important event in American history. It was the nation's first major overseas war, and made the United States the world's most powerful country. It was also one of America's bloodiest conflicts. According to official statistics, 116,627 Americans died in the war and another 204,002 were wounded. Only the Civil War and World War II resulted in more American casualties—and U.S. involvement in World War I lasted only eighteen months.

It is odd, then, that today World War I barely registers in the minds of most Americans. Battles like Belleau Wood or the Argonne Forest were once seared into the nation's consciousness, and seemed destined to be spoken of in the same breath as Lexington and Concord or the Alamo. Today, few Americans know much of anything about them. Americans have long demonstrated a willingness to travel to get in touch with their history, especially when it comes to the places their countrymen have fought and died. The Civil War battlefields of Gettysburg, Pennsylvania, alone attract three million visitors annually. For many Americans, no trip to France is complete without a stop at the D-Day beaches of Normandy. Even in the tropical vacationland of Hawaii, where people go to escape their cares, millions make the pilgrimage to Pearl Harbor and pay homage to the victims of the USS *Arizona*. Sadly, few put the Meuse-Argonne or Saint-Mihiel on their travel itineraries anymore. Browsing the shelves of any bookstore today, one can find numerous guides to the battlefields of the Civil War or World War II, but very few dedicated to World War I, and almost none specifically about the American experience in that conflict.

America and World War I: A Traveler's Guide is for those who wish to follow in the footsteps of the Doughboy—as the American soldier of the First World War was known. (The term's exact origins are unclear, but one common explanation stretches back to the late

1840s—namely, the doughlike dust that settled on U.S. forces as they marched through dry terrain during the Mexican-American War. Other possible origins include the large, globular buttons on nineteenth-century army uniforms, the dough that soldiers cooked while in the field, and the clay that soldiers used to polish their belt buckles and buttons.) It is a guide to the places the American soldiers themselves traveled during their tragic adventure, and to the monuments and memorials that sprouted up in their wake. But this book is meant to be more than just a travel guide. To help travelers better understand and appreciate the significance of the places they visit, it is also a history of the American experience in the Great War, focusing on the individuals who served, fought, and died. It incorporates the perspectives and insights of historians who study the conflict, but more importantly, it also gives voice to the Doughboys themselves. Through their letters, diaries, and memoirs, the Doughboys describe the places they visited, the way they saw the war, and how they felt about it. Soldiers were not the only ones who served, of course. The U.S. Navy did more that its fair share to achieve victory, for example, and service organizations like the Red Cross and the Young Men's Christian Association were often right up with the soldiers at the front. This book tells their stories, too.

Any travel guide to World War I must inevitably cover battlefields. In 1923, Congress established the American Battle Monuments Commission (ABMC) to mark the sites of America's most important Great War battles. During the 1920s and 1930s, the commission placed ten memorials across the Western Front, ranging from grandiose monuments to a small memorial plaque. The ABMC also erected memorials in Gibraltar and in Brest, France, ports from which U.S. Navy sailors conducted combat patrols. In addition to the memorials, the ABMC is also responsible for overseas military cemeteries. When the First World War ended, there were at least 75,636 American dead buried at as many as 1,700 places across Europe, from makeshift battlefield cemeteries to individual burials in remote fields and local graveyards. After the war, the federal government consolidated the dead. Families were given the option of having their loved ones reinterred in an overseas military cemetery, returned to the United States (at government expense) to be laid to rest in their hometowns, or left where they were. Most families opted to bring them home. On Memorial Day 1937, the ABMC officially dedicated eight overseas cemeteries in three countries, where 30,921 American soldiers and sailors now lie. In their memorialization efforts, the ABMC spared no expense. History's greatest war seemed to demand the greatest of all memorials. The commission engaged some of the top artists and architects on both sides of the Atlantic, who designed buildings and grounds of lasting, touching beauty. The Western Front from Belgium to the Swiss border is marked by a poignant trail of memorials and cemeteries. Those of the United States are among the most noteworthy and moving of them all.

But the ABMC cemeteries and memorials are just the start. Monuments to the Doughboy went up almost immediately after the armistice of November 11, 1918, that ended the war. Before leaving for home, several U.S. Army divisions placed small markers tracing their progress across France. Most are still there. Others, too, sought to recognize the American fighting man. The cities and towns the Doughboys liberated from German occupation erected heartfelt and grateful monuments to them. The governments of various U.S. states marked the places where their citizen-soldiers fought and died. Service organizations like the Red Cross and veterans groups, and sometimes even private families, built their own memorials.

Indeed, there were so many memorials being erected in the decades following the war that the ABMC actively discouraged the placement of any more of them, and even called for some to be demolished, concerned that battlefields overcrowded with monuments would appear undignified. Over the past century, some of these memorials have fallen into disrepair. A few have even been destroyed. Veterans' organizations and patriotic societies still maintain scores of them, and have even constructed new ones in recent years in time for the hundredth anniversary of the Great War. Small towns across Europe also maintain the memorials to America's World War I soldiers. Francophobia runs rampant in many quarters in the United States today, but small hamlets across France still care for Doughboy memorials with honor and affection, even if most Americans have forgotten about them.

Unlike many war-related travel guides, this book will move beyond the battlefield and explore the Doughboy's world behind the lines. Here the echoes of the war are more faint, but no less significant. Thousands of American soldiers served in rear areas during the war, and there are monuments big and small to them well behind the Western Front. Many cities, like the tourist meccas of London and Paris, are filled with places that were once U.S. hospitals, offices, or leave centers. Small towns and villages have them, too. Some of these buildings bear plaques noting their World War I connection. Most do not. The Americans inadvertently left scores of monuments behind. The U.S. Army constructed countless engineering works like roads and dams across Europe, some of them gigantic in scope. Their remnants are often still on the landscape, and in some cases still in use. Monuments away from the Western Front can be every bit as impressive as those on the battlefields. Scotland's Isle of Islay hosts one of the most evocative of all. Two troopships sunk off the island in 1918, killing more than 500 Americans. Soon after the war, the American Red Cross built a memorial tower in a field of heather on a rocky, windswept cliff overlooking the sea where one of the ships went down. Perhaps no war memorial anywhere in the world is more beautifully situated.

The traveler need not go abroad to appreciate America's Great War heritage. Legacies of the Great War are hidden in plain sight all across the United States. Training camps, for example, not only turned civilians into soldiers, but also left a profound mark on American society and culture. A draftee named Irving Berlin wrote some of the war's most memorable songs at one training camp, while another may have spawned the great influenza epidemic that ravaged the planet during and immediately after the war. Great War training camps sometimes evolved into important U.S. military installations. Others are now ordinary residential areas. Today thousands of Americans live on the grounds of Great War training camps, perhaps only dimly aware of the historical significance of their own backyards.

Indeed, Great War history can turn up in the most unexpected places. One of the most scenic hiking trails in Washington State's Olympic National Park, for example, has its origins with World War I aircraft production. There are World War I memorials in the United States every bit as spectacular as those in Europe, and even a few battlefields, though nothing approaching the likes of those on the Western Front. Tensions along the U.S.-Mexico border led to some Great War-related skirmishes in the deserts of the American Southwest, for example, and one small Massachusetts town even had an encounter with a German submarine.

Chapters are arranged chronologically, so as to follow the Doughboys through their wartime experiences. The book begins with an exploration of how and why the United States got involved the Great War, and then follows the soldiers from training camps to the battlefields and back again. Appendices provide a list of museums and historic sites—most of which are described in the text—that preserve the Great War heritage of the American soldier and sailor, as well as a select bibliography. The text gives heights and distances in the measurement system most commonly used in the country being described. The English system is used for Great Britain and the United States, and metric measurements for all other countries.

It has now been a century since the First World War. Though the history-minded traveler often overlooks this conflict, those who venture down the road the Doughboy walked will discover some of the most fascinating and significant places they are ever likely to encounter.

CHAPTER 1:
THE ROAD TO WAR

"You will be home before the leaves have fallen from the trees," Germany's Kaiser Wilhelm II told his soldiers as they marched off to war in the summer of 1914. The assassination of Austria-Hungary's Archduke Franz Ferdinand at the hands of a Serbian nationalist in Sarajevo on June 28, 1914, triggered Europe's first general war in almost a century. Europe had enjoyed decades of relative peace before 1914, but the Great War had been brewing for decades. The flames of nationalism and ethnic hatred burned across the continent. Ethnic groups that fell under the domination of larger empires struggled for independence, but nationalism also led to tensions between the continent's major powers, which were in constant competition for power and influence. Nationalist passion led to the unification of Germany in 1871, which upset the delicate balance of power that had reigned since the end of Napoleon. In an attempt to reestablish that balance, European nations entered into alliances with countries that had similar interests, concerns, fears, and hatreds. The assassination of Franz Ferdinand brought these nationalist tensions to the surface and triggered the alliance system. With the promise of German support, Austria threatened war against Serbia. Russia mobilized against Austria to protect its diminutive ally, which led Germany down the road to war with Russia. France then mobilized against Germany to honor its commitments to Russia. Germany's invasion of neutral Belgium on its way into France sparked British intervention. In the blink of an eye, Europe had gone to war, as the Central Powers (Germany, Austria-Hungary, and Turkey) fought the Allies (France, Great Britain, Russia, and, later, Italy). As European nations brought their overseas empires into the fray, the European conflict became the World War.

The Kaiser's prediction of a short war proved dreadfully wrong, but he was not alone in thinking so. Few expected a long conflict. Dreaming of martial glory, Europe's young men patriotically rushed to recruiting stations fearful they would miss out on all the action. But events defied such optimism. The sides were evenly matched, and neither could gain an advantage over the other. On the Eastern Front, the combatant nations hammered away at each other inconclusively, but it was on the Western Front in France that the war took on its most fearsome dimensions. Britain and France halted Germany's invasion just short of Paris at the Battle of the Marne in September 1914, and it was an extremely bloody affair. Machine guns and modern artillery increased the killing power of armies dramatically, and with industrialization these weapons appeared on the battlefield in great abundance. To protect themselves, soldiers on both sides dug in, and a vast complex of trenches emerged all across the Western Front, from the North Sea to the Swiss border. The leaves fell from the trees that autumn, but the soldiers had not gone home. Instead, they found themselves locked in a muddy, bloody stalemate. Each side tried mass infantry assaults to break through enemy lines, but they almost never worked. On the first day of the Somme Offensive, in July 1916, Britain lost 20,000 soldiers, but could not break through the German lines. That same year at Verdun, the French and the Germans lost nearly a million men combined, and each side had precious little to show for it. The Great War battlefields became the scene of little more than mechanized slaughter.

Four thousand miles away on the other side of the Atlantic Ocean, the United States watched the events unfolding in Europe with a sense of detachment. Americans had long believed that the oceans insulated them from the world's problems, and the war in Europe did not seem like any of their business. Most Americans paid little attention to foreign affairs. Granted, even in the late nineteenth century there were a few influential Americans, mainly wealthy Easterners, who pushed for an imperialistic foreign policy to show that the United States could keep up with its European economic competitors. In the Spanish-American War of 1898, the United States acquired Puerto Rico, Guam, and the Philippines. Hawaii came under formal American control that year, too, and the United States joined the imperial club. But Americans were by and large half-hearted imperialists, and paid much more attention to domestic affairs. The first two decades of the twentieth century comprised the heyday of the Progressives—political reformers who believed in the efficacy of government to solve problems and improve society. President Theodore Roosevelt, the Republican occupant of the White House from 1901 to 1909, gained the nickname "the trust buster" for breaking up corporate monopolies. He guided the nation through a wide range of other reforms, including consumer protection laws, irrigation projects to develop the West, and the protection of forests and wilderness areas. His successor, Democrat Woodrow Wilson, was also a Progressive, creating the Federal Reserve to shore up the nation's banking system, policing corporate behavior, providing aid to farmers, expanding America's highway system, and implementing a national income tax—just to name just a few of his accomplishments.

When it came to the war in Europe, President Wilson urged his countrymen to be "neutral in thought as well as action," but as the war dragged on and the casualties mounted, some Americans took sides. Most sympathized with the Allies. Ties of language, culture, and, in many cases, blood, connected Britain and America. France, the nation that aided the fledgling United States during its struggle for independence in the eighteenth century, also had a special place in the hearts of many Americans. Britain and France had representative governments and shared America's basic political values, whereas the Central Powers all had autocratic monarchies. German blunders, like the invasion of neutral Belgium, further elicited pro-Allied sentiments. The Central Powers, by contrast, had few supporters. Many German Americans sympathized with the Old Country, and sometimes raised money for German war relief. A few even returned to Germany to fight. Irish Americans, resentful of Britain's occupation of their island homeland, had no particular sympathy for Germany, but hoped that the weakening of British power might lead to the independence of Ireland. Very few Americans advocated entry into the war, but most hoped that the Allies would ultimately prevail.

Even more important than America's sentimental attachments to the Allies were its economic ties to them. Soon after it entered the war, Great Britain imposed a naval blockade on Germany, and the Royal Navy—the most powerful force afloat—enforced it with great vigor and effectiveness. American trade with Germany plummeted from $345 million in 1914 to $29 million in 1915 and just $2 million by 1916. Wilson claimed that as a neutral nation the United States had a right to trade with Germany and dutifully complained to the British, but Americans soon found that the trade it lost with Germany was more than offset by increased trade with the Allies. Britain and France wanted all kinds of things from America—chemicals, cotton, foodstuffs, steel—and when they ran out of cash, U.S. banks loaned them $2.3 billion so they could keep on buying. Indeed, American exports to those two countries jumped from $754 million in 1914 to $2.75 billion in 1916. Access to U.S. markets gave the Allies a significant advantage over the Central Powers. While the German economy slowly crumbled under the weight of the British blockade, the Allies received a steady stream of supplies from America—a fact that did not escape the attention of German leaders.

As the war continued month after bloody month, each side sought new "wonder weapons" to punch a hole in enemy lines and break the stalemate. All combatants used chemical weapons, for example. Usually delivered by artillery shells, these weapons came in many forms. Chlorine and phosgene gas asphyxiated. Mustard gas burned and blistered. Chemical warfare resulted in many horrifying and gruesome deaths, but simple countermeasures like the gas mask—ubiquitous with soldiers on the Western Front—rendered them less than decisive. In 1916, the British introduced an armored vehicle known as a "tank." Though impervious to rifle and machine-gun fire, the slow-moving giants were still vulnerable to artillery and land mines, and broke down frequently. The airplane also came into its own as an instrument of war. Armies had long used observation balloons to peer behind enemy lines, but fixed-wing planes gave reconnaissance operations much more speed, mobility, and flexibility. Commanders soon found many other uses for aircraft. Planes could attack enemy troops in tactical battlefield situations. They could also be used strategically to strike infrastructure and industrial plants behind the lines to undermine the enemy economy. And they could be used to bomb civilians, a tactic that, some decision makers thought, might undermine public morale. Tanks and airplanes showed more promise than chemical weapons, but commanders had to learn how best to employ them through a long and bloody process of trial and error.

World War I also saw the first major use of submarines. The idea of underwater naval craft had been around for a long time, but by the early twentieth century technological advances allowed submarines to dive deeper, stay under water longer, travel farther, and carry more ordnance. For Germany, unable to defeat the British Navy on the surface of the waters, the submarine, or "U-boat" (short for *Unterseeboot*, or underwater boat), offered a way to strike back. In February 1915, Germany declared the seas around Great Britain a war zone. U-boats prowled just below the waves, and when they encountered Allied ships bringing goods into Britain they surfaced and sank them. Wilson complained that the German submarine campaign, like the British blockade, violated America's rights as a neutral power, but given the volume of goods crossing that Atlantic to Allied ports, the threat Germany posed to the American economy was far greater. Not only was American property threatened, but U.S. citizens on Allied ships might also be injured or killed. Wilson warned Germany that it would be held to "strict accountability" for any loss of American life.

Wilson's concerns were well founded. On March 18, 1915, a U-boat sank the unarmed British cargo ship *Falaba* in the Irish Sea, killing more than 100 people, including an American engineer. The most shocking was the May 1915 sinking of the British passenger liner *Lusitania*. Part of the Cunard fleet, the *Lusitania* was one of the largest, fastest, and most luxurious ocean liners in the world. On May 1, the *Lusitania* pulled away from Pier 54 on Manhattan's West Side and headed out into the Atlantic bound for Liverpool. In the days before its departure, the German government placed advertisements in American newspapers, reminding travelers that British waters were a "zone of war" and that any Allied ship sailing in them was "liable to destruction." After a week at sea the *Lusitania* reached Ireland, and on the pleasant spring afternoon of May 7 was sixteen kilometers off the Old Head of Kinsale. Some passengers opened their portholes for fresh air. Others milled around the deck enjoying the spring sun-

The RMS *Lusitania*. (Courtesy of the Library of Congress)

shine and spectacular views of the rugged Irish coastline, unaware that a German submarine lurked nearby. At 2:10 PM, a torpedo slammed into the *Lusitania*'s starboard side, launching a geyser of water and debris into the air. Within minutes there was a second explosion, ripping a giant gash in the hull. The *Lusitania* sank in just eighteen minutes. Of the 1,959 people aboard, 1,195 lost their lives, including 128 Americans. Germany argued that the *Lusitania* was smuggling war goods was thus a legitimate target. Britain denied the charge, though it is now known that the ship was indeed carrying modest quantities of ammunition and other items destined for the Western Front. Debate still rages about just how much war material may have been on the ship, and who may have known about it.

As with Pearl Harbor, the Kennedy assassination, or 9/11, Americans vividly recalled where they were and what they were doing when they heard the news of the *Lusitania* attack. "The event left an indelible memory not just because it was a great disaster," wrote historian John Milton Cooper Jr., but because it "also raised for the first time the threat of American involvement in the war." Calls for action came quickly and loudly. The *New York Herald* characterized the sinking as a "cold blooded, premeditated outrage on a colossal scale," and demanded that President Wilson be true to his "strict accountability" pledge. "The sinking of the *Lusitania* was not only an act of simple piracy," declared former president Theodore Roosevelt, "but it represented piracy accompanied by murder on a vaster scale than any old-time pirate had ever practiced before being hung for his misdeeds." Roosevelt called for breaking diplomatic relations with Germany. A few American newspapers even wanted a declaration of war. Wilson did not see the incident as a *casus belli*, nor did the majority of Americans, but the president had to assert America's rights as a neutral power. He issued a series of strongly worded diplomatic notes to Germany, demanding an apology and reparations. Some thought Wilson's approach weak. Roosevelt complained that America could not confront Germany's "blood and iron" with "milk and water." On the other side of the spectrum, Wilson's secretary of state, William Jennings Bryan, thought the president's approach too belligerent. A devout Christian with a strong pacifist streak, Bryan resigned rather than risk war.

Further incidents on the high seas only intensified the debate. On August 19, 1915, a U-boat sunk the British passenger ship *Arabic*. Among the dead were two Americans. The incident led to another wave of diplomatic protests from Washington. A month later, Germany issued the so-called "*Arabic* Pledge," promising to warn passenger liners before attacking them, but Germany soon broke it. In March 1916, the ferryboat *Sussex* hit the bottom, and though no Americans were killed, several were injured. Wilson threatened to break off diplomatic relations with Germany unless it changed its behavior. "At this point," wrote historian Jennifer Keene, "Germany decided that the drawbacks of the United States joining the Allied side outweighed the benefits of continuing to indiscriminately sink boats in the war zone." Unwilling to take on yet another enemy, Germany made more promises. Under the terms of the "*Sussex* Pledge," Germany once again agreed to stop targeting passenger ships, and further agreed that before sinking merchant ships, it would stop them and remove the crew in order to spare lives.

Trouble on America's Southern Border

As tensions with Germany grew on the North Atlantic, trouble developed south of the border, in Mexico. The roots of this trouble stretched back years. After a disputed election in 1910, Francisco Madero had begun a revolution against the decades-long dictatorship of Porfirio Diaz. Madero's promises of economic reform resonated with Mexico's poor, and in 1911 he ousted Diaz from power. But when Madero's promises failed to materialize, the revolution continued, and in 1913 he was killed in a coup led by General Victoriano Huerta. As the situation in Mexico deteriorated, the U.S. Army beefed up its posts along the U.S.-Mexico border, such as Fort Bliss, Texas, and Fort Huachuca, Arizona, and established a series of camps at important border crossings. The United States, with its long history of interfering in the affairs of Latin American countries, attempted to influence events in Mexico. Most countries accepted the Huerta regime as legitimate, but President Wilson refused, stating that he would not "recognize a government of butchers." In 1914, a confrontation between the U.S. Navy and Huerta's forces in Veracruz led to the American occupation of that city. Wilson also secretly aided a group of anti-Huerta revolutionaries known as the Constitutionalists, led by Venustiano Carranza. Among the Constitutionalists was the charismatic José Doroteo Arango Arámbula, better known by his *nom de guerre*, Francisco "Pancho" Villa. A staunch Madera supporter, Villa was suspicious of Carranza but hated Huerta more. Battling Huerta's forces, Villa soon controlled Chihuahua and other areas of northern Mexico.

Though he often funded his operations through extortion and banditry, Villa, who frequently donned a sombrero and bandoliers, was a romantic figure and had admirers north of the border. Indeed, he even received military support from the United States.

Carranza and his Constitutionalists forced Huerta from power in 1914, but the coalition soon fragmented. Villa and others believed that Carranza planned to make himself dictator and turned their guns on their

Pancho Villa. (Courtesy of the National Archives)

former ally, plunging Mexico into further chaos. Villa, the only major revolutionary leader not to denounce the U.S. occupation of Veracruz, expected that his American support would continue. But as Carranza's forces handed Villa a series of stinging defeats, Wilson granted Carranza diplomatic recognition. Indeed, the United States began to intervene on Carranza's behalf. On November 1–2, 1915, Carranza's forces defeated Villa at the Battle of Agua Prieta, just across the border from Douglas, Arizona. American support for Carranza, such as transporting his soldiers by train through U.S. territory to get to the battlefield, was key to Villa's defeat. As the battle raged in Agua Prieta, U.S. Army commanders across the border in Douglas braced for a possible attack. It never came, though a stray bullet crossed the border, killing one American soldier, Corporal Harry J. Jones. In February 1916, the army named its camp at Douglas in the unfortunate soldier's honor. Camp Harry J. Jones kept watch on the U.S.-Mexican border throughout World War I, and remained an active U.S. Army installation until 1933. There is no sign of Camp Harry J. Jones today. It was located along the border on the southeast side of Douglas, roughly between Cavalry Cemetery and the airport. Much of the area today is residential or has returned to desert.

Feeling that Uncle Sam had betrayed him, Villa turned on his former ally. In late November, 1915, his men skirmished with American troops at Nogales, Arizona, sometimes crossing the border into the United States to do so, and another U.S. soldier, Private Stephen D. Little, was killed. The army camp at Nogales was named for Little. A small monument on the grounds of Nogales's city hall (777 North Grand Avenue) identifies the site of Camp Stephen D. Little. In January 1916, Villistas attacked a train near Santa Isabel,

Chihuahua, and killed sixteen Americans on board. But Villa's boldest move came two months later, with his cross-border raid on Columbus, New Mexico, on March 9, 1916. This prompted a U.S. military "punitive expedition" into Mexico to capture him and bring him to justice (see Chapter 2). The Carranza government, though no friend of Villa, objected strenuously to the Yankee incursion. By early 1917, the United States had managed to alienate both the Mexican rebels and the Mexican government, and there loomed the very real threat of a war on the southern border.

America Begins to Build its Military Muscle

Growing world tensions stimulated a sharp debate among Americans about military preparedness. Germany's flagrant disregard for American rights, preparedness advocates argued, was the result of U.S. military weakness. While the U.S. Navy was a formidable force, second only to the British Royal Navy, the U.S. Army was pitifully small, with just 126,000 officers and men. The National Guard added only 80,000 more. Leading the charge for preparedness was one of America's most distinguished soldiers, General Leonard Wood, a Medal of Honor recipient whose career included fighting in the Geronimo campaign in Arizona and the Spanish-American War. Harkening back to the days when all able-bodied men served in their local militia, Wood called for universal military training. He was especially concerned that the United States did not have enough competent officers to lead a mass army. As early as 1913, he organized military training camps for college students. In 1915 he expanded on the idea, setting up a camp for young business and professional men at the army barracks at Plattsburg (as per a common spelling at the time; today consistently "Plattsburgh") in northern New York state, on the shores of Lake Champlain. More than 6,000 attended. Volunteers often came from the nation's most powerful families. Unlike in later conflicts in which the wealthy systematically avoided military service, during the Great War America's fortunate sons often flocked to the colors, seeing it as their patriotic duty to defend the nation and set an example for the rest of society. Among those who trained at Plattsburg were three of Teddy Roosevelt's sons—Archibald, Quentin, and Theodore Jr. An emergency appendectomy prevented their cousin, Assistant Secretary of Navy Franklin D. Roosevelt, from attending.

Buoyed by the success of Wood's camps, preparedness advocates formed the Military Training Camps Association (MTCA) in January 1916 to expand the training program. "To send untrained troops into the field is manslaughter," the MTCA proclaimed, "but to dispatch troops with untrained leaders is murder in the first degree." When the MTCA training camps opened in the summer of 1916, they were filled to capacity. The largest and most important took place at Plattsburg Barracks, and the training initiative was often referred to as the "Plattsburg Movement." The trainees lived in a tent camp on the shores of Lake Champlain two miles south of Plattsburg. The views of Vermont's Green Mountains to the east were spectacular, but the trainees had little time to enjoy them. General Wood insisted on a training regimen so rigorous that it "would make the regular army buck." Reveille came at 5:45 AM. Calisthenics and drill occupied most mornings. Afternoons consisted of classes on military science and hands-on experience with weaponry. Camp conditions could be spartan. One trainee remembered that after a rainstorm the camp was "a big clay mud hole" and had "the odor of a first class pig pen." When not in their tent camp, the trainees went out on long hikes, sometimes lasting more than a week, and staged mock battles in the shadow of the Adirondacks. Villages around Plattsburg—like Chazy, Dannemora, Keeseville, and Rouse's Point—were taken and retaken in mock battles. "Plattsburg was definitely not an upper-class leisure resort," concluded historian Michael Pearlman. In all, more than 16,000 attended the MTCA camps, 90 percent of whom eventually saw service in World War I.

The training camp was located between U.S. Avenue (U.S. Highway 9) and Lake Champlain. A residential street called the Nevada Oval now rounds through the old camp. The tents are long gone, of course, but much of the army post the trainees would have seen is still around. Red brick buildings, dating to the late nineteenth century, cluster around the old parade ground known as the U.S. Oval, where the trainees often drilled. One building, the Old Stone Barracks on the south end of the post, dates to the 1830s. After serving as an army post for more than a century, Plattsburg Barracks became Plattsburgh Air Force Base in 1955, and some of the fields where prospective officers staged mock battles in 1915 and 1916 became a runway for B-52 bombers. The base closed in 1995, and the area today comprises a mix of municipal facilities, private residences, and businesses. The airfield itself is now an oversized local airport. Some of the old military buildings near the intersection of U.S. Avenue and New York Road now host museums, among them the Clinton County Historical Museum, which occasionally has exhibits about the Plattsburg Movement.

Most Americans still wanted no part of the European War, but in the wake of the *Lusitania* sinking and the troubles in Mexico, increasing numbers saw wisdom in beefing up the nation's defenses in other respects as well. Under the Naval Act of 1916, Congress authorized a major expansion in the number of ships in service, including battleships, cruisers, destroyers, and submarines. Proponents claimed this would make the American navy "second to none." The most important action was, however, a separate piece of legislation the same year, the National Defense Act of 1916. Approved in June, it authorized an expansion of the regular army to 175,000 troops and the National Guard to 400,000. This law provided states with money to expand their National Guard forces, but also exerted more federal control over them. Guard soldiers faced more training time and could now be sent overseas, for example, and officers had to meet more stringent qualifications. The law also established an enlisted and officer reserve corps, and created the Reserve Officers Training Corps (ROTC), through which college students could obtain officer training and commissions. Other provisions included greater federal control over the nation's economy in wartime, an expansion of the army's engineering corps and fleet of airplanes, and the creation of the National Research Council to keep the army up to date on the newest technologies.

From Doctoring to Fighting—and Flying—for the Allies

As Americans wrestled with the possibility of entering the Great War, several thousand of their countrymen and countrywomen were already overseas serving the Allied war effort, and in many cases even fighting. Americans went to the Western Front for a variety of reasons. Some simply wanted adventure, attracted by what they saw as the romance of war. Others strongly sympathized with the Allied cause. Like the Plattsburgers, those Americans who went to France tended to be wealthy and well-educated men and women from elite families, who had the means to travel overseas.

As German armies approached Paris in 1914, the American Hospital in Paris, located at 63 boulevard Victor Hugo in the suburb of Neuilly-sur-Seine, began taking in French casualties. The hospital soon became a rallying point for those Americans living in Paris who wanted to help France in her hour of need. American students studying in Paris volunteered their time, and wealthy businessmen provided money and medical supplies. In September 1914, the American Hospital in Paris set up a branch facility called the American Ambulance (in French military parlance, an *ambulance* is a hospital for ambulatory patients) in an unfinished school building at 21 boulevard d'Inkerman in Neuilly-sur-Seine, not far from the main facility. During the Battle of the Marne, as the sounds of battle reverberated through the streets of Paris, American volunteers evacuated wounded French soldiers from the front in donated Ford trucks hastily converted into ambulances. In 1915, an ambulance driver named A. Piatt Andrew arranged for American ambulance crews to work directly with the French military, and the American Field Service (AFS) was born. By 1916, AFS ambulances were evacuating wounded Allied soldiers all across the Western Front, from Belgium to the Vosges Mountains in eastern France. By early 1917 more than 2,500 Americans were working for the AFS. There were other opportunities to serve. Richard Norton, an American scholar in London, teamed up with French millionaire H. Herman Hartjes to form the Norton-Hartjes Ambulance Corps. In 1915, two American women, Isabel Lathrop and Anne Morgan (daughter of the Wall Street financier J.P. Morgan), organized the American Fund for the French Wounded (AFFW). Working out of a seventeenth-century chateau at Blérancourt in Picardy, the AFFW dispatched volunteers—nearly all of them women—to provide aid to wounded French soldiers and the hard-pressed civilians of France. French soldiers and civilians alike were often amazed to see intrepid female drivers of the AFFW delivering food and medical supplies to the areas just behind the front lines.

Life at the front was dangerous, and though they were noncombatants, American medical volunteers were close enough to the action to be wounded and sometimes even killed. After the United States joined the war in 1917, many of the ambulance crews became part of the U.S. military. Even after U.S. entry into the war, young Americans continued to serve in volunteer ambulance organizations. For enthusiastic men who were too old for military service or who did not meet the physical requirements of the army, ambulance companies provided one way to get to the front. Among such adventurous young Americans serving with the American Red Cross in Italy was a nearsighted writer from Oak Park, Illinois, named Ernest Hemingway (see Chapter 16), who after the war became one of America's greatest literary luminaries. Indeed, such ambulance corps attracted an unusually large number of individuals who would become important American cultural figures, among them writer John Dos Passos; the poet Edward Estlin Cummings, better known by his distinctively lower-case pen name, e.e. cummings; and cartoonist Walt Disney, whose animations revolutionized American popular culture. Among the AFFW volunteers were the expatriate American writer Gertrude Stein and her partner, Alice B. Toklas. Stein wrote of one trip to Perpignan, in southern France, to distribute "comfort bags" to wounded French soldiers. The soldiers were grateful, and Stein described her work as a "perpetual delight" and "a continuous Christmas."

The American Hospital in Paris still sees patients today, and the unfinished school in Neuilly-sur-Seine that hosted the American Ambulance is now the Lycée Pasteur. Many American ambulance companies served near Pont-à-Mousson in Lorraine, and when the city rebuilt after the war it paid tribute to the idealistic young Americans. Reconstruction plans called for the re-creation of an ornate seventeenth-century fountain at the place Duroc, in the center of town, but it was done with an American twist. The AFS financed the fountain, American architects William Bosworth and Roger Siegel

American Field Service Memorial, place Duroc, Pont-à-Mousson, France.

designed it, and the fountain was dedicated to the volunteers killed in the area. Completed in 1931, it still dominates the place Duroc today. After the war, Anne Morgan purchased the Château de Blérancourt, from which the AFFW ran its operations, and converted it into a museum dedicated to Franco-American friendship. The Franco-American Museum of the Château de Blérancourt is presently closed for renovations.

Yet other Americans signed up to fight in Allied armies. The sinking of the *Lusitania* outraged Arthur Guy Empey, an army recruiter in Jersey City, New Jersey. "The lights in the tall buildings of New York seemed to be burning brighter than usual," he remembered of the May evening he got the news, "with anger and righteous indignation." Empey expected a flood of young men clamoring to enlist, but in the weeks and months following the incident the recruiting papers on his desk, as he described it, were "covered with dust." Outraged with the apathy of his countrymen, Empey sailed for England and joined the British Army. Wounded in the Battle of the Somme, he returned to the United States and published a book about his experiences entitled *Over the Top*, which became a national sensation. Other Americans signed up for the French Foreign Legion, among them the poet Alan Seeger. After graduating from Harvard in 1910, Seeger went to New York's Greenwich Village, where he penned his verse and pursued a bohemian existence. Unpublished, he moved to the Latin Quarter of Paris in 1912 and continued his directionless ways. When war came to France he enlisted in the French Foreign Legion, and was killed in the Battle of the Somme on July 4, 1916. After his death, his poetry was finally published.

The French were grateful for the Americans who defended their country in the early years of the war, and in 1923—in the place des

États-Unis, a park in the 16th arrondissement of Paris that has been a symbol of Franco-American friendship since 1881—erected a monument to the American volunteers who died for their country. A statue of George Washington and the Marquis de Lafayette, the French nobleman who fought for the United States during the American Revolution, has

Monument to American Volunteers, Place des Ètats-Unis, Paris, France.

stood at the west end of this park since 1894. The memorial to the American volunteers graces the eastern end. On the front of the monument, a French soldier and an American volunteer reach out toward each other, holdings hands, while a winged angel embraces them both. On the reverse side are the names of several dozen Americans who died for France. It includes the names of thirty-four members of the American Field Service and twenty-four from the Foreign Legion. Among the names etched into the stone is Alan Seeger, whose poetry appears on the monument. A bronze statue of an American volunteer, based on a photograph of Seeger, caps the monument. After World War II, the names of three more Americans who volunteered for France and who died in that war were added.

Most of the names on the monument—sixty-four in all—are of those who died in the most famous American volunteer group, the Lafayette Escadrille. A few of the wealthy young Americans living in Paris when the war broke out had flying experience, and volunteered for the French air forces. Turned down at first, they signed up for the French Foreign Legion or joined ambulance companies, but by 1915 the French allowed some of them to fly. Meanwhile, enthusiastic American pilots began arriving in France seeking admission to the *Aéronautique Militaire*, as the French air arm was then known. In 1916, a group of American fliers led by Harvard-trained lawyer Norman Prince founded the *Escadrille Américain*, an air squadron bringing all American pilots into a single unit. The Americans gathered at an airfield at Luxeuil-les-Bains in the Vosges Mountains in April 1916, and it did not take long for them to get into action. (The site remains a French military air base today.) Kiffin Rockwell got the squadron's first kill on May 20, 1916, when he shot down a German observation plane over Hartmanswillerkopf in Alsace. Their first fatality came in June, when Victor Chapman lost his life in a dogfight over Verdun.

The Germans objected to the *Escadrille Américain*, claiming its existence was a violation of American neutrality. In response, the squadron changed its name to the *Escadrille Lafayette*, in honor of the Revolutionary War hero. Known back home as the Lafayette Escadrille, the daring young Americans captured their country's imagination, and inspiring more young Americans to fly for France. A group of wealthy French and American businessmen created the Lafayette Flying Corps, which recruited still more American flyers and integrated them in French air squadrons. Whether in the Lafayette Escadrille or the Lafayette Flying Corps, American pilots flew all over the Western Front and participated in some the war's most significant battles.

Lafayette Escadrille Memorial, Marnes-la-Coquette, France.

The wealthy and well-connected flyers inspired a number of monuments. Several in France are dedicated to a young American pilot named Ronald Wood Hoskier, who left his studies at Harvard in 1916 and served with the Norton-Hartjes Ambulance Company before making his way into the Lafayette Escadrille. He was shot down over Grugies, France, in April 1917. The town cemetery of Grugies, a small village just southwest of Saint-Quentin, has a monument to Hoskier. A cement pole on a granite base, it outlines the story of his death—in French. In Étalon, thirty-five kilometers away, the war memorial in the center of town also pays tribute to Hoskier, and the intersection it overlooks is called the place Ronald-Wood Hoskier. Stateside, there are at least two memorials to James Rogers McConnell, killed over Flavy-le-Martel in March 1917. One, an obelisk flanked with two cannon, is on the grounds of the Moore County Administration Building in Carthage, North Carolina, where McConnell once lived. Another, created by sculptor Gutzon Borglum (most famous for the presidential faces on Mount Rushmore), stands outside the Alderman Library at McConnell's alma mater, the University of Virginia in Charlottesville—a helmeted figure with wings reaching for the heavens.

Forty-eight members of the Lafayette Escadrille and the Lafayette Flying Corps are interred together at the Lafayette Escadrille Memorial in the Paris suburb of Marnes-la-Coquette. Nestled in a wooded park off boulevard Raymond Poincaré, the memorial is the work of French architect Alexandre Marcel. Dominating it is a stone archway, roughly half the size of the Arch de Triomphe in Paris, flanked by two porticoes and fronted with a reflecting pool. Dedications to the American flyers appear at the top of the arch—in French on the front and in English on the back. The names of the American pilots who died for France are engraved into the face of the arch, while the battles they flew in

Mosaic of Lafayette Escadrille emblem, Marnes-la-Coquette, France. The American flyers often used a swastika in their emblem, a Native American symbol of good luck.

appear above the portico columns. From the center of the archway, two staircases, one marked "Lafayette" and the other "Washington," descend to the crypts. Propellers, wings, and other symbols of flight appear in Marcel's Art Deco friezes and relief sculptures, as do Lafayette and Washington. Marcel used the Indian Head emblem of the Lafayette Escadrille in the stonework as well, and there is also a mosaic of the emblem on the small plaza behind the memorial. It was dedicated on July 4, 1928, and the Lafayette Escadrille Memorial Foundation has maintained it ever since.

America Joins the War

In November 1916, Wilson was reelected president with the campaign slogan, "He kept us out of war." But even before he could begin his second term, German leaders made a fateful decision. The limited submarine campaign, they concluded, was not sufficiently curtailing the flow of American supplies to the Allies. Only unrestricted submarine warfare, they concluded, would work. In fact, the German U-boat fleet had grown to more than 100 by early 1917, increasing their ability to sink ships. An intensified campaign, to include the targeting of American-flagged ships, they believed, could starve the British into submission within a year. Such a tactic was likely to draw the United States into the war, but the Germans had factored that into their thinking too. Aware of America's lack of military preparedness, they calculated that it would take the United States two years to build up the army needed to fight a war. By that time the war in Europe would be won, they believed, and even if it was not, U-boats would prevent an American army from ever reaching European shores.

Beginning in February 1917, the U-boats struck with unprecedented force. At the same time, Germany hoped to exploit U.S.-Mexican tensions to their advantage. In January 1917, German foreign minister Arthur Zimmermann sent a secret message to the German ambassador in Mexico, Heinrich von Eckardt. "We intend to begin on the first of February unrestricted submarine warfare," Zimmermann wrote. Should the United States join the war, von Eckardt was instructed to offer Mexico an alliance with Germany. The Germans promised Mexico "generous financial support," as well as the return of Arizona, New Mexico, and Texas—seized by the United States during the nineteenth century—to Mexican sovereignty. The Carranza government dismissed the proposal, but even worse for Germany, the British intelligence service had intercepted the message, decoded it, and turned it over to the United States. Just as outrage at home grew over the U-boat campaign, the so-called "Zimmermann Telegram" hit Americans like a lightning bolt. Despite the twin provocations, noninterventionist sentiment was still high. America should keep its ships out of the war zone, some argued, and suspicion that the Zimmermann Telegram was a forgery was widespread. Though the American public was still deeply divided about the wisdom of going to war, unrestricted submarine warfare and the Zimmermann Telegram had edged American public opinion in favor of entering the conflict.

When President Wilson went before Congress on April 2, 1917 to ask for a declaration of war against Germany, he spelled out America's motivations in highly idealistic terms. "We have no quarrel with the German people," he said, only with the "little groups of ambitious men" in the German imperial government "who were accustomed to use their fellow men as pawns and tools." The Great War was not about money or power, Wilson insisted, but rather about human freedom. Autocracy not only crushed liberty, Wilson believed, but led directly to instability and war. "Self-governed nations do not fill their neighbor states with spies," he contended, "or set the course of intrigue to bring about some critical posture of affairs which will give them an opportunity to strike and make conquest." German aggression not only threatened Americans, he argued, but the whole world, and the fate of freedom and representative government around the globe hung in the balance. "The world must be made safe for democracy," Wilson proclaimed, and argued that American involvement in the Great War was the only way to make that happen. "Our motive will not be revenge or the victorious assertion of the physical might of the nation," he said, "but only the vindication of right." Contentious debate rang through the halls of Congress for four days, but on April 6, Congress complied with the president's request. The United States declared war on Germany.

CHAPTER 2:
JOHN J. PERSHING

May 28, 1917, was a miserable day along the shores of New York Harbor. Mist and fog, occasionally punctuated by bursts of drenching rain, obscured the view of the Statue of Liberty and the city's famous skyline. Late on that dreary morning, a mysterious party gathered quietly on Governor's Island. Major General John J. Pershing, recently appointed commander of American forces in Europe, was about to sail off to the Great War. Out of concern that German submarines would hunt down his ship and sink it, Pershing's departure was supposed to be top secret. The general and his staff even dressed in civilian clothes to avoid detection by German spies. But according to historian Richard O'Connor, the departure "was one of the worst kept secrets of the war." Rumors of it had swirled around Washington for days, and crates with the general's name clearly stenciled on them had been piling up on the New York waterfront. At mid-day in cold and steady rain, Pershing boarded a ferry and headed out to the British liner *Baltic*, anchored in Gravesend Bay off Brooklyn. Unfortunately, the ship was not yet ready to receive him, and Pershing was forced to remain in his ferryboat bobbing up and down in the choppy waters for several hours. As the *Baltic* finally pulled out of the harbor just after 5:00 PM, the battery on Governor's Island fired an ill-advised salute in honor of the general, only further hinting to New Yorkers that something big was afoot. Major James G. Harbord, Pershing's chief of staff, reflected on "all sorts of wise bromides about bad beginnings making good endings" as the *Baltic* finally steamed out into the open Atlantic.

John Joseph Pershing was born on September 13, 1860, on a farm outside Laclede, Missouri. War touched his life at a very young age. The Civil War raged while he was a toddler, and the border state of Missouri saw some of its worst depredations as Unionists and Confederate sympathizers engaged each other in brutal guerrilla warfare. His father, John Fletcher Pershing, was an ardent Unionist who supplemented his farming income with a general store in Laclede. On the afternoon of June 18, 1864, Confederate raiders under Captain John Holtzclaw entered Laclede "with yells most terrific," as the local newspaper described it, and plundered the town. Pershing and his father were in the store when the raid began. The elder Pershing grabbed his shotgun, scooped up his three-year-old son, and went out the back door just as the raiders broke into the front. They made their way home and the elder Pershing prepared to take on Holtzclaw's men. Young Pershing remembered his father aiming his shotgun out the window while his mother begged him not to shoot. "You'll be killed," she pleaded, "let the money go." His father lowered his gun. Union forces arrived and chased Holtzclaw away, but not before two of the village's citizens had been killed. After the war, Pershing's father rebuilt his business, acquired more land, and became one of Laclede's leading citizens until the Panic of 1873 nearly wiped him out. At the age of thirteen, Pershing worked the family farm while his father took a job as a traveling salesman. Farming left little time for education, but the bright and persistent teenager managed to keep up with his schoolwork. As Pershing grew to manhood, he dreamed of becoming a lawyer. He took a job teaching at the Prairie Mound School ten miles from Laclede to support himself and attended classes at the Kirksville Normal School (today's Truman State University) to build his academic credentials. As a teacher, he gained a reputation as a tough but fair classroom disciplinarian, unafraid to apply a little corporal punishment now and then.

Young Pershing's world is preserved at the Pershing Boyhood Home State Historic Park in Laclede. The Pershing family moved into this home in 1866, when the future general was just six years old. The interior has been restored to its appearance in the late nineteenth century when Pershing grew from childhood into manhood. The Prairie Mound School House where Pershing once taught has been moved to the grounds as well, and now holds exhibits about his life and career. As a boy, Pershing fished and played along the banks of the Grand River just west of Laclede. Today two Missouri state parks preserve these lands as well. One is Locust Creek Covered Bridge State Historic Park, located just north of U.S. Highway 36. The bridge dates to 1868, and Pershing is known to have gone fishing and swimming there. The other is Pershing State Park, just south of the highway. The 3,500-acre park preserves an unusual fragment of northern Missouri's pre-settlement habitat, and appears much as Pershing would have seen it during his formative years.

It was the prospect of a free college education that attracted Pershing to the United States Military Academy at West Point. He passed the qualifying tests and was admitted to the class of 1886. Pershing's grades were unimpressive—French seemed to be the subject that bedeviled him the most—but his hard work and steely discipline won him the respect of his classmates. From the banks of the Hudson, Pershing traveled to the Western frontier for his first assignment, joining the 6th Cavalry at Fort Bayard, New Mexico. He arrived just as the war with Geronimo was winding down. His first "combat" assignment was an expedition to capture an Apache chief named Magnus. The troopers scoured the mountains of Arizona and New Mexico for days unaware that Magnus had already returned to the reservation. Pershing served at several other southwestern posts, including Forts Stanton and Wingate, both in New Mexico. In December 1890, Pershing went north to the Dakotas and played a minor role in crushing an uprising on the Great Sioux Reservation, patrolling the banks of the Cheyenne River in subzero temperatures in search of recalcitrant Native Americans. After a stint as military instructor at the University of Nebraska, Pershing served as an officer in the African American 10th Cavalry Regiment at Fort Assiniboine, Montana.

Pershing's footprints are still evident across the West. None of the posts at which he served are still active military bases, though remnants of them are still there, preserved by dedicated state and local historical agencies. Eight miles southwest of Havre, Montana, on U.S. Highway 87 is a state historical marker commemorating Fort Assiniboine, which notes Pershing's time there. The remnants of the fort are less than a mile south of the marker. Among the buildings still there from Pershing's time are the officer's amusement hall and the post library. Montana State University's Northern Agricultural Research Center now controls the grounds of Fort Assiniboine, which are open to visitors only through tours provided by the Havre Chamber of Commerce. The New Mexico forts can all be visited as well. At Fort Stanton State Historic Site, six miles southeast of Capitan off State Highway 220, the officers' quarters where Pershing lived still stand, as do several other buildings from Pershing's time there. The Fort Wingate site is twelve miles southeast of Gallup on State Highway 440. Fire destroyed much of the post in 1896, leaving little that Pershing would recognize, though one can still walk the parade ground. At Fort Bayard, nine miles east of Silver City, nothing but the parade ground remains of Pershing's time there, but those interested in the First World War will nevertheless want to pay a visit. The Fort Bayard Historic Preservation Society lovingly maintains a museum of post history in the old commanding officer's quarters on the west side of the parade ground. The museum covers Pershing's time at the fort, including his work establishing heliograph stations between Forts Bayard and Stanton. The museum also covers Fort Bayard's time as a hospital. In the early years of the twentieth century, the arid Southwest hosted numerous sanatoria for victims of tuberculosis and other lung ailments. During World War I, Fort Bayard was an army sanatorium for Doughboys who were victims of gas attacks, as well as those suffering from respiratory diseases. (Fort Stanton also served as a sanatorium during the war years, for the Merchant Marine.) The society gives guided tours of the post grounds, which include discussion of Lieutenant Pershing's years there and the World War I hospital. For those who cannot catch a tour or prefer to explore on their own, the society has also installed signage on the grounds.

Throughout his time in the West, the hard-working Pershing won the respect of his men and attracted the attention of his superiors, most notably General Nelson A. Miles, who brought Pershing back East to serve on his staff. In 1897, the promising young officer took the job of tactical instructor at West Point. It was one of the most disastrous episodes of his career. The cadets did not take well to Pershing's iron discipline, and called him "Black Jack" because of his service with African American troops. In the face of such resistance, Pershing's instinct was to clamp down even harder on the rebellious cadets. It was a vicious cycle that made his tenure on the West Point faculty a short one. When the Spanish-American War broke out in 1898, Lieutenant Pershing returned to the all-black 10th Cavalry and headed off to Cuba. The Battle of San Juan Hill near Santiago in July 1898 was Pershing's first real combat experience, and his stellar performance revived his reputation. Under withering Spanish rifle fire, Pershing rallied his men and led them forward. One observing officer recalled that Pershing was "as cool as a bowl of cracked ice," and his regimental commander, a Civil War veteran, called him "the coolest and bravest man I ever saw under fire." The 10th Cavalry played a crucial role in winning the battle, though it was the deployment of Gatling guns—early forerunners of the machine gun—that ultimately carried the day for the Americans.

Pershing's feats at San Juan Hill attracted the attention of some notable people, including Colonel Theodore Roosevelt of the famed "Rough Riders," who was soon to become President of the United States. After Cuba, Pershing took a number of different field assignments and staff jobs. He saw more combat in the campaign to subdue the Philippines. While in Washington, he met Frances Warren, the daughter of a Wyoming senator. They were married at Washington's Church of the Epiphany (1317 G Street NW) in 1905. That same year Pershing was appointed military attaché in Tokyo, and was a U.S. observer in the Russo-Japanese War. Pershing had amassed an impressive resume, but promotion was slow. In 1906, President Roosevelt took an unusual step by elevating

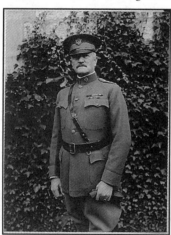

General John J. Pershing at his headquarters in Chaumont, France, 1918. (Courtesy of the Library of Congress)

Pershing from Captain to Brigadier General. Pershing returned to the Philippines for another campaign against the Moros, and served as military governor of Moro Province.

In January 1914 Pershing and his family moved to the Presidio of San Francisco, where the general assumed command of the Eighth Brigade. Having spent years in the Philippines, the Pershing family was glad to be back in the United States. To the children, America seemed like a strange and foreign land. The family enjoyed San Francisco's many cultural opportunities, including one outing to see Buffalo Bill's Wild West Show, where General Pershing recognized some of the Native American performers from his days in the Dakotas. Sadly, the family togetherness would not last long. In April 1914, as the revolutionary turmoil in Mexico intensified, Pershing and his brigade were ordered to Fort Bliss, Texas, on the Mexican border. He even met briefly with the Mexican rebel leader, Pancho Villa, before relations between Villa and the U.S. soured (see Chapter 1). As the deployment dragged on, Pershing made arrangements for his family to join him there, but then unimaginable tragedy struck. In August 1915, his wife and three daughters were killed in a fire at their residence at the Presidio. Only his son Warren survived. The tightly controlled disciplinarian wept inconsolably as he made his way from Texas to San Francisco to claim the bodies and bury his family. "Those who knew Pershing well said the tragedy changed him," wrote biographer Jim Lacy. Already rather diffident, Pershing grew even more withdrawn. "It became increasingly difficult for anyone to break through [his] hard outer shell," according to Lacy. The Presidio of San Francisco is now a national historic site. A tall flagpole in the center of the Pershing Square on the Presidio grounds marks the site where the home once stood.

Pershing Makes a Name for Himself in Mexico

Pershing returned to Texas and coped with the pain of his loss by throwing himself into his work—and there was plenty of it. Just before dawn on March 9, 1916, about 500 of Pancho Villa's men crossed into the United States and headed toward Columbus, New Mexico, three miles north of the border. The main body of raiders approached from the southwest shouting "Viva Villa!" and "Viva Mexico!" After rounding a rocky hill on the outskirts of the village, the column of attackers divided into two wings. One plunged into the streets of the town. The other descended on army camp near the Customs House and train station. A third force came toward the camp from the south along the drainage canal and the road that is now State Highway 11. As dawn broke across the New Mexico desert, Columbus erupted in violence. Villistas looted the Commercial Hotel on Lima Street, shot the proprietor and several guests dead, and burned it to the ground. The raiders also looted and torched the numerous shops and saloons along Broadway. Residents grabbed their guns and fought back, escaped into the desert, or took refuge in the town's sturdier buildings. Many retreated to the local schoolhouse on North Boundary Street. Others took refuge in the Hoover Hotel at the corner of Broadway and Missouri.

The 350 men of the 13th Cavalry stationed at Columbus sprang into action. As Villa's men rode into their camp, the troopers fought back as best they could. Cooks preparing breakfast threw boiling water at them. One defended himself with a baseball bat. Soldiers rushed to the guardhouse to grab their weapons. In one of the most heroic episodes, Lieutenant John Lucas, unable to find his boots in the confusion and early morning darkness, raced into battle barefoot. He positioned four Benet Mercié machine guns and thirty riflemen along the railroad tracks (present-day State Highway 9) on the south edge of town. Looking north into the village, the silhouettes of the raiders

appeared among the flaming buildings, giving his men excellent targets. Meanwhile, just to the northeast, Lieutenant James Castleman and several dozen riflemen set up positions near the Hoover Hotel and aimed down Broadway toward the raiders. The "Ben-A" machine guns jammed frequently, and the inexperienced soldiers sometimes loaded them incorrectly in the heat of battle, but Lucas and Castleman got the

Hoover Hotel in Columbus, New Mexico today. Once a refuge for local residents from Pancho Villa's raiders, it is now a private residence.

Villistas plundering the town in a murderous crossfire. After an hour and a half, local residents and the cavalry troopers gained the upper hand. A Villista bugler sounded the retreat, and the raiders dashed back into Mexico.

When it was over, eight soldiers and ten civilians were dead, and much of Columbus was reduced to smoking, bullet-riddled ruins. Villa's men got away with cash, valuables, and horses, though they lost an estimated ninety men in the process. Villa's motives for the raid were never clear. Some speculated that he wanted nothing more than revenge for what he saw as American betrayal. Others argue that he was motivated primarily by a need for money and supplies to keep his army going. Still others saw German fingerprints, and speculated that German agents in Mexico urged Villa to attack Columbus to distract the United States from events on the North Atlantic. The debate continues to this day. Some eyewitnesses put Villa in the streets of Columbus. Many historians doubt that he ever crossed the border.

President Wilson ordered the army to enter Mexico and capture Villa, and selected Pershing to command it. Within days of the raid, a force of 5,000 soldiers gathered at Columbus, and the army post, now known as Camp Furlong, swelled in size. The first elements of the so-called "Mexican Punitive Expedition" crossed the border on March 15, and from the beginning things went awry. Not only was the army unable to find Villa, but the Carranza government strongly objected to the invasion of Mexican territory

Political cartoon of the "Mexican Punitive Expedition" into Mexico to capture Pancho Villa, 1916. (Courtesy of the National Archives)

and refused to cooperate. Carranza denied the Americans the use of Mexican railroads, for example, forcing Pershing to move men and material with cars and trucks on Mexico's unpaved roads. By June, Pershing was using more than 300 vehicles. It was the first major use of motorized vehicles in U.S. military history, though it was an inauspicious beginning. The army lacked drivers and mechanics, and the vehicles frequently broke down in the desert dust and mud.

The U.S. Army also used reconnaissance aircraft. The 1st Aero Squadron—the only unit dedicated specifically to aviation—arrived in Columbus on March 15 by train with six aircraft in crates. Under the command of Major Benjamin Foulois, the men immediately assembled their planes and carved a crude airstrip out of the desert east of Camp Furlong. Four days later, Foulois and Major Townsend F. Dodd took off from Columbus in a Curtiss JN-3, nicknamed the "Curtiss Jenny," and flew thirty miles into Mexico scouting for Pershing's forces. It was the first time a U.S. Army plane had ever flown in a hostile operation—or over a foreign country. Foulois thought his mission a success, since he was able to report to Pershing that "there were no Mexican rebels within a day's march of the head or flanks of his infantry and cavalry columns." But like the army's motorized vehicles, the aerial operations soon ran into problems. There were mechanical maintenance issues. The engines of the JN-3 were not powerful enough for sustained operations, especially in high elevations of the Sierra Madre Mountains. Desert heat warped the propellers. Crashes were commonplace, and landings in rugged fields and in the valleys of the Chihuahua Desert took their toll on the machines. All of the squadron's planes soon became inoperable, and the new planes the army sent were not much better. As a result,

Foulois lamented, "we never again were able to perform useful field service with Pershing's forces."

By April 1916, the expedition penetrated as far south as Parral, Chihuahua, more than 400 kilometers south of the U.S. border. The Americans fought several skirmishes with Villa's forces, but were unable to find Villa himself. The cross-border raids from Mexico, which the expedition was intended to stop, continued, such as the attack on Glenn Springs, Texas, in May 1916. (Glenn Springs is now uninhabited, and lies in a remote area within the boundaries of Big Bend National Park.) On June 21, U.S. forces even engaged Carranza's Mexican regulars at the Battle of Carrizal. By the summer of 1916, Pershing's forces had grown to nearly 10,000 men. In May, Wilson mobilized the National Guard in Arizona, New Mexico, and Texas to protect the border in case of a full-scale war with Mexico. The following month, he called up units from across the country and sent them to the border. In all, more than 100,000 National Guard troops had been called to duty during the crisis. But neither side wanted war; Washington, in particular, had grown increasingly concerned about the Great War in Europe. Pershing began a gradual withdrawal from Mexico in January 1917. The last Americans departed Mexico on February 5 without ever finding Villa.

6th and 16th Infantry Regiments on the march in Mexico, January 1917. (Courtesy of the Department of Defense)

There are no monuments or historical markers in Chihuahua to mark the trail of the Pancho Villa expedition. U.S. intervention remains a touchy topic in Mexico, and few south of the border are interested in memorializing it. In 2009, an American named Ron Bridgemon rediscovered the graves of two U.S. soldiers from the Mexican expedition still buried in the cemetery of a remote ranch northeast of Parral (GPS: N 27.07484 W 105.38418). Cities and towns along the U.S.-Mexico border have sought to preserve the memory of the troubles. In the Mexican town of Puerto Palomas, just across the border from Columbus, an equestrian statue of Villa, racing forward with pistol drawn, occupies a small park at the corner of Avenida 5 de Mayo and Zaragoza. Just to the east of the statue, in a shopping plaza catering to American tourists, is another statue, this one of life-sized depiction of Pershing and Villa shaking hands. This portrayal of Villa puts him in a formal military uniform rather than thus typical sombrero and bandoliers.

The legacy of the Mexican expedition is perhaps best preserved in Columbus. Many of the buildings that played a prominent role in the raid are still there, such as the old school on Boundary Street and the Hoover Hotel, where Lieutenant Castleman set up his machine gun. Many are gone, like the Commercial Hotel, which was never rebuilt. The spot today is just an open space filled with weeds and broken concrete, and marked with an interpretive panel telling of its role in the raid. There are many such panels around town, highlighting the important events and remembering local residents who were killed in them. Several panels are near the old railroad station, which today hosts the Columbus Historical Museum and its exhibits about the raid. The grounds around the museum were the location of the 13th Cavalry's camp at the time of the raid. Along Highway 11 is a re-creation of the bandstand General Pershing used to review the troops marching back from Mexico in 1917. Also on the grounds is a monument with two bronze plaques. One lists the army dead from the Columbus raid. The other, on the reverse side, lists the civilians killed.

The grounds of Camp Furlong, on the west side of Highway 11, now make up Pancho Villa State Park. At the park entrance is a spacious museum that presents a comprehensive overview of the raid and consequent expedition from both American and Mexican perspectives. The museum features some interesting displays. Suspended from the ceiling is a Curtiss R2, the type of plane flying out of Columbus at the end of the expedition. Vehicles include an army truck (depicted, appropriately enough, stuck in the mud) from the Four Wheel Drive Auto Company of Clintonville, Wisconsin, and a bullet-riddled civilian automobile that survived the raid. Outside is another unusual vehicle, a Jeffrey Quad Armored Car—the U.S. Army's first armored vehicle, which was sent to Columbus in 1916 but never saw action. Just outside the museum is Cootes Hill, the high ground around which Villa's men rode, which then served as Camp Furlong's lookout post. The hill does indeed give a commanding view of the Mexican border. The park also preserves the Columbus Customs House, as well as a few old brick buildings left over from the camp, protected from the desert sun with corrugated metal shelters. Owing to the expedition's use of motor vehicles, there are also the remnants of an automotive repair facility. An interpretive sign in the park along Highway 11 notes that Foulois's airstrip was "just across the highway from this point." The statement is a little misleading. It was actually about a half a mile to the east of the sign, southwest of the intersection of Kansas and Jones Streets. Now covered with greasewood and mesquite, the site is today owned by a historical organization called the First Aero Squadron Foundation that plans to restore it to its 1916–1917 condition.

In retrospect, the Pancho Villa expedition was not a complete failure. Though Villa was never captured, his forces were dispersed and weakened. The mobilization also gave American military and civilian leaders valuable experience in the planning and execution of operations, which they would need in France months later, including the use of aircraft and vehicles. The expedition also made Pershing the only general officer in the army who had led such a large force in a hostile operation.

America Heeds Europe's Call

American entry into World War I in April 1917 came at a crucial moment. On the Eastern Front, Russia's Czar Nicholas II had been forced to abdicate the month before, and that war-weary nation's further participation in the war was uncertain. The fragile interim government kept fighting, but the Germans transported the communist revolutionary Vladimir Lenin from exile in Switzerland back to Russia in hopes of destabilizing it. On the Western Front, Germany settled in for the long haul, constructing a long line of formidable defensive positions across France that became generally known as the Hindenburg Line, after the German army's chief of staff, Field Marshall Paul von Hindenburg. France, by contrast, was still committed to the attack. Just days after the U.S. declaration of war, General Robert Neville, commander-in-chief of French forces, launched a massive assault in the Chemin des Dames region northeast of Paris. It began with British diversionary attacks near Arras early in the month, and then the main French attack came on April 16 between Soissons and Reims. The Neville Offensive was a disaster. In less than a month, France absorbed nearly 200,000 casualties but had barely bent in the German lines. The Poilu, or "hairy one," as the French World War I soldier was known, had reached the breaking point. Thousands deserted, and in late May and early June entire divisions refused to fight. Often described as a mutiny, the episode is best viewed as "a sort of military strike," according to historian John Keegan. French troops demanded better food, more leave, and an end to pointless attacks. The French army arrested thousands of mutineers, and even executed a handful of them for effect, but also acceded to many of the soldiers' demands. General Philippe Pétain replaced Neville, and called a halt to most offensive operations.

For the Allies, the only glimmer of hope that spring was America's entry into the war. Within weeks, both Britain and France sent high-level delegations to Washington to begin consultations with their new ally. Foreign Minister Alfred Balfour led the British mission. Former premier René Viviani and Marshal Joseph "Papa" Joffre, the hero of the 1914 Battle of the Marne, represented France. Britain and France did not coordinate their efforts, and in fact sometimes undercut each other, but each had one overarching goal in mind: Get American troops into the trenches as soon as possible. Three years of war had seriously depleted Allied manpower reserves.

France had already lost a million men. With America in the fray the Allies now had a vast pool of potential soldiers, though tapping into it proved elusive. The tiny U.S. Army was woefully unprepared and could not deliver troops anytime soon. Raising an army of millions might take years. Infantrymen could be trained fairly quickly, but the Allies expressed concern that an inexperienced American officer corps might lead their men to disaster. By the time America was ready to fight, they feared, Germany might have already won the war.

Each of the Allies conjured up plans to tap into American manpower. The British proposed that the United States send 500,000 raw recruits to Europe as quickly as possible. Under their plan, the American soldiers would simply be integrated into depleted British combat units and fight alongside the Tommy. Joffre had been thinking along similar lines, but understood that such a plan might offend American pride. He suggested that the United States send recruits to France in small units. The French army would train them and place them into their own divisions. As the number of American troops in France grew, Joffre argued, American units could then be pulled out of French divisions and brought together under an American commander. In the short run, Joffre requested that an American infantry division come to France *tout suite* to boost flagging civilian morale. He also asked for engineering, medical, and other badly needed specialty units.

The United States agreed to send a combat division and specialty troops as soon as possible, but civilian and military leaders alike argued that the amalgamation of American soldiers into British and French armies was unacceptable. Americans fighting and dying under a foreign flag would be deeply unpopular with the American public, they understood, not to mention with the troops themselves. American officers found suggestions that they might not be up to the job insulting. Amalgamation might also diminish American influence in the final peace settlement. If America was going to live up to President Wilson's pledge to make the world "safe for democracy," the United States needed to stand on equal footing with its allies, not as some kind of invisible junior partner. "When the war is over," warned General Tasker Bliss of the amalgamation schemes, "it may be a literal fact that the American flag may not have appeared anywhere on the line because our organizations will simply be parts of battalions and regiments of [other] armies." The American insistence on its own independent army in France meant that the effects of U.S. manpower on the Western Front would be delayed. Aside from boosting Allied morale, the American entry into the conflict would have no immediate impact on the battlefield.

Pershing Named to Lead an Army—But First to Build It from Scratch

The first step in creating the American Expeditionary Force (AEF) that would eventually sail for France was to select its commander. One leading candidate was General Leonard Wood, but his undisguised political ambitions and close association with Theodore Roosevelt made him unpopular with Wilson and Democrats. Thanks to his capable handling of the Pancho Villa expedition, Pershing saw his name go to the top of the list. The first hint of his new job came with a cryptic letter from his father-in-law, Senator Francis Warren, asking about his French language skills. Soon thereafter a telegram arrived from General Hugh Drum, army chief of staff, asking him to select four infantry regiments and one artillery regiment for immediate deployment to France. Drum added: "If plans are carried out, you will be in command of the entire force." Assuming he was to be a division commander, Pershing selected the 16th, 18th, 26th, and 28th Infantry Regiments, along with the 6th Field Artillery—all of which had served under him in Mexico. "I had scarcely given a though to the possibility of my being chosen as commander-in-chief of our forces abroad," he wrote in his memoir, but after heading to Washington and meeting with Secretary of War Newton D. Baker, the scope of his assignment became clear. "The thought of the responsibilities that this high position carried depressed me for the moment," he confessed. "Here in the face of a great war I had been placed in command of a theoretical army which had yet to be constituted, equipped, trained, and sent abroad." But, he added, "there was no doubt in my mind then, or at any other time, of my ability to do my part."

In characteristic fashion, Pershing got right to work planning for the massive endeavor. His first task was to put together a staff. Old friends and acquaintances came out of the woodwork requesting assignments. Pershing wanted only the best with him in France, and often bypassed older officers in favor of younger, more aggressive ones. In one heartbreaking decision, he turned down Teddy Roosevelt's request to form a volunteer regiment. Pershing was shocked at the appalling lack of military readiness. "It had been apparent to everybody for months that we were likely to be forced into the war," he wrote, "yet scarcely a start had been made to prepare for our participation." The army brass had done no serious contingency planning. The National Defense Act of 1916 had authorized a major expansion of the army, but by April 1917 little of substance had been accomplished. American companies had been supplying the Allies with war materials for years, but America itself had no real arms industry. To fight a modern war, the AEF needed mass numbers of artillery pieces, machine guns, and mortars, but the nation had no companies capable of mass-producing them.

The embryonic aircraft industry produced planes that by European standards were already obsolete. Few Americans had ever even seen a tank. Even if the United States had had enough weapons, there were not enough ships available to get them overseas. "The deeper we went into the situation," Pershing wrote, "the more overwhelming the work ahead of us seemed to be."

Pershing's days in Washington were also filled with meetings—at foreign embassies, with the Red Cross, and of course at the War Department. He was especially thrilled to speak with Marshal Joffre, though his admiration for the French warrior did not extend to Joffre's amalgamation proposal. "I was decidedly against our becoming a recruiting agency for either the French or British," he declared, and zealously supported the idea of fielding an independent American army. Four days before departing for France, Pershing paid a call on the White House and President Wilson. The meeting was brief and perfunctory. The president expressed confidence in the general and wished him well. Pershing admired Wilson's "poise and his air of determination," but was disappointed that he gave little guidance. "I had naturally thought that he would say something about the part our Army should play in the war in cooperation with the Allied armies," Pershing wrote of the encounter, "but he said nothing."

"I will give you only two orders," Secretary Baker told Pershing, "one to go to France and the other to come home." The reality was a bit more complex, but Pershing was indeed given broad powers to conduct the war as he saw fit. He was instructed to secure ports, establish lines of communication to the front, and prepare the army for combat. Pershing had complete discretion in battlefield operations. "Your authority in France will be supreme," said Baker. In dealing with the Allies, Baker told the general to cooperate with them but he also made abundantly clear that "in so doing the underlying idea must be kept in view that the forces of the United States are a separate and distinct component of the combined forces, the identity of which must be preserved." Pershing hardly needed to be reminded. Indeed, some believe Pershing may have written those instructions himself.

As the *Baltic* sailed eastward for England, Pershing and his staff worked feverishly to lay the groundwork for the AEF. He arrived at the Princes Dock in Liverpool on June 8, 1917, and was greeted with much pomp and ceremony. He was then quickly whisked off to London, where he established his temporary headquarters in the Savoy Hotel on the Strand. Among the many calls Pershing made while in London was to Buckingham Palace, where King George V told him, "It has been the dream of my life to see the two great English-speaking nations united in a common cause." After five days in London, it was off to France.

Of his landing at Boulogne, Pershing was to remember that "French troops, together with the assembled women and children from the town . . . presented a colorful picture." He made special note of the soldiers, whose "stripes and decorations indicated that every man had seen service at the front." His reception in Paris later that day was the most effusive yet. Arriving at the Gare du Nord, Pershing was brought by motorcade to the Hotel Crillon on the place de la Concorde. The route was one long scene of wild celebration. "Every housetop, wall, and window was filled with cheering crowds," reported the *New York Times*, "and it seemed everyone was waving an American flag, while cries of 'Vive l'Amerique!' became a sustained roar." "After our arrival at the [hotel] I was again and again forced to appear on the portico of my apartment to greet the dense crowds," Pershing wrote. "It was most touching and in a sense most pathetic," he later reflected, "and stirred within us a deep sense of the responsibility resting upon America."

He set up his headquarters at 27–31 rue Constantine, a stone's throw from the Hôtel des Invalides, on the Left Bank of the Seine. A home for retired soldiers founded by Louis XIV in 1674, over the years Invalides had evolved into a shrine to French military history, including the tomb of Napoleon himself. A bank, private residences, and the Colombian Embassy now occupy Pershing's rue Constantine offices. American financier and Paris resident Ogden Mills allowed Pershing the use of his eighteenth-century mansion at 73 rue de Varenne, just a few blocks away from AEF headquarters, as his residence. Pershing enjoyed the "magnificent garden" with its "century old trees," though he was also gratified that Mills had installed "all modern conveniences." Just down the street at 79 rue de Varenne, the aging sculptor Auguste Rodin maintained his studios. Pershing's one-time residence still stands, though it is privately owned and the mansion and gardens are concealed from public view. Rodin's studios are now the Musée Rodin, and there the traveler can stroll the gardens.

Hunched over their desks and burning the midnight oil, Pershing and his staff worked out the organization of the AEF. They envisioned a force of a million men. Some in Washington balked at such a figure, but by November 1918 the AEF had grown to twice that number. France and Britain graciously allowed the Americans to use their own military bases and training facilities. Pershing and Allied commanders also had to decide where the American army would concentrate its efforts. The obvious choice to all parties was the southern section of the Western Front, in the Lorraine region of France. The British put primary emphasis on guarding the English Channel ports in northern France that gave them access to the continent. In the center, France desperately wanted to protect its national capital, Paris. Pershing accepted the southern sector gladly, seeing there an opportunity for a decisive American offensive to end the war. He anticipated only limited offensive operations in 1917 and 1918 as the AEF grew in size and experience. To warm up the American war machine, he proposed to reduce the German salient into Allied lines near Saint-Mihiel in 1918. The major push would come in 1919, when U.S. forces would drive into Germany itself, taking Metz and the Saar region. This would cut essential German supply and communication lines, he argued, forcing a German withdrawal from large areas of Belgium and France. It would also deprive Germany of valuable coal and iron-ore resources, unhinging its economy. Coordinated with British and French operations to the north, this offensive would, Pershing believed, force Germany to surrender. In addition to strategic opportunities, the American takeover of the Lorraine sector also made logistical sense. Rather than using the congested roads and rails of northern France, the United States would bring its men and materiel through Atlantic ports like Bordeaux, Brest, and Saint-Nazaire, then transport them across central France.

In September 1917, Pershing moved his headquarters to Chaumont, in the Department of Haute-Marne, 280 kilometers southeast of Paris. His stated reason for doing so was to be closer to the Lorraine front where he expected Americans would one day fight. Chaumont, a small city of 15,000, lay near the end of the main American line of communication from Saint-Nazaire, and eighty kilometers behind the Saint-Mihiel salient. Pershing probably had other motivations for the move. "He thought that the newspapers at home and perhaps the French might say that the Americans were enjoying themselves in Paris instead of getting up to the front," wrote General Johnson Hagood, who added that Pershing "also thought

Chaumont, France by U.S. Army war artist Jules Smith. (From Jules A. Smith, *In France with the American Expeditionary Forces*, 1919)

that the bright lights of Paris would divert the officers, soldiers, and clerks from their legitimate duties." James Harbord, Pershing's chief of staff, also noted "the constant air of tutelage" from French officials in Paris, and suggested that he personally was glad to move from "the zone of the politicians to the zone of the soldiers."

Pershing and his staff took over the Caserne de Damrémont, home of the French 109th Infantry Regiment, on the north side of the city. The Château du Val des Écoliers, located in the woods and fields four kilometers south of the city, served as the general's residence. Chaumont may have lacked the excitement and sophistication of Paris, but Americans still found it charming. "Although the place is small and one could traverse its streets in a morning's walk," wrote Jules Smith, an official army war artist, "it has a dignity of architecture, and a distinct quality of ancient loveliness." "It certainly was a most delightful town," recalled finance officer S. Herbert Wolfe, "beautifully situated in a rolling section of France, traversed by quaint winding streets and its architecture appealing to Americans accustomed to the monotonous regularity of our buildings."

Today Chaumont has nearly 25,000 residents but has lost little of its charm. American visitors can find several reminders of their nation's presence there during the Great War. The Caserne de Damrémont is now a police training academy and closed to the public, but a plaque commissioned by the American Battle Monuments Commission is affixed to a building near the main gate. Thousands of Americans served in Chaumont during the war, and several hundred died there, mostly of disease. The dead were buried in the Saint-Aignan Cemetery, less than a kilometer to the southwest of the caserne, on the route de Neufchâteau. The Americans were exhumed and returned to America after the war, but a small memorial at the cemetery still commemorates them. In a park on boulevard Barotte near the central city stands the Monument to Franco-American Friendship. Commissioned by Chaumont and surrounding communities, it was dedicated in 1923 to great fanfare. French President Alexandre Millerand and Premier Raymond Poincaré were on hand for the ceremonies, as were thousands of locals. The *New York Times* described the lead-up to the dedication ceremony this way:

> Throughout the day people from the surrounding towns and many from Paris were constantly arriving, while the roads leading into the town from the countryside and all parts of the Department of Haute-Marne were filled with peasants in carts and vehicles of all descriptions. Some were camping in the streets and squares, and many spent the night in the town's beautiful park.

The marble sculpture consists of a woman, representing France, holding a French Poilu in one arm and extending the other to a youthful American soldier. Each soldier holds a gun, but careful observers will note that the weapons are lighter in color than the rest of the statue. During World War II, German occupation forces smashed the guns from their hands. They were replaced in 1973. Should travelers need a place to stay in Chaumont, the Château du Val des Écoliers, Pershing's former residence, is today a bed and breakfast.

Monument to Franco-American Friendship, Chaumont, France.

Pershing and "Open Warfare"

In late 1917 the war took more dramatic turns. During October and November, the Austro-Hungarians, bolstered by a contingent of elite German troops, smashed through Italian lines in the Alps of northeastern Italy. In this engagement, known as the Battle of Caporetto, the Germans experimented with new infantry infiltration tactics. Elite "storm troopers" punched through the Italian front lines, causing havoc in their rear, softening up their front, and allowing the second wave to sweep the Italians from their positions. German and Austrian forces pushed the Italians all the way to the Piave River and dealt them a devastating blow that threatened to knock Italy out of the war. In November 1917, Vladimir Lenin and the Bolsheviks, as his faction of Russian communists was known, seized power in Petrograd (present-day Saint Petersburg) and began peace negotiations with the Germans. With Russia effectively out of the war, Germany could now concentrate on the Western Front, where French and British armies remained bruised and under strength. As 1918 dawned, German victory was distinct possibility.

In the wake of Caporetto and the Russian Revolution, the thorny issue of amalgamating U.S. troops into Allied armies resurfaced. British and French diplomats in Washington began raising the issue, and British Prime Minister David Lloyd George cornered Edward M. House, President Wilson's friend and top advisor, while he was in Paris, about the matter. Wilson and Secretary Baker argued that amalgamation was a military issue and not a political one, and therefore it was Pershing's decision. The U.S. commander soon found himself face-to-face with Lloyd George and French Prime Minister Georges Clemenceau, who earned the nickname "the Tiger" for his tough determination. Discussions centered on a British proposal that the United States send 150 battalions of raw infantrymen and machine gunners. Britain offered to transport these men to Europe on its own ships, train them, and then attach them to its own divisions. While Lloyd George and Clemenceau badgered Pershing in Europe, their diplomats intensified British and French pressure on Washington. Wilson and Baker began to buckle, and let

Pershing know that they would accept some kind of amalgamation plan, but the general remained adamantly against it. In January 1918, the British agreed to Pershing's counterproposal, the so-called "Six Division Plan." Under the agreement, the British would to transport six American divisions—infantry as well as artillery and support troops—to France on their own ships. Britain would train these divisions, and they would serve in the British sector, though under American officers and under the American flag. Pershing also stipulated that should necessity demand it, these divisions would be turned over to American control.

Pershing's stubborn resistance to amalgamation stemmed in part from his opinions on European military thinking. The American commander believed that three years of inconclusive trench warfare had left European soldiers demoralized and their leaders fixated on defensive operations. To win the war, he argued, the Allies had to go on the offensive and fight it out in the open. Pulling the war out of the trenches required several things, opined Pershing. One was a fighting spirit. American soldiers, uninfected with the mentality of trench warfare, would reinvigorate morale across the front, Pershing believed, and give the Allies the edge over the Germans. Amalgamating Doughboys into British and French armies, he feared, would squander the precious gift of the American spirit the Allies would need to prevail. Success in the open also required the skilled use of the rifle and the bayonet—the traditional weapons of the infantryman. A soldier with steely discipline, a marksman's eye, and an indefatigable will to win, Pershing believed, was the most effective weapon of all. He dismissed machine guns as "weapons of emergency." Foot soldiers grew too dependent on them, he believed, sapping their fighting spirit. Pershing thought that other new weapons, like tanks and airplanes, were useful only in support of infantry forces. "In each succeeding war there is a tendency to proclaim as something new the principles under which it conducted," Pershing wrote after the war, but to his mind the Great War was not substantially different than any other. "The principles of warfare as I learned them at West Point remain unchanged," he declared.

Pershing's doctrine of open warfare, with the infantryman and his rifle playing the key role in the drama of the battlefield, expressed an American faith in the individual to meet challenges and overcome adversity, as well as an American tendency to dismiss European ways. It may also have betrayed a fundamental misunderstanding of warfare on the Western Front. Pershing's British and French colleagues were unimpressed with his doctrine of open warfare, thinking it naïve. But before Pershing's ideas could be proven or disproven, the United States had to field an army. In 1917, the mass army Pershing would lead into battle did not yet exist. The United States faced the immense task of raising a modern army from scratch.

CHAPTER 3:
TRAINING CAMPS

"Nothing more unmilitary in appearance can be imagined," thought army officer L. Wardlaw Miles as he watched draftees file into Camp Upton, New York, for basic training, "than the long columns of civilian-clad men, each with a paper-wrapped or rope-tied bundle, valise, or suitcase, which wound from the train to barracks." Examining their faces, Miles noted that "some looked very dejected" and "a few were boisterously drunk," but "the great majority accepted the situation with that practical American stoicism which is equally far removed from enthusiasm or despair." Such was the raw material of the Doughboy. If America was to make a difference in the war, these raw recruits had to be transformed into soldiers. When the war began, America's small army was scattered across the United States and in overseas possessions like the Philippines and Puerto Rico. It was also inexperienced. Most of its officers and men had never heard a shot fired in anger, and had little experience with weapons like tanks and poison gas. Germany certainly had reason to think that America would not be able to mobilize effectively for a long time. And yet within eighteen months of entering the war, the United States had 4.5 million men under arms, two million of them overseas. The creation of this mass army in such a short period of time was one of the greatest bureaucratic feats in American history and a crucial factor in the ultimate Allied victory.

The government's first task was getting men into uniform, and though there were lots of volunteers, Uncle Sam quickly turned to conscription. The Selective Service Act of 1917, passed on May 18, required all men ages twenty-one to thirty—later eighteen to forty-five—to register for the draft. The law ended the blatant favoritism toward the wealthy that made Civil War conscription so controversial. Gone were practices like hiring a substitute to serve in one's place, or paying a commutation fee to avoid service altogether. This time, men would be selected by lottery. It was then up to more than 4,600 local draft boards to determine the fitness of those in their own communities whose numbers were called. Registration began on June 5, the first draft calls went out on July 21, and selectees reported to training camps in September. There was considerable draft evasion. Roughly 10 percent of eligible men did not register, and in a few places there was armed resistance. Nevertheless, twenty-four million young men had registered for military service by 1919, of which nearly three million were inducted. The draft was so successful that by the end of the war the military suspended voluntary enlistments and relied solely on the draft for new soldiers.

These Doughboys-in-the-making needed leaders, but the army (including the National Guard) had only 18,000 officers. West Point accelerated its curriculum and the reserve officer programs scrambled to get organized, but with the first wave of draftees slated to hit the camps in September 1917 the army needed new officers right away. To meet the emergency, the army opened sixteen Officers Training Camps in May 1917 based on the Plattsburg model (see Chapter 1). The first opened at the Leon Springs Military Reservation north of San Antonio, Texas on May 8—a Texas Historical Marker on Boerne Springs Road near the Intersection with Interstate 10 commemorates this camp—and others soon opened at army posts across the country, from Plattsburg to the Presidio in San Francisco. The three-month program was rudimentary, emphasizing military discipline over cultivating leadership skills, but it was rigorous. Candidates drilled, dug trenches, and studied army manuals. "War isn't all brass buttons and cheering," officer candidate Frederick Edwards concluded. Teachers were sometimes barely more advanced than their students. Lieutenant Charles Bolté was an instructor at Fort Benjamin Harrison, Indiana. Preparing a lesson on the .45 pistol, he remembered that he "had to sit up all night long with a manual learning how you took it apart and put it together again" so that he could "try to teach this company how to do this very complicated task" the next day. "It was the blind leading the blind," wrote Bolté. Despite their shortcomings, the camps were essential. The draftees who showed up at the training camps in September 1917 "would have had no leaders at all," according to historian Garry Clifford, "had it not been for the officer camps." The army fine-tuned the program as the war went on. By November 1918, nearly half of all U.S. Army's 200,000 officers, and two-thirds of line officers, were products of the three-month officer training programs, often derided as "ninety-day wonders."

Officers and men entered an army thoroughly reorganized for modern war. The basic fighting outfit was the division—a combined arms unit composed of infantry augmented with machine gun, artillery, and various support units. Because the American army had little experience with the kind of fighting taking place in Europe, some units had to be completely re-equipped. Mounted cavalrymen, of little use in trench warfare, often became artillerymen or machine gunners. This meant learning to fight with weapons that were utterly unfamiliar to them. One coastal artillery captain was told by his commanding officer that he was to convert to a trench mortar battery. The young officer readily agreed, but asked, "What is a trench mortar?" "Damned if I know," replied his superior, "but you will soon find out." The U.S. Army developed a "square" division, which centered on two brigades composed of two infantry regiments each, for staying power in ongoing combat operations. As American planners envisioned it, one brigade would attack while the other remained in reserve. When the lead brigade became exhausted the reserves would move up, keeping constant pressure on the enemy. At roughly 28,000 men, the American division was twice the size of its European counterparts. The first five regiments sent to France (16th, 18th, 26th, and 28th Infantries and the 6th Field Artillery) formed the nucleus of the 1st Division, which was officially constituted in France. The 2nd Division, which included a brigade of U.S. Marines, was also organized overseas. All of the other divisions took shape in training camps in the United States.

Divisions fell into three categories. Regular army divisions took the numbers 1–20. The National Guard divisions were assigned numbers 26–42. The National Army was made up of draftees, and its divisions were numbered 76–92. The U.S. Army had never kept permanent divisions before. Many of the infantry and artillery regiments that were to compose them had long, illustrious histories, and members were often reluctant to subsume their identities into the new organizations. It was an especially tough pill to swallow for National Guard regiments, which had strong state identifications, though state and regional identities did not go away entirely. National Guard divisions were usually made up of regiments from the same part of the country. Guard regiments from the New England states made up the 26th Division, for example. National Army divisions also had regional identities. The 76th Division contained men from New England and New York state. The 77th was made up almost entirely of soldiers from New York City. But the practical demands of fighting the war quickly led to the weakening of these regional identities. The army combed through all units for promising leaders, and reassigned incompetent ones. As casualties mounted, replacements came into the divisions without regard to region.

The new divisions adopted nicknames that promoted unit cohesion. The New Englanders of the 26th Division called themselves the "Yankee Division." One National Guard division, the 42nd, was composed of units from across the country and took the nickname the "Rainbow Division." The 82nd Division, originally composed of men from the South, quickly attained such diversity that it became known as the "All-American Division." By war's end, the divisions also adopted distinctive shoulder patches. The emblem of New York City's 77th Division bore the likeness of the Statue of Liberty, and became known as the Liberty Division. The 1st Division's patch

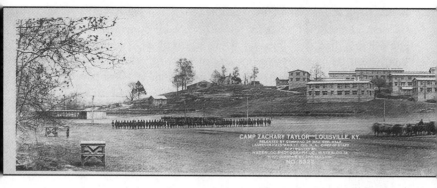

contained a red number one on an olive background. To this day, this division is known as the "Big Red One."

Existing army posts could not adequately handle the millions of young men now in uniform, so new training facilities had to be built. Creating the training camps was the responsibility of the U.S. Army Cantonment Division, established in May 1917. The commander of each military district in the United States was asked to scout appropriate training sites. The army leased or purchased lands, and in some cases accepted donations. There were thirty-two divisional camps in all. National Guard divisions would be trained at sixteen tent camps in the South. An additional sixteen cantonments were designated for the National Army, where men would be housed in wooden barracks. Regular army soldiers also trained at these new facilities. The camps were named for some of America's great military heroes—often with a local connection. Rockford, Illinois, for example, was home to Camp Grant, named in honor of Civil War general and Illinois favorite son Ulysses S. Grant. Camp Lee, near Petersburg Virginia, was named after Grant's Confederate rival and Virginian Robert E. Lee. Indeed, many camps in the South were named for Confederate Civil War leaders who half a century earlier had taken up arms against the U.S. government. Camp Gordon, Georgia, was named for Confederate General John B. Gordon. The general's widow even reviewed the troops at the camp named for her deceased husband.

Politicians and local civic groups scrambled to attract a camp to their community. In Pierce County, Washington, voters approved a bond of two million dollars to purchase more than 62,000 acres for a camp. The army accepted the gift, and Camp Lewis was born. Fort Worth, Texas, enticed the army to lease a site just west of the city by offering to improve roads, provide fire protection, and connect the camp to the city's water system. Camp Bowie soon sprouted from the prairies along Arlington Heights Boulevard. The first construction contracts were signed in June, and work began immediately with the goal of having them ready to receive troops by September.

Camp Zachary Taylor, Louisville, Kentucky.
(Courtesy of the Library of Congress)

Each camp was basically a small city—and had to be built overnight. Water, sewage, and electricity hookups had to be established. Rail and road links were needed too. Engineers usually followed existing roads and incorporated existing buildings into the camps. To meet the emergency, the army suspended competitive bidding and employed well-established contracting firms on a cost-plus-fixed-fee basis. Two hundred thousand workers labored throughout the summer in all kinds of weather to get the camps ready. In September the troops began to arrive, whether the camps were done or not. When Ray Fuller of the 32nd Division got to Camp MacArthur near Waco, Texas, he was surprised to find "nothing there but a big cotton field."

Some locations proved controversial. Community leaders in Chillicothe, Ohio, convinced the army to build a camp on farmlands along the Scioto River north of their city. The flat, level land with railroad access suited the army's needs, and the army offered to lease it from the owners with an option to buy. Camp Sherman was born, but not everyone was thrilled. Some farmers resisted giving up their prime river bottomlands for just $15 an acre. Local businessmen raised money to supplement the government offer, and appealed to the reluctant farmers' sense of patriotism and wartime sacrifice to accept the offer. Those who still resisted found that the government simply took their land through eminent domain. In addition, the northern edge of the camp contained a cluster of 2,000-year-old earthen mounds, the remnants of an ancient Native American culture known as the Hopewell. Archaeologists called this cluster the Mound City group, and it consisted of twenty-three conical and elongated mounds enclosed within an earthen embankment. Hopewell mounds were known to contain artistic treasures and trade goods from across the continent. Some contain human burials. The army planned to raze Mound City and put up barracks. The Ohio State Archaeological and Historical Society pleaded with the army to preserve the mounds; the army agreed to make some concessions for history. "We will construct the buildings in such a way on the mounds that they will not be destroyed," one army official promised, though he also took pains to note that "it will be necessary to run pipe lines through some of the mounds."

The World of the Training Camps

Army officials envisioned a training program of four months, but, with the desperate demand for men overseas, soldiers often received far less than that. Upon arrival, inductees were given uniforms and a physical examination. Then they were taught the soldiers' trade. There was lots of drill, calisthenics, and long marches. Soldiers dug miles of trenches and viciously attacked bundled corn stalks with their bayonets in order to prepare for what they might face in France. Experienced French and British instructors were on hand to pass on their combat expertise. The training could be physically and mentally challenging. "All of us wore gas masks and helmets," remembered Ray Johnson of the 37th Division at Camp Sheridan, Alabama. "We waded and slipped and struggled in mud that was two and a half feet deep in some places. Conditions were worse that we ever experienced before or after," he wrote, "even in France." American industry was just beginning to mobilize for war, so equipment shortages hindered training effectiveness. Early on, some units lacked rifles and drilled with wooden sticks instead. The army even had trouble getting uniform parts, and trainee clothing was often a hybrid of military and civilian items. One thing that was in plentiful supply was food. The average training camp ration was more than 4,600 calories a day.

Uncle Sam was very much concerned about the morals of the Doughboy. Historically, drunkenness and prostitution had plagued armies, and World War I was no exception. Alcohol could undermine discipline and combat readiness. Sexually transmitted diseases were a major problem in European armies. The British army recorded nearly half a million cases during the war. The French army had more than a million. The treatment of infected men took them off the line, diminishing combat effectiveness. The Progressives in the Wilson Administration believed they had the obligation to use the full power of the government to guide and alter the behavior of its fighting men. The Commission on Training Camp Activities (CTCA) stood ready to protect the soldier from himself. Noting how soldiers had been separated from their families and home communities—and the restraints those institutions normally imposed on their behavior—the commission strove "to furnish these young men a substitute for the recreational and relaxational opportunities to which they have been accustomed" and help them adjust to "the bewildering environment of a war camp."

To give soldiers a home away from home, the commission worked with numerous service organizations like the Salvation

Army, Knights of Columbus, and the Jewish Welfare Board, but foremost among them the Young Men's Christian Association (YMCA). Founded in London in 1844 to provide social services and wholesome recreational activities for young men migrating to cities, the YMCA had been well established in the United States by 1917, and its efforts dovetailed nicely with the military's needs. Every training camp—indeed virtually every U.S. military installation in the world—had a YMCA "hut" where any soldier of any faith could meet friends, write a letter home, or read the newspaper. Thanks to the CTCA and its partners, the Doughboy had many alternatives to boozing and whoring. There was a great emphasis on athletics, for example. Boxing was particularly encouraged, according to one committee publication, "because of its intimate connection to bayonet fighting." There were theaters for movies and stage productions. The CTCA published *Songs of the Soldiers and Sailors* in the belief that singing would build morale and camaraderie. The American Library Association made books and magazines available for the more studiously minded. To ensure that soldiers could purchase items on the post from a reputable source, the committee ran a post exchange. Soldiers would inevitably get off the post and head to the nearest town, but the CTCA followed them. The War Camp Community Service ran clubs for soldiers in nearby towns, sponsored dances with "respectable" local girls, and organized a "Take a Soldier or Sailor to Dinner" program as a way to meet the locals.

Under the authority of the Selective Service Act, the government closed taverns and red light districts in areas around the camps. Fort Worth, Texas, had a particularly vibrant red light district known as "Hell's Half Acre," which city leaders tolerated because of its economic benefits. When Camp Bowie came to town things changed. Few communities think their red light district worthy of historical commemoration, but Fort Worth does. A state historical marker near the intersection of Houston and 14th Street tells the story of Hell's Half Acre and notes how the First World War led to its temporary demise, which lasted only to the end of the conflict. Another marker at 14th and Commerce suggests that the district's infamous activities continued through the war years. Local entrepreneurs often complained about the restrictions, but in most cases community leaders applauded the moves. The *Milwaukee Journal* reported approvingly that Wisconsin's National Guard troops at Camp MacArthur were being closely monitored. "The military police . . . are patrolling every road and highway out of Waco on motorcycles, on horse, and on foot, and they keep the soldier population within bounds," the paper noted. "They are wise to the tricks of the soldier and cannot be fooled." Despite such bold pronouncements, some Doughboys found ways to obtain the services of prostitutes or enjoy the intoxicating pleasures of booze. John Barkley, who would later receive the

Congressional Medal of Honor for his battlefield exploits, smuggled whiskey into Camp Funston by train. As military police searched his car for contraband, Barkley wrote that he "raised my window and hung the bottles outside then closed the window." After the MPs had left, Barkley "opened the windows and pulled in [the] bottles." He later bragged that he "pulled off the trick repeatedly without being caught." Soldiers also received plenty of lectures, saw numerous films, and were given pamphlets on the evils of sexual promiscuity. In the camp YMCA hut, the soldier might see a poster telling him that "a German bullet is cleaner than a whore."

Formation portrait of President Wilson, Camp Sherman, Ohio. (Courtesy of the Library of Congress)

The training camps were an eye-opening experience for millions of young Americans. Many had never been away from their hometowns before or seen modern amenities like canned food, movies, and showers. A good many trainees were unable to read and write proper English. One army study estimated that 25 percent of soldiers were unable to read the Constitution or write a letter in English to the folks back home. Illiteracy rates were particularly high in men from impoverished regions of the South and West, and the army created programs to teach them to read and write. Not all trainees saw the benefits of literacy. One man complained to the chaplain that he was "going over there to shoot Germans, not write letters to 'em."

Many soldiers could barely speak English. The years before World War I saw an immense wave of immigration from Europe, and America's ethnic diversity was reflected in the ranks. Nearly 20 percent of the nation's servicemen were born in another country, and a good many more were the children of immigrants. The 77th Division from New York City had such an astonishing array of ethnic groups—Chinese, Czech, French Canadian, German, Italian, Jewish, Slovak, and Slovenian, just to name a few—that some called it the "Melting Pot Division."

Immigration complicated the draft. Naturalized citizens could be conscripted like anyone else. Selective Service ruled that those who had declared their intent to become citizens were also eligible, but non-declaring immigrants could not be compelled to serve.

The racist notions that prevailed at the time suggested that many of these men were physically and mentally inferior to Anglo-Saxons, especially those from southern and eastern Europe. Some doubted whether they could ever become good soldiers—or good Americans. There were also questions about loyalty. Many were "enemy aliens" who had been born in Germany or the Austro-Hungarian Empire. Would they serve and fight with America's interests at heart, or would they undermine the U.S. war effort and endanger the lives of their fellow soldiers?

Such fears proved to be unfounded. Immigrants typically became enthusiastic soldiers. Indeed, some non-declaring immigrants who were drafted by mistake opted to serve anyway. Those who hailed from the lands dominated by the Austro-Hungarian Empire were particularly anxious to fight, seeing service in the U.S. Army as a way to free their homelands. At Camp Gordon, Georgia, the army developed a system for training non-English-speaking immigrants, in which men were assigned to companies based on ethnicity and commanded by a bilingual officer. At war's end, a "Slavic Legion" was even being organized at Camp Wadsworth, South Carolina. Some saw in the war an opportunity to Americanize the immigrant. General Leonard Wood believed that military service might "heat up the melting pot." Immigrants were taught English and given a strong dose of Americanism, but the army was also respectful of the diversity in its ranks. Catholic, Orthodox, and Jewish chaplains served the spiritual needs of the men, and religious holidays were respected whenever possible. Thousands decided to become citizens, and Uncle Sam sped up the naturalization process for them. Beginning in May 1918, the government waived all naturalization fees, as well as the five-year residency requirement for those who could produce "evidence of loyalty," allowing them to become citizens immediately. By December 1918, 155,246 immigrant soldiers had taken the citizenship oath.

The training camps left an important cultural legacy. In 1918, the army drafted a thirty-year-old Russian Jewish immigrant musician named Irving Berlin. During the early twentieth century, music artists and publishers were concentrated on Tin Pan Alley, a stretch of 28th Street in New York City between 5th and 6th Avenues. Berlin was one of the district's brightest stars, and his being drafted made headlines, including one that proclaimed, "U.S. Takes Berlin." Sent to Camp Upton near Yaphank, New York, Berlin lived in the barracks, performed kitchen duties, and answered reveille like any other soldier—a far cry from the life of luxury he had known in Manhattan. He especially hated reveille, and expressed his feelings in a song entitled, "Oh! How I Hate to Get Up in the Morning," which he called his "bugle song." The camp commander asked the talented soldier to stage a musical production to raise money for a camp recreation center. The result was a play entitled *Yip, Yip, Yaphank*. With a cast made up almost entirely of Camp Upton soldiers—who played even the women's roles—the piece opened on August 19, 1918, at the Century Theater on West 62nd and Central Park West. (The building has since been demolished.) The production included Berlin's "bugle song," and concluded with soldiers in full combat gear marching off the stage singing, "We're On Our Way to France." His original draft of the musical included a song called "God Bless America," which Berlin cut from the final production but dusted off in 1938 as another war loomed. *Yip, Yip, Yaphank* had a run of thirty-two shows and raised more than $800,000, but the war ended before the recreation center could be built.

In 1917, an aspiring writer from Minnesota named F. Scott Fitzgerald left his studies at Princeton to become an army officer. Fitzgerald dreamed of glory on the battlefield, but proved to be a poor soldier. He attended officer candidate school at Fort Leavenworth, Kansas, where he daydreamed through lectures and focused mainly on writing a novel that would become *This Side of Paradise*. He often ran afoul of his commanding officer, Captain Dwight D. Eisenhower, and was known to his colleagues at Leavenworth as "the worst second lieutenant in the army." While stationed at Camp Sheridan, Alabama, Fitzgerald met a woman named Zelda Sayre, the daughter of a prominent judge, whom he would later marry. Camp Zachary Taylor near Louisville also left an impression on him, though he was only there for a month in the spring of 1918. His 1925 classic novel *The Great Gatsby* is set in New York, but Louisville and Camp Taylor are critical to the novel's plot. In the book, the title character Jay Gatsby is stationed at Camp Taylor, where he meets a young woman named Daisy Fay. Gatsby is soon sent to Europe, and he and Daisy lose touch. Later, rather reluctantly, Daisy marries a man named Tom Buchanan—indeed, Tom and Daisy's wedding takes place at Louisville's elegant Seelbach Hotel, which is today part of the Hilton chain. After the war Daisy and Gatsby meet again in New York, causing tension and trouble for all. Fitzgerald himself never left the United States, and frequently complained about missing the war. But perhaps it was a good thing. His literary contemporary, Ernest Hemingway, once quipped that had Fitzgerald gotten to the front he would probably have been shot for cowardice. Despite his shortcomings as an officer, Fitzgerald became one of America's greatest authors. He was among the leading figures of the "Lost Generation," whose writings expressed the bitter sense of disillusion that enveloped the country following the war. The seeds of some of the nation's finest literature were sown in the army training camps.

The camps also left a far darker legacy. The crowded and intimate conditions of military life often spawn disease. Indeed, disease was historically a much greater killer in wartime than combat. America's makeshift training camps brought in young men from across the nation, squeezed them into overcrowded barracks, and shuffled them around from place to place. One morning in early March 1918, a soldier at Camp Funston, Kansas, went to sick call just before breakfast complaining of a "bad cold." By noon, more than 100 others had come in with similar symptoms. Theories differ on the origins of the great influenza pandemic of World War I, but many believe that the events at Camp Funston that morning may have been the beginning of the global catastrophe.

Some of the men training at Funston came from Haskell County, Kansas, where there had been a spike in influenza cases earlier that year. These men may have brought the disease into the camp. From Funston, the disease spread to other army camps, and then to the civilian population. In Europe, initial cases were reported shortly after the arrival of the first Doughboys. By early April 1918, British and French troops began to fall ill, and by the end of the month so did the Germans. It also hit neutral Spain, where the publicity the disease generated led to it being called the "Spanish Flu." At first the outbreak did not seem particularly serious, but as the virus mutated it evolved into a strain far more deadly than anything science had ever encountered. For one thing, it spread unusually fast. Victims could go from onset of symptoms to death in just a few days. Standard influenza symptoms like aches, cough, fever, and nausea were much more pronounced. This strain also filled the lungs of victims with blood and other fluids, sometimes causing their skin to turn blue due to a lack of oxygen. In camps and in the trenches on both sides of the Atlantic, the deadly disease spread among military personnel. The close quarters on troopships were particularly conducive to spreading the disease. By the end of the war, more than 50,000 American soldiers and sailors had died of influenza, or complications of it like pneumonia. In Europe and America the pandemic reached its peak in late 1918, but it reverberated around the world until 1920. Possibly incubated in U.S. Army training camps and spread by the unusual conditions of war, the Spanish Flu was one of the greatest medical disasters in modern times, ultimately killing more than 600,000 Americans and anywhere from twenty to fifty million people worldwide.

The Training Camps Today

After the war, the training camps often served as demobilization centers, and many a Doughboy received his discharge papers at the very place that introduced him to military life. Once the soldiers had gone home, the fate of the camps varied. In many cases, the army quickly dismantled the buildings, sold them off or destroyed them, and returned the lands to their owners. Places that had once housed tens of thousands of soldiers vanished overnight.

The only reminders of many camps are lonely and neglected memorials or historical markers. Just a mile west of downtown Charlotte, North Carolina, for example, is a monument to Camp Greene, at the intersection of Wilkinson Boulevard and Monument Street. Just north of this is the Dowd House, which served as the camp commander's headquarters and now houses a small museum about the camp. In Montgomery, Alabama, a small stone monument stands in the middle of Johnson Avenue at its intersection with Lower Wetumpka Road, marking the location of Camp Sheridan's headquarters. The bronze plaque includes a relief map showing the camp's layout. At the intersection of Wade Hampton Boulevard and Artillery Road northeast of Greenville, South Carolina, stands a state historical marker dedicated to Camp Sevier. At the corner of Pike Knoll Drive and West Lee Road in the same city is another such marker, placed by the local American Legion in 1934. Camp Sevier stretched northward from these markers, but except for street names like Artillery Road and Warehouse Court that hint at the neighborhood's past, one would never know it. On the northern edge of Waco, Texas, there is little evidence of Camp MacArthur except for a forlorn historical marker in a shopping center parking lot at the corner of North 19th Street and Park Lake Road. Some former camps are not commemorated at all. Standing today at the intersection of 2nd Avenue and Holy Cross Road in the desert west of Deming, New Mexico, one sees only stretches of sand and greasewood with some mountains in the distance and a few farms nearby. There is no indication that Camp Cody once occupied these grounds.

Closed camps sometimes stimulated postwar suburbanization as real estate developers plugged into the water, sewer, and electrical systems the government left behind. Nourished by army infrastructure, the city of Menlo Park, California, grew quickly from the remnants of Camp Fremont. Just north of the Stanford University campus, the camp area is now covered with acres and acres of homes. Tiny Fremont Park, at the corner of Santa Cruz Avenue and University Drive, pays tribute to the camp, but walking or driving through these suburban neighborhoods the traveler will see nothing from Great War, though there is one last remnant of the Doughboys' presence not too far away. The MacArthur Park Restaurant in Palo Alto (27 University Avenue) was once the Camp Fremont YMCA Hostess House. For one dollar, the City of Palo Alto purchased the building, designed by the renowned architect Julia Morgan, and moved it to its present location in 1919. It is the only structure known to have survived from California's two World War I training camps.

A similar story unfolded at Camp Bowie, Texas. Once the army left the camp in August 1919, Fort Worth's suburban sprawl overtook

SIDEBAR I—WORLD WAR I TRAINING CAMPS

CAMP	NEAREST CITY	GPS COORDINATES
Beauregard	Pineville, LA	N 31.37569 W 92.38952
Bowie	Fort Worth, TX	N 32.74395 W 97.37976
Cody	Deming, NM	N 32.27500 W 107.80833
Custer	Battle Creek, MI	N 42.29250 W 85.32583
Devens	Ayer, MA	N 42.54502 W 71.61334
Dix	Wrightstown, NJ	N 40.01917 W 74.52278
Dodge	Johnston, IA	N 41.70306 W 93.71861
Doniphan	Lawton, OK	N 34.67922 W 98.42642
Fremont	Menlo Park, CA	N 37.44884 W 122.18621
Funston	Manhattan, KS	N 39.09626 W 96.72644
Gordon	DeKalb Co., GA	N 32.81178 W 83.54124
Grant	Rockford, IL	N 42.20833 W 89.08222
Greene	Charlotte, NC	N 35.22478 W 80.88249
Hancock	Augusta, GA	N 33.46639 W 82.03944
Jackson	Columbia, SC	N 34.03917 W 80.82222
Kearny	San Diego, CA	N 32.86778 W 117.14167
Lee	Petersburg, VA	N 37.23500 W 77.33278
Lewis	Tacoma, WA	N 47.09731 W 122.61510
Logan	Houston, TX	N 29.77149 W 95.42737
MacArthur	Waco, TX	N 31.58019 W 97.17261
McClellan	Anniston, AL	N 33.71722 W 85.78323
Meade	Odenton, MD	N 39.10694 W 76.74306
Pike	North Little Rock, AR	N 34.82513 W 92.28365
Sevier	Greenville, SC	N 34.89997 W 82.33698
Shelby	Hattiesburg, MS	N 31.18778 W 89.19917
Sheridan	Montgomery, AL	N 32.42651 W 86.28308
Sherman	Chillicothe, OH	N 39.37590 W 83.00650
Taylor	Louisville, KY	N 38.19708 W 85.70932
Travis	San Antonio, TX	N 29.45234 W 98.46094
Upton	Yaphank, NY	N 40.86230 W 72.88775
Wadsworth	Spartanburg, SC	N 34.93730 W 81.98078
Wheeler	Macon, GA	N 32.81186 W 83.54066

the area, drawn in by the water lines and improved roads the city built for the camp. The new residents did not forget the soldiers who once served there. Arlington Heights Boulevard was renamed Camp Bowie Boulevard in 1919—one local resident suggested "Hun's Defeat Boulevard," but that was rejected—and the site of the camp headquarters became a small park. Located at the 4,100-block of Camp Bowie Boulevard, Veterans Memorial Park contains two state historical markers, one about the training camp and another about the suburban growth that followed the war. Several other tributes to Great War veterans can be found in this park. On its western edge is a granite memorial to the 36th Division, the Texas National Guard unit that trained there. On the eastern edge is a memorial to veterans of all wars, but one with a Great War twist. Etched in the granite base is the famous World War I poem "In Flanders Fields," honoring the war's dead. It is capped with a bronze statue of a defiant Doughboy holding up a wounded comrade.

The Camp Taylor neighborhood on the southeast side of Louisville, Kentucky, grew up on the grounds of that cantonment. At first glance, there is little to indicate the area's military heritage. The historical marker on Poplar Level Road is easy to miss zooming down this busy commercial thoroughfare. But a closer look reveals more, such as a street named Grenade Avenue. Camp Taylor Park, once the heart of the army training facility, anchors this pleasant suburban neighborhood. Headquarters were located on the high ground just north of the park. A few World War I–era buildings remain in the neighborhood. The city is currently renovating the old camp motor pool building in the 1,200-block of Trevilian Way, for example. When the project is completed it will be known as the Camp Zachary Taylor Pavilion and host a small museum of the camp's history. There are several other surviving structures, though one has to know where they are. According to the Camp Taylor Historical Society, some local residents even live in homes that were once army latrines. Elongated one-story structures set in deeply from the sidewalk, these former commodes are usually found in pairs. Some can still be seen in the blocks just west of Camp Taylor Park. Near the corner of Lee and Grove Avenues was the "Naturalization Tree," the spot where many an immigrant soldier took his oath of citizenship. The tree has since succumbed to the ages, though a historical marker indicates where it once stood. Oddly, that marker is on private property.

Other camps were put to different uses. Camp Logan, Houston, became a park. After the war, wealthy Houstonians Will and Mike Hogg (the latter of whom served in the 90th Division during the war) purchased the Camp Logan grounds and resold it to the city for a minimal amount with the stipulation that it become a park dedicated to the World War I dead. The site is now called Memorial

Park. The term "urban oasis" is perhaps overused, but in the case of Memorial Park it is apt. This green island in the midst of city sprawl now contains a wide range of sporting facilities, including ball fields and a golf course where the camp parade ground once was. There are woodlands with hiking trails and an arboretum. Patches of trees around the golf course now bear names like "Artillery Woods" and "65th Infantry Woods," hinting at the area's former use. In the "Infantry Woods" just east of the railroad tracks and north of Memorial Drive, the cement foundations of camp buildings are still visible. The faint remnants of the trenches where soldiers once trained are still evident in the woods on the south end of the park. The Houston Archaeological Society, which is working hard to preserve the ruins, gives walking tours by request. At the intersection of Arnot and Haskell, near where the camp's main gate once stood, is a historical marker telling the story of the camp.

The open and level lands of many camps made them suitable for aviation, which flourished after the war. Portions of all three Georgia training camps became airports. Talk of transforming level lands of Camp Gordon in Chamblee into an airport began in the 1920s, though it took until 1941 to make it a reality. DeKalb Peachtree Airport is Georgia's second-busiest airport today. At the end of Airport Road near the terminal is Doc Manget Memorial Aviation Park, where one can watch the planes take off and land. At the park entrance are several historical markers, including one about Camp Gordon. Parts of Camp Hancock on the west side of Augusta became a municipal airfield known as Daniel Field in 1927. The U.S. Army Air Force trained pilots there during World War II. A portion of Camp Wheeler near Macon became the Herbert Smart Macon Downtown Airport. Other parts of the former Camp Wheeler are now industrial and residential. There are also some pleasant-looking woodlands in the area, but travelers should stay out of them. Camp Wheeler was reactivated during World War II as an infantry replacement training center. Unexploded ordnance and other hazardous materials from two world wars still lie in the woods, and the U.S. Army Corps of Engineers is currently cleaning up the site. A historical marker to the camp stands on Joe Tamplin Industrial Boulevard near its intersection with Riggins Mill Road.

Camp Grant, in Rockford, Illinois, also became an airport, though not until after World War II. The Illinois National Guard acquired the site in 1924, and it served as an induction center during World War II. It was closed for good in 1946, and the western portion of the camp is today the Rockford airport. Only fragments of Camp Grant remain today. Stone remnants of the main gate still stand at the foot of Kishwaukee Street at its intersection with Airport Drive. Tucked away between two airport runways is the Bell Bowl. Named for General George Bell, commander of the 33rd

"Prairie" Division from Illinois during World War I, this natural amphitheater hosted lectures, sporting events, and entertainment for the troops. Located at the end of Cessna Drive, the Bell Bowl has returned to its pre-settlement prairie environment, though it is occasionally still used for concerts. Composed of draftees from Illinois and Wisconsin, the 86th "Blackhawk" Division—named for the nineteenth-century Native American chief who fought the U.S. government in those two states—trained at Camp Grant, and Blackhawk Road is one of the streets than now runs through the area. The Camp Grant Museum occupies the only building from the Great War still standing. In addition to displaying a bewildering array of Camp Grant memorabilia from both world wars, the museum does double duty as a restaurant. Nearly every inch of wall space is covered with old photographs, posters, and banners from Camp Grant's venerable history. Inspecting the exhibits while inhaling the aromas of hamburgers and coffee, one might have the impression of having walked into some kind of militarized Hard Rock Café.

The most interesting remnants of Camp Grant lie in Seth Atwood Park, roughly two miles southwest of the museum. Straddling the banks of the Kishwaukee River, the park served as the Camp Grant rifle and mortar range during World War I. Shooters lined up on the bluff above the south bank and shot at targets across the river. Hidden in the woods along a roadway along the north bank are several concrete structures that, according to the Rockford Park District, date to the First World War. Below the hill from the Atwood Lodge is the target pit. Sheltered behind this elongated concrete barrier, soldiers raised paper targets for the shooters across the river. After the trainees shot, the soldiers in the pit then lowered the targets, calculated the scores, and telephoned them back to the firing line. Farther east along the road from the target pit is a series of smaller, lower concrete bunkers, which also sheltered those who tallied the marksmanship scores. The casual pedestrian or jogger would easily miss the bunkers, but peering into the edge of the woods they become visible. Some are crumbling, their roofs covered with moss, fallen leaves, and even some small trees. A few have caved in, leaving only a pile of rubble slowly disappearing into the woods. Bullets and ordnance are still buried in the nearby soils, and signs warn visitors to stay on the trails. The suburban area just north of Atwood Park between 11th Street (State Highway 251) and 36th Street was where the soldiers trained for trench warfare. "Fresh-turned earth ran snakily across the landscape for half a mile," noted the Blackhawk Division's official history. "Over this trench system was fought battle after battle. . . . The lines were occupied and evacuated, barraged, stormed, counter-attacked, until the sandy parapets and firing steps caved in under the strain."

Of the thirty-two World War I divisional training camps, seventeen are still in military hands. Over the years, the army upgraded many of them from the status of a camp (a temporary installation) to a fort (a permanent one). Further changes came with the end of the Cold War, when the Department of Defense closed many installations, downgraded others, and began combining neighboring military bases into single administrative entities. Fort Lewis and McChord Air Force Base in Washington State, for example, are now Joint Base Lewis-McChord. Fort Dix, New Jersey, merged with air force and navy bases to become Joint Base McGuire-Dix-Lakehurst. Seven former training camps are now National Guard or reserve facilities, and one belongs to the U.S. Marines. Camp Kearny near San Diego shut down in 1920, but the navy opened it up again as a dirigible base. The marines moved in during World War II and never left. The former Doughboy training camp is now the Marine Corps Air Station Mirimar.

Many of these active military bases still contain small remnants of the Great War training camps, though tight security prevents the ordinary traveler from poking around these interesting and historically significant places. With the exception of the occasional open house day and other public programs, civilians must have some kind of business on the base to gain admittance. However, many host historical museums that are free and open to the public, and most have exhibits about their World War I roots. To see them, travelers must meet certain security requirements, which can change suddenly based on prevailing threat conditions. Visitors are usually required to show government-issued photo identification and, if entering by car, vehicle registration and proof of insurance as well. On some posts, applications for a visitor pass should be filed several days in advance. Travelers would be wise to contact the museums beforehand.

The Fort Lewis Museum is located in one of the last surviving World War I buildings on the post. Originally called the Red Shield Inn, the Salvation Army constructed it in 1918 as a recreation center for soldiers and a hotel for their visiting relatives. The wood frame structure, now painted white, resembles an Old West frontier fort. In the foyer, the homey brick fireplace around which Doughboys once gathered, read newspapers, or chatted with their families before shipping out for France greets the visitor. Exhibits cover the entire history of Fort Lewis, and those dedicated to its Great War origins include some interesting displays; for example, a souvenir beanie from the 13th Division, which was just being formed at Camp Lewis when the war ended. The divisional emblem is rife with superstitious symbolism—an upwardly turned horseshoe, black cat, and of course the number 13—and one may wonder whether this unit was lucky or unlucky in never making it into the trenches. Near the Fort Lewis Visitor Center is a decorative archway that once stood above the camp's main gate. Made of fieldstones and logs, it too resembles the blockhouses of an Old West army post. In the spirit of patriotism, the workers who built the camp raised the funds to pay for the arch, constructed it themselves, and donated it to the army. It once stood on Lewis Drive not far from the Fort Lewis Museum, and was moved to its current location in 1957. Nearby are several memorials to units that have been based at Fort Lewis, and some commemorative trees. General Robert Alexander, commander of the 77th Division during the Meuse-Argonne Campaign in 1918, planted one of them. General Charles H. Muir, who commanded the 28th Division during that same operation, planted another one. Clear across the country from Fort Lewis, the Fort George G. Meade Museum in Maryland also has exhibits about that post's World War I connections. Exhibits include a collection of ornately painted combat helmets that bored but artistically talented Doughboys painted after the war.

Other installations host topical museums dedicated to specific aspects of the military experience, portions of which cover the Great War. Fort Dix, New Jersey, for example, is home to the Army Reserve Mobilization Museum, which outlines the story of America's reserve forces through the prism of the Fort Dix experience. The museum's exhibits on World War I at Camp Dix are fairly extensive, covering topics like camp construction, equipment, training, camp life, and demobilization. The open area behind the museum is called Doughboy Field, and was the original center of the camp. Fort Lee, Virginia, is home to the U.S. Army Quartermaster Museum. Spanning more than two centuries of army history, the museum explores the vast array of support services fighting men and women need, from food service to mortuary affairs. Many exhibits cover the World War I experiences and the Services of Supply that supported the Doughboys in France (see Chapter 9), but the museum also carves out some space for the origins for Fort Lee. Uniforms, pamphlets, souvenir items, period photographs, and (quite naturally) a quartermaster's truck tell the story of life at Camp Lee from 1917 to 1919. Next door is the U.S. Army Women's Museum. Interestingly, Fort Lee is located adjacent to the Petersburg National Battlefield, where Union and Confederate troops slugged it out in trenches that prefigured the First World War. Not far from the Civil War trenches, those the Doughboys dug in their training at Fort Lee still exist, but in a remote area closed to the public. Perhaps the most apropos museum for an old Great War training camp is the U.S. Army Basic Combat Training Museum at Fort Jackson, South Carolina, which has been training American soldiers for a century. The museum explores the process of turning civilians into soldiers, and devotes an entire gallery to the history of Fort Jackson, including its origins as a World War I training camp.

Three training camps were located on already-existing army posts, all of which remain important installations today. Camp Funston, on the eastern edge of Fort Riley, Kansas, contains two memorials to the Great War. One was built in December 1918 under the orders of the camp commander, General Leonard Wood. The fieldstone obelisk, dedicated to the men who trained there, is located just south of Huebner Road—a thoroughfare named, incidentally, after Kansas native Clarence Huebner, who served as a young officer in the 1st Division during World War I and commanded that same division during World War II. The other, just 700 feet to the northwest on the north side of Huebner Road, marks the spot of Wood's hilltop headquarters.

Camp Doniphan was located on the prairies on the west side of Fort Sill, Oklahoma. Nothing remains of it today, though a stone marker at the intersection of Randolph and Currie Roads stands at what was the northeastern corner of the camp. At the time of World War I, Fort Sill was one of the army's most important installations. It addition to hosting Camp Doniphan, Fort Sill was also home to artillery and infantry training schools, as well as an aviation base. The Fort Sill Museum, on the post Quadrangle in one of its oldest buildings, tells the story of the post's illustrious history, including its important role in the Great War. Camp Travis, Texas, trained Doughboys on the grounds of Fort Sam Houston outside San Antonio. The Fort Sam Houston Museum on the post also commemorates the men and activities of Camp Travis a century ago.

Monument at the site of Camp Doniphan, on the grounds of Fort Sill, Oklahoma.

The National Guard and reserve bases still hold some Great War history too. Camp Custer, now Fort Custer, is located on the west side of Battle Creek, Michigan. The Michigan National Guard still occupies much of the old Camp Custer site, but the main portion is now a public street. West Dickman Road—named after General Joseph T. Dickman, who commanded the 85th Division at Camp Custer before assuming command of the 3rd Division in France—was Camp Custer's main street in 1917 and 1918. It is mainly industrial now. Portions of the Fort Custer Recreation Area, a wooded area west of the post, were also part of the World War I training camp. The beach on Eagle Lake, a century ago crowded with Doughboys looking to cool off, is now a public beach. The camp hospital was located in the northern portion of the beach parking lot overlooking the lake. Similarly, the eastern portions of the old Camp McClellan, Alabama, are now part of the Mountain Longleaf National Wildlife Refuge, established in 2003. Several National Guard installations—like their active duty counterparts—have museums that tell of their Great War origins, such as Fort Devens Museum, outside Ayer, Massachusetts, which is on a portion of the old training camp no longer under military control. The museums on National Guard installations usually have a state focus. The Iowa Gold Star Military Museum is located on the grounds of Camp (now Fort) Dodge in the Des Moines suburb of Johnston. After World War I, the Arkansas National Guard took over Camp Pike near Little Rock, and in 1937 renamed it Camp Joseph T. Robinson. Today the facility hosts the Arkansas National Guard Museum. The Mississippi Armed Forces Museum is at Camp Shelby, five miles south of Hattiesburg.

Two former training camps remain in government hands but serve non-military purposes. Long Island's Camp Upton also served as a World War II induction center, and in 1947 it became the Brookhaven National Laboratory, today one of the nation's leading scientific research centers. Brookhaven is generally not open to the public, though frequent public programs, like the popular Summer Sundays, allow limited access to the grounds. Very little is left of Upton's World War I years. The high ridge in the center of the facility is still known as Headquarters Hill. On this spot, where the camp commander once surveyed his sprawling domain, now stands the Brookhaven Graphite Research Reactor, which produces neutrons for scientific research. But what's left of the Great War at Brookhaven is noteworthy. In a remote pine forest in the northeastern corner of the grounds, World War I training trenches remain etched into the earth. After a century, erosion has begun to fill them in, their bottoms now rounded and filling up with pine needles, but one can still make out their zigzag patterns as they stretch out across the forest floor. The camp's artillery range is now Brookhaven State Park. In front of the Brookhaven Center, a conference and banquet facility not far from the main gate, stands a small marker dedicated to Camp Upton's most famous Doughboy, Irving Berlin. It was dedicated in 1982 in honor of the musician's ninety-fourth birthday. "Camp Upton was a very important part of my life," he commented, "and having the plaque placed on the grounds of Brookhaven touches me deeply."

A small portion of Camp Sherman, Ohio, is now Hopewell Culture National Historical Park. Archaeologists began excavating the ancient Native American mounds even before Camp Sherman's buildings had been torn down. With their fieldwork completed and the camp dismantled, archaeologists then restored the mounds to their original appearance. In 1923, President Warren G. Harding declared the Mound City group a national monument, and in 1946 it gained full-fledged national park status. Today's Hopewell Culture National Historical Park encompasses several mound complexes in the Chillicothe area, but the visitor center is located at the Mound City site. Most people come to learn about the Native American past, but the park acknowledges the site's military interlude. The walls of the auditorium in the visitor center are lined with exhibits about Camp Sherman, and there is also an interpretive panel about the camp overlooking the Mound City complex. Today there are no signs of the World War I camp, and it's hard to imagine that rows of barracks once covered the green and mysterious mounds. Near the center of the Mound City group are three earthworks built close together—an elongated mound bracketed by two conical ones. Most barracks buildings here ran north to south, but on top of this particular cluster of mounds one building was raised and stood perpendicular to the others, interrupting the otherwise regimented appearance of the camp but preserving the mound for posterity. Archeologists still dig in the area, and World War I military items often turn up—buttons, buckles, and in one case even a pair of binoculars.

Mound City comprised just a small portion of Camp Sherman. State Highway 104—once known variously as Columbus Avenue or the Clarkstown Pike, and today called Camp Sherman Memorial Highway—was once the main thoroughfare through the installation. Much of the old camp land has returned to the plow. A veterans' hospital marks the northern end of the camp, and two separate correctional facilities also occupy the grounds. On Highway 104, just a little north of its intersection with U.S. Highway 35, is Camp Sherman Memorial Park. Next to a picnic shelter a small monument pays tribute to those who served at the camp. The camp extended as far south as Church Street in Chillicothe. The main gates were located at the intersection of Church and North High Streets. Four cement pillars still stand there, through which roughly 40,000 Doughboys passed. On Armistice Day 1980, local high school students affixed a small plaque to one of the crumbling and careworn pillars to acknowledge their historical significance.

Specialty Sites—from Chemical Weapons to Medical Training and Much More

In addition to the thirty-two divisional training camps, the army also expanded its professional education programs. Fort Sill was home to both the School of Musketry for infantry and the School of Fire for artillery, but as the army grew it soon became apparent that the post was not big enough for both of them. In 1918, the army purchased a genteel plantation outside of Columbus, Georgia, for the musketry school—renamed the School of Infantry—and transformed it into Camp Benning. Now Fort Benning, it is still home to the infantry school, as well as the National Infantry Museum. Fort Sill remained the home of the School of Fire (and the U.S. Army Field Artillery Museum is located there today), but several different training sites sprang up for artillery. In the pine barrens of central North Carolina the army established Camp Bragg in 1918. Fort Bragg is now home to the elite 82nd Airborne Division, and although nothing remains of the World War I camp, the Great War traveler will want to see the 82nd Airborne Division Museum, whose illustrious history began as the "All American Division" in World War I.

Ditto-Landsdale House in West Point, Kentucky. The building served as the canteen for Camp Knox, an artillery training facility. By the end of the war, Camp Knox was relocated to nearby Stithton, and is now Fort Knox. The building is now a private residence.

Another field artillery center, Camp Knox, was located on the banks of the Ohio River at West Point, Kentucky. The camp and the small town were closely intertwined. The Ditto-Landsdale House at 306 Elm Street, for example, served as the Camp Knox Canteen. (This building also saw government service as a hospital during the Civil War.) The tent camp stretched from the village south and west, generally following the Dixie Highway (U.S. Highway 60). Hemmed in between the bluffs to the south and the Ohio River to the north, the West

Point site proved inadequate for artillery training, and in August 1918, construction began on a new and improved Camp Knox near the village of Stithton, ten miles to the south. Today Fort Knox is one of the army's largest and most important installations. As home to the United States Bullion Depository, where the federal government stores its gold reserves, Fort Knox is synonymous with high security.

Some camps specialized in weapons and technologies that had no precedent in the American war experience. The brand-new Tank Corps, for example, began training at three facilities in 1918. One was Camp Tobyhanna in Pennsylvania's Pocono Mountains, which today is the Tobyhanna Army Depot and not open to the public. In Raleigh, North Carolina, the state fairgrounds became Camp Polk, now part of the North Carolina State University campus. A historical marker on the 2,500 block of Hillsborough Avenue in Raleigh commemorates both the fairgrounds and the tank camp. The most important Tank Corps training center was Camp Colt at Gettysburg, Pennsylvania, which opened in March 1918. Camp Colt occupied some of the most sacred Civil War soils, including the fields across which General

Pickett's men charged in their gallant but doomed attack on July 3, 1863. Looking out from the Copse of Trees on Cemetery Ridge in 1918, one would have seen rows of barracks, tents, and machine shops rather than fields of battle. The commander of Camp Colt was Captain Dwight D. Eisenhower. It was the West Point graduate's first independent command. Eisenhower never made it overseas in the Great War, but would become the top Allied commander in Europe during World War II and President of the United States in the 1950s. Amid the Civil War interpretive panels and monuments, two dedicated to Camp Colt are easy to miss. One National Park Service panel stands in a field with several Civil War markers near the intersection of Emmitsburg Road and Long Lane. About 600 yards south, on the east side of Emmitsburg Road, is a tall pine tree with a marker at its base. The World War Tank Corps Association planted the tree in 1954 on the spot of Eisenhower's Camp Colt headquarters. Eisenhower never forgot his time in Gettysburg. In 1950 he purchased a farm on the edge of the Civil War battlefield, which is today Eisenhower National Historic Site.

The United States also prepared for the ghastly horrors of chemical warfare. At American University in Washington, D.C., the Chemical Warfare Service was born. The army took over the university's McKinley Hall, built its own Chemical Warfare Building (where the Mary Graydon Building now stands), and transformed them into a chemical weapons laboratory. Known variously as Camp American University or Camp Leach, thousands of soldiers lived in barracks along the north side of Nebraska Avenue between Massachusetts Avenue and Tenley Circle, and along the west side of Massachusetts Avenue just north of the campus. The engineering troops assigned to the camp practiced many things, from camouflage techniques to using smoke as battlefield concealment, but learning the art of chemical warfare was the camp's *raison d'être*. During the Great War the area was sparsely populated, and the army sometimes tested its weapons in the nearby woods and fields, especially in an area just off campus known as Spring Valley, bounded by Loughboro Road, Massachusetts Avenue, and the Dalecarlia Woods. Troops released gasses over trenches to simulate battle conditions, and exposed dogs and other animals to various chemical agents to test their efficacy. Those living in the area sometimes complained. "From time to time clouds of gas are liberated which have produced sickness among the neighboring residents," noted one wartime army memo. Residents also complained that "the confined dogs create a great deal of unpleasant noise, and some of them from time to time . . . wander around the neighborhood in a more or less mutilated condition."

A century later these rural spaces are filled in with upscale homes, but the legacy of the Chemical Warfare Service still haunts the neighborhood. In 1993, more than 100 artillery shells, some containing hazardous wartime chemicals, turned up in backyards across Spring Valley. By 1999 the army had spent more than $200 million to clean up the site, but artillery shells, mustard gas, and other dangerous items kept turning up well into the twenty-first century. The search continues.

The hard realities of combat meant that the army needed more medical personnel, from physicians to stretcher-bearers. The most important medical training facility was Fort Oglethorpe, Georgia. A small cavalry post before the war, Fort Oglethorpe lay on the Chickamauga battlefield of the Civil War, but with the coming of the Great War the post mushroomed in size. Soon tents and barracks sprang up among the monuments to Civil War glory. Frederick Pottle began training as a combat medic there in January 1918. "We marched . . . down a long, straight, fairly hard road," he wrote of his arrival, "with numbers of great monuments rising on the right. . . . At brief intervals we passed trim metal signboards, lettered in white on black, telling what action in that long-ago battle had been fought at that point. Signs and omens, but at the time we did not perceive their meaning." Most medical training occurred in a part of the facility known as Camp Greenleaf, immediately east of the main post. In all, more than 160 hospital organizations representing nearly 30,000 doctors, nurses, and technicians, trained there. Fort Oglethorpe remained army property until after World War II, and is now a residential area. Barnhardt Circle in the city of Fort Oglethorpe was the center of the old post, and stately officers' homes still ring it. Camp Greenleaf is now a housing subdivision just west of Lafayette Road. Another important medical training facility was Camp Crane in Allentown, Pennsylvania. Built on the fairgrounds of the Lehigh County Agricultural Society, nearly 20,000 medical personnel trained there during the war. After the war the grounds reverted back to the agricultural society, and they now comprise the site of the Allentown Fairgrounds, which hosts fairs, concerts, and a farmer's market where one can pick up any number of Amish goodies.

The army needed still more specialist troops. The Veterinarian Corps trained at Camp Lee. The Signal Corps needed thousands of communication specialists, such as cryptographers, radio technicians, and translators. At Camp Benjamin Franklin, Maryland, next door to (and later absorbed by) Camp (today Fort) Meade, more than 400 women, specially recruited for their language skills and experience as switchboard operators, trained to operate the army telephone system. These so-called "Hello Girls" wore military uniforms and were subject to military discipline, but were technically civilian employees of the army. Camp Joseph E. Johnston near Jacksonville, Florida, trained quartermaster troops. The site is now the Jacksonville Naval Air Station. The Motor Transportation Corps trained at Camp Holabird in Baltimore, Maryland. The post closed in 1973 and is now an industrial park. A historical marker commemorating the camp stands at the corner of Dundalk and Holabird Avenues.

Germany never bargained that America would mobilize so fast. This was indeed one of the greatest feats of bureaucratic skill and organization in United States history, one that America's leaders would draw upon again when a second world war loomed two decades later. But for all of triumph, very real questions remained about how well this inexperienced army was prepared to fight a modern war. There was also the problem of transporting this army overseas. Never before had the United States sent so many soldiers to fight in a foreign war, and organizing that process would require even more bureaucratic skill.

CHAPTER 4:
PORT OF EMBARKATION

After several months of training, it was time for the Doughboys to head off to war. The 82nd "All-American" Division departed Camp Gordon, Georgia, in April 1918. "Beginning several days prior to our departure, relatives and friends flocked to the camp in all kinds of conveyances for farewells," reported the official history of the 328th Infantry Regiment. Though it was a hot day, the men were "wearing overcoats and heavy woolen underwear and the heaviest packs in captivity." It was a touching scene on the train platform. "Tear-stained wives, mothers, sweethearts and others of varying relationship, waved [at] us and embraced us till the old troop train pulled out." In all, American troops embarked for Europe from ten Atlantic ports, from Canada to Virginia. But by far the most important point of departure was Hoboken, New Jersey, across the Hudson River from New York City. Today Hoboken is perhaps best known as the hometown of crooner Frank Sinatra, who was born there in 1915. Sports fans know the city's Elysian Fields as the location of history's first documented baseball game. Still others may know it as the place where the classic 1954 film *On the Waterfront* was shot, or even as the home of Carlo's Bakery from the hit television show *Cake Boss*. During World War I, it was the last place many Doughboys ever set foot on American soil.

Hoboken was an ideal site for the shipment of troops to Europe. New York Harbor was America's largest and busiest port. At the turn of the twentieth century, both sides of the Hudson were jam-packed with miles and miles of wharves, and a cacophony of maritime sounds—growling engines, ships' whistles, seagulls—drifted across the waters. The New Jersey docks were especially suited for international trade. Being on the west shore of the river, they had direct access to the vast North American hinterland. Rail lines converged on the Jersey ports from across the nation, bringing the bounty of America's farms and factories to port for shipment overseas. Cities like Newark, Jersey City, and Hoboken became important entrepôts between the Atlantic world and the American heartland. When American factories began to supply the Allies with war materiel after 1914, much of it was brought to the docks of New Jersey.

As a place where the rails met the sea, Hoboken flourished as a transportation hub. By 1900, several transatlantic shipping companies had established their docking facilities there. Looking to get away from the crowded and expensive docks of Manhattan, Germany's Hamburg America Line relocated facilities to Hoboken as early as the 1850s. Another German line, North German Lloyd, soon followed suit. Hoboken became the first stop for thousands of German immigrants coming to the United States. Indeed, many never left. As the twentieth century dawned, the German language was commonly heard in the shops and on the streets of Hoboken. It was home to traditional German beer gardens. There were forty-two taverns on River Street alone. Scores of delicatessens, bakeries, and restaurants catered primarily to a German clientele. Germans worshipped at a variety of churches scattered about the town, and enjoyed a very active social life, ranging from singing societies to shooting clubs. By 1890, roughly 20 percent of Hoboken residents had been born in Germany, and the German connection was very important to the city's economy. Hamburg America and North German Lloyd dominated Hoboken's waterfront, their long state-of-the-art piers stretching far into the Hudson River between 1st and 4th Streets. Some of the world's largest ships docked here, such as the massive passenger ship *Vaterland* of the Hamburg America Line, which was the largest ship afloat when launched in 1914. Nicknamed "Little Bremen" for its connection to German shipping, Hoboken was filled with a genuine feeling of German *Gemütlichkeit*.

Being German American Isn't What It Used to Be as Suspicions Mount

But as war with Germany loomed, many Americans began to view their German neighbors suspiciously. The great majority of German Americans were loyal to their adopted country, but not all. German diplomats in the United States—in gross violation of international protocol—recruited a sabotage network to attack munitions shipments to the Allies. German sailors stranded in the United States due to the British blockade, German nationals working for German companies in the United States, and a few immigrants with strong sympathies for the Old Country—joined by a small group of Irish nationalists with a burning hatred of Britain—began setting fires at munitions plants and sneaking bombs onto ships bound for Allied ports. Their most devastating attack came at 2:08 AM on July 30, 1916, when a massive explosion occurred on Black Tom, an island off Jersey City from which munitions were loaded onto European-bound ships. The blast shattered thousands of windows in Manhattan, riddled the Statue of Liberty with shrapnel, and could be heard as far away as Maryland. At least twenty-six people died. On January 11, 1917, another explosion destroyed an ammunition factory of the Canadian

Car and Foundry Company in the Kingsland section of Lyndhurst, about ten miles to the northwest in the New Jersey Meadowlands. Investigations eventually tied both disasters to German saboteurs. Landfill connected Black Tom to the New Jersey mainland long ago, and it now occupies the southern corner of Liberty State Park. In a playground not far from the park headquarters, an interpretive panel outlines the events surrounding the deadly Black Tom explosion. Alongside a marshy area on Clay Avenue in Lyndhurst, a small plaque and flagpole marks the site of the Kingsland explosion. The plaque tells the story of Tessie McNamara, a cool-headed switchboard operator who stayed at her position, calling firefighters and warning her coworkers, as shells exploded around her. Perhaps as a result of her actions, nobody was killed in the Kingsland incident. Near the plaque a viewing platform looks over the marsh, where a solitary smokestack stands—the only surviving remnant of the factory.

After the U.S. entered the war in April 1917, life for German Americans changed drastically, especially in Hoboken. In the early morning hours of April 19, 1917, three companies of U.S. Army troops landed at Hoboken and seized the properties of Hamburg America and North German Lloyd. "Throughout the day groups of civilians gathered," the *New York Times* observed, "and watched the work of the soldiers with interest" as they took control of the docks. The government quickly transformed the port facilities into the U.S. Army Port of Embarkation to transport Doughboys to France. With ample warehouses, offices, and terminal buildings, the seized German port facilities were excellent, but after incidents like Black Tom and Lyndhurst, Hoboken's large German population raised security concerns. "The great docks . . . at Hoboken had always been a hotbed of sedition," claimed Lieutenant A. Reidell, a quartermaster officer assigned to the Port of Embarkation. "Along River Street, where the old Bock beer signs of the German occupation still marked the Deutsche Gartens and Kursaals," he wrote, "fat German saloonkeepers and their fraus and frauleins looked askance at this new invasion." German nationals were barred from the areas near the port, and soldiers conducted numerous raids around the city in search of enemy aliens and others of suspect loyalty. One raid, on River Street in November 1917, netted 200 suspects. "The soldiers went into stores, rooming houses, and stopped men on the street," reported the *New York Times*, "but the greater number of those seized were found in saloons." A few suspects were released, but most were spirited off to a detention facility on Ellis Island. The war devastated Hoboken's German community. Whether immigrant or American born, sympathetic to Germany or strongly pro-American, Hoboken's German community lived under a thick cloud of suspicion throughout the war years. Many left town altogether. Hoboken's *Gemütlichkeit* was gone.

Fears of wartime German sabotage also ran rampant across the Hudson in New York. One of New York City's greatest vulnerabilities was its water supply. The Croton Aqueduct carried water down to the city from northern Westchester County. More significant was the Catskill Aqueduct, which ran 100 miles from the Ashokan Reservoir in the Catskill Mountains. Cut these aqueducts or poison the water supply, city and state leaders believed, and America's largest city would be brought to its knees. As early as February 1917, the New York National Guard began patrolling the aqueducts, braving hip-high snowdrifts, but when those troops entered federal service the state formed a home defense force called the First Provisional Regiment to do the job. Composed mainly of teenage boys too young for the army and middle-aged men too old, the regiment patrolled the length of the aqueducts, guarding dams, pumping stations, and aerators against attack. Though these men and boys never left the Empire State, they nevertheless saw their service as vital to the Allied war effort, since an attack on New York City, as the regimental history noted, would "halt the flow of troops and munitions overseas" and "usher in the disaster." The men and boys patrolling the aqueducts reported a few suspicious incidents but never caught a saboteur. The regiment nevertheless suffered forty deaths, mostly from the Spanish Flu and associated diseases like pneumonia. A few died of accidental shootings, and one was struck by a train.

Eighteen-year-old Private Frank de Costa of the First Provisional Regiment died of pneumonia on December 3, 1918, but his family did not have the means to bury him. Touched by this sad story, William Rockefeller, son of the business tycoon John D. Rockefeller, donated a burial plot in the cemetery at the Sleepy Hollow Cemetery for de Costa. In the spring of 1919, the regiment selected a ten-foot-high boulder from Bonticou Crag near New Paltz—a landmark familiar to those who patrolled the Catskill Aqueduct—brought it down to Sleepy Hollow, and erected it near de Costa's grave as a memorial to all of its members who died during the war. The memorial stands today near the cemetery's main gate along U.S. Highway 9. Affixed to the stone are bronze plaques listing the constituent units of the First Provisional Regiment, and the names of all forty members who perished. Sleepy Hollow Cemetery is one of America's oldest and most famous burying grounds, and contains the final resting places of luminaries like Washington Irving, Andrew Carnegie, and William Chrysler. William Rockefeller lies in a mausoleum up the hill from the regimental memorial. Travelers frequently stop in to see the graves of the rich and famous, unaware of the World War I memorial, but the dead of the First Provisional Regiment are not forgotten. Every year since 1919, locals hold a remembrance ceremony at the monument on the first Sunday in May. Those interested in

following the footsteps of the
First Provisional Regiment will
enjoy some remarkable sylvan
beauty. Bonticou Crag is now
part of a natural area called
the Mohonk Preserve, popular
with hikers and rock climbers.
Hikers also walk along portions
of the Catskill and Croton
aqueducts. In fact, a twenty-six-
mile stretch of the latter is now
Old Croton Aqueduct State
Historic Park.

Monument to the 1st
Provisional Regiment, Sleepy
Hollow Cemetery, Sleepy
Hollow, New York.

Home defense units like the First Provisional Regiment formed
across the country during the Great War, guarding infrastructure
and factories, hunting down draft dodgers, and responding to disasters. Their work is all but forgotten today, but Sleepy Hollow is one
place where it is remembered.

The New York area was not alone in its fear of German ter-
rorism and espionage. A wave of anti-German hysteria gripped
the nation—fed by pernicious wartime propaganda—and reached
both ridiculous and tragic proportions. Sauerkraut received the
more patriotic-sounding name "liberty cabbage," and beer became
a threat to national security. "We have German enemies across the
water," one politician declared, adding, "we have German enemies
in this country too," and among the "most treacherous" were the
breweries of "Pabst, Schlitz, Blatz, and Miller." The passage of the
Eighteenth Amendment in 1919, beginning the thirteen-year-long
failed experiment to ban alcohol known as Prohibition, came in no
small part as the result of wartime anti-German hysteria. In many
communities, German immigrants were victims of vigilante violence. In Collinsville, Illinois, a mob lynched an immigrant named
Robert Prager in April 1918, and a jury acquitted all twelve men
indicted for the crime. "Nobody can say we aren't loyal now," one
member of the jury reportedly bragged afterward.

The Pleasures, and Displeasures, of the Embarkation Camps

The first military unit to leave from Hoboken was Base Hospital
No. 4, which departed on May 8, 1917. The regiments that would
form the 1st Division left on June 17. As the training camps and
cantonments began to churn out newly minted soldiers, more and
more trains snaked their way across the United States bound for
Hoboken. Many of these young men relished the opportunity to
see the country. For those on the West Coast, the trip could be

especially arduous, but a spirit of adventure prevailed nonetheless. It was "six days of tiresome, but interesting and jolly traveling," recalled Adolphus Graupner of the 91st Division of his journey from Camp Lewis, Washington. While en route to Hoboken, the Doughboys passed the time playing cards, singing, talking, or just watching the countryside roll by. Each day, the men were herded off the train cars for calisthenics, then herded back onboard. On occasion, they got to see the sights. The 61st Field Artillery Brigade, heading east from Camp Bowie, Texas, stopped to see Niagara Falls. "The soldiers left the cars to see the famous water falls," reported brigade member Rex Harlow, "and were much impressed by the wonderful sight." En route from the South, Ray Johnson of the 37th Division remembered "a beautiful moonlight view of the National Capitol as we passed through Washington." As the Doughboys headed to the port, America cheered them. "The trip overland was one continuous ovation," recalled Osborne de Varila, "which lifted our war spirit several more notches." Frederick Pottle described his train trip from Fort Ogelthorpe, Georgia, to New Jersey as "a triumphal procession. Red Cross women met us at the stations, showering us with gifts, whistles blew, and everyone shouted and waved flags." Writing a decade after the war, Pottle recalled that "we were intoxicated with glory" at the sight of the well-wishers. "It was, as far as purely pleasurable emotion was concerned, the peak of our war experience."

As troop arrivals increased, the army needed a place to prepare the men for overseas service and established several Embarkation Camps. The first and largest was Camp Merritt, ten miles to the north of Hoboken near Tenafly, New Jersey. Named after Civil War hero John Wesley Merritt, it was situated on a ridge between Cresskill and Dumont that the original Dutch settlers called the Schraalenburgh (scraggly hill). By 1917 suburbanization was beginning to encroach on this portion of the New Jersey countryside, but much of the area still retained its rural character. Farms and fruit orchards prospered, and pleasant wooded lots dotted the landscape. Shady oak and maple trees lined the roads that occasionally passed the landed estates of the wealthy. It was the very epitome of New Jersey as the "Garden State."

The government was not interested in such bucolic scenes, of course. Engineers thought the slope of the landscape would provide proper drainage for a large camp. But what the army really found attractive was the fact that rail lines ran on either side of the ridge— essential for moving troops in and out. Construction of Camp Merritt began in August 1917, and the first overseas-bound troops arrived on October 1. Centered on the intersection of Madison Avenue and Knickerbocker Road, Camp Merritt eventually covered 770 acres. It was roughly one mile long north to south along Knickerbocker Road, and three quarters of a mile wide east to west.

Most of the camp was devoted to barracks for the transient Doughboys. There were 611 two-story barracks buildings and a corresponding 189 lavatories. To feed the men, there were 165 kitchens and mess halls. To supply them, there were thirty-nine warehouses. "Life at Merritt was a succession of issues and reissues, trying on and taking off, inspecting and reinspecting [sic] clothing and equipment," according to Adolphus Graupner. Any clothing item that showed signs of wear from the months of training was replaced with a brand new one. It was here, too, that Doughboys received much of their overseas gear, such as their gas mask and their "tin derby"—the British-style broad brimmed steel combat helmet. Camp Merritt also meant a haircut. "Many a wonderful 'pompadour,' 'college cut,' and 'football special' went down in ruins," observed Walter Ingalls of the 27th Engineer Battalion. In addition to clothing and equipment inspections, there were more physical examinations. "These inspections took up only a fraction of the time," remembered Frederick Pottle, and "the greater part of the day we could use as we pleased." Camp Merritt had all the recreational opportunities the Committee of Training Camp Activities had to offer. The YMCA maintained seven separate huts located in various areas of the post. Near the center of camp was Merritt Hall, a massive recreation center for enlisted men. Here one could meet friends, play billiards, have a snack, write a letter home, check out a book in the library, or even take French lessons. As Frederick Pottle remembered, "Camp Merritt was probably the most comfortable camp in the United States."

As the Doughboys returned from Europe, Camp Merritt was converted into a debarkation camp, and was usually the first stop soldiers made upon returning to America. The camp was closed in 1920, its land returned to the owners and its buildings sold off and dismantled. The following year, as the deconstruction of the camp was underway, several fires broke out in the skeletal remains of the buildings. The first came in March 1921, when simultaneous fires broke out in the remains of the hospital buildings in the southern part of the camp. "Burning embers . . . were carried high in the air," reported the *New York Times*, and were "deposited, still blazing, many yards away." Because the camp's water supply had been shut off, the flames were difficult to contain, and the blaze was visible twenty miles away. After a third fire, in June, virtually nothing was left of the camp. The cause of the fires was never determined. Camp Merritt was gone, but not forgotten. On May 30, 1924, a memorial to the camp and the men who served there was dedicated at the intersection of Madison Avenue and Knickerbocker Road. Engraved on the sixty-five-foot high granite obelisk are the names of nearly 600 people who died at the camp, mainly due to the influenza epidemic. An estimated 20,000 attended the dedication ceremony,

Relief sculpture by Robert Aitken on the Camp Merritt Memorial, located on the border of Cresskill and Dumont, New Jersey.

including the state's governor and General Merritt's widow. None other than General John J. Pershing himself was on hand for the occasion.

Except for the monument, there is virtually nothing left of Camp Merritt to see. Once the epitome of Garden State agriculture, it is now the epitome of New Jersey suburbanization. The rows of suburban tract housing might remind some of the military regimentation that once reigned here, but these homes were built long after the Great War. A very small number of camp structures remain in the area, but they are unrecognizable to the casual observer.

The Hungry Peddler bar and restaurant (470 Knickerbocker Road, Cresskill) occupies an old Camp Merritt building. The Demarest Public Library, located about a mile north of the former camp (90 Hardenburgh Avenue, Demarest), is housed in a building salvaged from the camp and moved to its current location. On a walk through the neighborhood, one can see First World War-related names in the area—the Merritt Gardens apartment complex, the Merritt Shopping Center, and the Pershing Building—but nearly every trace of wartime activity is gone. The monument itself is located in a traffic circle, making it a prominent landmark but hard to see close up. There are no designated crosswalks leading pedestrians to the monument or stoplights at the intersection. Crossing over to the monument can be both difficult and dangerous, but it is worth it. Only close up can one appreciate the Art Deco relief sculpture on the base of the monument by Robert Aitken—a muscular, barechested Doughboy in the guise of an ancient Greek warrior with an eagle over his shoulder. One of America's top sculptors, Aitken is most noted for his work on the Liberty Memorial in Kansas City (see Chapter 18) and the west pediment of the U.S. Supreme Court building in Washington.

Camp Merritt could not handle the vast number of soldiers bound for Hoboken, and another embarkation camp sprang up across the Hudson in neighboring New York. Camp Mills was located on the Hempstead Plains, a vast prairie that stretched across much of interior Long Island. The army already had a presence in the area, maintaining an airfield near Garden City for the training of pilots (see Chapter 11). In a plot of undeveloped land not far from the airfield, Camp Mills sprang up. It began operations in August 1917 as a staging area for the 42nd "Rainbow" Division as it hasty prepared for overseas duty. After the Rainbow Division moved out, the 41st "Sunset" Division, composed of National Guard units from the northwestern states, moved into the tents they left behind. Conditions at the makeshift camp were far from desirable. Martin Kimmel, an artilleryman in the Sunset Division, arrived in November 1917. "This camp is a fright," he wrote home. "The low-lying flat country" was riddled with "depressions and hollows," and the cold autumn rain "makes a swamp out of this place." He continued:

> The tents were without floors & cold & chill without stoves. The Battery Street was a series of puddles. The kitchen was a shed open on 4 sides through which the wind carried the cold drizzling rain soaking the cooks, the food and the fire, which smoked dismally in the cold, grey dawn. Did you ever try rain soaked Cornflakes for your morning cereal? There were other things but why multiply the miseries?

The 41st Division moved on to Camp Merritt by the end of November, and Camp Mills was closed. But as the shipment of men overseas increased, the camp was brought back into service in April 1918. Like Merritt, Camp Mills hummed with the work involved with preparing men for overseas duty. Soldiers still lived in tents, but conditions had improved from the horrible days of 1917. The camp took on a more permanent appearance, with sturdy wooden buildings and recreational facilities like the YMCA hut. "The builders of Mills had seen to it that nothing was left undone to make the camp complete for the soldiers who passed through en route to Europe," Rex Harlow believed, but Camp Mills still generated more than its fair share of complaints. The 322nd Field Artillery arrived in June 1918. "We had to accustom ourselves to its outdoor conditions," reported the unit's official history, "the cold Long Island nights and the open-air showers of cold water." The 86th Division arrived in September and complained of "considerable discomfort" resulting from "the heat and the famous Long Island mosquitoes."

Today the Camp Mills site is located within the boundaries of Garden City, a bedroom community like many on Long Island. The main entrance of the camp was located near the intersection of Commercial and Clinton Avenues. A street named Rainbow Place splits off from Clinton Avenue near this intersection, forming a shady green triangular park known as Rainbow Division Plaza. Here a memorial to the division now stands. A fifteen-foot obelisk made of Alabama limestone, the monument lists the various units that made up this famed division, and carved into its base are depictions of the campaigns in which the Rainbow Division fought. Etched into one side of the obelisk is a lone bugler—forever playing taps for those who died, but also reminiscent of the reveille ceremony that occurred each morning on these grounds a century ago. The camp itself stretched out south and east from the monument. Once a field of tents, the area is now a tree-lined housing subdivision. The maturity of the trees on these quiet suburban streets testifies to the fact that much time has passed since this was a hastily built army camp on an open prairie.

Memorial to the 42nd "Rainbow" Division at the former site of Camp Mills, Garden City, New York.

Even with the addition of Camp Mills, the army still needed more space for processing overseas-bound troops. Camp Upton, a training camp on the eastern end of Long Island, was eventually pressed into service as an embarkation center, as was Camp Dix in central New Jersey.

Whether brought to Merritt, Mills, Upton, or Dix, the Doughboys were excited by the prospect of visiting New York City. Passes into town were often distributed liberally, but visits could be brief. "One cannot see much of New York in twenty-four hours," wrote Adolphus Graupner, "but reports from those who made the trip tended to show that there was some fast traveling in an endeavor to see the sights." Like ordinary tourists, the soldiers clamored to see the famous attractions, like Broadway, Fifth Avenue, and the Brooklyn Bridge. Men from rural areas found New York an especially eye-opening experience. "Everything they saw interested them," observed Rex Harlow:

> The magnificent automobiles speeding along the thoroughfares, the great street cars, packed and jammed at all times, people of all descriptions, from the poorest beggars to the most richly dressed inhabitants of Wall Street, the window displays, theaters, subways, and a thousand other things, all fired their imaginations and gave them a sense of bewildering exhilaration over being in the heart of the nation's metropolis.

Some ventured to Brooklyn's Coney Island, which had a reputation for booze, dance halls, and more tawdry forms of entertainment. But for the Doughboy, the most memorable of New York's many sights was the Statue of Liberty. Whipped up by red-hot wartime propaganda, many became emotional over seeing for themselves this symbol of American freedom—and a gift from France no less. "Oh, the thrill of seeing the Statue of Liberty," wrote John Warns of South Dakota. "I can't describe how I felt, but looking up to this great imposing statue just makes one feel safe."

Soldiers going AWOL (absent without leave) was a problem at the embarkation camps. "So acute had the situation in regard to men absenting themselves without leave grown," noted one official at Camp Merritt, "that it was found necessary that a stockade be built embracing sixteen barracks" which were usually "filled to overflowing." Reasons for going AWOL varied. Some men simply did not want to go the war. Many failed to return from their passes in a timely manner. Giuseppe Romeo of the 91st Division went to New York in search of "a good snort of demon rum." Unable to procure any in Manhattan, he and a buddy went to Coney Island, where they proceeded to "get wet." In fact, they both passed out on the beach. "We were supposed to be back at camp at 9 AM," he remembered, "but didn't get back until noon." Romeo drew company punishment and avoided the stockade, and in the end he characterized the experience as "worth it." Doughboys from the New York area sometimes sneaked away for one last goodbye with loved ones. The 82nd Division contained so many New Yorkers that when it arrived at Camp Upton "whole families besieged the Camp, begging and imploring passes for their relatives," according to the official history of the 328th Infantry Regiment. "The strain was too much for some who went home anyway."

The Final Journey to Hoboken and New York and Shipping out for Europe

Departing soldiers usually spent less than a week at the embarkation camps. Roused from their bunks in the early morning darkness, the Doughboys cleaned up their barracks or tents, gathered their things, and prepared to move out. From the Long Island camps they boarded trains to New York City, and then ferryboats to Hoboken. From Camp Merritt they usually marched to rail stations in nearby towns for the short ride to Hoboken. Frederick Edwards remembered that "the houses we passed were all dark" as he and his men left Camp Merritt, forming "a silent column that clattered over the road in their hob-nailed boots." Some marched as far as Alpine Landing on the Hudson River to catch ferries to Hoboken. For soldiers recovering from influenza, the march to Alpine could be grueling. Robert Mowry remembered that "many fresh from convalescent wards fell out of ranks from sheer exhaustion and were picked up by ambulances." After three miles the Doughboys reached the cliffs of the New Jersey Palisades, which tower nearly 500 feet above the Hudson. To reach the landing, they descended the cliff by way of a steep and winding trail, a "zig-zag road," as Adolphus Graupner described it. "At the end of that hike," recalled the official history of Company A, 102nd Ammunition Train, "all agreed that [Alpine Landing] had been fittingly named." Before reaching the ferries the soldiers passed the Kearney House, an eighteenth-century tavern that—they were told—was British General Cornwallis's headquarters during his 1776 invasion of New Jersey. Some Doughboys were inspired by the connection between the Revolutionary War and their own defense of the nation, but later research showed that Cornwallis probably never set foot in the house.

The exact route of the march from Camp Merritt to Alpine has been lost, but most likely followed present-day Hillside Avenue through Cresskill to the Palisades, then north to the cliff trail. In 2003, Cresskill erected a historical marker on Hillside Avenue, about half a mile from central business district, to commemorate what a local historian called the "march of the forgotten." Then as now, the cliffs are part of Palisades Interstate Park. Graupner's "zig-zag road" is today's the Closter Dock Trail, which one can still hike to commune with nature or connect with the past. Alpine Landing is a public marina.

Those arriving in Hoboken by train marched the short distance from the train station to the docks. Frederick Pottle was elated at his first sight of the ships. "An ocean liner always gives one a thrill," he wrote, "but oh! the thrill of seeing at last the boat which would take us to France." Whether arriving by train or ferry, Red Cross volunteers offering coffee and pastries usually greeted the men. Charles DuPuy of the 311th Machine Gun Battalion remembered that the Red Cross ladies had "great cauldrons of hot coffee, sandwiches, fruit, cigarettes, etc., in a kind of rolling buffet." The Doughboys were then usually led to warehouses—"vast echoing sheds," Pottle called them—to await boarding. "Many men stretch themselves out on the floor and go to sleep," wrote Philip Shoemaker of the 28th Division in a letter home. "Others roam around in the enclosure." Though having been awakened before sunrise to get to the docks, the men often found themselves waiting well into the afternoon to board the ships. It was the "hurry up and wait" experienced by soldiers in all wars. Ray Johnson remembered "a very aggravating delay of several hours," which he thought "very irksome to us in our keyed up condition."

But the moment finally came to board the ship. "The men were arranged in the order in which their names appeared on the passenger list," according to Adolphus Graupner. "The officers checked off each man as he walked up the gangplank." "This was rather grim business," recalled Christ Stamas of the 90th Division. "Around the docks guards were posted with order to keep anyone with unofficial business away." The guards also prevented soldiers with "gangplank fever" from escaping. "We found that we were virtually prisoners," according to DuPuy.

Due to congestion at Hoboken, the army utilized other piers in the New York area. Many departed from New York City's main ocean liner terminal at the Chelsea Piers, directly across the river from Hoboken on Manhattan's West Side. Today portions of the old Chelsea Piers are waterfront parks best known for being one of the city's prime recreation spots, home to ice skating, batting cages, and numerous other activities. Others went to Brooklyn. On December 31, 1917, the army commandeered the port facilities of the Bush Terminal Company, a major New York shipping company. Used mainly as a storage facility, the cargo piers also served the purposes of troop embarkation. The Bush Company is long gone, and the complex is known today known as Industry City. The piers themselves have fallen into disuse, but the old warehouses now host artist studios and a wide range of businesses.

Soldiers usually arrived at the Brooklyn and Chelsea Piers by ferryboat, which sometimes confused those inexperienced with ocean travel. Upon boarding the ferries for Manhattan or Brooklyn some "country lads . . . would suppose that they were already off to France," wrote General David Shanks, commander of the Hoboken Port of Embarkation, "and would make anxious enquiries as to the probable date of arrival." As at Hoboken, the Doughboys stood around for hours during the long boarding process, their troubles soothed by the Red Cross. "The ferryboats spewed forth their great throngs," wrote the authors of the 364th Infantry Regiment's official history, "which immediately filled the enormous pier buildings and began a savage attack on bushels of refreshments which thoughtful organizations had provided."

The moment finally came to set sail. As they left New York Harbor, the Statue of Liberty made a tremendous impression on the Doughboys. "The Statue of Liberty never looked so glorious to us before as it did on this memorable occasion," according to the official history of the 311th Infantry Regiment. "This Bronze Lady, the Queen of the Harbor, seemed very lifelike to us as she watched our departure, telling us in terms we could not misunderstand what she expected of us." For some, Lady Liberty evoked uneasy feelings. Margaret Rowland, a Red Cross nurse from Wisconsin, wrote that it gave her a "queer pang" to watch her "fading away in the distance." Leaving their country for a fate unknown was hard for some soldiers to take. "Many of them were so affected, as they knew a certain percentage of us must inevitably fall in battle," wrote Edward Alva Trueblood, "that they went below to spend a few hours by themselves in serious thought. I am not ashamed to say that I was one of those who sought solace for my feelings in thoughtful solitude." "I swore that if I ever came back, I would kiss the soil of America," vowed Christ Stamas, "even if the spot where I would first land was a dirty spot."

In all, 1.6 million—more than three quarters of the entire AEF—left for war from Hoboken or its subsidiaries at Chelsea Piers or Brooklyn. It would also be the place of return—if they were fortunate enough to do so. "Heaven, hell, or Hoboken" became a rallying cry for those serving in the AEF.

Hoboken's World War I-Era Heritage Today

Hoboken's days as a great port are long over. The city experienced a long, slow decline over the twentieth as industries and shipping companies moved out. By the 1960s, the abandoned docks of the Hoboken waterfront had become a postindustrial eyesore. But in recent decades Hoboken has undergone a major transformation. First artists moved in, attracted by cheap rents and proximity to Manhattan, followed by an influx of young professionals who gentrified much of the city. The streets of Hoboken are now lined with specialty shops and a wide range of trendy restaurants. Baby strollers are a far more common sight than longshoremen, and day spas and health clubs have replaced the taverns of River Street.

Despite Hoboken's renaissance, the city retains much of its working class roots. The new arrivals renovated many the old shop fronts and apartment buildings rather than ripping them down, giving the city a mature and historic feel. A few cobblestone streets and alleyways remain. Looking closely, one can even still spot a few remnants of Hoboken's German heritage, such as St. Matthew Trinity Lutheran Church, located on 8th and Hudson. A few German bakeries and restaurants remain as well, though walking the streets in search of dinner one is much more likely to find sushi than sauerbraten.

Travelers to Hoboken can also walk in the footsteps of the departing soldiers. The Erie and Lackawanna ferry and rail terminal, the 1907 Beaux-Arts building with its clock tower overlooking the streets, is the same one the Doughboys saw as they detrained and made their way to the waiting ships. A tree-lined waterfront esplanade has replaced the dilapidated docks, though one noteworthy remnant remains. Pier A still juts out into the Hudson River at the foot of 1st Street, one the last survivors of Hoboken's ocean liner heyday. Now a city park with a great lawn and shady trees, Pier A attracts summer sunbathers, office workers out for a little fresh air, and tourists looking for that million dollar photograph of the Manhattan skyline.

From this pier in 1917 and 1918, Doughboys walked up the gangplank and off to war. Where First Street ends, a boulder with a commemorative plaque serves as a memorial to those Americans who departed from Hoboken during the First World War. Dedicated in

1925 and originally located on River Street, the boulder was moved to its present location in 2003. A wrought-iron fence envelops the boulder, which local veterans keep decorated with flowers and American flags. Here one can look out over the park toward the river, and imagine what was going through the soldiers' minds as they arrived at the water's edge.

Memorial boulder at the former site of the U.S. Army Port of Embarkation, Hoboken, New Jersey.

Other Embarkation Ports

Hoboken was not the only port exporting troops. Merritt, Mills, and the other New York-area embarkation camps prepared soldiers who departed from several other East Coast ports, some of them hundreds of miles from the Big Apple. Forty-six thousand left from Boston's Commonwealth Pier or from the Boston Quartermaster Terminal (later Boston Army Base) just to the east, on Summer Street. The pier is now home to the Seaport World Trade Center, a conference and exhibition center. At the intersection of Summer Street and Drydock Avenue, two small memorials and a flagpole mark the site of the army terminal. Another 35,000 shipped out from Philadelphia. At the Port Richmond terminal of the Pennsylvania and Reading Railroad just north of downtown Philadelphia, giant piers stuck out like fingers into the Delaware River to ship Appalachian coal. The war increased the demand for coal, and throughout the war Port Richmond was a busy place, but by 1918, it was handling an even more vital commodity—Doughboys. Portions of the 79th Division arrived at Port Richmond in July 1918. "Awaiting them was the most nondescript collection of troop ships the men could imagine," according to the division's official history. Many of the division's men hailed from Philadelphia, and their friends and relatives lined the Philadelphia waterfront to give them a hearty sendoff. "In broad daylight the ship pulled out and passed down the river," wrote one soldier, "cheered by the crowds on ferry boats and pier heads. Next morning the hotels of Cape May loomed out of the mist off the port beam." The Port Richmond yards continued to supply America with coal until after World War II, but as oil and gas replaced coal as the nation's most important fuel the yards went into decline and closed in the 1970s. The docks are abandoned now.

Fifty thousand Americans sailed from Canadian ports like Quebec City and Halifax, but the majority passed through Montréal. For these troops, their departure from the United States came by land and not by sea. "We had our last look at the U.S.A. when passing over the line at Newport, Vt.," lamented Leslie Lane of the 26th Division. These Doughboys also experienced a foreign culture a little sooner than their cohorts. "One day's travel brought [us] into a strange country [where] the men came in contact with a foreign tongue," remembered Joseph Thornton of the 805th Pioneer Infantry. Most did not see much of Canada beyond the train window, though. "Detraining was done at the docks," remembered one soldier of his arrival at Montréal, and "no one was allowed to leave the ship after embarking." From Montréal, the troopships descended the St. Lawrence River to the Atlantic. "Sightseeing was far from being the objective," wrote Leo Noble of his trip down the river, "but the St. Lawrence was no undesirable or unpicturesque place to travel; a moon-lit night with the aurora borealis and distant light-houses, flaring at various intervals to right and left, illuminated a memorable passage."

The significance of Montréal's port has declined over the years, and much of the city's *Vieux Port* (Old Port) has been transformed into a park and waterfront promenade, though many of the piers remain and ships still use them. After the war, Montréal built a forty-five-meter-high clock tower at the eastern end of the port to commemorate the sacrifices of Canadian sailors during the Great War. Britain's Prince of Wales—the future King Edward VIII—laid the cornerstone himself. No memorial marks the passage of American troops through the port, though it is worth noting that one of the jobs of the sailors the clock tower commemorates was to ensure that the Doughboys made it safely across the Atlantic.

The second largest embarkation port was Newport News, Virginia, from which 288,000 soldiers left for Europe. The Virginia equivalent of Camp Merritt was Camp Stuart. Facing the waters of Hampton Roads—the massive natural harbor where the Elizabeth, James, and Nansemond Rivers meet—the site of Camp Stuart had already seen its fair share of military history. During the Civil War, the U.S.S. *Monitor* and the C.S.S. *Virginia* clashed just offshore. In these same waters in 1910, a pilot flew a plane off the deck of a U.S. Navy ship, heralding the birth of the American aircraft carrier. The routine at Camp Stuart was much the same as at the New York embarkation camps. "Here for thirty-six hours the principal event was a physical examination," observed a soldier. As always, the Doughboys had their complaints. "Life at Camp Stuart was not very interesting," according to the official history of Company C, 102nd Ammunition Train, "and some of the time the weather was exceedingly hot." "Camp Stuart afforded us fine accommodations and excellent food," wrote George Kelly of Company A, "but it also afforded full sway of inspecting officers and drill masters." A residential area today, the camp was located between Sugar Creek and Marshall Avenue, with 20th Street forming its western edge. An unassuming historical marker in the median on Roanoke Avenue at the intersection with 16th Street marks the center of the former camp.

Departure was much the same as well. "We started off on that eventful day at the early hour of three-thirty," George Kelly remembered, and "after a breakfast in the dark, a hurried fastening of packs and a hasty line-up, we were off in the still early hours of the dawn for our trip 'over there.'" From Camp Stuart, the departing soldiers marched down to the docks, just south of downtown Newport News—the site of today's Newport News Marine Terminal—and boarded the awaiting ships. Like Hoboken, Newport News became the return port for thousands of veterans. To welcome them back, Newport News built a Victory Arch. The structure was only meant to be temporary, but after the war nobody dared to tear it down. Renovated in the 1960s, it still stands at the intersection of 25th Street and West Avenue. Newport News has a distinguished military history, and its role as an embarkation port in two world wars is a very important part of it. Several local museums—including the Hampton Roads Naval Museum, the Mariners' Museum, and the Virginia Military Museum—have exhibits about the port's history during the First World War.

Whether from Hoboken, Hampton Roads, or Montréal, the ships carrying the precious cargo of Doughboys headed out into the vast Atlantic. Some troopships made one last stop at Halifax, Nova Scotia, to meet up with other transports and their cruiser escorts for the long transatlantic voyage. Most of Halifax had been laid waste by a massive explosion of an ammunition ship in December 1917, and as the soldiers looked out at the devastated city, it gave them a small taste of things to come. Despite the tragedy, which had killed some 2,000 people, the residents of Halifax welcomed the Americans warmly and gave them a hearty send-off when it came time to go. "Cheering crowds lined the shore as we pulled out," recalled one member of the 101st Machine Gun Battalion of their departure, "and ships dipped their colors, while the bands of British men-of-war played 'The Star Spangled Banner.' It was a wonderful send-off." The Doughboys were off to the Western Front, but in effect they entered the war zone as soon as they sailed into Atlantic waters. German submarines worked hard to ensure that America would be unable to make an impact on the war and, indeed, that the U.S. Army would never make it to European shores.

CHAPTER 5:
THE GREAT WAR AT SEA

Writing to his home church back in Milwaukee, Chaplain Gustav Stearns of the 32nd Division told his congregation of the moment he fully understood he was at war. As his ship, the U.S.S. *George Washington*, approached the British Isles, Stearns heard a whistle blow and "knew immediately that this was no ordinary warning." Rushing to his lifeboat station he heard a "thundering boom" and realized that "for the first time in my life, I have heard a cannon fired in actual warfare." When Stearns got to his station someone shouted: "There she is—right out there!" He peered into the grey Atlantic and "sure enough—only a short distance from where I was standing I could see very plainly something in the water. It was cylindrical and was standing upright and was apparently not moving with the waves." Guns opened up on the German submarine with vicious fury, and when "the object disappeared . . . there went up a mighty shout." He told the folks back home that "it was all over in a couple of minutes, but it convinced every boy on that boat of the fact that we are not travelling on a pleasure trip or an excursion boat and that when we reach the other side of the Atlantic it will not be for the purpose of joining any carefree tourist party of sightseers."

The Allies desperately needed the tons of material and millions of men that the United States could bring to bear against Germany, but these vital resources first had to cross 4,000 miles of ocean, where they were vulnerable to a growing fleet of German submarines. It was the job of the Blue Jacket—the U.S. Navy equivalent of the Doughboy—to get those supplies and men across and keep the U-boat menace in check. A forgotten part of a forgotten war, the U.S. Navy played a crucial, if not decisive, role in the ultimate Allied victory.

When America entered the war in 1917, the U.S. Navy was better prepared than the army. The country had begun an aggressive naval expansion in the late nineteenth century, and this accelerated rapidly under the presidency of Theodore Roosevelt in the first decade of the twentieth. By 1917, the U.S. Navy stood second only the British Royal Navy in sheer numbers of ships. It nevertheless faced some challenging problems when war finally came. One was an overemphasis on the battleship. In the minds of most American naval strategists, the battleship was the cornerstone of naval power, and the construction of smaller and faster ships like cruisers and destroyers took a backseat to the dreadnoughts. Navy traditionalists did not think much of submarines. "The submarine is not an instrument fitted to dominate naval warfare," declared an aging Admiral George Dewey of Spanish-American War fame. "The battleship is still the principal reliance of navies." Battleships did allow the United States to project its power over vast swathes of ocean, but the big, lumbering behemoths were of little use in combating the elusive submarine.

The navy also needed sailors. In April 1917, the navy had 60,000 men and 300 ships. Marine corps strength stood at 13,000 troops. Upon entering the war, the U.S. Coast Guard came under navy control, adding another 5,000 hands. Like the army, the navy needed to train officers and sailors quickly. The U.S. Naval Academy at Annapolis speeded up its curriculum, and hosted several rounds of crash officer training programs. Promising enlisted men were brought up from the ranks, and the navy combed college campuses for more leaders. Enlisted sailors trained at the Great Lakes Naval Station north of Chicago; the U.S. Marines, at Parris Island in South Carolina. All three of these facilities remain important bases today, and each has a museum that covers the experiences of navy personnel in the Great War. As when visiting U.S. Army posts, travelers should be prepared to meet all security requirements to gain admission to these naval installations.

But the expanding navy needed more places to train sailors. New York City patriotically offered the navy the use of Pelham Bay Park, on the eastern edge of the Bronx. Cooled by sea breezes, Pelham Bay was the site of numerous waterfront mansions until the city acquired the land in 1888. In 1917 the navy erected hundreds of barracks on a wooded peninsula in the southern portion of the park called Rodman's Neck. "Care was taken to preserve so far as possible the trees in the part of Pelham Bay Park taken over," reported city parks officials approvingly. The navy also moved into some of the surviving mansions. "The camp was treated as though it were a ship," reported journalist Willis J. Abbot, who wrote extensively about Great War naval affairs, "to leave its bounds was to 'go ashore,'" and "the recruit was taught to substitute 'aye, aye, sir' for the landsman's 'all right.'" In addition to training raw recruits, Pelham Bay also trained reservists and hosted an officer candidate school.

The navy dismantled the camp just as quickly as it sprang up. The woods remain to this day, but virtually no trace is left of the navy. After the war, a landfill connected Rodman's Neck with Hunter Island to the north, and Orchard Beach, a popular summer spot for Bronx residents, was constructed in the 1930s. Today, the New York Police Department uses the southern end of Rodman's Neck as a target range, and the area is off limits to the public. The foundations of many of the park's old mansions, including some that had been put to navy use, remain hidden away in the woods. The baseball diamonds between City Island Road and Rodman's Neck Road are located in the general area where the navy placed the base's own diamonds a century ago.

The United States needed these sailors quickly, too. U-boats brought the conflict right to the nation's doorstep, putting East Coast naval bases like the navy yards at Boston, Brooklyn, Philadelphia, and Washington on the frontlines. To beef up coastal defenses, the navy built new bases. To guard the entrance to Delaware Bay, for example, new installations emerged at Cape May, New Jersey, and Cape Henlopen, Delaware. In May 1917, the navy took over a disused amusement park at Cape May called the Fun Factory, on a peninsula known as Sewell's Point at the east end of town. The navy incorporated the amusements into the base, giving it a rather unusual appearance. The skating rink became a mess hall, and a five-ton cylindrical structure called the "Barrel of Fun" was outfitted with an iron door and became the brig. Fire gutted much of the base in 1918, necessitating the erection of more conventional buildings. Across the bay, the navy moved onto the grounds of a federal quarantine hospital near Lewes, Delaware. Minesweepers, patrol craft of various kinds, and even submarines filled Cape May Harbor and swarmed around the piers near Lewes. From these twin bases, the ships patrolled nearby waters for U-boats or any sea mines they might leave behind. Cape May remains one of New Jersey's most popular beach resorts, and pleasure craft now fill the harbor the navy once used. The site of the Great War naval base is today the basic training center for the U.S. Coast Guard and generally closed to the public. The Lewes site is now part of Delaware's Cape Henlopen State Park. The buildings of the old hospital-turned-naval-base are all gone now, but were located just east of the park's fishing pier. The military fortifications one sees in the park today date to World War II.

The naval bases guarding Delaware Bay also hosted seaplanes. Like the army, the navy and the marine corps also saw value in using aircraft for reconnaissance, both for coastal defense and fleet protection. In the years before World War I, navy experiments with "hydroplanes" (aircraft equipped with pontoons to take off and land on water) and with the launching of planes from the decks of ships seemed promising. During the American occupation of Veracruz, Mexico, in 1914, the navy used hydroplanes for reconnaissance—the first use of aircraft in a hostile situation in American history. Indeed, one plane was even hit with rifle fire. The navy opened its first air station at Pensacola, Florida, in 1914—now the site of the National Naval Air Museum, which has particularly good exhibits about World War I—and two years later established the Naval Flying Corps. Naval air stations sprouted up and down the East

Coast, patrolling coastal waters using hydroplanes, dirigibles, and fixed-wing aircraft. The southernmost of them was Key West Naval Air Station in Florida. Located on Boca Chica Key just east of Key West, it remains an important naval base today.

The most important naval air stations guarded the major cities and shipping lanes of the Northeast. Southern Long Island was studded with them. Rockaway Naval Air Station, on the Rockaway Peninsula at the southern extreme of Queens, guarded the entrance to New York Harbor. Just to its west was an army harbor fortification called Fort Tilden, also established in 1917. Seaplanes took off and landed from the Jamaica Bay inlet on the north side of the base, but Rockaway was perhaps best known as a dirigible station, launching blimps to scan the waters. Today the grounds of the air station and Fort Tilden are part of the Gateway National Recreation Area. Jacob Riis Park now occupies the site of the naval base. The vast oval parking area just to the north of the beach was the heart of the air station. The army abandoned Fort Tilden in the 1990s, and a few World War II and Cold War gun emplacements remain. All that is left from the Great War is the cement foundation of a dirigible hangar at Fort Tilden, located on the south side of Rockaway Point Boulevard about 300 feet from the intersection with Beach 184th Street.

Thirty-five miles to the east of Rockaway was the Bay Shore Naval Air Station, on the Great South Bay. Primarily a training base, it also launched U-boat patrols. Located in the village of Bay Shore at the end of present-day Garner Lane, it was to become the well-heeled residential area found there today, without a trace of its wartime past. At the far eastern end of Long Island was the Montauk Naval Air Station, where seaplanes used a small freshwater lake called Fort Pond. Navy dirigibles also operated at the far eastern tip of Long Island, in what's now Camp Hero State Park.

The string of naval air stations continued northward into New England. Chatham Naval Air Station, at the elbow of Cape Cod, patrolled the Massachusetts coast. The base was on a peninsula called Nickerson's Neck, which jutted out into Pleasant Bay behind the cape's barrier beach. The navy dismantled it soon after the war, and Nickerson's Neck now contains a country club and some pleasant waterfront homes. At the end of Strong Island Road in Chatham stands a diminutive boulder with a small bronze plaque, put up by the local historical society, marking the site of the camp but also an important event in aviation history. In 1919, U.S. Navy plane NC-4, which made the first successful transatlantic flight, paid a visit to Chatham. The plane took off from Rockaway Naval Air Station on May 8 and stopped in Chatham for repairs. Departing on May 14, the NC-4 flew to Nova Scotia, to Newfoundland, and then across the open Atlantic to the Azores, finally making it to Lisbon, Portugal, on May 27.

The northernmost U.S. Navy air stations were in Nova Scotia, Canada. Halifax Naval Air Station was located at Baker's Point on the harbor's Eastern Passage. The base commander there was Lieutenant Commander Richard E. Byrd, who later gained fame for his polar expeditions. When the U.S. Navy left Baker's Point, Halifax Naval Air Station became one of Canada's first military air bases, and is now Canadian Forces Base Shearwater. The Shearwater Aviation Museum, just off the base, covers the area's aerial history, and does not forget the American contributions. On the base, Canadian forces still use an old American seaplane hangar. It has been substantially refurbished and contains a plaque denoting its origins, but unless travelers have some connections with the Canadian military they are unlikely to ever see it. The base is not open to the public. Farther north, on Cape Breton Island, was the North Sydney Naval Air Station, located on a stubby peninsula just south of North Sydney known as Kelly Beach. Seaplanes flew from this same spot during World War II as well. Nothing from the base survives today, and the site is now Munro Park. A PBY-5A seaplane from World War II looms over the parking lot, and interpretive signage beneath the plane tells the story of Kelly Beach during both world wars.

The patrols off the East Coast were more than precautionary. Germany understood that the key to neutralizing America's role in the war was to prevent its ships from reaching Europe. As early as May 1917, U-boats began to send Allied ships to the bottom off the North American coast. One particular boat, U-156, caused plenty of trouble during the summer of 1918. One of the sea mines it laid sank the navy cruiser U.S.S. *San Diego* off New York's Fire Island on July 19, with the loss of six hands. The wreck still lies 13.5 miles south of Fire Island Inlet. On the hazy Sunday morning of July 21, the U-156 struck again, this time off Nauset Beach on the forearm of Cape Cod. Sunbathers staked out their places in the sand as the southbound tug *Perth Amboy*, with four barges in tow, steamed by. At 10:30 AM, as the procession passed Nauset Inlet, the U-156 opened fire. One shell ripped the pilot house off the tug. The crewmembers of the tug and barges, along with their family members accompanying them, boarded their lifeboats and headed toward shore, but not before the twelve-year-old son of a barge captain defiantly waved an American flag at the Germans as their shells screamed overhead. The fusillade continued for more than an hour. Several shells landed on the beach, sending the sunbathers scurrying for cover. The explosions were heard in the nearby village of Orleans. The Massachusetts State Guard mobilized for what it feared might be an invasion. Locals and vacationers rushed to the Nauset Heights overlooking the beach to see what was going on. "The submarine was plainly visible," one witness told the *New York Times*. "Its guns flared continually as it hurled shells at the tug and the barges." Planes arrived from the nearby

Chatham Naval Air Station, but the bombs they dropped were duds. By noon, the U-156 had submerged and slipped away. Three of the four barges were on the bottom, but the flaming tug stubbornly stayed afloat. From Nauset Beach, the U-156 headed north, sinking several fishing vessels off New England and the Canadian Maritimes before heading home.

Nobody was killed in the so-called "Battle of Orleans," though a crewman on the *Perth Amboy* lost an arm. Nauset Beach is now part of the Cape Cod National Seashore, and is more popular with sunbathers than ever. The best access to site of the engagement is at

the end of Beach Road, where the Town of Orleans offers parking and concessions. Those visiting in summer should expect long lines and crowded conditions. Visitors at any time of year should expect to see very little evidence of the 1918 engagement. The National Park Service has not erected any signage to commemorate it, though the rangers at the

Sign at Nauset Heights on Cape Cod, Massachusetts, indicating the site of the "Battle of Orleans," July 1918.

Salt Pond Visitor Center off U.S. Highway 6 in Eastham (the center closest to the engagement site) can usually give those who ask a rundown of the events. The only historical marker noting the attack is located at Nauset Heights—where spectators watched the battle unfold a century ago—on the wooden steps at the foot of Nauset Road leading down to the beach. The simple rectangular sign, placed there by the local neighborhood association, has an arrow pointing seaward toward the spot of the engagement and notes that Nauset Beach was the only place in the United States hit by enemy fire during World War I. A cottage near the head of the stairway, at 46 Nauset Road, played a role in the skirmish as well. In the wake of the attack, those pulled from the water were brought to this home to recover from their ordeal. That cottage, named Sea Fever, is now an upscale rental property.

Entering Europe's More Treacherous Waters

German raids along the East Coast raised Americans' feelings of vulnerability, but were little more than an annoyance. The real action was in European waters, where in the spring of 1917 the situation for the Allies was desperate. With Germany's unrestricted submarine campaign, the number of merchant ships being sunk rose sharply. At the outset of the campaign, in February 1917, U-boats claimed 520,412 tons of shipping. By April, the figure rose to 860,334.

Britain faced the very real possibility of starvation. In March 1917, as war with Germany looked all but inevitable, President Wilson sent Rear Admiral William S. Sims, president of the Naval War College, to London on a secret mission to discuss possibilities for Anglo-American naval cooperation. Congress declared war while he was en route. Soon after arriving in London, Sims learned just how serious the U-boat threat to Britain really was. "It is impossible for us to go on with the war if losses like these continue," British Admiral John Jellicoe told him flatly. Some in the British Admiralty quietly suggested that their country could only hold out a few more months. The U.S. Navy dispatched warships to European waters right away. A group of six American destroyers left the Boston Navy Yard (now part of the Boston National Historical Park) on April 24, 1917, and appeared ten days later at the Royal Navy base at Queenstown, Ireland. Asked when the American sailors would be ready to start hunting for U-boats, U.S. Navy Commander Joseph K. Taussig replied, "as soon as we are finished refueling." The can-do attitude impressed the British.

Sims established his headquarters in the American Embassy at 4 Grosvenor Gardens in London, but as his responsibilities and his staff grew he moved them down the street to 30 Grosvenor Gardens. The admiral himself took up residence at the nearby Carlton Hotel (90 Belgrave Road), and walked to work each day. Before long, Sims was promoted to Vice Admiral and appointed Commander, U.S. Naval Forces Operating in European Waters—essentially Pershing's naval equivalent. An iconoclast who did not suffer fools lightly, Sims made many enemies during his long career, but none doubted his abilities. He made a name for himself promoting gunnery accuracy, and was one of the few in the navy hierarchy to criticize the reliance on battleships. Unlike Pershing and his contentious fight for an independent American army in Europe, Sims placed his ships at the disposal of the Royal Navy. The British, respectful of American power and abilities, integrated the U.S. ships into their command structure. British experience in fighting the German navy was critical to the Americans, he believed, and building separate U.S. Navy bases would have been time consuming and expensive. Many in Washington grumbled, but Sims got his way. The arrangement worked well. "Sometimes we were commanded by British admirals, sometimes they served under my command," recalled U.S. Admiral Hugh Rodman. "There was never the slightest friction, misunderstanding, or petty jealousy. In fact our mutual association in this war's work has drawn us so close together that in the Grand Fleet it was instrumental in ripening friendship with brotherhood."

Stopping the U-boats was the first priority, and Sims had an idea. Up to this point, merchant ships were armed to protect themselves from attack, while destroyers and other warships patrolled the sea-lanes in search of submarines. Unfortunately, the German submarine commanders were usually able to evade the patrol boats, and merchant ships often failed to detect the presence of a U-boat until it was too late. Sims suggested the idea of a convoy, whereby merchant ships could be grouped together and escorted by a flotilla of protective warships. Not only would this better protect the merchant ships, Sims argued, but it would also attract the submarines to the Allied warships where they could be more effectively engaged. The British Admiralty had discussed the idea before and rejected it. Merchant ship captains objected, thinking the convoys would make them sitting ducks, and the Royal Navy did not feel it could devote enough ships to make the convoys effective. But with U.S. entry into the war, the Allies now had vastly more ships and opted to give it a try. After an experimental convoy had made it from Gibraltar to Britain without loss, the Royal Navy adopted the tactic.

American ships raced across the Atlantic and immediately began convoy escort duties. Long before significant numbers of Doughboys appeared in the trenches in France, the Blue Jackets were fighting U-boats on the high seas. Key to submarine operations was the destroyer—a fast, maneuverable, and well-armed warship that could close in on submarines before they could submerge and get away. Unfortunately, due to its love affair with the battleship, the U.S. Navy had few destroyers to spare, and building more would take time. In the emergency of 1917, the navy cobbled together an eclectic collection of fast and maneuverable ships. In August and September, six U.S. Coast Guard cutters made their way to Europe. Some wealthy citizens turned over their private yachts for military service, including such notable families as the Astors and the Harrimans. J.P. Morgan's steam-powered yacht *Corsair* became the destroyer U.S.S. *Corsair* and saw action off the coast of France.

Escort duty was long and hard, and North Atlantic seas were notoriously rough, especially in winter. Navy destroyers met incoming convoys about 500 miles off the European coast, then guided them into port. They also protected outgoing convoys headed to North America. "Our routine was five days at sea and three days in Queenstown," recalled Commander William Halsey of the USS *Benham*, "with five days for cleaning boilers after every fifth trip." When a U-boat was spotted, deck guns opened up on it. If it submerged, the destroyers dropped a "depth charge," sometimes called a "depth bomb," an explosive that blew up underwater at a selected depth where a submarine might be. After such an encounter the U-boat usually disappeared, though unless some wreckage or an oil slick was found the sailors never knew with certainty if they had destroyed their quarry. There were plenty of false alarms, too. On one patrol, the *Benham*'s lookouts spotted a large wake off the starboard bow. "Thought I surely had my Fritz," Halsey wrote, but just as he was about to drop his depth charges he discovered the wake was created by a "large school of fish." Halsey also recalled that "a porpoise has a strong resemblance to a torpedo." In addition to escort duties, destroyers patrolled the shipping lanes for U-boats. Supplementing the destroyers were small ships known as subchasers, which plied European waters in "hunting groups" armed with deck guns, depth charges, and an early version of sonar looking for the elusive U-boats. Wooden minesweepers cleaned up the ordnance the U-boats left behind. Within months of joining the Allies, the United States was playing a substantial role in the battle against the U-boats.

Allied navies graciously hosted American warships, no country being more welcoming than Great Britain. The U.S. Navy's main European base was the Royal Navy yards at Queenstown. Located on the southern coast of Ireland, Queenstown controlled the western approaches to the Irish Sea and the English Channel, and when war came in 1914 German U-boats found these waters prime hunting grounds. Among the scores of ships that fell victim was the passenger liner *Lusitania*, sunk off the Old Head of Kinsale in 1915 (see Chapter 1). The U.S. Navy's first combat patrols sailed from Queenstown in May 1917, and that force steadily grew. By November 1918, the U.S. Navy had installations all around Queenstown Harbor manned by 8,000 sailors. American destroyers, submarines, and even the occasional battleship moored alongside Royal Navy vessels at Ringaskiddy on the southern shore of the harbor, as well as on Haulbowline Island. A giant American warehouse sprang up just west of the railroad terminal at Deep Water Quay on the Queenstown waterfront. Subchasers established a base at Granary Wharf on the River Lee just south of Passage West. The navy hospital was located at a landed estate called Whitepoint House on a peninsula jutting out into the harbor southeast of the city center. Like all American bases, there were recreational facilities, like the large enlisted man's club at Lynch's Quay, just east of central Queenstown. Overlooking over it all was the Admiralty House on a bluff above the city's cathedral, where the Royal Navy's Admiral Sir Lewis Bayly commanded the multinational collection of warships. American officers made up an integral part of Bayly's staff. On one occasion, when Bayly left Queenstown for a short time, he placed Admiral Sims in command. "It was an international courtesy of an unprecedented character," journalist Willis Abbott explained, "for never before had a British fleet been put under the command of a foreign admiral."

American sailors got along well with their British counterparts, but relations with the native Irish were sometimes rocky. Ireland was part of the British Empire only by force, and seethed with revolutionary activity during the war years. In 1916 Irish nationalists staged an uprising in Dublin known as the Easter Rebellion, forcing Britain to bring in thousands of soldiers—badly needed on the Western Front—to crush it. By 1917 a political movement called Sinn Fein openly agitated for an independent Irish republic. Irish nationalists hoped that the arrival of the U.S. Navy in Queenstown signaled a weakening British grip on their country, and that American sailors of Irish ancestry would join with them. Such hopes were soon dashed, and the nationalists turned their hostility toward the Americans. For their part, U.S. sailors complained of the pro-German sympathies of many Irish. "I'm Irish myself," one Blue Jacket said, "and yet I'd give a month's pay to crack the head of a Sinn Feiner." Head crackings and other such confrontations between American sailors and Irish nationalists were not uncommon in Queenstown and in Cork, a nearby city popular with Blue Jackets on liberty. How much such violence was politically inspired is open to question. Admiral Sims noted that "the eternal women question also played its part," since the Americans "had much more money than the native Irish boys, and could entertain the girls more lavishly." Whatever the case, such incidents occurred so frequently that Sims placed Cork off limits to U.S. sailors, though some of Cork's young women regularly made their way to Queenstown on a train dubbed the "dove's express" to be with their Yankee boyfriends.

Ireland finally achieved its independence in 1922 and Queenstown assumed its Irish name Cobh (pronounced *COVE*), though Britain held onto its naval base there until the 1930s. Whatever Irish-American animosity there may have been a century ago, Americans are welcome there now. Indeed, Cobh celebrates its American connections. It was a major port of embarkation for Irish emigrants heading for America in the nineteenth century. After the *Lusitania* sinking, Cobh was the most important collection point for victims both living and dead. A *Lusitania* memorial stands among the pastel-colored buildings on Casement Square, and many of the victims are buried in the old church cemetery north of town. Perhaps most famously, Cobh was the last stop for the ill-fated *Titanic* in 1912. There is the *Titanic* Memorial, the *Titanic* museum on the waterfront in the old offices of the White Star Line, and *Titanic*-related walking tours. The Cobh Heritage Center, adjacent to rail station at Deep Water Quay, features exhibits about immigration as well as the *Titanic* and the *Lusitania*, making it one of Cobh's most popular attractions.

But Cobh has not forgotten the Blue Jackets. At the Cobh Museum, located in an old church on High Road overlooking Deep Water Quay, only the *Titanic* exhibit is larger than the one devoted to the American sailors of World War I. If one decides to take a walking tour of Cobh, the guides are all too happy to point out U.S. Navy-related sites. For those who wish to explore the world of the Blue Jacket on their own, there are only a few remnants of the

U.S. naval presence left. Ringaskiddy is now home to the National Maritime College of Ireland, and is also one of Ireland's most important industrial centers. The Irish navy has taken control of Haulbowline Island. The buildings of the subchaser base at Granary Wharf were torn down many years ago, and where American subchasers once operated is a waterfront apartment complex. Whitepoint House, located at a bend of a road named Whitepoint Estate, is now a private residence, the open grazing lands surrounding it at the time of the Great War today filled with homes. No trace of the American warehouse at Deep Water Quay remains. A tall red brick smokestack on Lynch's Quay is all that is left of the once-busy enlisted man's club. The Admiralty House is now a monastery for the Benedictine Sisters, who welcome visitors to stroll in their contemplative gardens.

On to the Mediterranean and France

Gibraltar, Great Britain's naval base at the entrance to the Mediterranean, also hosted American sailors. Operations against Turkey in the Middle East depended on Allied control of the Mediterranean, as did keeping supply routes open to Italy. The first American warships, among them the six Coast Guard cutters, arrived at Gibraltar in August 1917. To most Americans, their image of Gibraltar came from advertisements of the Prudential Insurance Company, which featured the company name superimposed on the famous Rock of Gibraltar. This imagery sometimes prompted a little sailor humor. Hilary Chambers, an officer on a subchaser, remembered that upon approaching Gibraltar "the older men who had been to sea before had the recruits all looking for the Prudential sign on the rock," and when "no letters could be made out, the green men would not believe it to be Gibraltar." The Allied naval force at Gibraltar was multinational. British, French, and Italian navies sailed out of Gibraltar, and there was even a group of Japanese ships. Americans just added to the mix. By the end of the war, roughly 5,000 Americans were based beneath the Rock of Gibraltar.

Blue Jackets also served in other areas of the Mediterranean. A contingent of subchasers joined with British and French ships operating out of a small cove on the Greek island of Corfu, for example. "Beautiful green grass ran to the edge of an embankment," wrote Hilary Chambers of the picturesque spot, and "olive trees grew on this embankment all the way up to the hills in the background. There were no buildings but a sheep herder's hut a few yards from shore." There are plenty of buildings there now. That cove, about a kilometer east of the village of Limni, is now lined with luxury resorts.

The American Battle Monuments Commission (ABMC) honors the service of the U.S. Navy in the Mediterranean with the Naval

Monument Gibraltar, located in the heart of the tiny British possession. An archway made of stone quarried from the Rock of Gibraltar overlooks a small plaza on Line Wall Road near the intersection with Parliament Lane. Above the cornerstone of the arch is bas-relief sculpture of an ancient seagoing ship, symbolizing Gibraltar's role as an important link between the Atlantic and Mediterranean worlds, and beneath it is an inscription celebrating Anglo-American naval cooperation. Steps descend southward from the arch into an even larger plaza on Reclamation Road, and locals know the monument simply as the "American steps." There is another less conspicuous reminder of the American Great War naval presence in Gibraltar at the former Royal Navy Dockyard along Queensway Road. Just west of the Ragged Staff Gate is an old office building with two plaques affixed to its façade, in honor of Gibraltar-based U.S. sailors lost during World War I. One plaque lists the names of the men lost in the sinking of the U.S.S *Chauncey* off Gibraltar in November 1917. The other is dedicated to two U.S. Coast Guard cutters, the *Seneca* and the *Tampa*. Eleven crewmembers of the *Seneca* died on September 17, 1918, in the rescue of sailors from the British ship *Wellington* in the Bay of Biscay. The story of the *Tampa* is particularly tragic. After completing an escort mission, she was traveling alone in England's Bristol Channel on September 26, 1918, when a U-boat spotted her and fired a torpedo. The entire crew of 155 was lost. None of the bodies were ever recovered.

Cooperation with the French navy was also superb. The main U.S. Navy base in France was at Brest. Sheltered in a rocky inlet at the far western tip of Brittany, Brest has long had military significance. The Château du Brest, perched on a cliff above the bay at the mouth of the Penfeld River, originated with the Romans and expanded over the centuries. In the seventeenth century, as France strove to be a major world power, Cardinal Richelieu transformed Brest into a major naval base. By 1700, the Penfeld River beneath the chateau was clogged with sailing ships. The Marquis de Vauban, France's master fortification builder, ringed the city with imposing ramparts. Brest played a role in the American Revolution. In 1780, the Comte de Rochambeau departed Brest with soldiers bound for America to help the United States win its independence, and the following year the Comte de Grasse led his fleet from here to beat the British at the Battle of the Virginia Capes.

With the German invasion in 1914, France devoted much of its military attention to land forces while Britain took the lead in naval matters, and the Brest naval base languished. The first American ships, a fleet of converted yachts, arrived in July 1917. The Blue Jackets found the place strangely quiet. "In the ancient port of Brest but a few remnants of the French fleet remained," noted one American account. "The streets of the gray town were deserted. Gone were the seamen that for centuries had given it its glory." The U.S. Navy found plenty of room to moor their own ships on the Penfeld River, and as at Queenstown, went right to work patrolling for U-boats. More and more American ships flowed into Brest harbor, and the Americans aggressively built up the port facilities. The city was not only a convoy escort base but also the most important troop transport center in Europe (see Chapter 6). The number of American sailors stationed at Brest steadily climbed, and by the end of the war the base was as large as the one at Queenstown.

American Naval Monument at Brest, France.

Brest remains an important French naval base today. The Château du Brest is now home to a branch of the Musée National de la Marine (National Maritime Museum), which chronicles the story of the French Navy from the Age of Sail to modern times. Admission to the museum also affords access to the chateau grounds, where one can wander the old stone ramparts and enjoy views of the port and the rugged Brittany seascape. The museum exhibits say nothing about the American presence, but the ramparts overlook the French naval yards on the Penfeld River, where American destroyers, converted yachts, and subchasers once docked. Just 500 meters east the maritime museum, along the leafy promenade called the Cours Dajot that follows Vauban's ramparts, is the American Naval Monument at Brest. Here a pink granite tower rises thirty meters above a wide plaza. Steel plates embedded into the cement in the adjacent plaza give a brief overview of the U.S. Navy's role in World War I. Originally built in 1932, it was blown up by the Nazis on July 4, 1941—five months before the United States entered World War II. The ABMC rebuilt it in the 1950s. Except for the chateau, the American naval monument is perhaps the most prominent landmark in Brest. To the south, below the bluff, is the old commercial port, where nearly a million Doughboys got off the transport ships and first set foot of French soil. To the north is a street called rue de Denver, named in honor of the Colorado capital, one of Brest's sister cities. Along rue de Denver, interpretive signs in English, French, and Breton (the people of Brittany are fiercely proud of their Celtic heritage and go to great lengths to preserve it) tell the story of the monument and the American presence in Brest during World War I.

Aircraft and Sea Mines vs. the U-Boats

Just as naval air stations dotted the East Coast of North America, so too did they cover the European coast. The first was a seaplane base at Le Croisic, twenty-five kilometers northwest of Saint-Nazaire. Work on the base began in July 1917, when German prisoners began to level the land on two small islands just off the village waterfront. The navy then built barracks and hangars, and the first patrols went out in November. The channel between the waterfront and the islands gave the seaplanes a refuge from the choppy waters, though the sharp tides sometimes made it necessary to lift the planes out of the water by crane. The channel is now filled with civilian vessels. One island of the former naval air station is now a fish market. The other is a parking lot. On the village waterfront today, affixed to the Salle Jeanne d'Arc facing the former seaplane base, is a plaque commemorating the U.S. Navy presence in the village. Since Saint-Nazaire was the most important French port taking in American shipping, Le Croisic was not the only U.S. air station in the area. At Paimboeuf, eleven kilometers upriver from of Saint-Nazaire on the Loire, was a dirigible base. Paimboeuf began as a French installation in 1916, and the Americans moved in after they entered the war. Today, in the middle of an ordinary-looking business park just a few hundred meters off the D723 highway on the route de Camp d'Aviation, are four concrete footings left over from the Great War. Nearby are three informational panels telling the story of the base and the principles of dirigible flight. Unfortunately for Anglophone travelers, they are only in French.

Several naval air stations in southwestern France watched over Mediterranean convoys and protected the ports of La Rochelle and Bordeaux. On eastern side of Cap Ferret, separating Arcachon Bay from the Atlantic, was a seaplane base called the Arcachon Naval Air Station. The site, at the foot of Allée des Grisets in the village of Bélisaire, is now a small but popular stretch of pine-shaded beach known locally as the Plage des Américains. Forty kilometers to the north was another seaplane base on an inland lake near the hamlet of Moutchic, six kilometers northwest of Lacanau. Once a French seaplane base, the Americans took it over in 1917. A monument to the Americans is located near the waterfront just west of the village on avenue du Docteur Pierre Arnou Laujeac. It is a simple cement obelisk with a plaque on its base listing the names of the Americans who died there. Fifty meters to the east of the monument is a dilapidated old mansion that once served as the base headquarters. Saint-Trojan Naval Air Station lay between the beach and a pine forest three kilometers south of the village of Saint-Trojan, on the Île d'Oléron. The site, in the area south of Chemin de Lannelongue, is now an experimental school. The seaplane ramps are still discernible, sticking out into the sea.

The navy guarded northern routes as well. A seaplane base operated on the far western end of the Brest naval base, for example. A concrete ramp running into the bay at the western end of rue de Courlis in Île Tudy, ninety kilometers south of Brest, once guided U.S. Navy seaplanes to their missions. Locals now refer to the ramp as the *Cale des Américains* (Dock of the Americans), and the Bretons launch their boats from it to harvest their world famous oysters. There was an American seaplane base on the island of Énez Terc'h east

Memorial to deceased U.S. Navy fliers at Moutchic, France.

of Plouguerneau, thirty kilometers north of Brest. The island, also known as the Île des Américains, is connected to the mainland during low tide, and concrete remnants of the U.S. presence there are still visible. However, the Nazis also occupied the island during World War II, and unexploded ordnance from that conflict remains a risk.

U.S. Navy air stations extended into the British Isles. At the massive Queenstown naval base there was a seaplane base at Aghata, on the southeastern shore of the bay. Located along the R630 highway, the grounds of the old air base now hold a tennis club and farmland. The remains of the airplane ramp and pier are still there. At Wexford, Ireland, a seaplane base operated out of the Slaney River estuary. The concrete slip is still visible in the Ferrybank section of town, across the river from central Wexford. Americans also helped the British patrol the North Sea out of a British naval air station at Killingholme, eight miles north of Grimsby on the River Humber. The site of the air base is today a nondescript open area east of the intersection of Rosper Road and Station Road.

The convoys and the U-boat hunting tactics worked splendidly. By November 1917, shipping losses had dropped by one third from the previous April, and kept falling through the remainder of the war. Though the U-boat peril was far from over, the Allied antisubmarine campaign had brought it under control. With the emergency past, the American and British navies turned to containing U-boats in the North Sea and keeping them away from Allied shipping lanes. Britain laid mines and aggressively patrolled the narrow Straits of Dover. The Germans usually found it prohibitively dangerous to pass through these waters, so most U-boats took the northern route around Scotland, where geography made containment more difficult.

The British thought it impractical to mine the nearly 300 miles of ocean from Scotland to Norway, but the U.S. Navy devised a plan to do just that. Beginning in March 1918, U.S. and British ships began laying the North Sea Mine Barrage. Based out of Inverness in northern Scotland, American Blue Jackets laid fields of mines under the cover of darkness, often with battleships keeping a protective watch for German ships. Though not completed by the time of the armistice, the barrier still produced results. Six U-boats are believed to have fallen victim to the barrage, including the U-156, which sank boats off the East Coast of the United States in the summer of 1918. In all, American sailors laid 56,000 mines in the North Sea and the British another 14,000. Inverness is just a few kilometers downstream from Loch Ness, where thousands of tourists head every year in search of the nonexistent Loch Ness Monster. The American base was located on the Caledonian Canal, just before it enters the Beauly Firth. The only remnant of the U.S. Navy presence today is a white building along the canal at 90 Telford Street, which served as the base sick bay.

Some of the battleships protecting the minelayers were American. A few of America's prized battleships came over and joined the Royal Navy in bottling up the German fleet in the North Sea. The first arrived at Scapa Flow in Scotland, the very heart of British naval power, in December 1917. Ensign Francis T. Hunter, aboard the USS *New York*, was awestruck as he passed through the submarine nets and "looked for the first time on the world's most stupendous sea force. . . . The Grand Fleet of Britain! How dignified, how powerful she looked." He was thrilled "realizing at last that we were actively a part of it." The American battleships saw little action. The British fleet smothered the German navy so effectively that the Germans were never able to break out of the North Sea. American battleships patrolled the North Sea with their British counterparts, and although German submarines got off a few shots at U.S. battleships, they all missed, and there was not a single battleship casualty as the result of enemy fire.

Getting the Doughboys across the Pond

The sea lanes were secured just as American industrial might began to ramp up, so as U.S. factories churned out vast quantities of war materials, they could be reliably transported across the ocean on what was called the "Atlantic Ferry." In all, more than seven million tons of goods streamed across the Atlantic, including 47,018 motorized trucks, 26,994 rail cars, 1,791 locomotives, and 68,694 horses and mules. Most important of all, more than two million Doughboys made the crossing. By early 1918, stateside training camps were beginning to produce soldiers in substantial numbers, but finding enough ships to get them to France was a challenge. Civilian ocean liners—much like the men they transported—were drafted into government service. The U.S. government chartered ships from neutral nations like the Netherlands and seized German-owned ships when it could. The massive ocean liner *Vaterland* of the Hamburg America Line, berthed in New York when Congress declared war, became the S.S. *Leviathan*, and transported 100,000 American troops across the Atlantic to fight its former owners.

Nearly half of all American troops crossed the ocean in British or Commonwealth vessels. Some were luxury liners like the *Aquitania* of the Cunard Line. Others were much less glamorous. The 301st Engineers traveled on the Australian liner *Katoomba*, which had also been used to transport cattle. "The odor of former four-legged occupants struck your sense of smell with such force that your nose unconsciously wrinkled in disgust," according to one account. France and Italy also provided some transport ships. Only 46 percent of U.S. troops crossed on American ships.

The voyage across the Atlantic usually took two weeks. Big ocean liners like the *Leviathan* were fast enough to outrun any submarine and traveled on their own, but most transports sailed across in convoys. Groups of transports sailed in formation, with cruiser escorts to protect them. "I was really amazed to count a whole fleet of ships—sixteen in number—headed by the cruiser *Montana*," wrote Christ Stamas, "ploughing the mighty Atlantic in an arrowhead formation and changing course every few miles." Along the East Coast, navy planes flew overhead searching for periscopes until the convoys passed out of their range. "The boys on the transport spent many an idle hour watching the aviators circle the ship time and time again," remembered William Bachman, "often coming within voice range of the transport's passengers." Fear of U-boats was high among the soldier-passengers, and out in the open ocean the cruiser escorts were a welcome sight. "The dark and sombre cruiser gave us more cheer than any craft," recalled Earl Searcy. "You have no idea what a sense of security it engendered." Ships also received camouflage paintjobs to deceive German submarines. "It looked as if an army of painters had gone wild," Searcy remembered. "Some of the vessels looked like huge swell crests; others appeared to be cut in half. They were easily discernible at close view, but at a distance, one would have been deceived as to the nature of many of the craft."

For most soldiers it was their first time at sea. Seasickness was common. "I didn't realize two months ago when I first entered the service that I would be out here on the Atlantic Ocean leaning over the railing of a deck heaving like a bellows," wrote Harland Osthagarp in his diary. "One of our own men while sick the first day rushed to the rail on the windward side," another soldier recalled, "and the deluge that he intended for the fishes was suddenly whipped back upon his person. The effect brought both a snort of disgust and a gale of laughter from the onlookers, and the man's appearance was anything but tidy."

Immigrant soldiers who had already made an Atlantic crossing often fared better. "I was not much bothered by seasickness," wrote Greek immigrant Christ Stamas, "and now considered myself a veteran." Seasickness usually abated after a few days, but the cramped quarters of the troopships did not.

Duties were minimal while aboard ship, and the Doughboys occupied their time in various ways. The men of Battery F, 135th Field Artillery spent much of their sea time playing "cards, loafing on deck watching the dolphin schools, desultory attempts at French, reading, very little writing, with each day pretty much the same," according to their official history.

When the convoys got within a few hundred miles of the European coast they reached the most dangerous waters, so Allied navies beefed up protection. Destroyers came out to meet them, and navy planes from shore flew overhead reassuringly. Land finally came into view—a welcome sight for the hungry, weary, and seasick soldier. The official history of Headquarters Company, 134th Field Artillery described the moment this way:

> On the horizon to port the craggy peaks of Scotland's hills loomed up in somber silhouette, their bases dipping into the very water's edge. . . . Green hills, seemingly suspended in the very air, checkered the grey hills beyond; and the low-hung haze, tenuous and purpled with the coming dawn, gave to it all the enchanting hue of fairyland. On our starboard was the Emerald Isle, wave lashed promontories and jagged headlands, that far northern part of untamable spirits and adventurous blood that so often infested our boy dreams. . . . There was unceasing movement from one side of the ship to the other, everyone eager to take it all in.

Most convoys crossed without incident, but several had some close U-boat encounters. "A periscope had been seen to emerge," wrote Earl Searcy of his crossing. "Three guns were trained upon it from the nearest ships. Presently, a little of the coning tower was visible, then the guns barked. A mess of black, oily water seethed in a moment, and a German submarine had been accounted for."

The Twin Tragedies of Islay

Allied navies did a remarkable job protecting the troops, but occasionally the U-boats scored a hit. The worst troopship disasters occurred in 1918 off the Isle of Islay (pronounced *EYE-lah*), the southernmost of Scotland's Hebrides chain. Islay lies on the North Channel connecting the open Atlantic and the Irish Sea. On a clear day Ireland is visible from the island, especially from a bulbous peninsula on its southern tip known as the Mull of Oa (pronounced *OH*), where stark cliffs rise more than 600 feet above the sea. Late in the afternoon of February 5, 1918, the German submarine UB-77, under the command on Captain Wilhelm Meyer, was on patrol in the North Channel when the crew detected a convoy steaming in under British escort. At the convoy's center were three massive ocean liners transporting American soldiers: the *Baltic* (the same ship that had brought General Pershing to Europe the previous year), the *Ceramic*, and the *Tuscania*. Meyer carefully calculated the convoy's course and speed, and positioned himself for attack. Just as dusk fell he launched two torpedoes. One missed, but the other slammed into the *Tuscania*, hitting her amidships on the starboard side between the engine and boiler rooms. There was "a decided shock which rocked the big ship from end to end," according to the official history of the 20th Engineers. "Simultaneously all lights went out and a deafening crash echoed and re-echoed through the ship."

The passengers remained surprisingly calm as they filed out of the bowels of the ship, but their situation was desperate. The explosion destroyed or damaged many of the lifeboats. The wounded ship listed about ten degrees, and some of the men on deck lost their footing and slipped into the sea. Waves swamped many of the over-crowded lifeboats, capsizing them. In one case, a lifeboat dropped onto another one already in the water, crushing some of its occupants and tossing others into the dark waters. *Tuscania* finally slid beneath the waves after four agonizing hours, but the horror continued all through the night. Rescue ships plucked many out of the wintry waters, but others succumbed to hypothermia and drowned. The dead, the dying, and those in undiscovered lifeboats drifted toward Islay. About fifty bodies washed up in Loch Indaal, a large inlet at the center of the island. At the Mull of Oa, several lifeboats crashed onto the jagged cliffs. "Moving sideways in the trough of the waves we were suddenly caught up in a big heave and sent crashing into an immense rock," recalled Arthur Siplon of the 100th Aero Squadron:

> The lifeboat turned upside down throwing everyone into the boiling, angry sea. As I reached the surface the boat was in front of me bottom side up. I could hear men screaming and praying all about me. With great effort I scrambled up on the bottom of the boat. My pal . . . came up near me . . . but in just a brief moment a huge wave drove us off, and into the raging sea again. It was then a matter of being buffeted about the bruising rocks, washed in with the waves, and out with the undertow. Just how long this pounding lasted there is no way to determine. . . . When it seemed my last breath was reached . . . I was struck forcibly in the chest. I grabbed with both hands. As the big wave went out I found I was on the point of a rock near shore. I gripped it with all my waning strength.

Everett Harpham of the 20th Engineers also landed on a rock, and as he lay there exhausted and bleeding he heard his friend Roy Muncaster shouting, "Cheer up, Harp, we'll get the Kaiser yet." Harpham never saw his friend again.

Cliffs of the Mull of Oa, just below the American Monument on Islay. Many victims of the *Tuscania* sinking died when their lifeboats crashed upon these rocks.

The people of Islay came to the aid of those who had washed up on their shores. A few soldiers managed to walk inland and take shelter in the cottages of local farmers and shepherds. When some showed up at the home of Annie Campbell, she baked scones for them over a peat fire. Locals quickly rushed to shore and searched for survivors. Robert Morrison, a coast watcher on the Mull of Oa, waded into the surf, threw a rope to struggling soldiers, and pulled them in. The next morning, survivors were taken to Port Ellen on horse-drawn carts and put up in the village's two hotels, the White Hart and the Islay Hotel. "Here the fallacy that the Scotch are tight was completely exploded," wrote Arthur Siplon. Villagers provided the survivors with food, shelter, and clothing. According to a Red Cross report, one local resident gave away so much of his own clothing that "when he arose the next morning he did not have any underclothes to put on." They also shared their whiskey, for which the island is famous. "Just outside the village was a distillery," wrote Siplon, "and I do not hesitate to say that I think the greater portion of a quart of this medicine is the reason I am still living."

In all, 166 Americans died in the disaster and were laid to rest on the island. "As the victims had come in at rather widely separated places," noted the American Red Cross, "they were buried as near as possible to these places in four cemeteries overlooking the sea." A rugged valley on the Mull of Oa known as Port nan Gallan had two small graveyards. One, on a grassy plain above the western edge of the valley, was called Killeyan. Another, known as Kinnabus, was just above the ruins of an old fishing village closer to the shore. Other victims were buried at the tiny seaside hamlet of Kilnaughton, two miles west of Port Ellen, immediately adjacent to the village cemetery. Those who washed up in Loch Indaal were interred in a cemetery along the shore just south of Port Charlotte, near a Bronze Age cairn. The islanders held reverent and heartfelt funerals for the Americans, perhaps most notably at Port Charlotte on February 9. Led by two pipers, the coffins were transported by truck and horse-drawn wagon down the main street while local residents joined the procession, following the cortege to the cemetery. "Every part of Islay seemed to be represented," one local newspaper reported, "and the sad proceedings seemed still more depressing through the drenching rain which fell in torrents." At the cemetery, a salute of gunfire rang out and bagpipes played as the boys were lowered into their graves.

Nearly seven months to the day of the *Tuscania* sinking, disaster struck again. On the stormy Sunday morning of October 6, 1918, another convoy entered the North Channel. Among the ships were two transporting Doughboys from New York, the HMS *Otranto* and HMS *Kashmir*. Sickness had already ravaged both vessels, which were sailing at the peak of the influenza epidemic, making the miseries of the Atlantic crossing even worse. But the transports then lost sight of each other in the strong gales and heavy seas, and in the confusion the *Kashmir* rammed the *Otranto*. The *Kashmir*, only lightly damaged, continued on, but the *Otranto* quickly took on water in the unrelenting waves. The British destroyer HMS *Mounsey* made heroic efforts to rescue the soldier-passengers. At one point, she pulled up alongside the *Otranto*. As the two ships bounced in the waves, some desperate men leaped thirty to forty feet from the sinking wreck of the *Otranto* onto the *Mounsey*. "Many suffered in the experience," reported the *New York Times*, "but fractured limbs were preferable to death." Not everybody made it. "Some missed their jump and met a terrible fate in the raging sea," the *Times* continued, "or worse still, were crushed between the vessels." Some refused to jump, and took their chances on the *Otranto*. For most, it was a fatal decision. Massive waves washed helpless soldiers out to sea, and winds pushed the *Otranto* toward Machir Bay, on Islay's northwest coast, where it broke up and sank about half a mile from shore. A handful of Doughboys managed to swim to shore, but most drowned or were smashed against the rocks and killed. The northwest coast of Islay was strewn with dead bodies and ship wreckage, all intertwined on a stretch of beach and in the rocky coves. Bodies washed ashore for days afterward. Once again, Islay residents made heroic efforts to save the men. In all, 351 Americans died in this disaster. The *Otranto* dead—British and American alike—were laid to rest at a British military cemetery near Kilchoman, overlooking Machir Bay.

The twin tragedies of the *Tuscania* and the *Otranto* broke the hearts of wartime Americans, but have long since been forgotten—except on the Isle of Islay. In 1920, the American Red Cross erected a monument on the Mull of Oa to honor the dead. The 65-foot cylindrical stone tower, known locally as the "American monument," is perched atop the cliffs overlooking the site of the *Tuscania* disaster. The memorial is the work of Glasgow architect Robert Walker, who designed it to resemble a cairn—a pile of stacked stones that in Celtic cultures serves as a memorial or grave marker for important people—and is made of rock quarried nearby.

Memorial to the victims of the *Tuscania* and *Otranto* disasters on Scotland's Isle of Islay, known locally as the American Monument.

Getting there is not easy. The nearest road ends about a mile away from the memorial, and from there one must hike. A trail leads through picturesque pastures filled sheep and shaggy cattle, then through fields of heather. The monument, now within the boundaries of a bird sanctuary, stands in a place of extraordinary beauty. Rare birds soar overhead, sheep and goats graze on the windswept heather, and the sound of waves crashing on the rocks below is occasionally punctuated by the barking of seals. Looking down on these stunning cliffs, it is hard to imagine that they were the scene of such pain and misery a century ago. The wreck of the *Tuscania* lies five and a half miles due south of the memorial in 345 feet of water.

Islay has a timeless quality, and today its villages, pastures, and one-lane roads appear much as they did when the unfortunate Doughboys washed up on the island's shores. The White Hart Hotel, facing Port Ellen's beach, still welcomes guests. The Islay Hotel, down the street near the ferry terminal, was demolished in 2007, rebuilt, and reopened in 2011. The Royal Society for the Protection of Birds, which maintains the nature sanctuary, offers summer walking tours of the Mull of Oa. In addition to providing a plethora of information about the area's flora and fauna, the guides also tell the tragic stories of the *Tuscania* and *Otranto* disasters. The Museum of Islay Life in Port Charlotte, housed in an old church, exhibits items from the island's long history, including some associated with the World War I sinkings. Perhaps the most evocative item in the whole museum is the bell from the *Tuscania*, which divers brought to the surface in 1997. Nearly all of the American dead have been removed from the island. Today, Britain's Commonwealth War Graves Commission maintains Kilchoman cemetery. The British victims—including the *Otranto*'s captain—remain there, but within the cemetery walls there are numerous open spaces where Americans once rested. All four of the *Tuscania* cemeteries were emptied as well. Robert Walker, the architect of the American memorial, proposed that small cairns be erected to mark the spots where *Tuscania* dead were buried, but this was never done. One American soldier remains buried on Islay. The family of Private Roy Muncaster of the 20th

Engineers requested that their son remain on the island, and he now lies in the British military cemetery at Kilnaughton.

Remembering the Sacrifices of the Blue Jacket

Many *Tuscania* and *Otranto* dead were brought to the Brookwood American Cemetery near London, along with the remains of other Doughboys and Blue Jackets who perished in and around the Britain Isles during the war. The London Necropolis Company established Brookwood in 1849 in response to the severe over-crowding in the city's urban graveyards. Located twenty-five miles southwest of London in the Surrey countryside, Brookwood was once the largest cemetery in the world. It even had its own rail line to bring mourners from the city. During World War I, Britain and Commonwealth countries began burying their dead at Brookwood, and when Americans arrived in 1917 they did the same. After the war, the ABMC took over that portion of the cemetery where the Americans were buried. The Brookwood American Cemetery and Memorial is the only U.S. Great War cemetery in Britain.

Brookwood no longer has its own rail line, but it is still easily accessible by train from London's Waterloo Station. The American portion of the cemetery is a five-minute walk from cemetery entrance at the Brookwood Station, on the west end of the cemetery grounds. The buildings and grounds of the American section are the work of New York architect Egerton Swartwout (perhaps best known for his design of the Missouri State Capitol) and his assistant, H.B. Cresswell. Covering 4.5 acres, the American section is surrounded by tall pine trees and lined with rhododendron. Swartwout and Cresswell arranged the graves in four sections, with a flagpole in the center. Most of the 468 service members buried there were naval casualties, or soldiers who died of disease or in shipwrecks. The chapel is made of white limestone quarried in Dorset, England, and has the appear-ance of an ancient Greek temple. The names of soldiers and sailors whose bodies were never recovered grace the interior walls—563 in all. (Those whose remains have since been recovered or identified are marked with a small rosette.) The majority of those named here are from naval incidents, and they are grouped by the ship on which they were lost. Particularly striking is the list for the *Tampa*, which lists all of the 115 American victims. One name on the west wall of the cha-pel is highlighted in gold. Osmond Ingram was a Gunner's Mate on the USS *Cassin*. While on patrol off Ireland in October 1917, Ingram spotted a German torpedo headed for his ship. Thinking quickly, he was able to jettison most of the ship's depth charges before the torpedo hit, saving the lives of many of his shipmates. Ingram was killed in the explosion, his body never recovered. He was posthumously awarded the Congressional Medal of Honor—the first sailor in World War

I to receive America's highest military decoration. Flanking the American cemetery are the graves of 5,000 soldiers from Britain, the Commonwealth, and Allied nations from both world wars. The Canadian section is particularly large.

By November 1918, the U.S. Navy had grown to half a million men. There were also 11,000 thousand enlisted women, nicknamed "Yeomanettes," who served mainly in clerical positions. Only a handful went overseas. At the time of the armistice there were 81,000 U.S. sailors serving in European waters on 370 ships and forty-seven different bases, from Ireland to Greece. Not a single troopship escorted by the U.S. Navy ever hit the bottom. Upon his return from London, Admiral Sims went back to his job at the Naval War College, but the remainder of his career was fraught with controversy. In his postwar tenure at the Naval War College he became a strong proponent of naval air power, and championed the development of the aircraft carrier to maximize the impact of the airplane in naval warfare. Traditionalists still wed to the battleship disliked Sims's ideas, but World War II proved him right. After a successful and controversial career, Sims retired in 1922 and settled with his family in a white clapboard home at 73 Catherine Street in Newport, Rhode Island. That home is now a bed and breakfast called the Admiral Sims House. He died in 1936.

Very few of America's World War I ships still survive. There are two places where one can walk the decks the Blue Jackets of the Great War once did, though neither has been restored to World War I conditions. The U.S.S. *Olympia* is part of the Independence Seaport Museum in Philadelphia. The cruiser is most famous as Admiral Dewey's flagship in the Battle of Manila Bay during the Spanish-American War, and has been restored to its 1898 condition. During World War I the *Olympia* prowled the East Coast in search of U-boats, but its greatest claim to Great War fame was its transportation of the Unknown Soldier to the United States from France after the war (see Chapter 18). Another is the U.S.S. *Texas*. Commissioned in 1914, the *Texas* patrolled the Gulf of Mexico during the Mexican Revolution, then joined the U.S. Navy contingent at Scapa Flow protecting the minelayers of the North Sea Mine Barrage. The *Texas* played a significant role in World War II, counting North Africa, D-Day, Iwo Jima, and Okinawa among its battle credits. Today the Battleship *Texas* State Historic Site preserves this veteran of two world wars on the Buffalo Bayou in the Houston suburb of La Porte. The *Texas* has been restored to its World War II conditions, though the Great War is not forgotten. Interpretive panels throughout the ship outline its contributions in the First World War. The ship is adjacent to San Jacinto Battlefield State Historic Site, where the Texans defeated Mexican forces and won their temporary independence.

U.S.S. *Texas* today.

"To our sister service we owe the safe arrival of our armies and supplies," General Pershing wrote in his final report after the war, but his statement understates the significance of the U.S. Navy to the Allied war effort. Its appearance in British waters at the height of the German U-boat campaign in the spring of 1917 may well have saved Britain from starvation. The American augmentation of the Royal Navy gave the Allies an insurmountable naval advantage over the Central Powers, whose economies were thus slowly ground to ruins. American sailors were fighting and dying on the seas just months after the U.S. entry into the war and did so along a battle front 4,000 miles long. The Blue Jacket is perhaps the greatest unsung American hero of the Great War.

CHAPTER 6:
ARRIVAL IN EUROPE

After a dozen days at sea, the ships carrying the first batch of American infantry to the Great War reached the coast of France. "In late afternoon an airplane appears, circles, and goes back," recorded Tom Carroll in his diary. "At dusk French destroyers join us. We must be close in." The sight of land evoked cheers from the travel-weary soldier-passengers. The first ships pulled into the port of Saint-Nazaire on June 26, 1917, carrying the 16th and 28th Infantry Regiments. "It was a beautiful sunny morning," recalled Captain George C. Marshall, the division's operations officer, "and the green hill slopes and little cottages along the northern shore gave us all an agreeable impression of what France was to be." But as Marshall's ship, the *Tenadores*, reached the dock, the young officer gained another perspective on wartime France. "A small crowd of French inhabitants collected along the edge of the basin at the end of the street to watch our arrival," he remembered. "Very few men were in evidence. There was not a cheer, and the general aspect was that of a funeral." France had endured three years of incomprehensible casualties, and in the spring of 1917 war weariness ran rampant across the nation. Her ally, Great Britain, had fared little better. One of the few bright spots for the Allies was the arrival of American soldiers. This small batch of inexperienced soldiers that landed at Saint-Nazaire, the nascent 1st Division, was the first of many to come—two million troops would make it to Europe over the next eighteen months. Would these Doughboys really help turn the tide of the war?

Company K of the 28th Infantry Regiment was accorded the honor of being the first U.S. Army combat outfit to set foot in France, and the ships disgorged the remainder of their human cargo over the next several days. From the docks, the men of the 1st Division marched to a camp on a hill about four kilometers west of the city simply known as Camp No. 1. "We were anxious that the men should make a good appearance in passing through the town," wrote Marshall, "but most of them were ignorant of the first rudiments of march discipline and were busy looking in shop windows and observing the French crowd." Construction of the camp had commenced just a few days before, and was still ongoing when the division arrived.

Ben Bernheisel recalled that when he got to Camp No. 1 "German prisoners were busy building barracks." "Poor accommodations and lots of confusion," complained Tom Carroll, "also raining." Mud was omnipresent. The men received work details soon after their arrival, which usually meant unloading the ships on which they had come. They also began drilling and marching. "Practice marches over the hills and along the seashore were taken daily," according to the official history of the 26th Infantry Regiment, "followed by a dip in the surf."

They also got to see a little of Saint-Nazaire. For the vast majority of the soldiers, it was their first time in a foreign land. "Everything seemed small," observed Ben Bernheisel, who had the sensation of stepping back in time. "The people were dressed quaintly and many wore wooden shoes," he observed, and thought the scene "not unlike a fairy story." The Nazaireans soon warmed to the brash strangers in their midst. "For the first two or three days the attitude of the French citizens was quite reserved," remembered George Bogert, "but the spontaneous, happy-go-lucky demeanor of the Americans seemed to inspirit them and they became more and more cordial and attentive as the days passed, especially the women and children." Booze and women seemed to be the main concern of many. U.S. laws prohibiting the serving of alcohol to men in uniform did not apply in France, and the Doughboys often took full advantage of this. Tom Carroll remembered that barbed wire surrounded the camp, but "guys were sneaking thru and getting loaded." "The day after the arrival of our troops three houses of ill fame were opened and packed with camp followers

Monument at Saint-Nazaire commemorating the arrival of the 1st Division in France.

from near-by sections of France," recalled Bogert, though the bordellos were soon shut down. With virtually no young men left in the city, most Americans did not have to turn to professionals for female attention anyway. Some Americans tried out their French, with mixed results. "I decided to initiate a policy of familiarizing myself with the French language by speaking French on every suitable occasion," wrote George C. Marshall. Riding in a staff car with a French officer, Marshall wanted to "comment on the wonderful morning," and turned to his colleague and said, "'Je suis très beau, aujourd'hui.'" Marshall quickly realized his mistake—he had said, "I am very beautiful today"—and wrote in his memoirs that "during the ensuing twenty-six months I never spoke French again except when forced to."

Saint-Nazaire has not forgotten the arrival of the Americans during those dark days of 1917. Hugging the shoreline of the city is boulevard du Président Wilson, and along the ocean side of the street is a lovely waterfront promenade, where one can enjoy cool ocean breezes and watch the ships begin their ascent of the Loire. Rising from a rock outcropping along the beach is a memorial commemorating the arrival of the 1st Division at Saint-Nazaire. Capping a stone pedestal is a bronze statue of an upright Doughboy on the back of an eagle with outstretched wings. The monument now hovering over the Saint-Nazaire shoreline is not the original. The first one appeared in 1926, but occupying Nazi troops destroyed it in 1941. The current incarnation was rededicated in 1989. Facing the statue along the promenade are French and American flags, along with several bronze tablets embedded in a stone base that tell the story of the monument and the U.S. arrival.

The French and the British Welcome the Doughboys

To get the biggest possible bang out of their propaganda buck, French officials proposed a massive parade of American soldiers through the streets of Paris on July 4, 1917, in celebration of America's Independence Day. General Pershing was hesitant. "We were not prepared to make much of an impression," he wrote, since about "two-thirds of the men were recruits." But the French insisted and the American commander relented. The 2nd Battalion of the 16th Infantry Regiment was brought up from Saint-Nazaire on July 3 to do the honors. It arrived at the Gare Austerlitz and marched to the Caserne de Reuilly (24 rue de Reuilly) near the place de la Nations on the east side of Paris. Parisians lined the streets to get a glimpse of the men the French began to call the "Sammies," as in Uncle Sam. On a few occasions "shop girls on their way to work slipped through the police lines and kissed the soldiers," reported the *New*

York Times, claiming that the soldiers expressed "great embarrassment" about it. Afterward, officers were treated to a banquet at the Cercle Militare (8 place Saint-Augustin). Enlisted men received a tour of the city, and spent the evening shining and polishing their equipment in preparation for the big show.

The following morning, the Doughboys boarded trucks and headed for the Hôtel des Invalides, where the parade was to begin. The ceremonies began in the Court of Honor at the heart of the Invalides complex. Spectators filled the balconies, and captured German weapons and equipment decorated the grounds. American troops lined the courtyard, while in the center French President Raymond Poincaré and Marshall Joseph Joffre officially welcomed Pershing to France with a stand of U.S. flags. "The impressive formalities were carried out with studied precision," Pershing wrote of the event. Tom Carroll, one of the participating Doughboys, had a different take on the proceedings. He remembered being "hot and sweaty, at attention mostly, for hours in the hot sun while the big shots made speeches." At the conclusion of the formalities, the troops began their march. "How the thousands did cheer," remembered Pershing aide James Harbord, "as the head of the column passed under the arch" of the courtyard and into the streets of the French capital.

The five-mile route went through the heart of the city and was fraught with historical symbolism. The soldiers of the great American democracy paraded past some of the most important sites of France's revolutionary heritage. They marched through the place de la Concorde, where the guillotine did its bloody work during the French Revolution. From there they marched east down the fashionable rue de Rivoli, passing the Tuileries Gardens and the Louvre, the former royal palace that became a public art museum. After a bit of rest at the Hôtel de Ville, it was on to the place de la Bastille, where the French people first rose up against royal authority. The Bastille prison, the symbol of the royal abuse of power that revolutionaries stormed on July 14, 1789, had been torn down long before, but the American troops marched past the giant obelisk that marked the spot where the French Revolution began. From there, the procession went down rue de Lyon and then turned east down boulevard Diderot, into a working class section of the city. The Doughboys turned right at rue de Picpus and marched to the grave of the Marquis de Lafayette in the Cimetiere de Picpus to honor the man who bound the two great democracies together.

Seldom has the Fourth of July been celebrated with more gusto than it was on the streets of Paris in 1917. Every inch of sidewalk was covered with cheering Parisians, as was every window, balcony, and rooftop. "As far as the eye could reach," remembered James Harbord, "the mass of French people stretched." "Females of all ages, young boys, old men, and tens of thousands of little children lined the streets," observed a *New York Times* correspondent, who also noted an "almost complete absence of young men." According to some estimates, perhaps a million people turned out. Giant American flags graced many buildings, and so many spectators held miniature flags that street vendors quickly ran out of them. The crowds were effusive too, shouting their encouragement in French and broken English. "The French went wild," wrote Ben Bernheisel, one the soldiers in the parade. He remembered that it was impossible to maintain any semblance of military bearing because their ranks were continually being "broken by the pressure of enthusiastic crowds." Young women ran up to the soldiers and festooned them with mounds of flowers. "With wreaths about their necks and bouquets in their hats and rifles," Pershing later wrote, "the column looked like a moving flower garden." The general, who was chauffeured along the parade route in a motorcar, got some flowers too. On boulevard Diderot, at the intersection with avenue Daumesnil, a young girl climbed onto the running board of Pershing's car and presented him with a bouquet, eliciting a smile from his otherwise stern visage. French soldiers on leave, with bandaged wounds clearly visible, emerged from the crowd and marched alongside the Sammies. French veterans of past wars lined the route as well. "It is a fact that tears streamed down many an old soldier's cheeks," wrote Ben Bernheisel, "not to mention us boys. It was a very emotional Paris that day." Pershing later reflected that "these stirring scenes conveyed vividly the emotions of a people to whom the outcome of the war had seemed all but hopeless."

The climax of the ceremonies came at Lafayette's grave in the Cimetiere de Picpus. Lafayette had helped America in a time of need during the eighteenth century, and in the twentieth century Americans had come to return the favor. After their long march through central Paris, the Doughboys went single file through the narrow cemetery gate. There were more speeches. Tom Carroll remembered Picpus as a "cool and shady" place where "we sat on headstones while the gab went on." That "gab" produced some of the most memorable words of the entire war. General Pershing spoke only briefly, assigning Colonel Charles L. Stanton to give the keynote address. Stanton spoke for about twenty minutes, but it was a single line in his speech that summarized the significance of the day. Standing before the grave of the marquis, Stanton announced: "Nous voila, Lafayette," which the press translated as "Lafayette, we are here." The remark became a battle cry and an enduring symbol of Franco-American friendship. It has long been attributed to Pershing himself, though the general never once took credit for it. "I have often wished that it could have been mine," he later wrote, "but I have no recollection of saying anything so splendid."

Located at 35 rue de Picpus, the Cimetiere de Picpus is the only private burial ground in Paris. Its inconspicuous entrance is easy to miss, but passing through the big brown doors one finds a peaceful respite from the frenetic pace of Paris. Lafayette's grave lies at the eastern end of the grounds, beyond the blue gates next to the chapel. Affixed to the gateposts are two plaques, placed by the Paris chapter of the Daughters of the American Revolution. One honors Lafayette, and the other commemorates General Pershing and the arrival of U.S. troops in France in 1917. Lafayette's grave is easily identifiable by the ever-present American flag above it. Numerous American patriotic societies have installed plaques on or near the gravestone, which is usually decorated with flowers and American coins. Pershing and Stanton were not the last Americans in Paris to pay to tribute to Lafayette.

Another parade took place in London on August 15. This one garnered fewer headlines than the Paris event, but the Doughboys were greeted no less enthusiastically. A smattering of engineer regiments, recently arrived at Liverpool, arrived at Waterloo Station that morning. They marched across the Thames, past the Houses of Parliament, and on to Wellington Barracks, where they ate a light breakfast with British counterparts. The main event took place at mid-day. As in Paris, prominent London buildings were bedecked with the Stars and Stripes. The skies were alternately sunny and cloudy, with an occasional light rain falling. From Wellington Barracks, the American army began the march through the streets of Westminster. They proceeded north along Horse Guards Road and through the Horse Guards Parade. As they turned north onto Whitehall, some of Britain's highest political officials waved to the Americans from the windows of the War Office on the east side of the street, including Prime Minister David Lloyd George and Minister of Munitions Winston S. Churchill. At Trafalgar Square, the Doughboys passed the statue of Admiral Nelson, the great British naval hero of the Napoleonic Wars, proceeded west on Cockspur Street, and then north to Piccadilly Circus, and from there down fashionable Piccadilly to the Wellington Arch.

All along the way, the streets were thronged with Londoners who, as the London *Daily Chronicle* put it, "forgot the silly traditions of British reserve." "I never saw so many people in all my life," wrote Walter Burrows of the 13th Engineers. "Every street and building, nook and crack, was just jammed full," he remembered, "and such noise as they made, one could not hear one's self think." "The Americans for the most part kept their eyes to the front," reported the *New York Times*, but occasionally a Doughboy could be spotted looking "to the right or left, grinning broadly or wiggling a hand in such a way the officers could not see." Others detected a more somber mood. British writer Stacy Aumonier watched the parade from Cockspur Street "by getting behind some shortish people and standing on tiptoe." Aumonier fancied himself a student of national characteristics and believed the Americans would exhibit a spirit of youthful exuberance, but was surprised to see instead "a curious set expression of purpose on their faces." As the ranks filed past him, the expression seldom varied. "They did not look at us or raise a smile," he wrote. Others around him noticed this, too, and Aumonier heard someone comment, "they're solemn-looking blokes, ain't they?" Some marchers reflected on the gravity of the task before them. "Now and then," according to the history of the 12th Engineers, the marchers "felt the fervid pressure of some old lady's hand on theirs and heard her entreaties to avenge the murder of her son or husband on Flanders' fields. There were few that day that did not repeatedly have to swallow a lump that rose in their throats." Robert Henderson of the 14th Engineers argued that "some of this solemnity was due to a mighty endeavor by green troops to keep in step."

From Hyde Park Corner, the parade headed south along Grosvenor Place to the American embassy at 4 Grosvenor Gardens, but the highlight of the day was yet to come. From there the parade headed north to Buckingham Palace, where the largest and most fervent crowds of all had gathered. "People climbed onto the Victoria Memorial," reported the London *Daily Chronicle*, but "police had orders to not interfere." The king stood on a reviewing stand in front of the palace, while soldiers and servants watched from the roof and the windows. As the American flag passed by, "the King and his party raised their hands in salute," reported the *New York Times*, and "the crowd roared approval so vigorously that the King was forced to smile." The Doughboys then filed into Green Park, across the street from the palace, where they were treated to lunch complete with linen tablecloths. As they ate, throngs peered into the park through iron gates, some begging for souvenirs. After an hour of rest, the men marched back to Waterloo Station. As in Paris, the events of the day lifted the spirits of war-weary Londoners. "Yesterday's enthusiasm was sufficient warranty," reported the *Times of London* the following day, "that the London public needs a spectacle like this every little while."

Sojourn in Britain

Americans continued to arrive in Britain and France in steadily growing numbers, and by 1918 the trickle of Doughboys crossing the Atlantic had become a flood. Of the more than two million American soldiers transported across the Atlantic, nearly half landed in Great Britain. Liverpool absorbed the lion's share, taking in 844,000. Most landed at Princes Dock on the River Mersey.

A century ago Princes Dock was one of the most important portions of the busy Liverpool docklands, taking in tons of cargo and thousands of passengers. But as Liverpool declined as a port Princes Dock fell into disrepair. In recent years Liverpool has revitalized its waterfront dramatically. Albert Dock, less than a mile to the south, is now one of the city's top tourist destinations, where one can have a nice meal or catch a Beatles tour. Among the attractions at Albert Dock is Merseyside Maritime Museum, which explores the city's vital connection to the sea. It includes exhibits about the 1915 sinking of the *Lusitania* (see Chapter 1), and even displays one of the ship's giant propellers outside, but is silent on the arrival of the Doughboys. Princes Dock now takes in cruise ships. Dilapidated piers still stretch out into the water, but in recent years high-rise hotels and office buildings have sprouted forth as well.

At first the American troops arriving at Liverpool were placed on trains near the docks and sent south, but in April 1918 the army opened a rest camp on the eastern outskirts of the city at Knotty Ash to give them a chance to recover from the arduous sea voyage. The soldiers got there by foot, marching the five miles to the camp through the streets of the city. "Our hobnails on the cobblestones, wet with frequent showers, made difficult footing," wrote Edwin Tippett, but he also noted that "we got a royal welcome" from the locals. Miniature American flags seemed to materialize out of nowhere, and many Doughboys remembered the march as an almost constant chorus of cheers. "Some of these good people brought and gave us cakes and tiny meat-pies," he recalled, while "those who could not afford that carried us pitchers of cold water." "The women rushed out to shake our hands with faces all aglow," noted the official history of Battery F, 135th Artillery, "and the bright-eyed, rosy cheeked girls smiled frankly at us." But it was the city's children that seemed to demand the most attention. The artillerists also noted that some kids picked out a Yank, "adopted him as their own and trudged along bravely in the rain for a mile or more, hand in hand with their hero. The whole affair made us warm up to these Britishers." Some were less enamored of the Liverpudlian youth. "Those kids beat anything I have ever seen for begging," recalled L. S. Wanamaker. Indeed, some noticed how the war taken a toll on England. For members of the 134th Field Artillery, the march through Liverpool was where they first sensed the "awful curse" of war. Their official history noted "hundreds of children, ragged and unkempt" and "untold numbers of young men, one-legged and one-armed, [who] favored us with a smile wistfully sad in contemplation of the fate that awaited many of us."

The Knotty Ash neighborhood had once been dotted with the country estates of wealthy Liverpool businessmen, though by 1900 urbanization had begun to encroach into the area. By the time of World War I, Prescot Road, which stretched westward out of Liverpool, still retained a largely rural character, dotted with farms and some hamlets that consisted of a few cottages and pubs. Little Bongs, near the intersection of Prescot and Eaton, even boasted several inns and a brewery. The Cheshire Line Railroad ran north to south across the area. Where it intersected Prescot Road was Knotty Ash Station. Immediately to the east of the station was Springfield Park. Alder Hey Hospital, just north of Springfield Park at the corner of Alder and Eaton Roads, was completed in 1915. The open spaces and railroad access made Knotty Ash attractive to the American army looking for a rest camp site. In all, the camp at Knotty Ash covered an area of about sixty-three acres lying north and east of the intersection of East Prescot Road and Queens Drive, encompassing Springfield Park and abutting the Alder Hey Hospital grounds.

Most soldiers spent no more than forty-eight hours at Knotty Ash before moving on. They were initially housed in tents, which many found to be uncomfortable. According to Fred Witt, the tents were "of a thickness and state of repair that gave the rain and wind easy access," and "the floors were covered with wet mattresses of straw onto which we threw our wet packs." "We were handed out sleeping boards which were just about the size of a man," stated the official history of Battery F, 135th Artillery, but these boards "were neither conducive to sleep nor rest, and the term 'Rest Camp,' after this first experience, was a matter of jest for us." The army constructed wooden barracks by the end of the war. There were numerous complaints about the food, especially the British fare that was often served. "We almost starved after eating cod fish and some other junk about like that," recalled one hungry Doughboy. As L. S. Wannamaker quipped, Knotty Ash was a place "where only our stomachs had a rest."

Few of the Doughboys ever got to see much of Liverpool beyond their march into camp. Officers had more freedom to come and go, but enlisted men were usually restricted to the grounds. Walls and fences surrounded the camp, and one member of the 332nd Field Artillery complained that Knotty Ash "reminded me more of a stockade than anything else." The fence did not deter some of the troops from getting to know the area. "We found a weak spot in the camp guard," remembered Fred Witt, "leapt a wall and gained a practical knowledge of English currency in pastry shops and ale houses—paying well, no doubt, for the instruction." "There was a little 'pub' just outside the camp called the 'Black Horse,'" according to the history of Battery F, 135th Artillery. "It was an odd little joint with small rooms, a little bar and English bar-maids. The place was jambed [sic] with English and Americans, and it was a struggle to get service." "Many men succeeded by various methods to scale the fence and get out by running the guard," claimed the historian of the 88th Division, "but one night about 250 were caught getting back in again."

As in stateside training camps, the YMCA had a major presence at rest camps like Knotty Ash. It maintained several huts on the grounds, and there was an officers' club housed in the Oakville mansion nearby. Camp Hospital No. 40 commenced operations at Knotty Ash in April 1918 as a contagious disease facility. The influenza epidemic continued to bedevil the army, as the Doughboys carried the virus with them from stateside training camps to Europe. One particular convoy, which arrived in Liverpool on September 29, brought in so many cases that barracks buildings had to be converted to hospital wards to accommodate all of the sick, and some were sent to nearby English hospitals. "Deaths occurred daily" during those dark days, according to Camp Hospital No. 40's annual report. At first, the hospital operated out of triple marquee tents erected along Prescot Road in Springfield Park. When this quickly proved inadequate, the army began construction on a more permanent 500-bed facility next to Alder Hey Hospital, suited for both contagious diseases and general medical needs, which saw its first patients in December 1918.

After their brief stay at Knotty Ash, soldiers were marched to the rail station, placed on trains, and sent south to the English Channel for transport to France. The U.S. Army closed the Knotty Ash camp in 1919, but it was not empty for long. Postwar Liverpool saw a severe housing crunch, so the local housing authority purchased the wooden barracks and converted them into dwellings for civilians. The first residents had moved in by December 1919, and within a few years perhaps 2,000 people lived at the former American post. Young mothers pushing their prams replaced marching soldiers, and tidy garden plots grew along the old barracks. With electricity and indoor plumbing, the housing conditions in Knotty Ash were an improvement for many working class Liverpudlians. By the 1930s, the old barracks had been torn down and replaced with the new housing units one sees there today. There are no visible remains of the American camp, nor is there a plaque or historical marker to indicate the area's former use. Even the Oakhill mansion is gone, the grounds now occupied by the Alder Sports Club. Knotty Ash is now an unremarkable suburban area. Except for the fact that the cars are driving on the left side of the road, one might mistake Queens Drive for Queens, New York. The Cheshire Line tracks that took the troops away from the camp have been converted into a bicycle path. Today one can walk down the pedestrian ramp that brought soldiers to waiting trains or bike under the same Prescot Road bridge that their trains passed under on the way to the front. Alder Hey Hospital construction has encroached on Springfield Park in recent years, occupying grounds that once comprised the American rest camp. There is little there that the Doughboy would recognize, although the Black Horse Pub still pours pints.

Then it was off to southern England. For most of the Americans, the rail journey was their first opportunity to see the English countryside, and they were enthralled by it. Having been bombarded with British history and writers like Shakespeare while in school, they were interested to see the land they had so often read about. "Until dark we drank in the quaint poetic scenes of 'Merrie England,'" wrote Fred Witt, "they were all that our books, our songs and our artists had tried to portray to us—and more." The Doughboys of Company F, 135th Field Artillery admired the "verdant green meadows, sleek cattle, shining waterways, carefully kept hedges, thatched cottages, large estates, manor houses with their parks, every square inch used for one purpose or another, all flashed by the carriage windows." "I never saw such beautiful country as old England," wrote Edwin Tippett. "All the fellows gave it their heartiest praise, even the greenest of the Irish." Occasionally stopping along the way, the Americans elicited the curiosity of locals wherever they went. "The people seemed as much amused with our pronunciation as we were with their queer English," wrote Joseph Minturn of one stop in Birmingham. He recalled one Yank commenting: "Don't see why they couldn't be taught to speak correctly while they were about it."

The next destination was usually another rest camp closer to the English Channel. The army opened a rest camp on the Southampton Common in September 1917, but it quickly proved inadequate and in November the Americans took over a British training and transit camp nine miles to the north, in the Hampshire countryside just east of Winchester. Winchester is one of England's most historic cities. An ancient Roman administrative center, it served as the de facto capital of England for a time during the Middle Ages. Winchester is perhaps best known for its magnificent cathedral, which has the longest nave of any Gothic cathedral in Europe. The rest camp near this city, which the British called Morn Hill, was actually several distinct camps that stretched out on a mile-long segment of Alresford Road, with Magdalen Hill Cemetery at its center. To the west of the cemetery, the Magdalen Hill section straddled Alresford Road. A medieval leper hospital once stood just to the north of the roadway, but all visible traces of it were gone by the Great War. Just to the north of Magdalen Hill, along what is now Fair Lane and Long Walk, was the Winnall Down section. The camp area east of the cemetery was called Avington Park. As the Americans streamed across the ocean, the old British camp grew even larger, swallowing up more and more of the green English countryside. Soldiers arrived at the Winchester train station and marched to the camp. There was so much U.S. military traffic coming in that in 1918 the army built a rail spur into the camp. By war's end, Winchester was the largest U.S. Army installation in Britain. By one estimate, more than 700,000

American troops passed through Winchester on their way to France.

Most found Morn Hill an improvement over the spartan conditions at Knotty Ash, though hardly luxurious. "The place was worthier than Knotty Ash of the name 'rest camp,'" observed Fred Witt. "In wooden barracks we laid rows of slats across two pieces that kept us from the floor, secured mattresses of straw, and slept soundly." "The men are quartered in 'Huts' [made of] sheet iron with plaster veneer, 40 to a hut," remembered Carl Penner, while "officers are in buildings of similar construction, two to a room." Though preferable to Knotty Ash, the Doughboys still found plenty to complain about. Edwin Tippett remembered that the men "slept on dirty straw ticks placed on three boards which were, in turn, laid on two little trestles about four inches from the floor. If you wish to approximate this novel bed, try a snooze on an ironing board." Once again, there were incessant complaints about the food. "We were all on a diet of British rations," recalled Edmund Arpin, "which to our standards seemed very meager." "All belts have been taken up a few notches," wrote Penner, who noted that some began referring to Winnall Down as "Dwindle Down." As at Knotty Ash, the men were kept busy with various tasks. "The morning usually devoted to washing and cleaning up," recalled Penner, "and the afternoon to marches." "Our daily practice hikes took us over old Roman roads," wrote Arpin, which he thought "still bore evidence of sound construction and excellent drainage." For the homesick soldier, Morn Hill could be a lonesome place. John Taber described the men of the 168th Infantry Regiment there as "a hungry, cold, dejected, home sick lot."

Whenever possible, the Doughboys went into Winchester. The main destination was the cathedral, which held services for soldiers every evening at 6:00 PM. It was unlike anything most of these young Americans had ever seen. "The medieval Cathedral with its historic relics and associations aroused the respect, if not the admiration, of the youthful sightseers from the Middle West," claimed Iowa's John Taber. Other historic sites turned soldiers into avid tourists. At the Great Hall at Winchester Castle, the Americans were interested in a wooden object billed as King Arthur's Round Table, though many doubted its authenticity. One young man was overheard to say that he would "bet a dollar that the storied table was made in a Jersey City antique shop." Some took the opportunity to explore the nearby countryside. "We have been on many walking trips visiting the nearby towns," wrote John Acker, such as the hamlet named Easton, which he thought a "quiet, sleepy, beautiful village." Acker and his cohorts patronized Easton's pubs, like the Cricketers and the Chestnut Horse, where he remembered drinking "very weak ale" that was "four pence a pint and spirits a shilling a small drink." Unfortunately, the Doughboys' eternal quest for alcohol and women sometimes led to strained relations with the locals. "Some

Yanks immediately preceding the arrival of the 353rd Infantry had torn up the town in Winchester," recalled the regimental history. "As a result of their hilarity, passes to Winchester could be had for groups only and an officer must be in charge of each group." Carl Penner complained that officers were "exploring the historic corners of Winchester including taverns with their pink cheeked bar maids," while he and other enlisted men were "not permitted to leave camp except in formation."

Morn Hill had particularly good recreational facilities. The Americans inherited two huts from the British, but expanded their own facilities greatly after taking over. "Being less than two hours' journey by rail from London," noted the official wartime history of the American YMCA, "it was possible to secure the best of talent" for camp shows. "At one time or another," the organization bragged, "every crack British band played at the camp." At Morn Hill the Y also maintained eight libraries, offered classes in topics ranging from French to Bible study, and provided tours of Winchester. Athletic opportunities included "eight baseball diamonds, five basket-ball courts, two football fields, and an athletic field with quarter-mile track," according to the YMCA official history, "besides ample facilities for other sports." There was even a golf course on the south edge of the camp. Doughboys generally had kind things to say about the Y at Winnall Down. "The Y.M.C.A. here is also very good," remembered Edwin Tippett, "It sells goods very reasonably." From one recreation tent, he remembered playing cards and enjoying a view of the English countryside. "From our seats, we looked out across a valley toward a clump of trees on a high hill, a landmark for miles." John Taber contended that "the only bright spot in camp was the Y.M.C.A."

Morn Hill attracted its share of high-profile visitors. British writer Rudyard Kipling came to dedicate the new YMCA officers' club in July 1918. The legendary author, who had lost a son at the Battle of Loos in 1915, expressed his satisfaction at seeing American troops come to the aid of the Allies. "None of you can have been in England more than a day," he said to a gathering of enlisted men, "without discovering for yourselves how most heartily welcome you all are." In a similar vein, he told the officers gathered at the hut dedication ceremony that "you could not annoy us if you started to build pyramids." Kipling was impressed with the fighting spirit of the Americans. "They are marvelous simple and modest," he wrote a friend, "and they say, quite sincerely, that their desire is to 'kill Germans.' Now we've been at war four years and it isn't good form to say that yet." In September 1918, Secretary of War Newton Baker paid a visit. According to the *New York Times*, Baker inspected the medical facilities, living quarters, "lunched with a big crowd of [soldiers] in the mess tent beside a little woodland stream," and "listened to Red Cross 'Jazz' bands at practice." At one point, he expressed a wish to try on a soldier's pack. "He trudged back and forth two or three times, carrying a seventy pound load," the *Times* reported, "while a pair of heavy hob-nailed trench boots, swinging from the bottom of the kit, banged against his legs." Others passing through Morn Hill would achieve notoriety later in life. In the cemetery of the Winchester Cathedral, the gravestone of an eighteenth-century soldier who, as the epitaph described it, died after "drinking Small Beer when hot" caught the attention of an artillery officer with a drinking problem named Bill Wilson. Wilson claimed that years later the memory of his experience at the cathedral opened his eyes to the transformative power of God, and inspired him to found Alcoholics Anonymous. Frank Buckles, America's last surviving World War I veteran, was an ambulance driver at Camp Hospital No. 35 at Morn Hill for a time before heading off to France.

The peak of the influenza epidemic in the autumn of 1918 hit Morn Hill especially hard, as it did other U.S. Army camps in the area, like the Southampton rest camp, the pilot training base west of Winchester at Flowerdown (located on Sarum Road half a mile west of the intersection with Romsey Road), and the rest camp at Romsey (located near the intersection of Braishfield Road and Sandy Lane north of the village), which opened to handle the overflow from Morn Hill. In late September, the troopship *Olympic* delivered another boatload of Doughboys to England. The flu "blazed out during the last days of the voyage," according to one medical report, and the infected overwhelmed the camp hospitals at Morn Hill and Romsey, as well as Base Hospital 204 in Hursley (a spot now occupied by IBM offices on Hursley Park Road), which was also filling up with battle casualties from the Western Front. The disease then spread from the hospitals and by the time the disease had run its course, hundreds of soldiers were dead. The majority of those Americans who died while in Hampshire were buried at Magdalen Hill Cemetery at Morn Hill. By 1919, more than 500 Americans had been interred there, their graves along Alresford Road just east of the sexton's house. After the war nearly all of them were removed and reburied at home or at the Brookwood American Cemetery, but two Americans are still there—Sergeant Newton H. Lovell and Private Herman Blise. Their bodies were reburied up the hill in different parts of the cemetery.

Driving down Alresford Road today one would never guess that it was once the main thoroughfare through a bustling military camp. Faint remnants of the railroad spur are still discernible north of the road to those who look closely. There are only a few known structures left from the World War I camp, though their wartime connection is not immediately evident. Adjacent to the parking lot for Magdalen Hill Cemetery is a red brick home, for example, that once served as an U.S. officer's mess. It is now a private residence and has undergone substantial modification. Little else exists of the camp—at least aboveground. The medieval leper hospital at Magdalen Hill has attracted the attention of archaeologists, including the British television program *Time Team* and scholars from the University of Winchester. In their excavations, the archaeologists have found not only the ruins of the hospital but also remnants of the Great War camp, including building foundations, drainage ditches, and gravel walkways. Most notably, they uncovered the brick foundation of a large theater in 2010. The Magdalen Hill Archaeology Research Project at the University of Winchester continues to work the site, and travelers might well see them in action. The portion the camp south of Alresford Road is now Magdalen Hill Down Nature Reserve. Restored to its natural chalk grassland environment, the grounds are renowned for the wide range of butterflies they attract. At the end of the war there was talk in Winchester of placing a memorial to the thousands of soldiers who passed through the Morn Hill camp, but nothing came of it. The camp went uncommemorated for nearly a century until a local historian named Tony Dowland resurrected the plans for a memorial. His organization, To Honour A Promise, formed in 2012, has placed interpretive signage at the site of the camp, and a memorial to the camp and all of its soldiers—including the Yanks—on the grounds of Winchester's Great Hall.

Grave of Private Herman Blise, a victim of the influenza epidemic, who died at Morn Hill, England in 1918 and remains buried there.

From Morn Hill, the transient soldiers headed to Southampton for their trip across the English Channel to Le Havre. At the docks, the Americans met many British and Commonwealth soldiers returning to France after leave, or going over for the first time. "The average Tommy was obviously war-weary," claimed Fred Witt, "liberal with neither optimism nor smiles, and a bit reserved." By contrast, he thought Australians and Canadians were "fine, cordial fellows with whom we fraternized at once." To minimize the possibilities of U-boat attacks, the crossings took place overnight. For many, the English Channel was more harrowing than the Atlantic. The boats were much smaller than the ocean liners that brought them to Europe, with no sleeping quarters. The conditions were more crowded than any had ever experienced. As Witt described it, soldiers were "massed on the stairs, choking the passage-ways, huddled on top of, around and under every fixture in the lavatories, every post, every wall, every railing, either suffocating inside from the heat of our own breath or chilled to the bone on the cold steel decks, were intertangled legs, arms and bodies." Edwin Tippett claimed that in his ship the "air could not have been staler or viler, without passing into the category of solid substances." Storms added to the miseries. "The men who had stood the trip across on the *Vaterland*," wrote Edmund Arpin, "were almost to a man violently sick on this little voyage." As he remembered it, "every bit of floor space was nothing but a slippery mess."

Bienvenue en France

The boats usually reached Le Havre about dawn. "The dock was a cosmopolitan scene," according to one soldier account, "with coolies working on the boat, English officers, French kids, American soldiers, German prisoners, and a few Belgians about. It reminded us of the fact that the Boches were fighting nearly all the civilized peoples." From the docks, Americans marched several miles through the city to British rest camps in the village of Sanvic, on the hill above Le Havre near the Saint-Adresse fortress. One soldier, having been through this routine several times before, complained that "for some unknown reason all rest camps were located as far as possible from the railhead." Passing through docklands filled with innumerable ships, the Doughboys entered the streets of Le Havre. Fred Witt remembered marching through a poor section of the city, where "droves of poorly-clad children begged us for money." He also sensed the French desire to defeat the Germans. "Our first impression of the French," he wrote:

> was furnished by a thick-set elderly woman of the peasant class early on her way to work. She was very happy to see us and spoke a greeting of which we recognized only the word "American." Then, raising a husky arm, she grabbed the throat of an imaginary foe, her face distorted with intense hate. With a heavy cane held in the right hand she bayoneted her victim repeatedly in vivid pantomine [sic] and cast his corpse aside.

"Everything we saw was strange to us," wrote L. S. Wanamaker. "The language we, for the most of us, could not understand. The signs we could not read. We could hardly walk upon the cobbled streets. But we liked it all just the same." From the densely packed center of the city, the Doughboys then marched along the shore. "Between us and the water on our left was a bathing beach," recalled Joseph Minturn, "and to our right a long, high bluff, thick with casinos, terraced gardens, and elaborate architecture." Then they marched up a steep slope beneath the fortress to the British camps on the high ground above the city.

The official history of the 332nd Field Artillery noted that Rest Camp No. 1, to which they were marched, "was situated at a considerable elevation and commanded a majestic view of a portion of the city of Le Havre, its harbor and the Channel beyond." Though the views were terrific, the camps were far from desirable. Edwin Tippett complained of "inadequate sleeping and practically no bathing accommodations," but what he disliked the most was the fact that soldiers were put to work digging ditches. Relations with the British Tommy were sometimes less than collegial. "In the English Y.M.C.A. I met an English soldier who asked me in broad Cockney why the American troops had come to France," wrote William Brown. "We can't whip Fritz," he was told, "so, it's a cinch, you can't." Le Havre, it was also clear that the war was much closer. "With monotonous regularity, trains carrying wounded from the fiercely contested battle around Cambrai passed through the camp," remembered John Taber. According to Fred Witt, "through the stillness of the night we heard for the first time the thud of heavy guns in distant battle." Le Havre remains a workaday port city, and Sanvic has long since been incorporated into it. The Saint-Adresse fortress still keeps watch over the English Channel, but Sanvic is now densely residential, and there is no longer any trace of the British rest camps.

A slim majority of U.S. troops—1,057,000 of them—went directly to France. Of them, nearly 200,000 came in through Saint-Nazaire. A deep water port at the mouth of the Loire River, Saint-Nazaire was the AEF's main supply port (see Chapter 9), but took in its share of troops as well, especially early in the war. The leading elements of the 1st Division arrived here in June, and other troops soon followed in their footsteps, marching from the docks to Camp No. 1 outside of the city. "Paraded the Regiment ashore today and we received a regular ovation," recalled artillery officer George Leach of the 42nd Division. "Everyone got flowers and the people gave us a great welcome. A bunch of children marched the whole way, delighted with the band, and under my feet most of the time." Subsequent arrivals found Camp No. 1 little more commodious than the 1st Division did. "The short sojourn at Billet Camp No. 1 was disagreeable to the entire personnel," wrote George Studley of the 31st Railway Engineers, who complained that the "the Camp was muddy and sloppy." "Camp No. 1 consisted of a few wooden barracks of rather hasty construction, built in ankle-deep red clay," wrote Henry Stansbury of the 117th Trench Mortar Battery. Alvin Binswanger of the 364th Field Hospital remembered the barracks as "long, one-story buildings with tar-paper roof and earthen floor, a row of double-deck bunks extending the length of the building on either side." Conditions were sometimes "a prolific source of profanity," he recalled.

The routine at Camp No. 1 was much like that experienced in the English debarkation camps. There was "drill in the midst of sleet-storms," recalled George Shively of Ambulance Company 585, and plenty of hikes in the surrounding countryside, though these hikes offered interesting new scenery. "We became thoroughly familiar with the 'shining roads of France,'" Shively wrote, "with the hedges and little thatch-roofed *chaumières*, the wayside shrines, the hospitable *buvettes* that marked the crossroads, and the blackberry lanes through which we wandered, eating that forbidden fruit." Soldiers were also put to work. "Our ten days' stay here was designated as a rest period," wrote Henry Stansbury, "and so that we might enjoy our rest we built roads, tore up roads, repaired roads, built stone walls, tore down stone walls, repaired stone walls." As the location was a major supply port, many soldiers did stevedore duty. The 23rd Engineers also worked on the docks, as well as on a dam. After one day of hard work the men were treated to the movies. "One picture we saw showed the 'Goddess of Liberty' and it faded and a dough-boy took her place," stated the Company A's official history. "About that time some in the 23rd shouted, 'Where's her pick and shovel?'" Debarking soldiers often got to see a little of Saint-Nazaire. Like their 1st Division predecessors, booze and mademoiselles were often the first priority. "Lack of space prevents enumerating those who succumbed to the wiles and guiles of J. Barleycorn and came back to camp in a pitiable condition," wrote Alvin Binswanger after his company got passes into town, "it would merely be a repetition of the company roster."

The area of Camp No. 1 today is an ordinary residential area of Saint-Nazaire. Roughly speaking, the camp extended north-west from avenue Hector Berlioz to boulevard Georges Charpak. The southern border of the camp was just north of rue Jacques Offenbach and route de Fréchets. The combination roadway of rue Saarlouis, boulevard Sunderland, and rue Gabriel Fauré comprised the approximate northern border. The area is today filled with small white homes and drab apartment buildings. The fields of sticky mud the soldiers complained so bitterly about have been transformed into tidy little gardens and schoolyards. No plaques, statues, or historical markers indicate the area's former use.

By far the most important troop importation center in France was Brest, which took in nearly 800,000 Doughboys. Located on the far western tip of the Brittany Peninsula, Brest offered the shortest convoy route directly to France. Already an important U.S. Navy base (see Chapter 5), it was the logical choice for troop traffic as well. The beauty of Brest harbor sometimes awed the arriving soldiers. "Of all lands and cities," wrote Frederick Pottle about his arrival:

> is any lovelier than Brittany or more picturesque than Brest? As we sailed up the estuary, no wider than a river between its

tall banks of emerald green, we watched the graceful maneuvers of the little boats with colored sails that skimmed the water all about us, and wondered what lay behind those hills for us, . . . France at last!

"The sight was a magnificent one," recalled Oliver Quane, "with shipping all about and the city crowning a high hill."

Once the transports entered the safety of Brest harbor, lighters converged on them, offloaded the soldiers, and carried them to the docks below the Cours Dajot. The soldiers then began the march to the rest camp at Pontanézen, five kilometers north of the waterfront. The march began by ascending the bluff—the very same one on which the American Naval Monument now stands (see Chapter 5). After two weeks at sea, "many of the men were so weakened that they were unable to march more than half a mile up the steep slope," recalled Ben Chastain, "before they were compelled to fall out and rest." As in other ports, the march to the rest camp gave the soldiers their first look at a foreign land. "Most everything . . . that met our eyes had a decidedly foreign look," wrote Edward Alva Trueblood. "The freight cars have a diminutive look," he observed. "They are only about half the size of American cars [and] the locomotives are much smaller than ours." He also thought that "the dress and the habits of the people differ materially from those of America." He was surprised to see the working classes wearing wooden shoes called *sabots*, and noted that "the men wear large loosely fitting trousers and tight jackets" and "a peculiar hat, with a tightly fitting crown, a broad round brim, and two streamers of black ribbon about eighteen inches long hanging down in back." Middle class people "dress more like Americans," he thought, "though not with as well made clothes." Trueblood also noted that "women from the windows gave us a hearty welcome, waving flags and calling 'Vive les Amerique,'" [sic] as well as the townsfolk "offering cakes and nuts for sale [and] begging white bread from us. It was here that we first heard those two French words that became so familiar to us before we left France, 'Donnez moi.'"

The French military presence at Pontanézen dated to the French Revolution, and arriving Doughboys often referred to the small walled complex as the "Napoleon Barracks." When American troops began arriving in Brest in November 1917, the French graciously allowed the U.S. Army use of the grounds and adjacent farmlands as a rest camp. "The surrounding country was mostly pastureland," recalled Ray Johnson of the 37th Division. "There were a few high-gabled, red-tile-roofed, whitewashed stone houses within sight, but apparently the land was devoted solely to dairy farms as indicated by the small herds of cows. In the distance could be seen a couple of church spires, marking the sites of villages." As troop shipments steadily increased, Camp Pontanézen engulfed more and more of the Breton countryside, especially north and east of the Napoleon Barracks. The Brest-Gouesnou Road just east of the barracks formed the main axis of the American camp.

Brest may have been well situated for the arrival of troop convoys, but the climate of Brittany made Camp Pontanézen the muddiest and least pleasant of all the AEF rest camps. Cold rain fell nearly continuously from November through April, and summers had their fair share of precipitation as well. Disease made things even worse. The soldiers complained bitterly about conditions at the camp. Ray Johnson arrived in June 1918. "We marched three miles through the cold, heavy mist that was rolling in from the sea, and finally pitched pup-tents haphazard in a wet field," he wrote. "The morning sun revealed a chaos of confusion that the night had shrouded; pup-tents set at random, equipment scattered everywhere, and piles of rations and field kitchen impedimenta lying on the ground. Everything was cold and soaked with dew." The 36th Division arrived a few months later, but found conditions no better. "These fields were covered with manure and were wholly without sanitary necessities," recalled Ben Chastain. "The only baths to be had were at the old Barracks and were not adequate, although for those who were able to get under them, they proved a blessed relief." There was "a constant downpour of rain," he wrote, but "the only shelter available was the shelter tents the men carried in their packs." "The barracks were for the hard-fighting quartermasters; not for us," noted Oliver Quane sardonically. "We were guided to a hedge-bordered field, inches deep in mud." "American troops wallowed in ooze," complained Major Smedley Butler of the 13th Marines, who arrived in September 1918. Pontanézen was "acres and acres of mud flats with dripping, dejected khaki-colored tents," he observed, "shivering cold, bleak, death-stricken—a hell of a place."

Butler soon got the job of cleaning up the mess at Pontanézen, which by the fall of 1918 had become a national scandal. The son of a Pennsylvania congressman, Butler was one of the most colorful figures in U.S. military history. He lied about his age to become a marine officer during the Spanish-American War. He did not see any action in 1898, but got plenty of it in America's turn-of-the-century imperialist adventures, fighting in the Philippines, China, Latin America, and the Caribbean. He remains one of a handful of Americans to receive the Medal of Honor twice—first at Veracruz, Mexico, in 1914, and a year later in Haiti. By 1917 Butler had become a marine corps legend, but clashes with superiors kept him from a frontline command. Butler expected to see action when he arrived in France with the 13th Marines, but Pershing had other plans. The commander-in-chief promoted Butler to brigadier general and assigned him the commander of Camp Pontanézen. "For twenty years I had worked hard to prepare myself for a big war,"

Butler lamented, and "it nearly broke my heart that I wasn't allowed to go to the front. To sit in the rear and run this dirty mud-hole was the first in a series of jolts that finally destroyed my enthusiasm for soldiering." He thought Pontanézen "as far from the Front as it was possible for me to be without jumping into the ocean."

Despite his disappointment, Butler threw himself into the work of improving the camp. "I planned to erect a semi-permanent camp and run it like a big hotel," he later explained. Butler revamped the camp hospital, constructed more barracks, and set out to conquer the ever-present mud. Supply warehouses at the docks held miles of duckboards—wooden slats laid at the bottom of muddy trenches for footing—but the local quartermaster refused to let the rest camp have any of them. The red tape and small-mindedness infuriated Butler, who soon found a way around the problem. When the U.S. commander at Brest went away for a short time and put Butler in temporary command, Butler marched his men down to the warehouses and carted away the duckboards, as well as some construction supplies to boot. "Late in the afternoon the strangest column that ever marched through France trudged along on its way up the hill," Butler recalled. "Some of the men heaped pots and pans on the duckboards and carried them like stretchers." The general was not afraid of a little hard work himself. On the way back to camp he encountered a soldier who did not recognize him in the early evening darkness and complained that he had signed up "to fight, not to carry chicken coops." "You're perfectly right," Butler told him, but persuaded the young man to shoulder his fair share of the burden. The soldier grabbed one end of a duckboard, Butler the other, and together they carried it toward the camp. "As we started up the hill," recalled Butler, "several soldiers who knew me gathered around us and guyed the life out of the boy for letting a general carry his pack." Thanks to Butler, conditions at Pontanézen improved noticeably, and he received decorations from both the army and the navy for his efforts—only adding to his chestful of medals. Proud of his accomplishments, Butler nevertheless remained bitter about not seeing the front. "Cleaning up a concentration camp was not soldiering," he believed. "The job could have been handled by any enterprising hotel-keeper or circus manager."

The daily routine for the soldiers-in-transit at Pontanézen was like that of the other rest camps, including marches through the countryside and work details at the docks. There were occasional trips into Brest. Inspecting the city's fortifications, Ben Chastain was interested to see the "moat and walled defenses that characterize so many European cities." Near the old French barracks, he saw what he believed to be "many of the relics of the day when Napoleon's troops had lived there," including "a guillotine then in use." To Chastain, rural Brittany seemed a charming but backward land:

Not far from the camp were several chateaux which were inspected with the greatest interest. The strange garb of the priests as well as the peasants and their combination houses wherein the stock as well as the family found residence, were the subject of every letter written home, and the use of the antiquated flail by the peasants in threshing their grain was so astounding that many of the troops declared the land to be not worth fighting for.

Just outside the camp were a few cafés, which, as Chastain remembered, were allowed to sell "light wine" but no hard liquor. "In spite of these regulations however it was not difficult to obtain any and all varieties of drinks in the evening," he wrote. "Some of the officers as well as the men attempted to sample all of the known varieties in one evening with disastrous results." Not all were so charmed. "When night fell there was nothing to do but to go to bed," recalled Leslie Baker. "There was no place worth going A.W.O.L. to visit."

By the time of the armistice, Camp Pontanézen could hold up to 75,000 soldiers in tents and corrugated iron barracks. There were fifteen mess halls, three large bathing facilities, several amusement halls, and a permanent cadre of 13,500 men. The most important rest camp for arriving soldiers in the AEF, Pontanézen became the

Pontanézen light rail stop in Brest, France. Camp Pontanézen, a rest camp for Doughboys arriving in France, was located just to the north.

primary embarkation point for troops heading back to the United States. Little remains of it today, and there are no historical markers or monuments to commemorate it. The old French barracks are still there, located at 167 rue du Général Paulet, and now serve as a police and army facility. A few older buildings nearby may well have known Doughboy boots a century ago, but what characterizes the area today is newness. Once well outside the city of Brest, the area is today known as the quartier de l'Europe and comprises its commercialized outskirts. Along boulevard de l'Europe (much of which did not exist during the World War I) are scads of retail establishments, particularly automobile dealerships. The KFC and McDonald's in the area represent later American influence. The American tents and barracks were located north of boulevard de l'Europe between rue du Général Paulet and rue Gustave Zédé, with the D112 expressway forming the camp's approximate northern border. Rue de Gouesnou (present-day highway D788) was its main thoroughfare. Light rail connects quartier de l'Europe with central Brest. One stop just south of boulevard de l'Europe is named Pontanézen. What Brest residents know today at the Pontanézen neighborhood is located just outside the former American camp. One stop away is Mesmerrien, located on rue de Gouesnou. Near this rail stop the main entrance to Camp Pontanézen once stood.

After a few days and rarely longer than a week, the Doughboys marched out of the French rest camps to the nearest rail yards to begin the journey to a training facility. "All the night before it had rained," wrote Oliver Quane of his departure from Pontanézen. "We rolled our packs in the rain, and marched down to the station in it." "Some of us managed, with the help of sailors, to fortify ourselves for the coming trip with bottles of wine, chocolate and fruits," remembered Leslie Baker, also leaving Pontanézen. "The wine, of course, was strictly forbidden, but that fact seemed only to enhance its flavor, when presented in contrast to the cold dry rations which were to suffice each car for the coming thirty-six-hour ride."

The train ride would not be a comfortable one. The first thing the Americans noted was the small size of French train cars. "The cars looked like toys compared with the big American box cars," observed artilleryman Leslie Bucklew. "Our freight cars will make two French cars with some room to spare," thought Private Joseph Feingold of the U.S. Marines. Officers rode in what Edmund Arpin described as "unheated, third-class coaches." He complained that "there were six of us in each compartment, which provided barely enough room for all of us to sit down at one time." Enlisted men fared far worse. Once at the rail station, the Doughboy encountered small box cars labeled "*hommes 40, chevaux 8*" (40 men, 8 horses), into which they were herded for the ride to the training camp. The "Forty and Eight" cars, as the American soldiers called them, were infamously unpopular. Joseph Feingold recalled that his car actually contained forty-two men, along with "our rifles and our rations." "We had fifty men in our car," according to William Brown of the 2nd Division. To top it all off, Fred Witt noted "many indications that 'Chevaux 8' had been our very recent predecessors."

The men coped as best they could. They chatted and watched the French countryside roll by. Some got into trouble. The soldier-passengers lit fires in their cars to keep warm, though it often burned holes in the floor and sometimes set the whole car ablaze. Edmund Arpin recalled that some of his men began to ride on the roofs. "We passed through . . . occasional tunnels," he wrote, "which were disastrous to the men who were still on top." Others disappeared whenever the trains made stops. By the time his train arrived at its destination Arpin estimated that "about half our men were missing," and noted that "some of them were never accounted for." For most, it would not be their last ride in a Forty and Eight car. In fact, it would be their primary mode of travel across France.

William Brown remembered his first Forty and Eight ride to be a "real hardship" but, writing after the war, he also remembered that at the time he "didn't know what the months would bring." The hardships were indeed just beginning. The Doughboys received such a hearty welcome in Britain and France because their people were desperate for the war to end, and the appearance of the Americans meant that their long nightmare might soon be over. Ultimately, the Americans came to fight, and combat on the Western Front was an exceedingly grim business. For most, training camp, the transatlantic voyage, the rest camps, and the Forty and Eight cars were little more than an unpleasant imposition. Upon setting foot on European shores, the Doughboys got down to the real business of fighting a war. They were about to find out that they still had a lot to learn.

CHAPTER 7:
FIRST BLOOD

The first U.S. service member killed in action during World War I was a noncombatant charged with healing the wounds of war. Base Hospital No. 5, a medical unit organized at Harvard University, arrived in France in May 1917. It set up shop with a British military hospital between the villages of Dannes and Camiers in the Pas de Calais region. The Dannes-Camiers rail station lay just west of the camp. There was a cement plant immediately to the north, and a little farther up the road was an ammunition dump. German planes had been operating in the area for months, raiding Allied positions along the French coast and as far away as England. On the clear and moonlit evening of September 4, 1917, a German plane approached the illuminated grounds of the hospital. "We know not what was on the minds of the Germans," wrote medic J. Philip Hatch, but at about 11:00 PM the plane dove in toward the hospital tents and dropped several bombs. The first one landed just inches from the tent of Lieutenant William T. Fitzsimons, a physician from Kansas who had arrived just two weeks earlier. The young doctor was "literally blown to pieces by a bomb that fell at his feet," according to the hospital's official history. Seconds later, more explosions killed three U.S. enlisted men, Privates Rudolph Rubino, Oscar Tugo, and Leslie Woods, along with several British soldiers recovering in the hospital wards. In Kansas City, Missouri, the William T. Fitzsimons Memorial Fountain, at the corner of 12th Street and The Paseo, keeps alive the memory of the young doctor. Fitzsimons was the first of 53,513 Americans to die in hostile action during the First World War. Britain and France were desperate to get their new Allies on the front line as soon as possible, but American soldiers arrived woefully unprepared for what lay ahead of them. For the Doughboy, the first stop in France was a training camp, where Allied instructors gave them an intensive tutorial on trench warfare. Part of their training included on-the-job training in the trenches, and it was not long until other Americans joined Fitzsimons on the nation's honor roll.

General Pershing and his staff developed a three-stage training regimen to get his soldiers up to speed. The program began at a training area behind the lines, where they worked alongside experienced Allied soldiers. This stage of training reinforced basic military skills, but it also gave them hands-on experience with weaponry they seldom saw in the United States. Divisions were usually broken up during this stage, with artillery training in a different facility. The second phase involved actual experience in so-called "quiet sectors" of the front. Americans would enter the trenches alongside Allied soldiers, who would orient them to the world of combat. Though these sectors saw little action, fighting did occur. The learning curve on the front lines was steep, and the soldiers were also killed, wounded, or taken prisoner. As the Doughboys' competence in the trenches grew, their Allied comrades would gradually withdraw, leaving Americans in control of small portions of the Western Front. In the third phase, all elements of a division would be brought to a single training area where they would learn to work together as a division without Allied trainers. For Pershing, this was the most important phase of the process. Here, without the influence of the British and French and their emphasis on trench warfare, Pershing wanted the third phase of training to stress his open warfare tactics, which he believed would the deadlock on the Western Front and play the decisive role in ending the war.

The first to undergo the process was the 1st Division, which in the summer of 1917 came together near the village of Gondrecourt-le-Château, fifty kilometers northeast of Pershing's headquarters at Chaumont and forty kilometers south of the front lines at Saint-Mihiel. The training grounds covered a triangular area between the villages of Gondrecourt, Boviolles, and Villeroy. Local chateaux and other prominent buildings became headquarters for various American units. At first there were no barracks, so soldiers lodged with local farmers. Officers typically stayed in the farmers' homes, while the enlisted men slept in the barns and stables that were filled, according to the division's official history, "with the untouched cob-webs of years, and with decayed roofs through which the rain, snow and wind entered freely." Making the barns habitable for soldiers was not always easy. "We removed countless wagon-loads of dirt and junk accumulated over centuries," complained the official history of the 1st Engineers. Rural French life in was far different than the images of Parisian sophistication that filled the minds of so many Americans. Particularly shocking was the *fumier*—a large manure pile found in front of every farmhouse. General Robert Bullard, who assumed command of the division in December 1917, noted that for the French farmer the *fumier* was "the sign of his thrift and even of his wealth," but for the American it was "a disagreeable thing, irritating and dangerous in the dark, and a kind of front yard ornamentation to which our soldiers could never grow accustomed." The engineers went to work building proper barracks for the men, but when completed they offered little improvement. One account described them "uncommonly flimsy" buildings "constructed of thin boards not tightly joined." The artillery trained at the French military base at Valdahon, thirty kilometers southeast of Besançon near the Swiss border. Conditions there were considerably better than Gondrecourt. Corporal Osborne de Varila reported "real mattresses and real pillows" in his sleeping quarters.

The elite and battle-tested 47th Chasseurs Alpins, nicknamed the "Blue Devils," drew the assignment of instructing the green American troops. The Doughboy and his French counterpart, the Poilu, got along well. "More courteous, indulgent and patient teachers could not be imagined," according to the official history of the 26th Infantry Regiment. The camaraderie went beyond professional matters. Ben Bernheisel remembered that the French soldiers "would sit at tables and have friendly chats over their wine," and that "they always welcomed [us] as a part of their group." The French may have been friendly, but they had hard lessons to teach. Expectations for the Americans were high, and the training was difficult. Bernheisel remembered that drill began "the following morning" after their arrival, and "drilling we had in plenty from then on." They normally trained eight hours a day, six days a week. During July and August, training focused on physical conditioning, marksmanship, and chemical warfare. The troops also got instruction about weapons such as flamethrowers, grenades, and machine guns—which were unfamiliar to them. By September, a patch of countryside between the hamlets of Demange-aux-Eaux and Delouze became known as "Washington Center," where the Doughboys received an intensive tutorial on the arts of trench warfare. They etched countless trenches into the ground, then practiced learning how to assault and defend them. Barbed wire entanglements, dugouts, and other features made the training as realistic as possible. "Nothing was omitted or left to the imagination of the soldier," recalled Bullard. "Almost everything except the actual bursting of shells or the passing of projectiles in his immediate neighborhood was offered to the man undergoing instruction."

The First Doughboys Fall

After three months of training at Gondrecourt, the 1st Division went to the front—specifically, the Sommerviller sector, about ten kilometers east of Nancy. The area had seen no significant action since 1915. Both Germany and France used the area as a place of "rest" for exhausted combat units, and the fighting was limited to artillery barrages, patrolling no-man's land under cover of darkness, and occasional trench raids. Paired with the French 18th Division, the Americans entered the trenches for the first time in early morning hours of October 21, and took up positions north and east of the tiny village of Bathelémont-lès-Bauzemont, between Athienville and the Rhine-Marne Canal at Parroy. Alongside their French instructors, the Americans manned listening posts and machine-gun positions, and conducted night patrols of no man's land.

Despite the wretched rainy weather, the Americans were itching for action. According to reporter Floyd Gibbons of the *Chicago Tribune*, artillery batteries "were struggling in the mud of the black gun pits to get their pieces into position in the quickest possible time, and achieve the honour of firing that first American shot in the war." Battery C of the 6th Field Artillery, under the command of Captain Idus R. McLendon, won the competition. Though rain fell "with tropical violence," Corporal Osborne de Varila of Battery C was "filled with a kind of fierce exhilaration" to get his gun in place, dragging and pushing it through darkness and mud so thick that he thought his "arms would jump from their sockets." In the early morning darkness of October 23, McLendon's men dragged their French-made 75mm gun up a small hill, and at 6:05 am Sergeant Alex L. Arch fired the U.S. Army's first shot of the land war in Europe. "There was not an American within sound-range who did not whoop with exultation when the first shot for liberty rang forth," wrote de Varila, who equated the event to "the ringing of the old Liberty Bell in '76." Floyd Gibbons recorded the spot of the first shot as being "one kilometre due east of the town of Bathelemont and three hundred metres northeast of the Bauzemont-Bathelemont road." Other accounts put it just 400 meters east of the village. As for the gun itself, Captain McLendon suggested that it be sent back to the United States. Today it is on display in the Large Weapons Gallery at the West Point Museum, just a stone's throw away from the United States Military Academy, in Highland Falls, New York.

The Germans soon learned of the American presence and decided to welcome the Doughboys to the Western Front. In the early morning hours of November 3 they conducted a raid on a position known as Strong Point Artois, atop a hill known as the Haut de Ruelles, about one kilometer northwest of Bures. Around midnight, the 2nd Battalion of the 16th Infantry Regiment descended into the trenches to relieve the 1st Battalion. Little did they know, a German raiding party was creeping across no man's land toward them. At 3:30 AM, the Germans unleashed a box barrage—an artillery attack that isolates a position by surrounding it with a bombardment, preventing escape or reinforcement. A party of Germans then blasted through the barbed wire and poured into the trenches. The raid took just minutes, and when it was over the enemy had dragged eleven American prisoners back to their lines and left five Allied soldiers dead, three of whom were Americans—Corporal James Gresham of Evansville, Indiana, and Privates Thomas Enright of Pittsburgh and Merle Hay of Glidden, Iowa—the first American combat soldiers killed on the Western Front.

The following day, the bodies were taken to Bathelémont. After a religious ceremony on an improvised altar in the village, the bodies were buried in a meadow near the local chateau, alongside French dead. The burial was a solemn and moving affair. French artillery shells whistled above on their way toward German positions as the commanding general of the French 18th Division gave the eulogy. He predicted that the graves of these Americans would become a pilgrimage site for liberty-loving people. "The passerby will stop and uncover his head," he said. "The travelers of France, of the Allied countries, of America, and the men of heart, who will come to visit our battlefields of Lorraine, will go out of their way to come here to bring to these graves the tribute of their respect and gratitude." "The entire ceremony was one of the most impressive I have ever witnessed," reported the division's operations officer, Captain George C. Marshall, "and made a profound impression on all who were present." Within a year of the raid, the citizens of Lorraine had constructed a monument to the fallen Americans in the center of the village, across the street from the church and just to the east of today's town hall. Bearing the Lorraine cross, the monument listed the names of the three men killed, and described them as "worthy sons of this great and noble Nation" who "fought for Justice, Liberty and Civilization against German Imperialism, the scourge of mankind." The bodies of the three men were returned to the United States in the early 1920s and reburied in their hometowns. When the Germans took the village in 1940, they did not appreciate the anti-Teutonic tone of the memorial and destroyed it.

Nestled in an unusually picturesque corner of rural France, Bathelémont today has fewer than seventy residents, but it is proud of its place in American history. In the center of town an information shelter stands atop the ruins of a cement blockhouse left over from the Great War. Interpretive panels inside give a rundown of local history. One focuses on the village itself, another on the World War II tank battle that took place to the east at nearby Arracourt. A third panel tells the story of the Big Red One in the village during the First World War. The texts are in French only. Just to the east of the village, a road called Chemin des Américains splits off from the main road and leads eastward. Doughboys quartered in the ruins of Bathelémont during their tour of duty here walked this road on their way to and from the trenches. Somewhere in the hills nearby was where Sergeant Arch fired his gun on October 23, 1917. The Haut de Ruelles, the scene of the first three deaths, is unmarked and reachable only by narrow dirt farm roads. The Nazis may have destroyed the original memorial to Enright, Gresham, and Hay, but after World War II the villagers erected a new one. A large granite block, it stands at the entrance to the local cemetery at a crossroads just a few hundred meters west of the village. The inscription lists

Chemin des Américains at Bathelémont-lès-Bauzemont, France.

the names of the three men, and suggests (in French) that they still lie in the soil of Lorraine, though they have long since been returned to the United States. At the base of the monument is a small plaque, placed there by the American Legion in 1967, marking the 50th anniversary of the deaths. An interpretive kiosk, in French, English, and German, tells the story of the first three Doughboys killed.

On November 20, 1917, the entire division—artillery and all—proceeded back to Gondrecourt to begin its third and final phase of training. Here maneuvers focused on open warfare and making sure that components of the division worked together seamlessly. "It was inspiring to see the Division in battle formation, stretching away over a front of more than two thousand meters, and a depth of more than three thousand meters," noted the division's official history. The intensity of the training increased. "Have been drilling madly since coming back," Tom Carroll wrote in his diary. The approach of winter added further challenges. "Old torn uniforms, no gloves, just barely enough food, and no forage, with the bitter cold and never ceasing manoeuvres on the bleak 'Washington Centre,' brought many a comparison with the winter at Valley Forge," recalled Alban Butler. "A final maneuver of the whole division was held in a blizzard," recalled General Charles P. Summerall. "We experienced great difficulty in moving the guns through deep snow and over ice, but the guns were placed, and simulated fire was conducted in a gratifying manner."

Aside from a plaque at Gondrecourt's town hall (15 place de l'Hôtel de Ville), there is little there today to suggest its important place in the history of the AEF. The countryside of Washington Center has long since returned to crops. Older buildings in Gondrecourt, nearby villages, and the surrounding countryside were familiar to the soldiers of the Big Red One, though there is no outward indication of this. The village hall in Abainville (3 rue Saint Martin) served as the headquarters of the 1st Engineers. The Château de Beaupré, once the headquarters of the First Field Artillery Brigade, still stands west of the village of Chassey-Beaupré, seven kilometers southwest of Gondrecourt. It is on private property. Driving through the countryside around Gondrecourt and looking at the old barns and farmhouses, one can only speculate which ones the Doughboys may once have called their temporary homes. Valdahon, where the Big Red One artillery began its training, remains a French military base.

More Doughboys Undergo Training, and Fall in Battle

As more divisions made their way to France, they also gathered at training grounds in Lorraine and went through much the same process. In October 1917, the elements of the 2nd Division (the only other division formed overseas) coalesced in the rural hamlets surrounding Bourmont. The 26th "Yankee" Division, the first National Guard unit to arrive in France, gathered near Neufchâteau in September, and the 42nd "Rainbow" Division near Vaucouleurs in November. By mid-1918, nearly two dozen divisional training areas had been established within an eighty-kilometer radius of Pershing's headquarters in Chaumont. Conditions at all of them were similar to those at Gondrecourt. The U.S. Army took over local chateaux and soldiers slept in barns and farmhouses. William Carter, a marine in the 2nd Division, wrote that in Blevaincourt, ten kilometers southeast of Bourmont, "we were billeted in stable lofts or houses, in groups of from ten to a platoon." "In the rocky soil of this part of France trench digging was more of a mining than an agricultural operation," noted the official history of the 32nd Division, which trained near Prauthoy. Martin Hogan of the Rainbow Division remembered "a very small village" in the Vaucouleurs training area "that was filled with mud and despair. The streets of this place had never been cleaned and so, in the rainy season, one plowed deep through generations of refuse and pollution. Even the cows, pigs, and geese seemed depressed over the condition of the place." Not all took such a dim view of rural France. Richard Derby, a physician in the 2nd Division, thought Bourmont "a picturesque small town" with "the houses clustered together on the hilltop." Derby noted that many soldiers became friends with their hosts, and when they got leave later in the war "many of our men . . . would return to visit some devoted French family." Friendships may indeed have been strong, but virtually no trace of the training areas remains today. One place that commemorates them is Bourmont, where a granite monument to the 2nd Division stands in a plaza along rue du Général Leclerc. The road below the plaza is boulevard des États-Unis.

Artillery continued to train separately at French army posts, such as Saint-Cyr Coëtquidan near Guer in eastern Brittany. Saint-Cyr Coëtquidan remains an active and important French military post today. Portions are publicly accessible, most notably the Musée du Souvenir (Museum of Remembrance), dedicated to the French officer corps. The grounds of the installation are strewn with war memorials, and even some German bunkers left over from the World War II occupation, but no markers indicate the American Great War presence there.

Camp de Souge, located on the sand flats west of Bordeaux, also hosted American artillerymen. Milton Goodman of the 306th Field

Artillery, 77th Division, described it as "an endless line of brown barracks [that] stretched on an endless yellow road through a drab and endless desert of sand. There were trees here and there, as there are oases in the Sahara." The camp was not without its pleasures, though. Goodman enjoyed "the strange county-fair colony that clustered outside the gate," with push carts, curio salesmen, portable cinemas, and a stationery shop selling copies of *La Vie Parisienne*, a popular erotic magazine. "But most interesting of all were the wine shacks," he wrote, including one named Café New York "certainly in preparation for us." The training was hard, but worthwhile. "We had come to Souge a regiment of rookies," noted Goodman, but left "a trained and powerful fighting force, well-organized, well-taught, well-equipped, ready to take our place in the line." Adjacent to the Bordeaux suburb of Martignas-sur-Jalle, Camp de Souge is also an active French military base partially accessible to the public. As at Saint-Cyr Coëtquidan, there is no indication of the onetime U.S. presence. The French know Camp des Souge for the World War II atrocities that took place there. During the German occupation, the Nazis used the wilds of the camp as an execution ground. A memorial to the more than 300 victims now stands in a remote area of the camp near the site of the massacres.

About thirty kilometers southwest of Camp de Souge was another artillery training ground, Camp du Corneau, just north of Cazaux. The camp originated as a transit point for riflemen brought up from France's African colony of Senegal. Conditions there were awful. Electricity and running water were nearly nonexistent. Barracks were overcrowded and poorly constructed. Adding to the miseries of these colonial troops was the climate, which was cold and damp compared to their native West Africa. Beginning in 1916, pneumonia cut through the Senegalese ranks, killing a thousand of them, their bodies buried in a mass grave in the sandy forest west of the camp. In 1917 Russia dispatched 16,000 soldiers to fight in France, but when their country spun into revolution that fall many of them refused to fight. The French sent 6,000 of the rebellious Russians to Courneau, where a dozen of them died of disease, their bodies added to the Senegalese mass grave.

In January 1918 the French turned Camp de Courneau over to the Americans, who renamed it Camp Hunt and used it for artillery training. The Russians and Senegalese were still around when the Americans first arrived—"a queer mixture of troops," thought Edmund Arpin—but the French soon moved them out. Disease continued to haunt the camp, this time the Spanish Flu. Eighty-seven Americans were buried across the road from the Senegalese mass grave, most of them victims of influenza, though a few were airmen who died in accidents at the nearby Cazaux air field (see Chapter 11). Today, the Camp Hunt site is part of a French Air

Force base closed to the public. The Senegalese/Russian mass grave is now a military cemetery known as the Nécropole du Natus, located in the forest a few hundred meters west of the intersection of the D112 and D256 highways. After the war, the American dead were returned to the United States or reburied at the Suresnes American Cemetery outside Paris. However, there is a small memorial where the American cemetery once was.

After completing the first phase of training, the Doughboys boarded the infamous Forty and Eight trains and headed off to a quiet sector of the front. The 26th "Yankee" Division took up positions along the Chemin des Dames northwest of Reims in February 1918. Ten months earlier the area had seen some of the war's bloodiest fighting, but when the Yankee Division arrived things were fairly quiet. The American fighting spirit impressed the French, though they found the Sammies quite naïve about war. The Americans sometimes acted more like tourists than soldiers, exploring the battlefields and collecting souvenirs. "The French were first amused, and then alarmed by the inordinate curiosity of the Yankees," wrote Frank Sibley, a Boston newspaperman accompanying the division. In one way, the men of the Yankee Division had an advantage over other Doughboys in the trenches. The limestone bluffs of the Chemin des Dames were riddled with quarries, which both sides used for storage and soldiers' quarters. The Germans and French had fought many subterranean battles in these quarries, but when the Yankee Division arrived they provided safe and relatively comfortable quarters, as well as command posts and storage facilities. Arriving at the front, James Duane was directed to a "dug-out," which he imagined was "a small hole in the ground covered with a few feet of dirt." Upon entering, he was surprised to find "electric lights, then a stable containing about twenty horses and many wagons, a blacksmith shop, a canteen, a hospital, and a chapel."

FAMOUS AMERICAN SPORTS ABROAD
SOUVENIR HUNTING

Like the 1st Division, the 26th took its first casualties along the Chemin des Dames, though they were light. "Later on when we were fully baptized to enemy shell-fire we used to laugh and joke at our uneasy

Like most Americans traveling in Europe, the Doughboys liked to pick up souvenirs, though in the war zone the practice could lead to injury or even death. (From Co. "A," Twenty-Third Engineers, 1919)

feelings on this night," remarked one Yankee Division soldier of his first night in a combat zone, "and when we compare it to some of our later exploits it certainly was tame." The Yankee Division spent just six weeks at the Chemin des Dames before pulling back for more training. Today, the woods and fields of the Chemin des Dames are strewn with monuments and war memorials. Among the smallest and most obscure of them is one dedicated to the 26th Division, located off a remote dirt road northwest of the village of Braye-en-Laonnais. It stands at the entrance to the Carrière de Froidmont, a quarry that Yankee Division troops once occupied. This particular quarry has been the victim of souvenir hunters and vandals and is closed to the public, but nearby is the Caverne du Dragon museum, where one can tour another quarry and get a sense of the war's subterranean dimensions.

Many divisions got their baptism of fire at the Saint-Mihiel Salient south of Verdun. Elements of the 2nd Division entered the lines near Sommedieue on March 17. Casualties came quickly. On the evening of March 23, 1918, Lieutenant Moses Taylor led a raid on a German machine-gun position. He was severely injured in the assault, and the Germans took him prisoner. He died of his wounds and was buried in the village cemetery at Vigneulles. Although his body was later returned to America, the village still remembers him. Like every community in France, Vigneulles has a memorial to its Great War dead, but the one on the town square here also pays tribute to the fallen American. On the south face of the monument is a statue of Taylor, with a dedication to his sacrifice. The square itself is named place Taylor.

The 42nd "Rainbow" Division's introduction to the trenches came on a long segment of the Western Front in Lorraine known as the Lunéville Sector. Attached to three different French divisions, the Rainbow Division soldiers occupied scattered sections of the front from Lunéville in the north to Baccarat in the south. This division saw its first deaths on March 7 in the Bois de Rouge Bouquet, in the Fôret de Parroy east of Lunéville. The 165th Infantry Regiment holding the sector was one of America's most distinguished units. Originally the 69th New York Infantry, the "Fighting 69th" was composed mainly of Irish Americans. During the Civil War, it amassed an impressive combat record. It played a major role at Bull Run in 1861, and was present at Lee's surrender at Appomattox in 1865. The prestigious regiment, led by a group of politically well-connected officers, completed its Beaux-Arts-style armory at 68 Lexington Avenue in New York City in 1906. (The building remains in the hands of the New York National Guard, and is still one of the city's most distinctive architectural landmarks.) In the reorganization of forces that came with the U.S. entry into the Great War, the regiment became the 165th Infantry, but it retained its strongly Irish character and it was still known to its members as the Fighting 69th.

At 3:20 in the afternoon on March 7, the Germans began an artillery barrage on the American lines in the Rouge Bouquet. One shell scored a direct hit on an American bunker, trapping its occupants underground. Despite continued shelling, Rainbow men rushed to the bunker to dig them out, among them Major William Donovan—who in World War II would lead the Office of Strategic Services, the forerunner of today's Central Intelligence Agency. The rescuers could hear the voices of their trapped comrades as they furiously dug and cleared away logs and other debris, but the heavy German barrage made their efforts impossible. In the end, only two men were pulled out alive and another five bodies recovered. Fifteen remained trapped below ground, the bunker becoming their grave. The Fighting 69th placed a tablet above the bunker to mark the site, and the division's beloved and legendary chaplain, Father Francis P. Duffy, gave the last rites. One member of the regiment, Sergeant Joyce Kilmer, composed a poem for the occasion entitled "The Wood Called Rouge Bouquet." A graduate of Columbia University, Kilmer was a rising star in the world of American poetry, his work noted for its emphasis on nature and Roman Catholic spirituality. Kilmer signed up for the New York National Guard shortly after America's entry into the war, and though college educated, he insisted on serving in the ranks. At St. Patrick's Day services that year, Father Duffy read Kilmer's poem aloud while the sounds of buglers playing "Taps" echoed through the woods. It brought tears to the eyes of many tough fighting men.

Sadly, the exact spot of the ill-fated bunker is no longer known with any precision. The Forêt de Parroy was the scene of especially bitter fighting during World War II, which destroyed most vestiges of World War I. Post-World War II logging operations further deteriorated the site. The tablet the Fighting 69th placed above the bunker is gone, its fate unknown. It may have been shattered into a million pieces during World War II or nabbed by souvenir hunters. Perhaps it still lies buried somewhere in the soil with the soldiers it commemorated. The Rouge Bouquet is located 3.8 kilometers south of Mouacourt, on the east side of a paved but rugged logging road. There are no signs to mark the spot. In 1937, New York City dedicated a portion of Times Square to Father Duffy. Located along Broadway between 46th and 47th Streets, Duffy Square contains a statue of the famed priest in military uniform with a Celtic cross in the background. Incidentally, nearby is a statue of another famous Irish American of Great War fame, the popular-music composer George M. Cohan. A contemporary of Irving Berlin (see Chapter 3), Cohan was a leading figure on Tin Pan Alley. Swept up in the patriotic wave that overtook America when it entered the war,

Cohan wrote what was to become the nation's most popular war song, "Over There."

The 5th "Red Diamond" Division took up position in the Vosges Mountains south of Saint-Die in the Anould Sector in June 1918. A month later, it moved a little farther north, occupying a line immediately east of Saint-Die. On August 17, the 5th Division even undertook a small offensive to reduce a salient in the Allied lines near the village of Frapelle, nine kilometers east of Saint-Die. Their artillery opened up on the Germans at 3:54 AM, and the infantry stepped off soon afterward. "Evidently the enemy was prepared for the attack," stated the division's official history, because German artillery plastered the second and third waves of advancing Americans, and when the Doughboys reached the village they found that most of the enemy had evacuated the town. The troops of the Red Diamond Division held Frapelle through German artillery barrages and counterattacks lasting several days. "Frapelle was the first operation of any kind that the Division had engaged in," noted the official history, "and the men went through it splendidly, like veteran troops." After the war, the 5th Division erected twenty-six cement obelisks, each decorated with a red diamond and a plaque, to mark the sites of their most important actions. One such obelisk stands in front of the village hall in Frapelle. The original cement marker had become weathered over the years, and in 2000 local officials in Frapelle erected a new granite memorial.

Americans also went to quiet sectors in Alsace, at the southern end of the Western Front. This bicultural region had long been part of France, but Germany took it after the Franco-Prussian War in 1871. The 32nd Division, composed of Wisconsin and Michigan National Guard troops, took up positions in Alsace east of Belfort, at the southernmost end of the Western Front. Here the French penetrated several kilometers into German territory in 1914 and held their ground for the rest of the war, so when the 32nd arrived there in May 1918 its members bragged of being the first U.S. troops on German soil. Here, too, the Yanks showed their naïveté about life in the trenches. "The troops used to climb the trees for cherries," wrote Lieutenant Paul Schmidt. "They would be fired on by the German snipers, but fortunately no one was hit." Schmidt believed the German-speaking area was riddled with spies. On their first morning at the front, for example, his men "looked over the parapet of the trenches to observe a long banner stretched over the German trenches, reading, 'Welcome 32nd Division.'" Though suspicious of the locals, many of these Midwesterners were of German ancestry and felt oddly at home. "Many of our men could speak German," noted the division's official history, "and accordingly one of the difficulties of being a stranger in a strange land was made less acute." Alsace became part of France again after the war, but the region retains much of its German heritage. There are no memorials marking the 32nd Division's brief time in Alsace, though remnants of some of the trenches its troops occupied still remain, such as in the Bois de Gildwiller, between the D25 and D26 highways north-west of Ammerzwiller.

Once the training cycle was completed, the divisions were put on another quiet sector of the front for more seasoning. The 1st Division took up positions on the southern face of the Saint-Mihiel Salient late in January 1918. But getting the divisions combat-ready was just one of Pershing's problems. In order to be effective the soldiers needed qualified leaders, but many officers had little more military experience than the average draftee. Managing a two-million-man AEF also required administrative skills few Americans officers had. In addition, modern war required Americans to learn about weapons and technologies with which they had little if any experience. To get his army up to speed on these vitally important tasks, Pershing embarked on a massive educational program for the AEF.

One French Town and Pershing's Grand Plan to Train the AEF

One of Pershing's biggest headaches was a shortage of staff officers who could perform the myriad administrative tasks necessary to run the AEF—from GHQ in Chaumont down to the divisional level. Pershing pleaded with Washington to send more staff officers, but sufficient numbers never materialized, so the commander-in-chief founded his own schools to create them. The AEF General Staff School was located in Langres, thirty-five kilometers southeast of Chaumont. Perched on a limestone bluff above the upper reaches of the Marne, Langres is reminiscent of an Italian hill town. It is the birthplace of the Enlightenment philosopher Denis Diderot, whose statue graces the town's main plaza. Its location on a bluff above the Marne's headwaters made Langres an important ancient and medieval military center, as the 3.5 kilometers of stone ramparts surrounding the town, some dating back to the Romans, attest. Its location in eastern France made it important for border defense. In the nineteenth century the French army built a huge citadel less than half a kilometer south of the walled city, and filled the surrounding countryside with scores of subsidiary forts, artillery batteries, and ammunition magazines.

The General Staff School commenced classes in November 1917 with seventy-five students enrolled for an intensive three-week course. Subsequent classes grew in size. The school was housed in the Caserne Carteret-Trécourt, a French army barracks on the city's eastern ramparts. In the shadow of Saint-Mammès Cathedral, the facility was a convent until Napoleon turned it into an army

Countryside east of Langres, France. The orientation table in the photograph points to some of the nearby French military installations where Americans learned the art of warfare.

barracks a century before the Great War. American officers there learned to tackle problems common to army staff work—writing orders, locating headquarters and command posts, preparing for movement, quartering troops, and a host of other such concerns. Since few American officers had staff experience, the British and French agreed to supply some of the faculty. Many General Staff School students came from the nearby Officer Candidate School, located at the Caserne Turenne in the Langres citadel, which began classes in December 1917. Here promising enlisted men got a crack at becoming an officer. By the fall of 1918, the Officer Candidate School had grown so large that Fort de la Bonnelle, Fort de la Pointe de Diamant, and Fort de Cognelot, all located on the outskirts of Langres, began absorbing the officer candidate training overflow. Dormitory space quickly ran out, and students boarded in homes in Langres and surrounding communities. By October 1918, there were nearly 5,000 American officer candidates at Langres.

The General Staff School and the Officer Candidate School were just the beginning of Pershing's educational efforts. Langres also hosted nearly a dozen specialty schools, promoting professionalism and technical competence in a wide range of military occupations, some of which had no precedent in the American military experience. Several were located within the ramparts of Langres. In addition to the General Staff School, the Caserne Carteret-Trécourt also hosted the AEF School of the Line, which emphasized combat tactics, as well as the Intelligence School and the Gas School. The Sanitary School trained medical personnel across the street at a girls' school along the east ramparts. At Fort de Plesnoy, twelve kilometers east of Langres, the Infantry Specialists School taught topics like bayonet use, hand grenades, sniping, and a host of other combat skills. The engineering school operated at a hilltop bastion known as Fort de Saint-Menge, 7.5 kilometers north of Langres. Machine-gun officers learned their deadly trade at Fort de Peigney, just two kilometers east of the city. Pigeon handlers trained at Fort de la Bonnelle, 2.5 kilometers southwest. In the fields five

Lieutenant Colonel George S. Patton Jr. at his tank school at Bourg, south of Langres, France. (Courtesy of the National Archives)

kilometers south of Langres, near the tiny hamlet of Bourg, the Tank School trained Americans to operate this brand new weapon of war. The commander of the school was George S. Patton Jr. A protégée of Pershing, Patton had served with the general in Mexico, and Pershing took a shine to the aggressive young officer. Among the party that accompanied Pershing to Europe in May 1917, Patton had served on Pershing's staff, but jumped at the chance for a combat role. Patton knew nothing about tanks, but saw in them the opportunity for promotion and publicity, believing them "a great drawing card in the papers and illustrated magazines." They also fit his aggressive nature. After spending just two weeks at the French tank training center near Compiégne, Patton began preparing American armor for war.

This vast educational complex, Pershing hoped, would produce officers capable of running the ever-expanding AEF and inculcate them with his open warfare ideas. Designed to protect France from an enemy invasion, Langres instead experienced an Allied one. "Its cobble-paved streets and narrow sidewalks became thronged with thousands of alert young officers whose collars bore the insignia of every branch of the American army," wrote intelligence officer E. Alexander Powell, and "the clumsy, two-wheeled carts of the peasants, drawn by shaggy ponies, were crowded from the roads by staff cars and trucks and ambulances and motor-cycles painted in the olive drab of the Expeditionary Forces." American music soon filled the streets, American officers crowded the "smoke-filled, garlic-scented restaurants," and the Americans "introduced to Langres Charlie Chaplin and Fatty Arbuckle and Douglas Fairbanks, and all the heroes of the screen." Powell thought that "if the war had lasted a year or two longer Langres would have become as American as Schenectady or Montclair." The existence of the schools was supposed to be top secret. Langres was never mentioned by name in any communications, and referred to only by its army postal address, APO 714. Given the size of the U.S. presence in Langres, concealing the schools was probably pointless. "To believe that the Germans were ignorant of all this was severely to strain one's credulity," opined Powell.

The American presence in Langres may once have been mighty, but there is little evidence of it today. Outside of Bourg on the west side of the D974 highway, near its intersection with the D51, stands an easy-to-miss memorial to Patton. During World War II, Patton returned to the area at the head of the U.S. Third Army and liberated it from the Nazis. No other marker or memorial to the U.S. military schools exists in the area. The Caserne Carteret-Trécourt has been returned to the Catholic Church, and is today the College Lycée Jeanne Mance. The building that once housed the Sanitary School is now a primary school. The Citadel just south of Langres is now controlled jointly by the city of Langres and the French military. The Caserne Turenne is on the civilian side of the facility and is falling into disrepair. Many local watering holes that served U.S. officers, like Hotel de la Poste and Cheval Blanc, are still around. Many of the subsidiary forts where Americans once trained have since been sold off and are now in private hands. Forts Bonnelle, Pointe de Diamant, and Cognelot are still accessible, but only by booking a tour with the Langres tourist office. Tours are only available April through September and only in French.

In the end, Pershing was never able to fully realize his ambitious vision for training the AEF. The programs suffered from a chronic lack of equipment and qualified instructors, especially in the early phases of U.S. involvement. Pulling experienced American troops from the frontline units to train the neophytes proved a double-edged sword. While trainees greatly benefited from their instructors' combat know-how, fighting prowess was also needed on the battlefield. The constant reshuffling of personnel also inhibited the development of unit cohesion. But the main problem was simply time. Britain and France wanted the Doughboys to join them in the trenches as soon as possible, and let Pershing know it. A series of German offensives beginning in March 1918 forced Pershing to delay (and eventually scrap) his cherished three-stage training program, and get Americans into the fight during one of the most critical stages of the entire war.

Germany Seeks a Knockout Punch

By early 1918, Germany was in a position of great peril but also of great opportunity. Thanks in large part to the U.S. Navy, the submarine campaign that brought America into the war had failed to knock Britain out of the war. Instead, Germany had acquired a powerful new enemy with almost inexhaustible resources while its own economy teetered on the brink of collapse. On the other hand,

Russia was effectively out of the war, allowing the German military commanders Field Marshall Paul von Hindenburg and his top strategist, General Erich von Ludendorff, to focus their attention on the Western Front. The year 1918 might be Germany's last chance to strike a decisive blow and win the war, Ludendorff thought, "before America can throw strong forces into the scale."

Ludendorff decided to concentrate his attentions on the British, whom he saw as the more deadly adversary. His plan was to "roll up" British lines in northern France, seize the channel ports, and drive the Tommies into the sea. In the months before the attack, Ludendorff brought in tons of artillery, as well as some of Germany's best divisions. He also planned to employ the new "storm trooper" infiltration tactics that Germany had been developing in Russia and Italy. Ludendorff launched his offensive, dubbed Operation Michael, on March 21. After a five-hour artillery barrage that included a generous amount of poison gas, seventy-six top-notch German divisions smashed into twenty-eight British divisions of varying quality across a seventy-kilometer front between Arras and La Fére. Stunned British forces fell back. According to historian John Keegan, Britain "had suffered its first true defeat since trench warfare had begun three and a half years earlier." German advances continued in the following days. By March 24 they had reached Péronne, and kept right on going toward the critical rail junction of Amiens. The lack of coordination between British and French forces made the situation even more dangerous. Haig wanted reinforcements from the French, but instead Pétain moved to defend Paris and prepare for an anticipated German offensive near Verdun. By March 26, the Germans had taken Noyon, threatening a complete separation of French and British lines, and were within twenty kilometers of Amiens.

The Allies struggled to respond. French and British leaders met in the city hall at Doullens on March 26 and promptly began pointing fingers at each other. Hope for some kind of coordinated response seemed lost until General Ferdinand Foch, the French chief of staff, took the floor. "We must fight in front of Amiens," he thundered, "we must not now retire a single inch." Inspired by his defiance, the Allies agreed to create a unified command to coordinate their actions, and put the fiery Foch in charge. Another conference at Beauvais fine-tuned the arrangement further, making Foch "Commander-in-Chief of Allied Armies" and giving him "direction of strategic operations." General Pershing did not attended the Doullens Conference, but was present at Beauvais. "I am in favor of a supreme commander," said Pershing, assenting to General Foch as the man for the job.

Fortunately for the Allies, the German drive stalled just short of Amiens. With each passing day German momentum slowed.

Ludendorff's decision to add the objective of separating British and French forces diluted the impact of his armies. Allied troops also put up a heroic defense outside of Amiens, and among the troops on the line there was a small contingent of U.S. Army engineers who were working with the British when the attack came (see Chapter 16). German casualties were enormous. They lost perhaps a quarter of a million dead and wounded, including some of the country's best troops. By the first week of April Ludendorff's forces had ground to a halt, but he refused to admit defeat. On April 9 he launched Operation Georgette in Belgium and northern France, hoping to divert Allied attention northward. Results were much the same as with Operation Michael—the Germans took lots of territory and opened a sizable salient in the British lines, but lost the initiative. Ludendorff had taken more territory than anyone since 1914, but he could not land the knockout punch he sought.

With the Germans on the march, the question of amalgamating U.S. troops into Allied divisions surfaced yet again. Britain argued that in light of the emergency, the January 1918 "Six Division Plan" for training American troops (see Chapter 1) was no longer adequate. Britain wanted more Doughboys. France also clamored for American troops. "Pershing is getting all the meat," Clemenceau once complained. "I want some of the meat." At a conference in Abbeville on May 1, Allied leaders—among them Clemenceau and Lloyd George—ganged up on Pershing to get him to accede to some kind of amalgamation plan. "Are you willing to risk our being driven back to the Loire?" Foch asked him pointedly. "Yes, I am willing to take that risk," Pershing responded. The meeting went on for two days, and in the end Pershing bent a little, but got more than he gave. He agreed to assign priority in troop shipments to infantry and machine-gunners to get Yanks on the line as soon as possible. In exchange, he extracted a formal commitment from the Allies to the creation of an independent American army.

Pershing's dogged commitment to an independent American force did not mean he was unwilling to help stem the German advances. Indeed, he was itching to get his boys into the fight and was a little embarrassed that he could not contribute more. In late March, Pershing told Foch that "the American people would consider it a great honor for our troops to be engaged in the present battle," and said that "all we have is yours, use them as you wish." But Pershing did not have much. In March 1918 there were only six full U.S. divisions in France, and only one of them, the 1st Division, had completed all three stages of the training cycle. When the Germans launched their March offensives, the Big Red One occupied a quiet sector on the south face of the Saint-Mihiel Salient for more seasoning. As darkness fell on March 31, the 1st Division pulled out of the trenches near Saint-Mihiel and began its journey north to Picardy to join the First French Army near Amiens. The 26th Division, which had just completed a stint along the Chemin des Dames and was undergoing the third phase of training, hastily moved into the 1st Division's positions.

As April began, the Yankee Division occupied a front that ran roughly from Apremont-la-Forêt in the west to Flirey in the east. The Germans had been in the area since 1914 and knew it well. From their fortified position on a nearby hill known as the Butte de Montsec, the Germans controlled the vast plain below. Today an American war memorial occupies the top of Montsec (see Chapter 12), and from here one can fully appreciate the commanding position the Germans enjoyed. During the first weeks of April, the Yankee Division absorbed a constant stream of artillery and poison gas. "The Germans seemed to resent the intrusion of these newcomers," wrote Carroll Swan of the 101st Engineers, "and threw a lot of supplies over that were not on our bill of lading." One artillery position at a bend in the road just south of the village of Beaumont received so much attention that it assumed the nickname "Dead Man's Curve." The Germans also probed the American lines vigorously. Beginning on

Trench remnants in the Bois Brûlé near Apremont-la-Forêt, France. The 26th "Yankee" Division fought in the area in April 1918.

April 10, the 104th Infantry Regiment from Massachusetts endured some spirited assaults in the Apremont Woods, also called the Bois Brûlé, in the hills northwest of Apremont-la-Forêt. In an attack on April 12, the Germans temporarily drove the Bay Staters from their trenches, but by the end of the day the Massachusetts regiment had wrestled them back. "It was a fight of sections and platoons," recalled Emerson Taylor, "in a tangle of broken trenches, twisted wire, and thick underbrush . . . where individual grit and fighting ability counted for everything."

On April 20, the Germans launched an even bigger assault against the village of Seicheprey, less than a kilometer behind the front line. Intelligence picked up signs that a German attack was imminent, but when it came the Americans were unprepared. At 3:00 AM, German artillery and gas began raining down on American positions. It was a "bombardment as the Division had not yet even dreamed of," wrote Emerson Taylor. The Germans hit the U.S. front line as well as key roads behind it, including the Paris-Metz high-way that ran behind the U.S. lines (the present-day D907 and 958 highways between Apremont and Flirey) and Dead Man's Curve. At 6:00 AM ambulances arrived at Dead Man's Curve to take away the wounded. Accompanying them was Father William J. Farrell, a chaplain with the 101st Field Artillery. The Roman Catholic priest offered last rites to the dead and dying as the battle raged, but Farrell's actions at that day went beyond the spiritual. He carried one wounded man on his back to the closest aid station. He brought ammunition up to the gunners, and when the crew of one gun fell to an enemy shell he manned the gun and kept it firing until he was wounded himself. One of the few chaplains decorated for bravery under fire, Farrell became a legendary figure in the AEF, and was known forever afterward as the "Fighting Parson."

At 5:00 AM, the Germans isolated Seicheprey with an artil-lery barrage and sent in the storm troopers. They attacked in three columns. One moved into the Bois de Remières east of the village. Another came directly toward Seicheprey down the road from Saint-Baussant (the present-day D28A highway), and the last one came in from the west along the road from Richecourt (now the D119). The Doughboys in the first line of trenches then began to see Germans emerge out of the fog behind a rolling barrage—an artillery attack that moves forward just in front of an infantry assault to screen the soldiers' forward movement. The brunt of the attack fell on the 102nd Infantry Regiment, made up of Connecticut men. The men in the front trench line put up stout resistance despite being vastly outnumbered, but by 7:00 AM the Germans had entered the ruins of the village. Vicious fighting ensued as the New Englanders held on to every shell-hole-ruined basement they could. The attack caught a group of soldiers in the village on a kitchen detail, but they fought too, one charging at a German soldier with a meat cleaver. The Germans thought the Americans foolhardy for clinging so tena-ciously to the insignificant pile of rubble that was Seicheprey, but they admired their spirit and raw fighting abilities. Paul Ettighoffer, a German soldier who became a noted novelist after the war, believed that Yankees put up "stubborn resistance, which neither the exhausted French nor English would be able to put up any longer." Examining the American dead, he was also impressed with the "big, athletic physiques" of the Americans and their "wonderful uniforms and rubber boots." Indeed, the supply-starved Germans carted away as much American materiel as they could. "We had to drag off copi-ous quantities of blankets, tins, groceries, sweet-tasting cigarettes, baffling chewing gum, rare coffee beans and delicious white rice," Ettighoffer recalled.

By noon French troops had arrived to help out and the Allies began to organize a counterattack, but the Germans pulled back

View of Seicheprey, France by war artist Lester G. Hornby, 1918. (Courtesy of the National Archives)

after nightfall. When the counterattack came early in the morning of April 21, the Germans quickly fell back to their original lines. In all, eighty-one Americans had been killed, 401 wounded, and 187 taken prisoner. After the engagement, German intelligence concluded that "the American is most courageous individually and resists desperately to the last with pistol, knife and hand grenade," is a "cunning and ruthless adversary in close-quarters combat," and "can only be beaten by reckless action." Even after the beating they received, the Americans remained defiant. The New Englanders often compared their experiences to their forefathers in the American Revolution. Referring to the drubbing the Patriots received on the Lexington Green before the victory at Concord in April 1775, Clifford Markle, a medic taken prisoner during the raid, predicted that Seicheprey "will go down in American history as the Lexington of the World War."

Though the fights in the Apremont Woods and Seicheprey were comparatively minor ones, those tiny French hamlets remained dear to the Yankee Division. Preserved trench remnants still fill the forest floor where the Massachusetts soldiers fought in the Bois Brûlé northwest of Apremont, just south of the D907 highway. A narrow road splits off from the highway about a kilometer outside of the village, leading to the trenches, many of which are cut out of the bedrock. Interpretive panels nearby tell of the fierce fighting that took place here between the French and Germans in 1914 and 1915, though the presence of the Yankee Division in 1918 is not mentioned. The Bay State's contribution to victory in the area is not forgotten, though. After the war, the citizens of Holyoke, Massachusetts, built a monument to their fallen sons in Apremont in the form of a new village water works. Dedicated in 1922, the facility still stands today, just off the main square of the village, which the villagers graciously named the place d'Holyoke. In Seicheprey, a small fountain erected by the State of Connecticut in 1925 commemorates the men of the 102nd Infantry Regiment that defended the village in April 1918. Dead Man's Curve, site of Father Farrell's heroics, is now part of the D907 highway just south of Beaumont. The curve remains a feature of the roadway, though the area now comprises peaceful fields. In addition to memorials on the battlefield, the fight at Seicheprey is commemorated in the Hamden Memorial Town Hall at the corner of Whitney and Dixell Avenues in Hamden, Connecticut. The building has many remembrances of local soldiers going all the way back to the Revolution. Perhaps the most interesting of them are four stained glass windows commemorating the life and service of A. Frederick Oberlin, an officer in the Yankee Division who received the Croix de Guerre for bravery at Seicheprey. One window depicts the fight at Seicheprey, complete with the cleaver-wielding cook.

The Doughboys Show That They Can Take the Offensive

Despite the hard fighting of the Yankee Division, Seicheprey raised questions about the readiness of American forces. If the Doughboys could not hold their own in the field—and do so soon—calls for the amalgamation of U.S. troops into French and British divisions would undoubtedly intensify. Pershing wanted to put American troops on the offensive, and believed that the 1st Division, in the reserve of the French First Army in Picardy, would provide the best demonstration of U.S. military prowess. On the night of April 24–25, the Big Red One took up positions in the Montdidier Sector, about twenty kilometers south of Amiens, relieving an exhausted Algerian unit. Their task was to take a small village named Cantigny. Located in a shallow German salient in the Allied lines, the village stood on high ground that dominated the surrounding countryside. The Germans had taken it the previous month in the Michael Offensive, and when the offensive petered out the Germans and Algerians battled furiously for the most advantageous positions. When the Americans arrived, the Allied front line, less than a kilometer west of the village, consisted of little more than some loosely connected shell holes. Seizing Cantigny would suppress German artillery and provide the Allies with a better defensive position in the area, but "the rationale for the attack rested more on psychological than operational advantage," according to historian Allan Millett. Everyone wanted to see if the Doughboys were up to it—the Germans, the Allies, and most of all, Pershing. The French agreed to supply some artillery and other combat support units, but Cantigny would be an American show. Before the 1st Division departed for the front, Pershing impressed upon its men the gravity of their task. The fight was about more than just a village, he told them. "You will represent the mightiest nation engaged," he said. "Our future part in this conflict depends on your action."

The Doughboys' first task was to dig proper trenches. Because the Germans had the American lines under constant surveillance from the high ground, the work had to be done at night. "By day the infantry lay in shallow fox-holes," wrote Alban Butler, "and during the short night, while the one meal of the day was brought up, they dug furiously in the hard chalky soil to connect these holes into a trench line." The Germans vigorously probed the U.S. lines and sent over lots of artillery fire, including copious amounts of mustard gas. "For sixteen hours I worked with my gas mask on," wrote Howard Cooper, "and man after man kept falling to the ground." But the Big Red One pressed on with their work. The Americans gave as good as they got. Franco-American artillery pulverized German positions, as well as the village itself—its residents having evacuated long ago—in order to deny the Germans any cover. Tom Carroll wrote in his diary that "Cantigny was a comparatively pretty place when we arrived," but within days "most of the trees had been stripped by shellfire, and the few stumps left standing were full of jagged pieces of high explosive shells." The Americans probed the German lines too. Carroll recalled one patrol soon after his arrival. He and his party reached the main road through the village, he recalled, when the Germans detected their presence and a firefight ensued. "Grenade hit my back," he wrote, "but didn't explode." Carroll went on another patrol a few nights later. "Ran into 34 Boche laying in wait for us," he wrote. Carroll took a bullet to the head, but noted with satisfaction that "I saw two Boche go down before the blood started to run into my eyes, blinding me."

D-Day was set for May 28. The 28th Infantry Regiment, under the command of Colonel Hanson E. Ely, drew the assignment of making the assault. The plan was to seize the village and then penetrate several hundred meters beyond it and occupy the high ground. Though Cantigny was less than a kilometer from U.S. lines, reaching it would be difficult. After crossing open ground in front of German positions, the attackers then had to ascend a ravine before reaching the village. The day before the operation was to begin, it was nearly scrubbed. On May 27, the Germans launched another major offensive in the Chemin des Dames region, this one called Operation Blücher-Yorck. Using their storm trooper tactics, the Germans penetrated twenty kilometers on the first day of the offensive and raced toward the Marne. If the Germans crossed that river, Paris would be in serious jeopardy. Just hours before the assault on Cantigny was to begin, the French announced that they were pulling out most of their forces to stem the latest German offensive. Their artillery and tanks, they said, would stay for the initial assault, and then leave. After that, the Americans would be on their own.

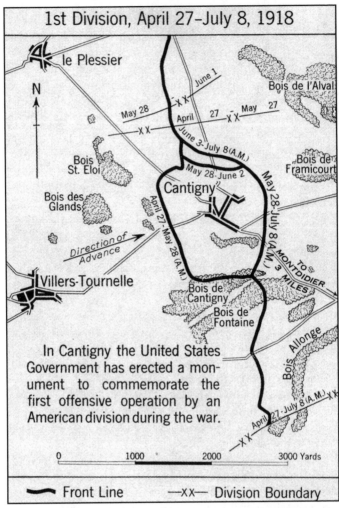

1st Division, April 27–July 8, 1918

le Plessier

N

June 1

Bois de l'Alval

May 28

April 27

May 27

June 3-July 8 (A.M.)

Bois St. Eloi

May 28-June 2

Bois de Framicourt

Cantigny

Bois des Glands

April 27-May 28 (A.M.)

May 28-July 8 (A.M.)

Direction of Advance

Villers-Tournelle

Bois de Cantigny

Bois de Fontaine

TO MONTDIDIER 3 MILES

Bois Allonge

In Cantigny the United States Government has erected a monument to commemorate the first offensive operation by an American division during the war.

April 27-July 8 (A.M.)

0   1000   2000   3000 Yards

━━ Front Line   —xx— Division Boundary

At 4:45 AM, as the glow of sunrise made its appearance on the eastern horizon, Allied artillery opened up on the Germans, hitting their trenches, their artillery, the ruins of the village, and key crossroads behind the lines. "The shells kept right on going overhead in one steady screeching yowl," recalled Dan Edwards, "and Cantigny just began to boil up. . . . The air was full of trees, stones, timber, equipment, bodies, everything you can imagine, all smashed up and whirling around with the dirt." In the early morning haze two hours later, the Doughboys went over the top behind a rolling barrage. French tanks and flamethrowers came with them in support, and French planes provided air cover. The Germans contested the attack fiercely, but the Big Red One proved irresistible. "Cantigny was ours in thirty-five minutes," bragged Howard Cooper, who reported that the Germans "were indeed surprised to see us." Lieutenant Clarence Huebner—who would serve as commanding general of the 1st

Division during World War II—witnessed the horrifying work of the flamethrowers clearing the shattered cellars and shell holes of Cantigny. "Just as I had seen rabbits in Kansas come out of burning haystacks," he later reflected, Huebner saw one unfortunate German soldier who emerged from the ruins and "ran ten to fifteen yards [and] then fell over singed to death." By 7:30 AM, the Americans reached their objectives, and began digging in along the ridge about 500 meters to the east of the village.

Getting into Cantigny had gone rather well, but staying there was an entirely different matter. The French withdrew their artillery and tanks as promised, leaving the Americans on their own. Repeated German counterattacks came for days afterward. "Holding the village against seven counter attacks during the next three days was a far greater task than its capture," observed Alban Butler. Colonel Ely, a tough-as-nails West Point football star, was determined to hold on to the smoking ruins of Cantigny, but in the face of constant German pressure even he began express doubts. "Front line pounded to hell and gone," he reported back to headquarters. Pershing, paying close attention to the fight, urged Ely to hold. Bullard sent in a few companies from the 16th Infantry Regiment to shore up the line, but under those conditions a full relief of the 28th was nearly impossible. Fortunately for the Americans, the Germans never recovered from the initial shock of the attack, and failed to coordinate their infantry and artillery attacks effectively. After three days of unsuccessful counterattacks, the 16th Infantry Regiment moved into Cantigny in relief. Cantigny had been liberated, but destroyed at the same time, and the 1st Division took nearly 5,000 dead and wounded. Vinton Dearing called his experiences at Cantigny "some of the most strenuous hours of my life."

The village that Dan Edwards once saw boiling with dirt, stone, and bodies is now a remarkably quiet French country community of barely more than 100 residents. Red brick homes, a few farm buildings, and a modest church cluster around a pleasant green village center. Evidence of the battle comes in the form of memorials, and Cantigny has several of them. The road leading into the village from the west, along which the 28th Infantry Regiment attacked, is now called rue du 28 Mai 1918. Less than a kilometer southeast of the village center on the D26 highway stands a memorial erected by the veterans of the 1st Division—one of five marking their major battlefields across France. The square column is capped with a sculpture of an eagle perched atop the division's emblem. Plaques on the sides of the monument list the names of those who died in the village and surrounding fields. Dominating the center of the village is the Cantigny American Monument, erected by the American Battle Monuments Commission. The monument, a square limestone shaft

Cantigny American Memorial. American troops attacked from the fields in the distance.

with Art Deco-style eagles decorating each of the upper corners, rises from a plaza in the center of the village. Barely fifty meters to the east is a memorial to the 28th Infantry Regiment, the first U.S. troops to enter the village. The monument consists of a charging Doughboy statue mounted on a black granite base. Inscriptions on the side of the monument tell the story of the 28th Infantry Regiment at Cantigny. Embossed on the front is the figure of a lion. After the Battle of Cantigny, the regiment adopted an insignia of a black *lion rampant* on a white shield, based on the lion found on the Picardy coat of arms. To this day, the 28th Infantry Regiment is known as the "Black Lions."

Just a few meters to the east of the Black Lions monument is a simple plaque on a concrete base that recounts the story of one of the 1st Division's most prominent members, Robert R. McCormick. President and publisher of the *Chicago Tribune*, McCormick came from one of Chicago's wealthiest and most prominent families. When the Great War broke out in 1914, "Bertie" McCormick traveled to Europe and interviewed the likes of Czar Nicholas II and Winston Churchill for his newspaper. Upon his return to Chicago he joined the Illinois National Guard and saw service on the Mexican Border. After U.S. entry into the war, Major McCormick served as an intelligence officer on Pershing's staff in France. McCormick found staff work uninteresting and lobbied ceaselessly for frontline duty, landing a spot commanding the 1st Battalion of the 5th Artillery Regiment, 1st Division. He saw action at Bathelémont and the Saint-Mihiel Salient, where he gained a reputation as an aggressive fighter, but also for being egotistical and difficult. "McCormick frequently skated over the thin ice of insubordination," wrote his biographer Richard Norton Smith.

McCormick's regiment saw plenty of action at Cantigny. Like everyone else in the division, he spent the days leading up to the attack in muddy shell holes and musty ruined basements dodging German artillery. In one incident, an exploding shell rendered him unconscious. Even in the midst of the May artillery duels, McCormick kept angling for promotion, dreaming of one day wearing a general's star. He even left the front and spent three days in Paris pleading his cause while his battalion's guns blazed away on the Picardy plains. On May 13 McCormick came down with the Spanish Flu. He remained seriously ill for the next several weeks, but when the assault on Cantigny came at dawn on May 28 he was at his post skillfully directing fire on the German lines and providing part of the rolling barrage that covered the advancing infantry. But by noon that day McCormick could function no longer, and he was evacuated to the rear. McCormick spent much of the summer of 1918 in command of the 122nd Field Artillery Regiment of the 33rd Division (Illinois National Guard) as it trained for combat. In August, he received a promotion to full colonel and orders to return to the United States to train more artillery units. McCormick begged to remain in France. "I don't care about the colonelcy if I can have a regiment," he told Pershing, but the commander-in-chief did not budge. McCormick would thereafter be known as "The Colonel," but his fighting days were over.

After the armistice The Colonel returned to his sprawling estate named Red Oaks in the Chicago suburb of Wheaton. Although McCormick became a staunch isolationist after the war, he was fiercely proud of his wartime service. The 1st Division remained especially close to his heart. McCormick renamed his estate Cantigny in honor of the division's first major fight, and warmly hosted division reunions there. Today the estate is open to the public. Cantigny Park, owned and operated by the Robert R. McCormick Foundation (the same group that placed the plaque in the village of Cantigny), is a green oasis in the suburban sprawl of Chicagoland. The 500-acre grounds contain restaurants, a golf course, a band shell, a parade field, and twenty-nine acres of some of the Midwest's finest gardens. McCormick's home is now a museum dedicated to his life and works. His grave is nearby. In a grove of trees just south of the gardens is the First Division Museum, devoted to the history of the Big Red One from the Great War to the present. The exhibits include a life-sized diorama of the village of Cantigny, smashed up and ravaged, much like the 28th Infantry Regiment saw it as they took the village and held it. Military vehicles litter the woods in front of the museum, including an American-made M1917 tank. Based on the French FT-17 Renault tank, none of these U.S. knockoffs ever saw action in France. On the eastern end of the parade field, not far from Bertie's Coffee Shop, is a statue of a Doughboy—an exact replica of the Black Lions statue in Cantigny, France.

"Cantigny, in itself, was a small fight," conceded the victorious general, Robert Bullard, but in some ways it was one of the most important battles of the war. It was the first U.S. offensive, and it demonstrated that American soldier could indeed fight. American confidence soared. "It was a matter or pride to the whole A.E.F.," Pershing later wrote, that the Big Red One "displayed the fortitude and courage of veterans, held their gains, and denied the enemy the slightest advantage." Cantigny impressed the Allies as well, and gave them hope that victory could in fact be achieved. After Cantigny, calls for amalgamating American troops into Allied armies dropped off dramatically. Pershing was unsure if any of his other divisions were combat-ready, but he would soon find out. As significant as the Cantigny was, it was soon overshadowed by a bigger battle in a far more desperate situation. The German offensive of May 27 would throw even more American troops, partially trained, into the thick of the battle. For the AEF, it would be the ultimate test.

CHAPTER 8:
AMERICANS ON THE MARNE

Ludendorff's northern offensives of 1918 had taken a lot of territory, but had failed to knock the British out of the war. On May 27, he launched another assault, Operation Blücher-Yorck, in the Chemin des Dames region northwest of Reims along the Aisne River. Originally meant simply to pull French reserves away from the north—the Germans knew the French would defend Paris at all costs—the attack was more successful than Ludendorff expected. In just a few days, the Germans had advanced sixty kilometers, putting them just sixty kilometers from Paris. "The opportunity seemed too good to miss," wrote historians Robin Prior and Trevor Wilson, and Ludendorff decided to make Paris his main effort. The Marne River, which flowed west and emptied into the Seine just south of Paris, was of critical strategic importance. If the Germans could control the Marne Valley, the gates to the French capital lay wide open. For the Allies, there was now no choice but to send in untested American troops, and the Doughboys played a crucial role in stopping the offensive. Indeed, this engagement, known as the Second Battle of the Marne, may have been the turning point in the war. American military records divide the operations into two distinct phases. The Marne Defensive involved halting the Germans at the Marne. The Aisne-Marne Offensive meant pushing them back.

As German forces raced toward the Marne, Pershing handed over two divisions to Foch, neither of which had any significant combat experience. The 2nd Division, under the command of General Omar Bundy, was stationed near Chaumont-en-Vexin north of Paris when the attack occurred; it had been preparing to replace the 1st Division at Cantigny. On May 30, the division got word that it was headed to the front. At 5:00 AM the following morning, its members boarded a fleet of trucks and headed to Meaux, a city on the Marne that lay in the path of the German advance. It was a chaotic scene. The men boarded trucks driven by Vietnamese, who raced down narrow roads clogged with refugees fleeing the German advance. "Lucky if we don't get killed before reaching the front," wrote one officer. James Harbord, Pershing's former chief of staff who had recently been promoted to general and given command of the marine brigade of the 2nd Division, reflected on the sad trail of refugees in his diary. "Men, women, and children hurrying toward the rear; tired, worn, with terror on their faces," he wrote, some "driving carts piled high with their little possessions," and a few with "little flocks of sheep, occasionally a cow, and sometimes a crate of chickens on a cart." The division reached Meaux by nightfall. Today the city is home to the Musée de la Grande Guerre, which opened in 2011 and immediately became one of the most impressive of all World War I museums. One gallery pays tribute to the American role in the war. Just north of the museum is a monument that the American Friends of France erected in 1932, marking the farthest German advance in the First Battle of the Marne in 1914. From Meaux, the 2nd Division was assigned to the French Sixth Army and hastily assembled a defensive line in the hills and farms west of Château-Thierry on June 1.

The 2nd Division had spent some time training at the front along the Saint-Mihiel Salient, but the other division called up, the 3rd, had practically no frontline experience at all. The division had been organized at Camp Greene, North Carolina, in 1917, but its various elements trained at ten other installations across the United States. The division did not come together until it reached the training area at Châteauvillain in the Haute-Marne region in 1918. The 6th Engineers had seen some action with the British in northern France (see Chapter 16), but nearly all the rest had only walked through a trench at training camp. Commanding the division was General Joseph T. Dickman. A member of the West Point Class of 1881, Dickman was one of the army's most experienced and well-traveled officers. He had served in the Apache Wars in Arizona, and had fought at San Juan Hill in Cuba. In Asia, he had seen action in the Philippines and during the Boxer Rebellion in China. The 3rd Division also got word on May 30 that it was being thrown into the fight, and immediately boarded Ford trucks heading up to the Marne.

The first American unit to get into the fight was the 7th Machine Gun Battalion of the 3rd Division. After traveling for twenty-four hours over 117 kilometers of dusty and bumpy French rural roads, the battalion arrived in the streets of Château-Thierry in the late afternoon of May 31, 1918. A city of 8,000 straddling the Marne, Château-Thierry lies eighty kilometers from Paris. Its military history is a long one. Romans, Huns, English, Spanish, Prussians, and Russians have all marched through its streets. The Germans held it briefly in 1914 before pulling back. Château-Thierry derives its name from the ruined castle on the hill above the town. During the 8th Century, Frankish strongman Charles Martel held King Thierry IV prisoner there. The Marne flows east to west through the city, and it was the two bridges that crossed the river there that gave the city its military significance. The western bridge, located in the heart of town, was part of Château-Thierry's main north–south thoroughfare. The roadway running north from the bridge was called rue du Pont. (Renamed rue du Maréchal Pétain after the war, it is now rue Charles de Gaulle.) The market square and the city are just a few hundred meters north of the bridge, and the castle ruins just beyond that. To the south, rue Carnot led from the bridge to the countryside south of town. Upstream, about a kilometer to the east, a railroad bridge spanned the river, connecting local farmers to the rail hub on the south side of the city. Retreating French forces wanted those bridges to evacuate to the safety of the Marne's south bank. The Germans, meanwhile, wanted to establish a bridgehead across the Marne on their way to Paris.

As darkness fell, the 7th Machine Gun Battalion took up positions along the south bank of the Marne between the two bridges, placing their guns in the windows of riverfront buildings or in hastily erected barricades. One detachment of Americans, under Lieutenant John T. Bissell, a recent West Point graduate, joined French forces on the north side of the river to help cover the French withdrawal. Bissell's men set up their machine guns in a circular medieval tower at a crossroads about 300 meters northeast of the western bridge, and prepared for the Germans to come. They did not have to wait long. As the American machine-gunners and French infantry prepared their defenses during the night of May 31, German artillery rained down on Allied positions, and German troops filtered into the northern fringes of the city. From the predawn hours of June 1 and all through the day, fighting raged in the hills and woods north of town. American machine-gunners near the eastern bridge poured lead into German infantry formations advancing along the north side of the river toward the city. By evening the Germans had taken the chateau, giving them a commanding position above the city streets. By early evening, vicious house-to-house fighting developed in the market square, and the Germans threw up barricades across rue du Pont. They were within meters of the west bridge. The Germans even converted the city's clock tower into a machine-gun nest. By nightfall on June 1, much of the once-picturesque town was battered into dust and rubble. The Allies fought valiantly, but by the end of the day their grip on Château-Thierry was untenable. French engineers prepared to blow up the bridges to prevent the Germans from using them.

Sometime around midnight, Bissell and his men joined the withdrawal back across the Marne and headed for the western bridge. Unbeknownst to them, German forces had gathered in considerable strength at the northern foot of bridge and were preparing to drive across to the south bank. French engineers blew up the bridge before the Germans could reach it, inadvertently killing some Senegalese troops crossing the span. The premature explosion also left Bissell and his men stranded. When Bissell's party arrived on the scene, the blown-up bridge was just one of their problems. German machine guns opened up on them. Bissell and a rag-tag collection of stranded French and American survivors made their way under fire through the ruins to the eastern railroad bridge. Here the American gunners, unable to tell who was approaching the bridge in the darkness, began shooting. As both enemy and friendly fire raged all around him, Bissell shouted over the din to the Doughboys on the south bank, convincing them to hold their fire as he and about thirty other U.S. and French soldiers escaped across the bridge. That bridge was blown up hours later. For his actions, Bissell received the Silver Star. After the war he made the army his career, and during World War II, General Bissell served as artillery commander for the 89th Infantry Division as it rolled into Germany.

The battalion held its position on the south bank for several more days, enduring punishing artillery barrages and snipers, but the Americans could not be budged. Enduring heavy combat after many days with no sleep and little food, the 7th Machine Gun Battalion played a critical role in preventing the Germans from crossing the Marne at Château-Thierry and blunting Ludendorff's offensive. For more than a year, the Allies had waited anxiously for the Americans to get into the fight, and when the moment finally came the Doughboys delivered. The remainder of the 3rd Division arrived in short order, and took up positions along the south bank of the Marne from Château-Thierry eastward.

The ruined bridge at Château-Thierry, France, by war artist Lester G. Hornby, 1918. (Courtesy of the National Archives)

Today a small city of 15,000, Château-Thierry rose from the ashes of the Great War. Residents repaired or replaced the damaged buildings, and rebuilt the two bridges. Remnants of the bridge blown up in 1918 became sacred war relics, and some of them ended up in the United States. One is today in New York City on the grounds of the Bronx County Clerk's Office at the corner of East 161st Street and the Grand Concourse—just three blocks from Yankee Stadium. Sadly, Château-Thierry suffered significant damage during World War II. As Nazi troops approached the city, the French once again blew up the bridges, though this time doing so failed to stop the invaders. After World War II the west bridge was reconstructed yet again, but the railroad bridge was not. Despite the ravages of two world wars, visitors today can still see portions of the Château-Thierry the Doughboys once knew. The castle ruins still crown the city. Lieutenant Bissell's stone tower still stands at the bend in the road where avenue Joussaume Latour becomes rue de la Barre. At the riverfront, the Palais de Justice at the corner of avenue de Soissons and avenue Jules Lefebvre near the riverfront survived, and the city hall still overlooks the market square. At the foot of avenue de Soissons on the north bank of the river is a small granite monument decorated with carvings of Poilu accoutrements and capped with a French combat helmet. Known as a *Borne Vauthier*, it is one of 120 such markers erected in the 1920s to mark the front lines as they stood at the German high-water mark of July 1918. The project was the brainchild of French sculptor and World War I veteran Paul Moreau-Vauthier, who designed the monuments and persuaded the touring clubs of France and Belgium to finance and erect them. Visitors to Western Front battlefields today are likely to encounter any number of the ninety-seven that still exist. The one in Château-Thierry is the oldest of them all, dedicated on November 10, 1921. The fact that the monument lies on the north side of the Marne is due in no small part to the work of the U.S. Army's 7th Machine Gun Battalion during those uncertain days in June 1918.

Château-Thierry remembers its American defenders in several ways. After the war the plaza in front of the Palais de Justice, known as the Champ de Mars, was renamed place des États-Unis. Today, it is little more than a parking lot. At the east end of the plaza stands a statue of French poet and hometown boy Jean de la Fontaine. After World War I, this was the site of a memorial to the 3rd Division. The 1940 destruction of the bridge irreparably damaged the memorial, but after World War II a new one was built about 200 meters to the west on avenue Jules Lefebvre. The new monument commemorates the division's role in both world wars—the division fought in southern France during World War II. Just across the street from the Fontaine statue at 2 place des États-Unis is the Maison de l'amitie Franco-Américain, or the House of Franco-American Friendship.

The institution originated with the Methodist Episcopal Church in the United States, which pledged to help France rebuild after the war. The church purchased an old hotel on the site and converted it into a community center and war memorial museum. The original structure was razed in 2009, and is currently being rebuilt into a much larger facility. The Methodists no longer run the museum, but they still have a presence in Château-Thierry. On the market square just a few steps from the city hall is the American Memorial Church, opened in 1924. A bas-relief sculpture above the entrance depicts an angel blessing a Doughboy and a Poilu, and the stained glass windows include a romanticized portrayal of General Pershing's arrival in France. The church is normally open only on Sundays.

The Marines Prove Their Mettle at Belleau Wood

The Germans failed to cross the Marne at Château-Thierry, but Paris was far from safe. A few kilometers west of the city the advance continued. In the first few days of June, the hamlets of Vaux, Bouresches, and Belleau fell into German hands. Most importantly, the Germans seized a prominence known on military maps as Hill 204, which offered a commanding position above Château-Thierry, the Marne, and the nearby countryside. On June 1, Franco-American forces under the command of French General Jean DeGoutte hastily established a jagged resistance line west of Château-Thierry. The U.S. 2nd Division held a critical portion of that front. Its 3rd Brigade dug in from a point south of Vaux, across the main Paris-Metz highway (present-day D1001) to Triangle Farm, roughly one kilometer south of Bouresches. The line of the 4th Brigade, made up of U.S. Marines, extended from Triangle Farm west along a low ridge just north of Lucy-le-Bocage, then curved northwest into the woodlands toward Campillon. In front of the marines lay a wooded ridge that once served as the hunting ground of a local nobleman. Known as the Bois de Belleau, Americans referred to it by its anglicized name, Belleau Wood. Today's A4 expressway, which cuts across the battlefield area, roughly marks the boundary between the American brigades. As the Americans established their lines, French troops fighting a rear-guard action passed through their positions. The first fighting between the Germans and the Americans took place at Triangle Farm on June 2, and intensified over the next several days as each side jockeyed for the most advantageous ground. German commanders, upon learning that they were facing untested Americans, urged their men to fight with particular vigor to break Doughboy morale. The Americans were just as eager to prove themselves as warriors. When a retreating French officer told Captain Lloyd Williams of the U.S. Marines that he and his men should pull back with him, Williams allegedly retorted, "Retreat? Hell, we just got here." The words became legend throughout the AEF. The fighting along the 2nd Division front "was very bitter," according to *American Armies and Battlefields in Europe*, "and the casualties on both sides were out of all proportion to the amount of ground which finally changed hands."

By June 5, DeGoutte and Bundy agreed that the time had come for a counterattack. The onus fell on Harbord's marines, who attacked in two phases. The first came at 3:45 AM on the morning of June 6. Supporting a French attack to their west, the 5th Marines went over the top, heading for a high spot known as Hill 142 southwest of Torcy. The marines were on the hill and in the nearby woods by 8:00 AM, and held it in the face of determined counterattacks. Then at 5:00 PM, attacks came against the village of Bouresches and the Belleau Wood. Allied commanders believed that only a handful of German troops occupied the woods, and saw the operation as a simple one. The Americans fought bravely and enthusiastically, but they also showed their inexperience. Attacking the woods from the south and west, the marines charged across open wheat fields in line, as one might have seen in the American Civil War. "They fought the way men fought in the West Wood near Antietam," wrote historian Edward M. Coffman, "and in the little clump of trees on Cemetery Ridge at Gettysburg." Such tactics resulted in extraordinarily heavy casualties, and by sundown the gains were disappointing. The Americans held just fragments of the southern portion of Belleau Wood, which the Germans contested fiercely. One bright spot was the fact that the 6th Marines took Bouresches. All told, the marines took 1,087 casualties that day.

Marine attacks in Belleau Wood resumed the next day, and the next, but the Germans gave little ground. On June 9, the marines temporarily withdrew from the woods and saturated them with artillery. When they went back on the following day, the Germans were still there, fighting as tenaciously as ever. Every tree and stump, every trench and shell hole, were bitterly contested. Machine guns and artillery did their bloody work, but combat was often hand-to-hand. "In the fighting that now confronts us, we are not concerned about the occupation or non-occupation of this or that unimportant wood or village," one German commander told his men, "but rather with the question as to whether Anglo-American propaganda that the American Army is equal or even superior to the Germans, will be successful." The 7th Infantry Regiment of the 3rd Division was brought in to help the marines, but progress was still painfully slow. By June 11, the Americans firmly held the southern portion of the woods. It took another two weeks before American forces had cleared the woods and controlled them in their entirety. The Germans were impressed with the tenacity of the marines. One German after action report called

Marine Corps recruiting poster. The marines earned the nickname "Devil Dogs" after the fierce fight at Belleau Wood in June 1918. (Courtesy of the National Archives)

them "vigorous, self-confident, and remarkable marksmen." According to legend, some of the 1,600 German prisoners taken in the woods referred to their captors as *Teufelhunde*, or "Devil Dogs," because of their fighting prowess. The story is most likely apocryphal, but it was a name the marines gleefully appropriated.

Soon after the battle, France officially renamed the site the *Bois de la Brigade de Marine* (Marine Brigade Woods), but it is the name Belleau Wood that lives on in American military annals. For the U.S. Marine Corps, it instantly became sacred ground. The American Battle Monuments Commission now controls 200 acres of the woodlands where most of the fighting occurred. The trees have grown back over the last century, but the forest floor is still pockmarked with countless shell holes and etched with the remnants of trenches. The tall oaks shading visitors today are survivors of the battle. Locals refer to them as "the Veterans," and—at least so the story goes—woodsmen refuse to cut them because they are filled with bullets and shrapnel. The Marine Memorial stands in a clearing in the center of the woods. Sculptor Felix de Weldon created this bronze relief of a shirtless, rifle-toting marine on a black marble slab, which was dedicated in 1923. De Weldon's association with the marine corps only grew after World War II, when he designed the famous Marine Corps War Memorial, based on Joe Rosenthal's immortal photograph of the flag-raising on Iwo Jima, and which now stands outside Arlington National Cemetery. Artillery pieces from the battle surround the memorial, and a few steps away is a series of brass plaques placed by a United States Marine Corps (USMC) officer training class in 1998. Dramatically situated near some shell holes, the plaques contain a map and texts that give a narrative of the Battle of Belleau Wood. Numerous hiking trails cross through the woods, and Belleau Wood can be a sylvan delight. The distance that it took the marines the better part of a month to cover can be walked in little more than twenty minutes. Birds sing and squirrels rustle across the forest floor, but the sight of a trench line jolts the hiker back to the historical realities of this place. Standing at the western edge of the woods one can look over the fields and get a sense of what the Germans saw as the marines charged toward them Civil War-style on June 6, 1918.

The surrounding countryside contains other reminders of the battles around Belleau Wood, though the casual observer is likely to miss them. For example, a weathered old pear tree stands forlornly at the crest of a ridge along the D82 highway just north of Lucy-le-Bocage, along what was once the front line of the 2nd Division. As a nearby interpretive panel explains, American troops killed in Belleau Wood were temporarily buried underneath this tree. Indeed, the panel contains an image of the improvised cemetery, and goes on to note that during World War II the German occupiers used this ridge as an aerial observatory.

Marine Corps Memorial in Belleau Wood, France.

In the village of Bezu, eight kilometers southwest of Lucy-le-Bocage, the local fifteenth-century church served as a field hospital during the fight at Belleau Wood. Lieutenant Colonel Richard Derby, surgeon with the 2nd Division (and son-in-law of Teddy Roosevelt) recalled the scene inside the church late in the evening on June 6:

> The interior presented a weird and somber picture. The whole floor space, except for three aisles running the length of the church, was filled with blanketed figures lying upon stretchers. The church was lit by candles upon the altar and pulpit railing. The chancel was occupied entirely by prisoner wounded, placed there for the ostensible purpose of guarding against their escape. This refinement in their security was hardly necessary judging from the serious nature of their wounds. Seated on a bench against one of the side walls was a long row of slightly wounded men.

Derby's descendants later donated money to restore the church bell tower. A plaque inside the church notes its role in the Great War, and thanks the Derby and Roosevelt families for their generosity.

Travelers might also notice large white boulders with a star embossed on them scattered across the area. After the war, the 2nd Division veterans placed the cement boulders to mark the places they fought. Some are well maintained, and still bear a plaque noting the dates the division was in the area. Others are in various states of disrepair. Being the site of the division's first major campaign, the area around Belleau Wood has several of these memorials. Some mark the starting line for the division in that campaign. One of them stands near a lonely bus stop just east of the hamlet of Le Thiolet along the D1001 highway. Another graces a pleasant little park in the center of Lucy-le-Bocage. Others track the division's movements. There is a memorial at the edge of Belleau Wood, for example, on the road connecting Bouresches and the village of Belleau. Another one is just north of Bouresches. This particular boulder is located on rue du Lieutenant Osborne. A navy dentist attached to the 6th Marines, Lieutenant (Junior Grade) Weedon Osborne, received a posthumous Medal of Honor for his heroic efforts evacuating the wounded near the village on June 6. Osborne plunged into the thick of the fight to evacuate the wounded, and was killed carrying an officer off the battlefield.

More Doughboys Get into the Fray

With Belleau Wood securely in U.S. hands, the heaviest fighting shifted eastward. On July 1, Franco-American forces launched another major assault in the area of the vital Hill 204. The 2nd Division drew the assignment of taking the village of Vaux at the base of hill. To avoid the intelligence failures that made Belleau Wood such a bloody affair, the Americans planned the Vaux operation to the letter. The locations of the German troops were meticulously tracked. Refugees were questioned about the layout of the village in great detail, so that invading troops knew the location of each street, house, barn, and garden plot. "Every platoon and squad leader . . . was given a map of the town," remembered William Brown, "with the particular cellar his squad was to capture, designated in red ink." After twelve hours of artillery preparation, the assault commenced at 6:00 PM. "In twenty-five minutes," Brown recalled, "we had taken the village and advanced our line about a thousand yards." The operation cost the Americans 200 casualties. The Germans lost about 300 killed and 600 captured. The Doughboys were elated. "This was my first real battle," wrote Brown, "and it really meant more to me than any of the others." A 2nd Division boulder on the east edge of the village is the only reminder of the American action there today.

On July 9–10 the 26th "Yankee" Division relieved the battered and bruised 2nd Division at the north edge of Belleau Wood. In a little more than a month, the 2nd Division lost 9,000 killed, wounded, captured, or missing. Given the intelligence and tactical mistakes, the battle was more costly than it should have been. More marines died at Belleau Wood than had been lost in the USMC's entire history up to that point. However, American troops had played a significant role in blunting the German advance in a major engagement, and once again proved their battle worthiness.

American confidence skyrocketed. The Germans began to appreciate that they had acquired a powerful new enemy.

The American presence was just one of many reasons the German offensive on the Marne had failed. Logistical problems, the ravages of influenza, and determined French resistance also took their toll. Despite the setback at Belleau Wood, Ludendorff still saw the opportunity to win the war, and in July he launched two more offensives. On July 8, the Germans attacked in Picardy between Montdidier and Noyon in an attempt to pressure Paris from the north. The offensive sputtered out quickly. The other, which the Germans dubbed the *Friedensturm*, or "Peace Offensive," came on July 15 on both sides of Reims. An important rail and road junction, Reims was at the center of a salient that stuck out like a thumb into the German lines. Capturing it would help the Germans shorten their lines, relieve logistical problems, and provide a better springboard to Paris. All efforts to take Reims frontally had failed, so Ludendorff planned a pincer movement to surround it. Simultaneous attacks would occur in the Champagne region to the east of Reims and along the Marne to the west, with the two wings meeting up south of Reims.

Crucial to the German plan was the Surmelin River, which emptied into the Marne ten kilometers east of Château-Thierry near Moulins. The Surmelin Valley provided the Germans an avenue through the hilly terrain along the south bank of the Marne, crucial to their planned envelopment of Reims. The Marne-Surmelin confluence resembles a capital T, with the Surmelin running vertically south to north and the Marne capping it horizontally east to west. Rich bottomlands bordered the Marne, and a railroad line snaked across the fields near the south bank. Two bluffs stood high above the Surmelin. On the east side was the Moulins Ridge, offering a commanding position over both the Marne and the Surmelin. The high ground to the west was known as the Bois d'Aigremont. Defending the Surmelin Valley was the U.S. 3rd Division, under General Joseph T. Dickman, who organized a defense in depth. Soldiers along the banks of the Marne stood ready to contest any German river crossing, but Dickman also fortified the bluffs bracketing the Surmelin to control movement along its banks. He established several more defensive lines father upstream to slow any advance through the valley. Dickman's plan was sound, though it stretched his troops dangerously thin. To the right of the 3rd Division was the French 125th Division, along with elements of the American 28th Division training with them.

Allied intelligence had learned of Ludendorff's imminent offensive, so as German infantry marshaled on the north bank of the Marne on the evening of July 14, Allied artillery hit them with a vicious barrage, slowing but not stopping their plans. The German guns answered just after midnight, and troops crossed the Marne on boats and pontoons just after 2:00 AM. During the early morning hours of July 15, particularly brutal fighting took place in the bottomlands near the hamlet of Mézy, especially along the railroad line. The Yanks put up a courageous defense. Some infantry companies were nearly wiped out. Valiant though they were, the Americans could only slow Ludendorff's men. The German river crossings near Varennes were more successful, and by afternoon the Germans were inching their way up the Surmelin Valley. To the east, the French 125th Division had given up ground as well. Indeed, east of the Moulins Ridge the Germans had penetrated more than five kilometers in some places. But in the crucial Surmelin Valley, Dickman's troops held. After two days the Germans had slogged their way to the northern fringes of Connigis, but could go no further.

Doughboys also helped to slow the momentum of the *Friedensturm* in Champagne (see Chapter 15), and Ludendorff's fifth and final offensive ended in failure like all the rest. For its dogged defense of the Surmelin Valley, as well as its equally courageous stand at the Château-Thierry bridges, the 3rd Division earned the nickname "Rock of the Marne." Despite the importance of the Surmelin Valley to American military history, and indeed to the Allied cause in World War I, there are almost no memorials to the Doughboys in the valley today. On the sidewalk in front of the mayor's office in Moulins (27 avenue Champagne) is a brass plaque on a low granite base commemorating the role of the 38th Infantry Regiment, which held the Moulins Ridge above the village.

The Aisne-Marne Offensive

Foch had been planning a counteroffensive before the *Friedensturm*, and as Ludendorff's July 15 attack faltered, he scheduled his strike for July 18. The plan involved several coordinated assaults. The main thrust would come from the French Tenth Army against the west face of the German salient between the Aisne and Ourcq Rivers. At the same time, the French Sixth Army would hit the nose of the salient west of Château-Thierry, and the French Fifth Army would strike the east face. The assault was dubbed the Aisne-Marne Offensive, and the U.S. Army would be a big part of it.

By July 1918 the AEF had grown to one million men, with 10,000 arriving at ports like Brest and Liverpool every day. Pershing had new divisions becoming available, and he threw the best of what he had into the fight. After more than a year of building up and preparing its forces, the United States was finally in a position to impact the course of the war.

The Tenth Army struck at 3:45 AM on July 18 south of Soissons. Spearheading the attack was the French XX Corps, which contained two battle-tested U.S. divisions, the 1st and 2nd. The Big Red One's line of departure was about two kilometers east of Coevres-et-Valsery. The 2nd Division, now commanded by General Harbord, began farther south from the Forêt de Retz. Between them was the 1st Moroccan Division, which included a regiment of the French Foreign Legion. XX Corps had several objectives. One was to cut important German communication lines. The main Soissons-to-Paris rail line traversed the area, as did the Soissons-to-Château-Thierry highway (the present-day D1), which the Germans found vital for moving men and equipment behind their lines. The highway ran across the high ground south of Soissons, which was the second major objective. From these hills, Allied artillery could threaten the entire German pocket. This high ground also provided an excellent launching pad for an assault deep into German lines, which could allow the Allies to hit the rear of the German forces along the Marne and envelop them. Reaching the objectives would not be easy. While much of the area consisted of rolling wheat fields, sharp ravines cut across the XX Corps line of advance, giving the Germans excellent defensive positions.

To keep the American presence a secret, the Doughboys only reached the line of departure during the night of July 17–18. Elements of the 2nd Division did not arrive until just minutes before the attack, scrambling through the dark and rainy woods to reach the starting line. The attack commenced at 3:45 AM as scheduled. Artillery preparation was minimal, but more than 500 French tanks went forward with the infantry. Germans troops were caught off guard, and at first the attack went well, as the Franco-American forces waded through fields of waist-high wheat. By 7:00 AM the 1st Division reached its first major obstacle, the Missy Ravine and the village of Missy-aux-Bois at its head. Here the division met stiff resistance, both in the ravine and on the high ground to the east of it known as Hill 166. By this time most of the French tanks had been knocked out, forcing the infantry to fight without significant armor support, stymieing the rapid advances of the early morning. The 2nd Division penetrated as far as Vierzy, eight kilometers from its starting point, successfully cutting the rail line but also getting bogged down in a sharp ravine.

Recovering from their initial shock, the Germans stiffened their resistance on the second day, and each division gained little more than a kilometer. After having taken 4,000 casualties in two days, the exhausted 2nd Division was relieved in the early morning hours of July 20 just shy of the village of Tigny. The 1st Division fought on. By July 21 it had severed the Soissons-to-Château-Thierry highway, reached the high ground above the village of Buzancy, and held on in the face of German counterattacks. In three days, the Big Red One had taken 7,000 casualties.

The Soissons operation was a great success, though the casualties were enormous. "Battalions looked like companies," noted General Beaumont Buck, one of 1st Division's battalion commanders, "[and] companies looked like squads." French soldiers thought the Sammies still had a lot to learn. "They don't take sufficient care," remarked Pierre Teilhard de Chardin, a stretcher-bearer in the 1st Moroccan Division, "they're too apt to get themselves killed." Teilhard de Chardin nonetheless admired their fighting spirit. "They're first-rate troops," he hastened to add, "fighting with intense *individual* passion . . . and wonderful courage." He especially admired how the wounded "hold themselves upright, almost stiff, impassive, and uncomplaining. I don't think I've ever seen such pride and dignity in suffering." At the intersection of the D1 and D1240, just west of Buzancy, is a 1st Division memorial to mark its triumph. A 2nd Division boulder lies on the west end of Tigny, marking that unit's farthest advance.

The French Sixth Army also attacked on the morning of July 18 west of Château-Thierry. This operation marked an important first in the history of the AEF—an American corps occupied a segment of the Western Front. The U.S. I Corps took control of a section of the front line west of Château-Thierry on July 4. The date was not coincidental. It consisted of just two divisions, the U.S. 26th Division and the French 167th, under the command of American General Hunter Liggett. Some thought that the portly sixty-one-year-old Liggett was physically incapable of a field command, but Pershing had complete trust in him. From their starting line at the northern edge of Belleau Wood, the Yankee Division attacked German positions in Torcy and the village of Belleau. The fighting was bloody and progress was slow. From their position on a hill north of Belleau known as Hill 193, the Germans made the New Englanders pay dearly for every inch of land they took that day. "I saw rows of wounded boys on stretchers," recalled Carroll Swan, "with every conceivable kind of wound—some with legs or arms blown away, some with eyes shot out, many with chins gone, others with every muscle in their bodies shaking as with palsy, shell-shocked, some with bodies burned by gas so badly that they were all black."

But Ludendorff quickly realized that his position on the Marne was untenable. The attack at Soissons had destroyed his most important communication lines in the salient, and his forces on the Marne faced envelopment. Allied armies, energized with fresh American troops, proved invincible. On the night of July 19–20, the Germans began a phased withdrawal from the Marne salient, setting up defensive lines along ridges and rivers to cover their retreat. The Allies followed in hot pursuit. By July 24, American and French troops reached the high ground above the Ourcq River, fifteen kilometers north of the Marne. The Yankee Division had pushed north and east from Belleau to the Forêt de Fére southeast of Beuvardes. East of Château-Thierry, the 3rd Division had cleared the Germans from the south bank of the Marne in their sector, and then pushed north of the river, reaching Le Charmel by July 24.

Pershing now put fresh new divisions into the fight. The 42nd "Rainbow" Division replaced the Yankee Division on the cold and rainy night of July 25–26. On the line less than a day, the Rainbow Division took on the Germans in a sharp and bloody fight at La Croix Rouge Farm, in the woodlands between Beuvardes and Fresnes-en-Tardenois. The farm lay directly in the path of the American advance, so the Germans beefed up their positions there, converting the farm buildings into a citadel and planting well-concealed machine-gun nests in the surrounding woods and fields. The day was cold and drizzly and German artillery pounded the Doughboys all day, but at 4:50 PM the 167th Infantry Regiment, a National Guard unit from Alabama, attacked from the woods to the west. In just fifteen minutes scores lay dead, the survivors pinned down in the open fields. An hour later they attacked again. The "rebel yell" rang out as the grandsons of Confederate soldiers charged across the muddy fields of France. By 7:00 PM the Alabamians had reached the ruins of the farm, and bloody hand-to-hand fighting erupted among its remains. Meanwhile, the 168th Infantry Regiment from Iowa pressed in from the south. The attack was poorly coordinated and the 168th took enormous casualties, but a few Iowans reached the farm as well. The day's drizzle turned into a steady rain as night fell, and the Doughboys gathered up their wounded in the muddy darkness while German artillery fell with the raindrops. The farm lay in disrepair for nearly a century, but in 2011 the Croix Rouge Farm Memorial Foundation erected a memorial on the site to honor the Alabama men who fought and died there. The site is on the D3 highway eight kilometers south of Fère-en-Tardenois. Dominating it is a bronze Doughboy, three meters high, holding a dead comrade in his arms, with clothes tattered and limbs hanging limply. Not far away is an ivy-covered wall, the only remnant of the farm buildings that witnessed such bloody combat. The countryside today appears much as it did back on July 26, 1918. The woods and fields remain in nearly the same configuration. Standing there on a cold, drizzly day, it is easy to imagine the horror that unfolded in the surrounding fields.

On July 27 the Germans pulled back behind the Ourcq. The Rainbow Division followed them to the banks of the river, but heavy artillery and machine-gun fire prevented their crossing that day. In the early morning darkness of July 28 the division got across the Ourcq, but with the Germans holding the high ground north of the river, gains were small and costly. For the next several days, fighting seesawed back and forth on the north bank of the Ourcq, and the casualty list grew precipitously. The 165th Infantry

Regiment—the former New York National Guard's "Fighting 69th"—experienced particularly fierce fighting at Meurcy Farm, south of Seringes-et-Nesles. Lieutenant Oliver Ames was reconnoitering German positions with his battalion commander, Major William Donovan, when a sniper hidden behind a dead horse shot him dead. At Meurcy Farm today, and the end of a road called Le Moulin Colas off the D2 highway, is a stone memorial to the young officer. Sergeant Joyce Kilmer was also victim of a sniper's bullet at Meurcy Farm. The promising young writer, famous for the poem "Trees" and who penned "The Rouge Bouquet" in honor of some fallen comrades (see Chapter 7), was scouting a German machine-gun position when he took a bullet clean through the head. There are several memorials to Kilmer in New York City today. On the Mall in Central Park, a tree is dedicated to the author of "Trees." Just north of the Bronx County Clerk's Office—and the piece of the Château-Thierry Bridge on its grounds—is Joyce Kilmer Park. The Garden State honors him too. On the New Jersey Turnpike near his hometown of New Brunswick is the Joyce Kilmer Service Area, and several schools across the state also bear his name. Kilmer memorials are not limited to New York and New Jersey. The Joyce Kilmer Memorial Forest preserves a patch of Appalachian woodlands near Robbinsville, North Carolina, 100 miles west of Asheville.

As the battle on the Ourcq intensified, more American divisions entered the fray. Just to the east of the Rainbow Division, the 28th Division relieved the French 39th Division near Courmont on July 28. A National Guard unit from Pennsylvania, the "Keystone Division," was training with the French west of the Surmelin Valley when the Germans crossed the Marne a few weeks before, and consequently some of its members had seen a little action. From Courmont, in conjunction with the 3rd Division on its right, the Pennsylvanians launched several attacks on a wooded highland called the Bois de Grimpettes beginning July 28. None succeeded. On July 30, the 32nd Division (Wisconsin and Michigan National Guard) relieved the 3rd Division, and joined the Pennsylvanians in its attack on the woods. The Bois de Grimpettes finally fell to the Americans, though the cost in blood was high. In just three days the Keystone Division took more than 1,400 casualties, and was withdrawn from the line. Assuming the front line of the 28th Division, the 32nd Division was able to press a few kilometers north the following day, taking the village of Cierges and digging in on the northern end of a patch of woods known as La Jomblets. The Bois de Grimpettes and La Jomblets are still discernible on the landscape today. The former is about 500 meters east of the D14 highway between Courmont and Cierges and visible from the roadside. The D14 cuts through the latter just north of Cierges. Both are now pleasant woods that give no indication of their bloody past.

During the night of August 1–2, the Germans pulled back to the Vesle River, roughly fifteen kilometers north of the Ourcq, with the American divisions once again following close behind. On the morning of August 2 the 32nd Division took the village of Chamery, where its members found the grave of Lieutenant Quentin Roosevelt, pilot and son of President Theodore Roosevelt, who had been shot down over the village on July 14 (see Chapter 11). The remnants of Roosevelt's plane were still lying near the grave but quickly disappearing. When Glen Garlock visited the site he noticed "souvenir hunters rapidly carrying away the remains of the plane." The Germans had apparently taken its control panel, but "inside of 48 hours our soldiers had removed everything left except the largest pieces of metal too big to carry or cut up." The 32nd Division pressed northward from Chamery, liberating the villages of Coulonges, Cohan, Dravegny, Saint-Gilles, and Mont Saint-Martin. By August 4 they reached the high bluff above Fismes, a small city on south bank of the Vesle, and moved into its streets that afternoon. French commanders marveled at the fierce and effective way the 32nd Division advanced to Vesle, and took to calling them *Les Terribles* (the terrible ones). On August 3, the 4th Division replaced the exhausted 42nd, which had taken 5,400 casualties since it entered the line on July 25. Elements of the Ivy Division (a play on words for the Roman numeral IV) fought on the left of the 32nd Division, taking the villages of Mareuil, Dôle, and Chéry-Chartreuve. They reached Saint-Thibaut on the Vesle on August 4. The Germans blew up the bridges over the Vesle, preventing an immediate American crossing.

With the Germans pushed back across the Vesle, the huge salient they opened up on the Allied lines on May 27 had effectively disappeared. The Aisne-Marne Offensive officially came to an end on August 6, though the fighting was far from over. Responsibility for the front at Fismes now fell to the American III Corps, the second U.S. corps to control a section of the front. It came under the command of General Robert Bullard, who led the 1st Division to victory at Cantigny. Bullard's goal was to establish a bridgehead across the Vesle, but the Germans had prepared a stubborn defense for him. On August 6, the 4th Division launched an assault across the river near Bazoches with the intent of cutting the highway along the north bank of the river (present-day N31). Bitter fighting continued for days in the wooded bottomlands along the river near an estate known as the Château du Diable, which changed hands several times during the fighting, but the Ivy Division was unable to establish itself on the north bank. A 4th Division monument stands today on the N31 highway roughly halfway between Fismes and Bazoches, marking the farthest point of its advance. On August 7 and again on the August 10, the 3rd Division attempted to cross the Vesle east of Fismes. The Germans turned back all of them.

The Keystone Division, replacing the 32nd, took some particularly heavy losses. The Pennsylvanians gained a foothold on the north bank of the Vesle on August 8 in Fismette—a village across the river from Fismes—and two days later controlled the entire village, but German counterattacks were unrelenting and Fismette was never entirely secure. On August 27, the Germans took it back. Using a box barrage, German artillery blocked the Doughboys' escape routes across the river, and entered the village in force with flamethrowers blazing. Only a few Americans managed to swim back across the river to U.S. positions on the south bank.

The Fismes area occupies a special place in Pennsylvania's war annals. The town of Meadville, Pennsylvania, forty miles south of Erie, placed a bronze plaque at the entrance to the Fismes town hall to commemorate the sacrifices of Company B, 112th Infantry Regiment, which originated in that community. In 1927, the Pennsylvania Battle Monuments Commission erected the 28th Division Memorial Bridge over the Vesle between Fismes and Fismette to honor its fallen sons in the fight along that river. On the Fismes side, two columns rise from either side of the roadway, each capped with a classical female figure. Artwork at the bases of the columns includes images of a buffalo, Doughboy faces, and the emblem of the 28th Division. Decorative brass lamps adorn the Fismette side. Philadelphia architects Thomas Atherton and Paul Philippe Cret designed the structure. Cret was a French-born architect who accepted a professorship at the University of Pennsylvania in 1903. Visiting France when the war broke out, he joined the French army and fought for his homeland. After the war he returned to Philadelphia and devoted much of his time and talent to designing U.S. war memorials. Indeed, he became a consulting architect for the American Battle Monuments Commission (ABMC).

Statue on the 28th Division Memorial Bridge at Fismes, France.

On August 18, Foch—by this time promoted to Field Marshal—launched another offensive against German positions north of Soissons. Dubbed the Oise-Aisne Offensive, direct American participation was not very extensive. The 32nd Division, now attached to the French Tenth Army, attacked the Germans at Juvigny on August 28. They seized the village on August 30, taking an important rail line from the Germans, and by September 2 had reached the Saint-Quentin-Soissons Road, cutting an important highway. The Oise-Aisne Offensive made the German positions north of the Vesle vulnerable, and the Germans began a fighting withdrawal back behind the Aisne River. The 28th Division reached Basilieux by September 4, and pressed on a bit beyond the village in subsequent days. The 77th Liberty Division—the first National Army division to participate in a major operation—pressed north across the Vesle, reaching Villers-en-Prayers on the Aisne by September 6. It took 4,600 casualties in the process. The 370th Infantry Regiment, an African American unit of the U.S. 93rd Division and attached to the French 59th Division, fought the Germans in the area of Vauxaillon during the middle and latter part of September (see Chapter 16). Its members were the last Americans fighting in the region. By September, the Germans had withdrawn to the starting line they had at the beginning of the Blücher-Yorck offensive in late May.

American Remembrance along the Marne

To commemorate America's role in the defense of the Marne, the ABMC erected a memorial on Hill 204 just east of Château-Thierry. Dedicated in 1930, the Château-Thierry American Monument is a roofed double colonnade of marble fifteen meters high and forty-five meters long running north–south among the woods and vineyards of the hill. On the west side of the monument, facing the forested hilltop, are two figures in classical garb, hand in hand, representing France and the United States. The dedication below— in French and English—states that the U.S. government built the monument "to commemorate the services of her troops and those of France," and to be "a last-ing symbol of the friendship and cooperation between the French and American armies." It was the brainchild of Franco-American architect Paul Cret, who wrote that his design was "inspired by Greek simplicity" but combined with "American traditions of the post-colonial period" and "the spirit of our own times." The sculptures

Château-Thierry American Memorial.

were the work of Frenchmen Alfred-Alphonse Bottiau, who like Cret, was a French army veteran of the Great War.

The east side of the monument overlooks the Marne Valley and the city of Château-Thierry. The bridge where the 7th Machine Gun

Battalion made its legendary stand is clearly visible, and off in the distance is the Surmelin Valley, where the 3rd Division, the "Rock of the Marne," made another heroic defense. A massive American eagle in Art Deco style adorns the monument's east face, and engraved in the stone below it is a map of U.S. operations during the battles along the Marne that summer. Below that is an orientation table, pointing toward the sites of important engagements and providing the distances to them in kilometers. One arrow points toward Château-Thierry, just two kilometers away; and another to Mézy, ten kilometers in the distance. Steps lead from the orientation table down to a great lawn, where one can have a contemplative walk through the grounds, look out over the Marne, or take in different perspectives on the colonnade. Above the austere square columns on all four sides of the monument are etched the names of places where the Doughboys fought and died, such as Belleau Wood, Bois de Grimpettes, Fismes, Mézy, and Vaux. Below the columns on the west face are the names of the American corps and divisions engaged in the Marne battles, as well as their unit emblems.

More than 8,000 American dead rest in two U.S. military cemeteries a short distance from Château-Thierry. Eight kilometers to the west of the monument, on the D9 highway, is the Aisne-

Chapel at Aisne-Marne American Cemetery, Belleau, France.

Marne American Cemetery at Belleau. The cemetery is located on the northern edge of Belleau Wood, right at the spot where the 2nd Division halted its advance through the woods and handed the front line over to the Yankee Division. The site was one of several makeshift burial grounds that army graves registration units established in the wake of the fight there. Congress selected the Belleau Wood location to be a permanent overseas cemetery in 1921, and construction began shortly thereafter. The prestigious Boston architectural firm of Cram & Ferguson designed the chapel and grounds. The William F. Ross Company, also of the Boston area, designed the exterior decorations, and Alfred-Alphonse Bottiau crafted them.

The cemetery is set back 200 meters from the D9 highway. A driveway, lined with trees and beautifully manicured flower beds, leads from the highway to the visitor center, where the traveler can find help locating specific graves or learn more about the battles in the vicinity. Beyond the visitor center is a plaza with two flag-staffs, and sweeping out in an arc on either side of the plaza are two fields of graves, following the curvature of the Belleau Wood hill. There are 2,289 headstones, 250 of which mark the graves of the unknown. One Medal of Honor recipient rests here, navy doctor Weedon Osborne. Anchoring the grounds is the Romanesque-

Column capitals depicting battle scenes, chapel of the Aisne-Marne American Cemetery, Belleau, France.

style chapel built of native limestone, which lies directly atop the old front line. Above the oak double doors is a relief sculpture of a medieval crusader, representing righteousness, in a tangle of oak branches. Shields representing France and the United States appear on either side of him. Decorative columns flank the doorway, with capitals depicting Great War combat scenes in Art Deco style—some Doughboys shoot rifles and machine guns, while artillery observers peer out toward their targets through binoculars. The chapel's exterior suffered some battle damage during World War II. Most

of the scars have been repaired, though a hole is still visible to the right of the entrance. Inside the chapel, in the alcoves on either side of the vestibule, the names of 1,060 soldiers and marines whose bodies were never recovered or identified line the walls, along with their units and home states.

The village of Belleau lies just north of the cemetery and hosts a number of sites of interest to the American traveler. Most notable is the 26th Division Memorial Church just

Stained glass window depicting a Doughboy and a *Poilu*, 26th Division Memorial Church, Belleau, France.

across the road from the cemetery. In the fight to liberate Belleau on July 18, the village church became one of the battle's casualties. After the war, Yankee Division veterans raised funds to rebuild it. Completed in 1929, it stands today as a memorial to the New Englanders. The names of the Yankee Division's dead are inscribed on the walls, and the stained glass windows highlight centuries of Franco-American amity. Washington and Lafayette stand side by side. So do a Doughboy and a Poilu. Jacques Marquette and Samuel de Champlain, French explorers of North America, appear as well. New England veterans' organizations still support the maintenance of this church. About 150 meters to its north is an easy-to-miss, knee-high fountain dedicated to Pennsylvanians who perished at Belleau Wood.

The village hall is located on small plaza in the center of town called the place du Général Pershing, and inside is the Musée de la Mémoire de Belleau (Belleau Remembrance Museum). The museum is small but worth a look, and it offers guided tours of the battlefields. Across the street is the chateau of the Count and Countess of Belleau, where a peculiar ritual of U.S. military culture takes place. On the grounds of the estate is a fountain with an old bronze spout in the image of a mastiff dog. Exactly how the ritual started has been lost in the mists of time, but somehow the legend emerged that any marine who drinks from this so-called "Devil Dog Fountain" will have his life extended by twenty years. The chateau grounds are closed to the public, but the count and countess allow U.S. Marines onto their property to drink from the fountain.

Twenty kilometers from the Château-Thierry memorial, and two kilometers east of Fére-en-Tardenois, near the village of Seringes-et-Nesles on the D2 highway, is the Oise-Aisne American Cemetery. Located at the heart of the Rainbow Division's fight to cross the Ourcq in July 1918, the cemetery began as a temporary burial ground for the division's dead. The visitor center is located on the south side of the highway, and the graves area lies to the north of it, on the slope of a hill looking over the Ourcq Valley. The cemetery is divided into four sections with a flagpole in the center, and well-groomed plane trees line the mall separating the quadrants. Oise-Aisne is the second largest of America's Great War overseas cemeteries. Most of the 6,012 buried here (597 of whom are unidentified) died in the fighting that along the Ourcq, Vesle, and Aisne Rivers that terrible summer. In addition, after the war many who perished of disease and accidents behind the lines were reburied here. Perhaps the most notable soldier resting on the grounds is the poet Joyce Kilmer, who met his end by a sniper's bullet just a few hundred yards from his final resting place. Overlooking the graves at the north end of the cemetery is the memorial, a semicircular peristyle of pink sandstone with a marble alter in the center. The peristyle columns are made of granite. Their capitals contain the emblems of the divisions that fought in the region, along with various soldier accoutrements—items ranging from a machine gun to a mess kit. At the right end of the peristyle is the chapel, containing the names of 241 men missing in action. At the left end is the map room, showing the progress of U.S. forces in the Aisne-Marne region. The friezes on the chapel's exterior contain the insignia of various army branches, as do the map rooms. Combat arms like infantry and artillery are represented, but so are branches like the Engineers, Signal Corps, and even the Inspector General. The U.S. Marine Corps and the American Field Service are represented as well.

The Second Battle of the Marne was a crushing defeat for Germany. In addition to the vast amounts of irreplaceable men and materiel Ludendorff expended on his failed grab for Paris, his hopes of victory before the Americans could get onto the battlefield in force were dashed. Not only did the American soldiers play a crucial

Oise-Aisne American Cemetery, Seringes-et-Nesles, France.

role defending the Marne, but thousands more poured across the docks and Brest, Saint-Nazaire, and Liverpool every day—each one another nail in the Kaiser's coffin. American success during the Second Battle of the Marne made Pershing's greatest dream finally come true. On August 19, 1918, the American First Army was officially formed, with Pershing at its helm. In early September, most American divisions packed up from their positions along the Aisne and headed back to Lorraine to take control of the front near Saint-Mihiel. Pershing could now shift from defense to offense. Since arriving in France in June 1917, Pershing had been planning for a decisive American offensive to win the war for the Allies. By August of 1918, the pieces of that plan were coming into place.

CHAPTER 9:
BEHIND THE LINES

After the brutal fight at Soissons, the 2nd Division received some well-deserved rest, but for General James Harbord, its commanding officer, the recuperative period did not last long. One day at lunch he received a call from Pershing's staff in Chaumont, asking him to come at once. It was an uncomfortable five-hour trip by automobile, and "all through the journey," Harbord recalled, "my mind was full of conjectures as to what could be the subject of the conference." Upon arriving at Pershing's residence, the "Big Chief" got right to the point. The Services of Supply (SOS), the branch of the AEF responsible for sustaining the Doughboys in the field, was not keeping up with demand and Washington was worried. As Pershing's chief of staff when the war began, Harbord won praise on both sides of the Atlantic for his administrative acumen. As a proven combat leader, he garnered great respect throughout the AEF. Pershing said he needed someone who could whip the SOS into shape, and "all these things pointed me out as the man for the place," Harbord wrote. Expressing a "heavy heart" at losing his division, he dutifully accepted the unglamorous but vital job. Many ordinary soldiers assigned to the SOS felt much the same way. As the lyrics of one song popular in the AEF went:

> Mother, take down your service flag,
> Your son's in the S.O.S.
>
> He's S.O.L., but what the hell,
> He never suffered less

By November 1918, 644,540 troops were assigned to the SOS—roughly one third of the AEF's total strength—engaged in the vital tasks of administration, procurement, construction, and distribution. Their work may not have provided the glory of battle, but the entire American war effort depended on them.

"Before a commander can even start thinking about manoeuvering or giving battle," wrote historian Martin van Creveld, "he has—or ought—to make sure of his ability to supply his soldiers." Pershing was well aware of this fact, and establishing a logistical system was one of his top priorities. He created a logistical command called the Line of Communication in July 1917, shortly after arriving in France.

Briefly renamed the Service of the Rear, the organization assumed the name Services of Supply in March 1918. The SOS was hardly a refuge for second stringers. Behind the lines, Pershing benefitted from some of America's top talent. The resume of his top railway engineer, Colonel William Wilgus, included designing New York's Grand Central Station. His chief procurement officer was General Charles Dawes, a prominent banker in civilian life who would later serve as Vice President of the United States under Calvin Coolidge. The SOS divided its operations into three geographic regions, each successively closer to the front. A base section was established around every major port bringing in supplies from the United States. Here the goods would be offloaded, sorted, and prepared for movement inland. From the ports, the supply chain moved toward the Intermediate Section, a vast area stretching across central France. Here troops stockpiled supplies, and performed a wide range of support services, from food service to motor repair. From there, supplies moved up to the Advance Section, where depots behind the front distributed supplies to forward units. The SOS made its headquarters at Tours, 200 kilometers southwest of Paris, in the Loire River Valley. Tours comprised its own special administrative district within the SOS command structure, as did Paris.

The Base Section Ports

Base Section No. 1 at Saint-Nazaire commenced operations on June 22, 1917—just days before the men of the nascent 1st Division arrived (see Chapter 1). A deep-water port at the mouth of the Loire River, Saint-Nazaire suited American purposes well. The port had five ship berths sheltered in two interconnected boat basins that France was willing to turn over immediately. Among them was the passenger terminal of the Compagnie Générale Transatlantique (CGT) on the Bassin Saint-Nazaire, which could accommodate the traffic in troops. In addition, smaller and lighter ships could proceed fifty kilometers upriver to Nantes, where four berths were available. From Saint-Nazaire, rail lines ran east to the American bases in Lorraine. Though nearly 700 kilometers from the port, the railway avoided the clogged and overburdened lines of northern France. The Americans quickly turned Saint-Nazaire into a beehive of activity. "Our army and navy engineers seized on that quiet French fishing village and made it something which the old inhabitants could not recognize," observed journalist Willis J. Abbot. The Americans went right to work improving port facilities, building piers and breakwaters, and erecting warehouses. Labor was a constant problem. Thousands of African American stevedore troops did the lion's share of the work on the docks (see Chapter 10), but they were hardly alone. Newly arrived soldiers destined for the front often took a turn at the docks.

The Bassin Saint-Nazaire by war artist Jules Smith. (From Jules A. Smith, *In France with the American Expeditionary Forces*, 1919)

French men were serving in the country's army, but French women sometimes worked in the shops. There were contract laborers from China and the French colony of Vietnam. German prisoners of war were a common sight as well.

American military installations quickly sprouted up around the city. Most important was Camp No. 1, located four kilometers west of Saint-Nazaire. Built for the 1st Division, which arrived in June 1917, the camp continued to serve as a transit point for the thousands who followed (see Chapter 6). It was the first of nine U.S. camps in the immediate environs of Saint-Nazaire. Most were located in the countryside west of the city, within a few kilometers of Camp No. 1. Camp No. 2, another transit facility, was located between rue de Pornichet and the ocean just south of Camp No. 1. Camp No. 3 occupied portions of what is now place du 19 Mars 1962, a park commemorating the end of the France's long war in Algeria, and was home to engineers. Just to the east was Camp No. 4, located north of rue de Pornichet at avenue de Lesseps. This camp was home to 8,000 African American stevedores, who marched daily from the camp to work on the docks. Today's Jardin de Plantes, a pleasant waterfront park, occupies a portion of the U.S. Army remount facility, through which 42,000 horses and mules passed on their way to AEF stations across France. Camp No. 7, located on present-day rue Jean Gutenberg north of Camp No. 1, was a reception center for motor vehicles, which were brought there from the docks to be uncrated, reassembled, and registered. A motor repair center, known as Camp No. 8, was near the intersection of boulevard Albert 1er and rue Benjamin Franklin on the waterfront. By 1918, the western fringe of Saint-Nazaire had become a veritable *Petit Amérique*.

Once off-loaded from ships, materiel had to be collected, classified, stored, and prepared to be sent farther inland. Several camps, mainly for engineering units, were closer to the docks. Camp No. 6 hosted a detachment of railway engineers. This small camp, according to the history of the 31st Railway Engineers, "consist[ed] only of four barracks in a corner of the Saint-Nazaire train yards" near the CGT passenger terminal. It was located along boulevard Paul Leferme about 100 meters north of the intersection with rue des Frères Pereire—named for the founders of the famous French shipping company. Two were located a bit farther north. Camp No. 5 was near the intersection of rue de Trignac and a street known today as Voie Américains. Camp No. 9, hosting a detachment of the 19th Engineers, was located north of the intersection of rue des Chantiers and avenue de Penhoët.

Today's Saint-Nazaire would be unrecognizable to the Doughboy. During World War II, the Germans demolished the docks of the Compagnie Générale Transatlantique and built a massive submarine complex there. The presence of the U-boats soon attracted streams of Allied bombers that obliterated most of the city. The devastation of World War II was so complete that upon rebuilding Saint-Nazaire the old street pattern was sometimes abandoned altogether. Saint-Nazaire has precious few buildings more than seventy years old, though oddly enough, one of them is the Nazi submarine complex, which withstood the bombers with its concrete roof eight meters thick. The very structure that prompted the city's destruction is now one of its major attractions, and hosts museums, restaurants, art exhibits, and a tourist information center within its cold, gray walls. One improbable survivor of the bombings is a U.S. Army refrigeration plant from the Great War, known locally as "le frigo," just south of the submarine pens, on boulevard René Coty. The building is still used for its original purpose, though it has been substantially altered over the years. The area north of the boat basins is today mainly industrial. The lands west of the city, where the Americans established the bulk of their camps, are now filled with quiet suburban streets. Driving past block after block of small single-family homes and apartment buildings, one sees not a trace of the U.S. presence, and there are no monuments or historical markers to identify the camp locations. The American monument commemorating the arrival of the 1st Division in 1917 (see Chapter 6) is the only overt indicator of the American presence in Saint-Nazaire during World War I.

The port facilities at Saint-Nazaire were overwhelmed within months of the American arrival, and ships backed up in the harbor waiting to be unloaded. To break the supply logjam, the army constructed a massive supply depot and docking facility at Montoir, a small town immediately east of Saint-Nazaire. Construction began in December 1917. Engineers leveled and filled four square miles of land along the riverbank, and then built row after row of warehouses. By the time of the armistice, the depot had 138 ware-houses providing 3,446,740 square feet of covered storage space. In addition, many items, such as coal, lumber, and metals, were stored in the open. An ingenious system of railroads, designed by Colonel Wilgus, integrated the entire complex. The rail complex included reception, classification, and storage yards, as well as a state-of-the-art repair facility. On its northwest end was a massive departure area dubbed the Wilgus Yard, where trains were prepared for the journey eastward. By November 1918, the Montoir storage facility contained 134 miles of tracks, making it perhaps the largest rail yard in the world at the time.

The Montoir storage depot hummed constantly with the com-ing and going of trains, and was continually expanding as Pershing geared up for his anticipated 1919 offensive. Captain J. F. Mollenkopf of the 17th Engineers reported that at the Montoir site "there are steam shovels, cranes, pile drivers, switch engines, concrete mixers, and all the other machines used in great construction jobs, even a saw and planing mill to cut and dress the lumber." Mollenkopf wrote that "the speed with which the Americans progressed" was "a constant marvel to the French population," and observed that "peas-ants come for miles to see the steam shovels devouring a hill and see track-laying gangs put down rails." In June 1918 construction began on a long pier into the Loire near the mouth of the Brivet River to bring goods directly from the ships into the facility. The pier was to be 3,230 feet long, 119 feet wide, and have eight berths for incom-ing ships. It was only half completed by the armistice of November 1918. Army engineers anticipated that the completed project would contain more than four million square feet of covered storage, nearly ten million square feet of open storage, and 268 miles of railroad tracks.

Virtually nothing remains of the Montoir storage depot. After the war, it was dismantled nearly as fast as it was built. Rail lines running across the area today only hint at the engineering accomplishments that once occupied this site. The level, wide-open spaces the U.S. Army created became the Saint-Nazaire airport. The giant European aircraft manufacturer Airbus now has an assembly plant where the Wilgus Yards once dispatched train after train to the Western Front. A few cement foundations of warehouses and other buildings still lie in the fields around the airport runway and adjacent private lands. Driving around the airport perimeter, one can still occasionally see some concrete footings or nondescript piles of cement rubble—the only physical remnants of the once-great storage yards. The Pont de Saint-Nazaire crosses the Loire at the approximate site where the American docking pier once jutted out into the river. Boulevard des Grandes Rivières (the D100 highway) roughly marks what was once the southern edge of the American depot. In the years after the war, the port of Saint-Nazaire reclaimed land south of that road from the river estuary and transformed it into expanded port facilities, as the giant lift cranes, warehouses, and storage tanks dominating the riverside indicate.

Still other communities in the Saint-Nazaire area saw an American invasion. U.S. Navy air stations at Le Croisic and Paimboeuf protected incoming convoys from U-boats (see Chapter 5). At Savenay, twenty-six kilometers east of Saint-Nazaire, Base Hospital 8 took over a local schoolhouse in September 1917. With its proximity to the ports of Saint-Nazaire and Nantes, the Savenay facility became an important link in the medical chain that brought sick and wounded soldiers from the front lines back to the United States. The hospital quickly outgrew the confines of the school, so the army built numerous outbuildings for the burgeoning facility. There were special psychiatric and tuberculosis wards, and a convalescent camp. By March 1919, nearly 62,000 patients had passed through Base Hospital 8, making it one of the biggest and busiest

U.S. Army hospitals in France. Most of the hospital buildings are now gone, replaced by residential housing, but the school building around which Base Hospital No. 8 grew still stands. The fieldstone structure is today the Lycée Jacques Prevert (17 rue Joseph Malegue). Affixed near the entrance to the school is a granite tablet in French, English, and German, noting the American Great War occupation of the school.

Lycée Jacques Prevert at Savenay, France, once home to the U.S. Army's Base Hospital No. 8.

The U.S. presence vastly overtaxed the existing local infrastructure. Saint-Nazaire's water system could not meet the increase in demand, for example, but once again American engineers tackled the problem. The army built a reservoir in the Bois de Joalland, a pleasant wooded area just to the west of the American camps. Some roads had to be moved and houses condemned, but when completed the reservoir held 1.5 million cubic meters of water—and still does. Known locally as the Étang du Bois Joalland, it is today a popular spot with Saint-Nazaire residents for hiking, boating, and fishing. But more water was needed. North of the city lay the Brivet River Valley, a marshy wooded area sprinkled with farms. The Americans saw the area as a fine source of water, but locals objected to losing prime agricultural land. The project went ahead when the U.S. agreed to dismantle the dams after the war. In the farmlands roughly fifteen kilometers north of the city, American engineers built several reservoirs for Saint-Nazaire. One, just northeast of Pontchâteau, was created with a one-meter-high dam made of shipping crates filled with stones. It was not pretty, but it provided 1.75 million cubic feet of water. American-built pumping stations all along the river valley then streamed the water toward Saint-Nazaire and Montoir. The Pontchâteau

Étang du Bois Joalland, an American-built reservoir, outside Saint-Nazaire, France.

reservoir is now gone. The area that once supplied the Doughboys with water is today the rich bottomlands that lie between the villages of Drefféac and Sainte-Anne-sur-Brivet. Two small Brivet Valley reservoirs remain: the Lac de la Roche-Hervé and the Étang du Gué aux Biches, located west of Saint-Gildas-des-Bois along the D2 highway. Base Hospital No. 8 at Savenay also needed water, and the Americans dammed the Mabille River just east of the village. This dam was not made of shipping creates, but cement, and held thirteen million cubic feet of water. That structure and reservoir are still there too. A pleasant 2.5-kilometer hiking trail hugs the wooded shoreline of the Lac de la Vallée Mabille, along which one can get a close-up look at the century-old American dam. To find it, drive east on rue du Lac from the center of the village.

By early 1919, roughly 60,000 Americans were stationed in the lower Loire region. Saint-Nazaire had civilian population of 40,000, but hosted 31,000 American troops. Savenay had 2,000 people, but hosted nearly 4,000 Americans. The U.S. hospital there had more beds than the village had residents. The numbers in Montoir were even more skewed, with 1,000 inhabitants in the village and 12,000 Americans in surrounding camps. Nantes had 10,000 Americans, but with civilian population of 180,000 their effects were much less pronounced. The American presence sometimes created tensions. Big-spending Sammies fostered inflation, for example, and their quest for alcohol and female companionship sometimes led to trouble. The rate of sexually transmitted diseases shot up in Saint-Nazaire soon after the Americans arrived. Prostitution was legal in France, and lusty Doughboys soon lined up at the city's *maisons tolérée*. A horrified Pershing declared the brothels off limits to U.S. troops, threatened the infected with court martial, and held officers directly responsible for disease rates among their men. The French thought the policy unrealistic and puritanical, and complained that placing the *maisons tolérée* off limits only encouraged the harassment of local girls, as well as the illicit sex trade that incubated disease. The situation in Saint-Nazaire reached the highest levels of government. French Prime Minister Georges Clemenceau offered to establish *maisons tolérée* for the exclusive use of U.S. troops. When Clemenceau's memo reached Secretary of War Newton Baker in Washington, he reportedly exclaimed: "For God's sake . . . don't show this to the president or he'll stop the war." Not all sex was of the commercial variety, of course. True love could also be found in the midst of war. In 1919, 19 percent of all marriages registered in Savenay were between Americans and local women. The same year, the figures were 21 percent in Saint-Nazaire and 22 percent in Montoir. Indeed, one should be careful not exaggerate the dimensions of Franco-American tensions. The French were genuinely glad to see the Doughboys, and found their enthusiasm and optimism inspirational after the long years of terrible war. As the plaque on the former hospital in Savenay states, the Americans "came as Allies and left us as friends."

The story of the Americans in Saint-Nazaire was repeated in the other base section ports. The second leading port for American shipping was Bordeaux (Base Section No. 2). Bassens, below Bordeaux on the Gironde River, was the largest port development project that AEF engineers undertook. Construction began in November 1917, just north of a pre-existing French dockyard and industrial facility. The American port received its first ship in April 1918, and by the armistice there were ten berths at the Americans docks, and another ten at the French. Railroad tracks went up to the riverbank, where state-of-the-art Gantry cranes scooped up cargo right from the ships and placed it into waiting rail cars. After the war the French took over the American facilities, and Bassens remains one of France's most important ports. The former American Great War docks lie on the northwest edge of the city. Bounded by railroads on the north, east, and south, rue Lavoisier runs through its center. Despite the U.S. contribution to the building of that port there is no monument to it and no obvious trace of the American presence.

From Bassens, trains brought the U.S. war goods eastward to the Saint-Sulpice Depot—Bordeaux's equivalent to Montoir. Carved out of vineyards above the Dordogne River between Saint-Sulpice et Cameyrac and Vayres, the depot had 110 warehouses, 2.6 million square feet of covered storage, 5.7 million square feet of open storage, and 92.6 miles of track. Once again, there is virtually no sign of the American presence today. The former depot grounds, split between the municipalities of Izon and Vayres, lie between avenue d'Izon on the north and the railroad tracks to the south. The site now hosts a French military base and an industrial area. A few vineyards are still there too. Eight kilometers west of the Saint-Sulpice depot was the Saint-Loubes Ammunition Depot. Located between the rail and the river east of the village of Saint-Loubes, the area was "almost equally divided between meadows and vineyards," according to one engineering report, "and traversed in all directions by drainage ditches." Warehouses for the explosives were spread far and wide in case of an accidental detonation, and the sprawling depot covered more than 500 hectares. Base Section No. 2 hosted numerous other American installations. Naval air stations lined the coast around Bordeaux (see Chapter 5), and army pilots trained in the area as well. Camp de Souge and Camp de Corneau trained artillery units (see Chapter 6).

Shortly after the war, France began construction on the Monument to the Glory of the Americans at the tip of the Pointe de Grave, where the Gironde meets the Atlantic. A memorial lighthouse seventy-five meters tall, it was dedicated to the memory of both the Marquis de Lafayette as well as American participation in the Great War. It was officially christened in 1938, and among those attending the ceremony was John F. Kennedy, the son of the U.S. ambassador to Great Britain. Sadly, the memorial stood fewer than five years. In 1942, German occupation forces blew it up, and put up some of their ubiquitous Atlantic Wall fortifications on the sandy spit of land. In 1947, a more modest monument replaced the massive original, which can be found just a few meters away along Allée du Sémaphore. In French, its inscription explains that this was the site of a larger monument. At the bottom in English, it reads: "They have destroyed it. We shall restore it."

By the time of the armistice, there were six other base section commands across Europe. The northern ports (Base Section No. 3, headquartered in London; Base Section No. 4, headquartered in Le Havre; and Base Section No. 5, headquartered in Brest) dealt mostly with troop traffic. Southern ports (Base Section No. 6, headquartered in Marseilles; Base Section No. 7, headquartered in La Rochelle, and Base Section No. 8, headquartered in Padua, Italy) mostly handled weapons and supplies. During the occupation of Germany after the war, Base Section No. 9 opened in Antwerp, Belgium. The AEF promoted a healthy competition among ports, awarding leave time to units that unloaded the most supplies in the shortest amount of time.

The Intermediate Section

From the base section ports, American lines of communication stretched inland into the Intermediate Section. Several corridors emerged, all based on existing rail lines. The main line went east from Saint-Nazaire through Saumur, Tours, Bourges, Nevers, and Dijon, then up to the Advance Section. From Bordeaux, American rail traffic went northeast through Perigueux, Limoges, Châteauroux, and joined with the main communication line at Bourges. From Brest, trains passed through Rennes and Le Mans to meet the main line at Tours. As a modern industrial nation, France already had a well-developed rail network. Indeed, it had a higher rail density per square mile than the United States. To speed up the American impact on the battlefront, France allotted certain rail routes for the exclusive use of U.S. forces, routes that would be run in an American way. The French rail system nevertheless posed many problems for the American military. For one, railroads in the southern and central parts of France had been neglected during the long years of war. Second, the French system operated rather differently from the American. Signals and switches were entirely different, as were traffic management practices. Locomotives and rolling stock were also dissimilar. The French used a hand break system, while the Americans used air brakes.

U.S. Army engineers undertook hundreds of construction projects to upgrade the French rail lines and make them conform to American standards. They built roundhouses, sidings, and switching facilities. To speed traffic, the Americans laid new tracks parallel to existing lines, or built cut-offs to shorten routes. They also set up locomotive and car repair facilities, the most important of which was located near Nevers, an important rail hub in the upper Loire Valley. In 1914, the Paris-Lyon-Méditerranée Railway was in the process of constructing a new repair facility along the tracks in the Nevers suburb of Vauzelles. When the war came it suspended the project, which was only 40 percent complete. In June 1917, the French offered the incomplete facility to the American army. "The proposition was quickly accepted," recalled Pershing's top railway engineer, Colonel William Wilgus. Work began that fall, but power and equipment shortages delayed completion. The locomotive repair shop began operations in June 1918 and the car repair shop three months later. Though the facility had the capacity to service 100 locomotives a month, Wilgus thought that figure inadequate, and laid plans to build another repair yard near Paris until the armistice saw them cancelled. The massive building that housed the repair facility still stands at 1 rue Benoît Frashon in the municipality now known as Varenne-Vauzelles. The French national railway maintains its trains there now.

Nevers was also the site of the army's most ambitious rail construction project, the Nevers Cut-Off. All train lines converged on the city center, leading to congestion, delays, and headaches for traffic managers. Commenced in June 1918 and completed in October, the eight-kilometer bypass began just south of the hamlet of Les Argougniaux and ran eastward through Plagny, across the countryside between Sermoise and Le Crot de Savigny, and on to the Loire. The project required cutting through bedrock in some places and raising the roadbed in others in order to make the tracks as level as possible. It also meant building a 427-meter-long bridge across the

Loire. Wooden support piles driven into the riverbed supported the steel-girder rail trestle above. The bypass shaved 13.5 kilometers and precious time off the trip to the front. After the war, the tracks were abandoned. Looking south from the D265 highway on the eastern edge of Les Argougniaux, one sees an ordinary-looking line of trees pointing northeast. This was the western terminus of the bypass. A short stretch of the D907A highway north of Sermoise follows the old rail route. Near its intersection with the D13 there is another line of trees trailing off to the northeast—another stretch of the old rail. A rustic dirt farm road called route du Pont des Américans follows the south bank of the Loire, and ends where the American bridge once spanned the river. When water levels are low, wooden pilings are still visible.

World War I occurred at the dawn of the Automobile Age, and trucks also helped to get war goods to the front. The Motor Transportation Corps (MTC) ferried trucks and other vehicles by road in convoys from the base ports to the front lines, a journey that took five days on average. To relieve congestion at the ports, the convoys carried as much materiel as they could take toward the front. Like the army railroads, the MTC also had a network of maintenance and repair shops. Some of the most difficult work was done at Motor Reconstruction Park 772. Originally based at the Caserne Pittié in Nevers (a now-abandoned French army barracks on rue de 13E de Ligne that is currently under renovation), the unit moved to a sprawling camp at Verneuil, forty kilometers east of Nevers on the main rail line, in July 1918. Recruited for their mechanical abilities, the MTC's skilled craftsmen repaired and rebuilt damaged vehicles, many fresh from the front. "Here is assembled the maimed and battle-scarred equipment brought down by rail," wrote journalist Isaac Marcosson, who observed their operations. "You see motor-cycles that are merely twisted bundles of steel; passenger cars riddled with holes; trucks that are wire-gashed and shrapnel-torn. Crimsoning these vehicles is the good red blood of the American doughboys who stuck to the steering-wheel until death released their grip." The spot, once a virtual automobile factory, is now an ordinary farmer's field just east of the D169 highway between the river and the railroad tracks.

The AEF's widely scattered bases needed to talk to each other. By November 1918, the U.S. Army had opened 282 telephone exchanges, 133 telegraph stations, and had strung 100,000 miles of wire across Europe. Among those who made this vast system work were members of the Signal Corps Female Telephone Operators Unit, better known as the "Hello Girls." The Signal Corps worked with the YWCA to house these women. In Paris, the Hello Girls lived at the Hotel Petrograd (now the Hotel Saint-Petersbourg), at 33–35 rue de Caumartin, where they were closely chaperoned to keep them from meeting the wrong element of men. Hello Girls also served in other AEF administrative centers. In Tours, they stayed in the Central Hotel (21 rue Berthelot), and in Chaumont at the Château la Gloriette (62 place Aristide Briand).

American lines of communication converged in the central Loire Valley, a region with a front row seat to French history. In 732, Charles "The Hammer" Martel defeated the Moors there at the Battle of Tours. During the Hundred Years War, Joan of Arc rallied the French against the English invaders at the siege of Orléans, turning the tide of the war in France's favor. The Renaissance kings of France called the Loire Valley home. The region is known around the world today for its stunning chateaux, like Chambord with its busy roofline of ornate towers, and Chenonceau, which hovers gracefully over the Cher River. During the Great War, the Loire Valley saw a remarkable concentration of U.S. military installations. American troops did their crucial work in the shadow of—and sometimes inside—the world famous Loire chateaux.

About 200 kilometers south of Paris was the Gièvres Intermediate Supply Depot, the largest storage yard in the AEF. During the summer of 1917, American soldiers began churning up farms, filling in marshlands, and cutting down the forests on the flat sandy plain north of the village of Gièvres on the Cher River. Some residents complained about the wholesale destruction of the countryside. The Americans were "taking over forests, and even vineyards, without authorization," one local official complained to Paris. Most understood that the sacrifice would help the war effort, and when the depot began generating thousands of jobs such complaints ceased. The depot grew continually, swallowing up more and more woods and farms. By November 1918, there were 132 warehouses along the Cher, storing everything from foodstuffs to ammunition. Huge round tanks stored oil and gas. In addition to storage, Gièvres performed many other vital functions. There was a bakery and coffee roasting plant. Two remount stations and a veterinary hospital serviced more than 2,500 horses and mules. Perhaps most remarkable was the refrigeration plant, which, when completed on May 1, 1918, became the third largest in the world. Its ice plant could produce 500 tons of ice a day, and its beef storage warehouse was capable of handling fifteen million pounds of meat, though it never actually contained that much.

In addition to the Gièvres depot, there were other American bases in the area. An automobile reconstruction park operated between Gièvres and Romorantin (a city that has since merged with neighboring Lanthenay) where the present-day D724 highway meets the E85 expressway. The army's largest aircraft assembly plant (see Chapter 11) operated on the grounds a French airbase now occupies.

To perform its myriad functions and to keep up with the constant expansion, 25,000 American troops were stationed at Gièvres. Another 20,000 civilians also worked there, including local French residents, French colonial workers from Vietnam, and contract laborers from Portugal, Spain, and China. The refrigeration plant alone had a workforce of 12,000. The influx of big-spending Sammies boosted the local economy, as cafes and shops opened up in Gièvres, Selles-sur-Cher, Romorantin, and surrounding cities and towns to service them. As at Saint-Nazaire, the Doughboys soon became an important part the community. In 1919, nearly half of all marriages in Gièvres involved local women and American soldiers. A particularly moving example of the American soldiers' connection to local communities is found inside Notre-Dame-la-Blanche Church in Selles-sur-Cher. The church dates to the 6th century (though rebuilt numerous times) and holds the remains of Saint Eusice. Joan of Arc once prayed in this church during the Hundred Years War. Inside the church is a statue of her, with a plaque on the wall explaining its origin. "To Joan of Arc," it says in French, from "American Catholic soldiers in memory of their stay in Selles-sur-Cher."

The area of the Gièvres depot is today rhomboid-shaped and bounded by the D796 highway on the northern border and the railroad line on the south. In the century since World War I, the warehouses have disappeared and the woods and farms have returned. The refrigeration plant, dismantled and sold to Mexico after the war, was located not far from the D796 highway just west of Les Arpents Farm. During the war the south side of this road was lined with barracks and warehouses. Homes have since replaced them. A few scattered remnants of the AEF storage depot remain. Two of the gas tanks, right along the D796 on the eastern end of the grounds, still exist. Surrounded by newer tanks, they now store alcohol. To see some remnants requires very close inspection. Walking through the woods north of the village one can still stumble upon concrete slabs poured by U.S. troops a century ago. Remnants of the American rail system remain too. In the woods about 500 meters south

Joan of Arc statue donated by U.S. troops in the Notre-Dame-la-Blanche Church, Selles-sur-Cher, France.

of the old gas storage facility, some of the rails still bear the name of their manufacturer, Carnegie, and the date of their production, 1917. Gièvres has two small memorials to commemorate the presence of the U.S. Army. Where rue de Romorantin (D128 highway) meets rue du Camp Américain, a low granite marker, dedicated in 1987, stands near the center of the old U.S. Army camp. In addition, in a traffic circle near the center of town (where the D128 and D54 intersect), the flags of the French Republic, the European Union, and the United States flap in the breeze. As a stone marker nearby explains, the American flag commemorates the U.S. camp that once dominated the town.

The Loire Valley was also home to major personnel classification centers. One was located in the impossibly picturesque city of Blois. The Château de Blois, which dominates the city on a bluff above the river, is one of the most beautiful and famous in the region. Constructed over many centuries, its architecture exhibits classical, Gothic, and Renaissance styles. In 1588, King Henry III had his archrival, the Duke of Guise, assassinated in the chateau—one of the most notorious episodes in French history. The typical American found the name Blois hard to pronounce, and simply called it "Blooey." The city still contains many narrow streets and half-timbered buildings, making it one of the most charming in all of France.

Blois was home to the Casual Officers Depot and Replacement Center. Officers arriving in France without assignment reported to the Caserne Maurice de Saxe, a French army barracks about a kilometer northeast of the chateau, for evaluation. Wounded officers who were no longer able to perform combat duties but capable of administrative roles reported to Blois for reassignment. Caserne Maurice de Saxe also processed casual enlisted men, who went through a process there that Issac Marcosson called "The Chute." Comparing their situation to the processing of cattle at the Chicago stockyards, Marcosson described how, soon after arrival, each such soldier "emerges in a few hours bathed, shaved, fully equipped, financed, with bulging barrack-bag in his hand, and a little card in his pocket which assigns him to a job that is both useful and congenial." For these Americans, Blois could be a pleasant place. "Nature must have had some vague intimation long ago that in this restful verdant nook the maimed veterans of America's Army of Freedom would come for sanctuary and to get a fresh grip on usefulness," Marcosson wrote. At least a few agreed. "We were allowed out of the concern (barracks) every day from 1:30 until 9:00 PM," recalled Corporal William McGinnis of the 26th Division, injured in the Aisne-Marne Offensive. "Each man was placed on his honor." McGinnis found Blois to be "a very interesting city." He especially enjoyed the chateau, and "a stairway in this castle that tourists from all parts of the world travel to and admire."

But for some, Blois was a place of fear and dread. Most American officers had been in uniform only a short time, a fact that caused great consternation in Chaumont. "Pershing was a hard man," wrote historian Richard S. Faulkner, and "fully realized that his personal reputation as well as that of the army and the nation were inextricably linked to the results attained by the AEF." To weed out incompetent officers, Pershing issued General Order 62. Those of questionable abilities were sent to the Casual Officers Depot at Blois, where they faced an examination board. It was a grueling and humiliating process. "Courageous men who led their soldiers in battles against the Huns have emerged from the inquisitorial chamber shattered wrecks," according to one news report, "in tears, crushed, humiliated, and broken in spirit. Others have come out like roaring lions, swearing vengeance. Others have departed meekly, convicted by their own records." Of the 82,000 officers in the AEF, more than 1,800 endured such proceedings, nearly all of them from combat units. Some were discharged. Some were sent back to the front. Most were assigned noncombat jobs in the SOS. Harbord called Blois a "human salvage plant." Most officers knew it as the "canning factory" or "the morgue." Many were sent to Blois for justifiable reasons, but other cases were less clear. National Guard officers, for example, complained of prejudicial treatment from regular army officers. Constant fears of being sent to Blois may have sapped the individual initiative of some combat officers. There was no doubt that being sent to Blois was a career killer. It was "the AEF's version of making him wear the scarlet letter," observed Faulkner.

Blois was so notorious among AEF officers that it actually enriched the English language. According to the Oxford English Dictionary, the adjective "blooey" means to go awry or amiss—a new word that emerged during the war. The French army abandoned the Caserne Maurice de Saxe, on avenue du Maréchal Mounoury, in 2001. The city of Blois has plans to renovate some of the buildings and convert the grounds to public areas and green spaces, but progress has been slow. The caserne buildings presently stand in a dilapidated condition. The U.S. Army used several other buildings around Blois, such as a marketplace called Halle aux Grains (2 place Jean-Jaurès), just down the street from Caserne Maurice de Saxe, as a motor repair facility. The Halle aux Grains nearly met the wrecking ball, but in 1970 the city transformed it into a concert and exhibition center. A plaque on the building tells the story of its near demolition, but does not mention the brief U.S. Army presence.

Forty kilometers south of Blois and twenty kilometers west of Gièvres, on the Cher near the medieval village of Saint-Aignan, was the 1st Replacement Depot, the largest replacement camp in the AEF. When the 41st "Sunset" Division (a National Guard unit from the Northwestern states) arrived in January 1918, its members received some shocking news. Rather than going off to combat training, they would be redesignated the 1st Depot Division and cannibalized by the rest of the AEF when manpower ran low. The sun had set on the Sunset Division. The camp was actually across the river from Saint-Aignan at the village of Noyers-sur-Cher, in the fields north of the railroad tracks, but the camp made its headquarters at the Château du Saint-Aignan, on a bluff above the Cher. "The task of the Division in its new role as a depot," wrote the camp's first commander, General Robert Alexander, "was to receive the replacements forwarded from the United States or transferred to us from other divisions or hospitals, provide for their equipment, administration and training while under our control and send them forward in an orderly, systematic manner as they were called for." The camp steadily grew as America stepped up its war effort, engulfing more of the fields and farms north of the Cher. Doughboys sometimes spent days and weeks waiting around for their assignments. Morale was often low, and the impatient soldiers sometimes referred to Saint-Aignan as "Saint Agony." By the end of 1918, nearly 240,000 Doughboys had passed through the 1st Replacement Depot.

Little remains of the American presence in Saint-Aignan and Noyers-sur-Cher, but what's left is among the most interesting non-battle remnants of the AEF. The Château du Saint-Aignan, one of the lesser-known treasures of the Loire Valley, is still the property of a local nobleman, though the grounds are open to the public. Standing in the courtyard and looking north over the river, one can appreciate General Alexander's bird's eye view of his sprawling camp. From that same spot today one sees only Noyers-sur-Cher and the farmlands beyond it. There is little obvious sign of the American presence in Noyers-sur-Cher now, but a close look at some of the older buildings along rue de Blois and rue de Ricoisnes on the north end of the village reveals some intimate echoes of the Great War. Bored Doughboys carved graffiti into the soft sandstone of several buildings. Many just left their names. Others included their hometowns—Baltimore, Maryland; Fort Worth, Texas; Lafferty, Ohio; and "NYC" are among the places represented. More creative soldiers left artwork. There's a gun, an American flag, and a Native American head. Time has taken its toll on the Doughboy etchings. Some visitors in later years felt inspired to add their own graffiti to the collection—including German soldiers during World War II who left a few swastikas behind. To preserve the memory of the rapidly deteriorating graffiti, a local historian reproduced some of the better examples and placed them on a rectangular monument in a rest area at the intersection of the D796 and D796B highways in Noyers-sur-Cher. On the bridge between the two villages—in the shadow of the chateau—is a memorial to the American camp. The obelisk with gilded lettering gives the dates the camp was in operation, and notes that more than 800 died while waiting for assignment in these two charming rural French villages.

SOS headquarters was located at Tours, a city on the main communication line roughly halfway between the ports and the front. For an administrative center, the French army offered the SOS the use of the Caserne Baraguay-d'Hilliers on boulevard Thiers. It was home to the French 66th Infantry Regiment, which was quite naturally away at the front, and the Americans simply called it "Barracks 66." The demand for office space led the Americans

Graffiti art left behind by bored Doughboys, rue de Ricoisnes, Noyers-sur-Cher, France.

to invade another French barracks, the Caserne Rannes, right next door. Engineers, the Medical Department, the Signal Corps, the Quartermaster Corps, and other support services directed their complex operations from these buildings. So did General Harbord, although he spent much of his time traveling across France on inspection tours. The ever-growing AEF also took over a newly built cavalry barracks called the Caserne Beaumont Chauveau on rue Plat d'Etain, one kilometer west of Barracks 66. Today boulevard Thiers is called boulevard Jean Royer, but the SOS headquarters buildings at the Baraguay-d'Hilliers and Rannes look much as they did a century ago—and still perform vital administrative functions for the French armed services. Among other operations, they host a training command and the human resources directorate of the French army. Historical plaques on the street-facing buildings of the casernes tell of their significance to French military history, but not of their American role. The "Beaumont Barracks," as the Yanks called the Beaumont Chauveau facility, is now the property of the University of Tours and is undergoing renovation.

In addition to SOS headquarters, several other bases sprang up in the Tours area. In the suburb of Saint-Pierre-des-Corps, railway engineers operated Camp de Grasse just east of the city's train station. Trackside warehouses nearby housed Salvage Depot No. 8, where damaged clothing and equipment was brought in, repaired or recycled, and then shipped out again. "The colossal establishment reeks with a movement that is only surpassed by the odor from the tons of waste that are dumped daily at its doors," observed Isaac Marcosson. French civilian women did most of the work of repairing and cleaning shoes, boots, blankets, leather goods, and countless other items, though a good number of Doughboys participated as well. "Nothing is thrown away," Marcosson remarked. "The garments incapable of restoration are dyed green for our prisoners of war." The recycling effort saved precious space on transatlantic cargo ships, and General Harbord estimated that the salvage plant at Saint-Pierre-des-Corps alone saved the AEF four million dollars a month. As an important rail hub, the town suffered terribly from Allied bombings during World War II, which destroyed an estimated 85 percent of the city. The area just east of the main train station, where the rue Jean Moulin viaduct crosses over the tracks, was the center of American activities. By November 1918, the Tours area was home to 20,000 Americans.

The SOS and the Fighting Man

From the Intermediate Section, supplies were passed on to an Advance Section depot, which, according to historian Steve Waddell, was "the most important link in the supply chain." Here supplies were offloaded and organized for shipment to specific frontline units. The typical American division at the front needed about twenty-five French rail cars of supplies a day—everything from bread to bullets. Sundry items like mail—the soldier's lifeline to the folks back home—had to be delivered, too. Replacement troops also followed this chain. It was the job of the advance depots to put those supply trains together. Once assembled, the trains went up to the railhead that each division maintained behind the front. From there the supplies got to the fighting man in numerous ways. Narrow gauge railways reached the front. Trucks were most common, since they could travel over open ground and shell-damaged roads. Horses and mules did their fair share of the burden as well, much as they had in past wars. The advance depots were much like those at Montoir and Gièvres, though being closer to the front made them potentially subject to enemy attack, so they had the protection of anti-aircraft batteries.

American forces used French advance depot stations throughout the war, but given Pershing's insistence on an independent American army, U.S. engineers went right to work building their own near their bases in eastern France. The first and largest was Advance Depot No. 1 at located at Is-sur-Tille, twenty-five kilometers north of Dijon. Construction began in September 1917, and by the armistice the depot had forty-eight warehouses in two separate storage yards serviced by 18,000 troops. In Is-sur-Tille today the American depot is remembered quite graciously. The former main street of the facility is now called route du Camp Américain, located on the eastern end of town. The storage and transfer yards occupied the farmlands on either side of this road. Some portions of the old camp serve as an industrial zone. In 2008, Is-sur-Tille erected a historical marker on route du Camp Américain to commemorate the U.S. presence there. An even more touching monument stands in the central part of the town. Like every French community, Is-sur-Tille has a memorial to its Great War dead. This one also pays homage to the American soldier. On the front are two bronze medallions, one with the image of a Doughboy and one of a French Poilu. Foch and Pershing make appearances too. On the back of the monument are the names of the 238 American soldiers at the depot who died in the camp hospital.

The U.S. Army built a second advance depot closer to the front at Liffol-le-Grand, eighty kilometers south of Saint-Mihiel. Planning for it began in December 1917, but getting the Liffol-le-Grand project operational proved difficult. "The plans adopted in conformity with the wishes of the French placed the yards in a waste land," complained one engineer's report, "much of which was swampy, thus complicating construction." The shortage of supplies created by the German offensives of mid-1918 further delayed construction. Liffol-le-Grand did not open until October 12, 1918, and construction was ongoing when the war ended. Barely a trace of the Liffol-le-Grand depot exists anymore. The area of the camp, just north of the D674 highway between Liffol-le-Grand and its diminutive twin, Liffol-le-Petit, is now an ordinary-looking farm field. Spur lines from the tracks running parallel to the road along the south side brought the supply trains into the complex, and camp buildings once lined either side of the road.

As supplies were brought up to the front, battle casualties were evacuated to the rear. From the combat zone, the wounded Doughboy went through a chain of mobile medical facilities each progressively larger and more comprehensive. Field medics collected casualties at an aid post just a few hundred meters behind the lines. Stretcher-bearers then carried them (those capable of walking did so) to a dressing station. From there, an ambulance whisked them to a field hospital, where they were triaged based on the severity of their wounds. For those in need of more care, an ambulance took them to an evacuation hospital several kilometers behind the lines, and from there they often boarded a special hospital train bound for a stationary medical facility in the SOS Intermediate Section. Not all soldier-patients were combat casualties. There were training accidents. There were motor vehicle and train collisions. Falling crates might injure supply workers or stevedores at the port. In the soldier's world, the possibilities for accidents seem endless. Influenza and other diseases ravaged the ranks as well.

At the time of the armistice, there were 231 functioning hospitals in the AEF, caring for 184,421 patients. Nearly every post in the AEF had a camp hospital that handled the soldier's everyday medical needs. The larger base hospitals dealt with more complex cases and long-term care. In several cases, base hospitals were grouped together into "hospital centers." Women nurses played a vital role at base hospitals. The military was very much a man's world during the Great War, but as nurses women found a place to serve near the front. The Red Cross recruited 21,000 women for the Army Nurse Corps, about half of whom went overseas. Nurses held an ambiguous position in the army's rank system. "Although a part of the army," explained the official history of the army's medical department after the war, nurses "were considered neither as enlisted or commissioned personnel." They were subject to military discipline and treated as officers, but without official rank they could not give orders. Hospital orderlies sometimes refused to follow their directions, and doctors demanded dates. No nurses died in combat during World War I, although many got close enough to the front to receive citations for bravery under fire. On the west side of the American Red Cross on 17th Street NW in building in Washington, DC is a memorial to Jane Delano, the founder of the Red Cross Nursing Service and superintendent of the Army Nurse Corps, who died of disease at the U.S. Army hospital at Savenay in 1919. The memorial features a bronze female figure with outstretched arms, and is dedicated to all 296 American nurses who died in World War I.

Hospitals sprang up all along the American lines of communication. Many moved into French hospitals and schools, such as Base Hospital 43, composed of medical personnel from Emory University in Atlanta, which worked out of widely scattered buildings across Blois. The Americans took over the city's municipal hospital. Located just below the chateau on the banks of the Loire, the building had a colorful history. It began as a Benedictine monastery and the Saint-Laumer chapel (later renamed Saint-Nicholas) in the twelfth century. Over the centuries the buildings and grounds were modified and rebuilt several times, and during the French Revolution the monastery became a hospital. "It is sheltered by the pointed steeples of the old church," reported Katherine de Monclos of the American Red Cross, "around which rooks fly and caw incessantly. The square-paned windows overlook the Loire and the quaint box-bordered alleys of the garden." The hospital also absorbed several other buildings in the city, most notably the bishop's residence at the Saint-Louis Cathedral about a kilometer to the east, with its finely manicured gardens overlooking the river.

Charming as the scenery was, medical officers saw things differently. "All these buildings were old, dirty, fitted with inadequate and out-of-date sanitary appliances," noted one report. The bishop's residence, in particular, was "converted with considerable difficulty, owing to the almost total absence of plumbing." Two barracks buildings were erected in the bishop's gardens overlooking the

Loire to house enlisted personnel. But once the renovations were completed, Blois afforded Doughboys a fine place for recovery. "The patients who are convalescent and able to come down love to sit here under the shady lime trees or sun themselves seated on the low wall," Monclos reported about the riverfront hospital site.

The men and women of Base Hospital 43 found Blois a pleasant place to work, though the city posed its challenges. "To one raised on dry territory it came as a shock to see on every corner in the little wine-shops men, women and children, soldiers and civilians," observed the hospital's official history, which however reported that "to the honor of the men of Base Hospital 43 this liberty was not abused." And yet "the buvettes gave that foreign spice to our life over here that made it all the more bizarre." The riverfront hospital is today a French government office building on quai du Foix at the intersection with and rue de 3 Marchands. It is not open to the public, though a historical plaque is affixed to the gate. The plaque describes the history of the site from medieval times to the French Revolution, but skips the Great War. The bishop's residence is now the Blois city hall (9 place Saint-Louis). The gardens just to the east still afford picturesque views of the Loire.

Other hospitals began completely from scratch. Relatively close to the front and accessible by rail, the Nevers area had several major hospital facilities for wounded soldiers. In February 1918, construction began on a massive 20,000-bed hospital center near Mars-sur-Allier, fifteen kilometers south of Nevers. "The work of this center has embraced every phase of medical and surgical practice," its commander reported. By the armistice, the fields between the villages of Saint-Parize-la-Châtel and Magny-Cours contained 700 buildings covering thirty-three acres. The grounds of the Mars-sur-Allier hospital are now a motor raceway known as the circuit de Nevers Magny-Cours. All that remains of the U.S. hospital there is a stone water tower on route du Circuit (the D58 highway). A memorial once stood along the N7 highway where the camp cemetery was located. It has since been relocated to the village cemetery on route d'Azy on the southeast edge of town. In a field thirty-five kilometers north of Nevers, in the farmlands just east of Mesves-sur-Loire, was another hospital center. Work began on this facility in April 1918. "When construction was first commenced wheat was just beginning to sprout in some of these patches," noted one report, "while in others native peasant women tended their white cattle, which browsed quietly over the fields." The bucolic scene did not last long, as buildings went up at a rapid pace. The multicultural workforce included Americans, French, Spanish, and Chinese, creating what one report said was "a parallel organization to the Tower of Babel." The first patients arrived at Mesves on July 19, and the complex was busy for the rest of the war. The hospital was located east of the railroad tracks and south of the D125 highway between Mesves and Bulcy, and not a trace of it remains today save one thing. When constructing the camp, the army spared the buildings of Les Asserts Farm, which stood in the middle of the facility and became the commander's headquarters. The farm remains on a rural road a few meters south of the D125.

The Doughboy gets a Little R&R

Pershing demanded a lot from his men, but he also understood the necessity for a little rest and recreation to keep up morale. Like at stateside posts, service organizations such as the Red Cross and the YMCA stood ready to entertain the Doughboy—and keep him out of trouble. Nearly every station in the SOS—even the smallest of them—had a YMCA hut, usually staffed by American volunteers. Camp Marcy, a small outpost of the 39th Railway Engineers a few kilometers west of the Verneuil motor repair facility, housed just three companies of soldiers to maintain the nearby rails, but the YMCA was there with them. Indeed, the only trace of the camp that remains is the brick chimney of the YMCA hut, located in a farmer's field on the south side of the D918 highway five kilometers east of the intersection with the D979 highway. Service organizations worked close to the front, and the men and women working there were very dedicated, such as Thomas Rodman Plummer of New Bedford, Massachusetts. Born in 1862, Plummer was too old to enlist, so in 1917 he offered his services to the American Red Cross. He ran a mobile canteen service in Moyenmoutier, a small community in the Vosges Mountains, where many combat divisions received their introduction to the trenches (see Chapter 7). Many days saw Plummer right behind the front, giving weary soldiers comforts like hot chocolate, tobacco, and writing paper. His hard work and tireless dedication impressed not just the American troops, but the French locals as well. Shortly after the armistice, an exhausted Plummer fell ill and died. Today there is a plaque to Plummer's memory on the village hall in Moyenmoutier. His grave is in the local cemetery just up the hill, and is still kept decorated with American and French flags. The plaza in front of the cemetery is named in his honor.

Under AEF policy, each soldier was entitled to a seven-day furlough for every four months in Europe—battle conditions permitting, of course. But where to spend it? "The French soldiers could spend their well-earned 'permissions' at home," wrote Franklin S. Edmonds of the American YMCA in France, and "the British soldiers could be transported across the English Channel to 'Blighty' . . . but the American soldier was in a foreign country." Giving the Doughboys the opportunity to roam freely around Britain and France would make it hard to recall them in an emergency, and many commanders feared they would roam to the nearest pub or *maison tolérée*. In close partnership with the army, the YMCA established leave centers in resort areas of France and Britain, were the men could unwind in a wholesome, structured environment.

The YMCA set up its first leave area in the Alpine resort of Aix-les-Bains in February 1918. The Y took over the Casino Grand Cercle and "converted [it] into a club house for the American doughboy," as a postwar YMCA report explained. The organization furnished it with everything the soldier, so it was thought, needed to unwind. "With theaters running, several movie performances a day in the cinema hall, dancing in the ballrooms, continual canteen service in several parts of the casino, rough and tumble frolics every night after the show, athletics in the form of baseball, volley ball, soccer, hikes in the mountains, boat excursions on the lake, thermal baths—the soldier's vacation was a continuous round of fun." Special trains carried the soldier-tourists to Aix-les-Bains, and YMCA officials met them at the station and guided them to their billets. The army and the YMCA established numerous other leave areas. The French Riviera, the playground of royalty and the wealthy, was especially popular with the Doughboys. The YMCA rented casinos for soldier recreational use, and rooms in local hotels to house them. In Nice, for example, the YMCA took over the famous Jetée Promenade, an ornate casino built on a pier into the Mediterranean, as a recreation center for enlisted men. Sadly, the Germans tore it up for scrap metal during World War II, and all once sees there today is a lonely fragment of a pier off Promenade des Anglais at the foot of rue du Congrès. After the armistice, the neutral principality of Monaco also opened its doors to the American troops. By 1919, the YMCA had acquired accommodations for 6,000 officers and 10,000 enlisted personnel on the Rivera.

Many soldiers gravitated toward big cities, and the YMCA was waiting there for them. One of the most impressive facilities was the Eagle Hut in London, a recreation center for enlisted men. Located in an open semicircle at the intersection of Kingsway and the Strand, the Eagle Hut was open twenty-four hours a day for Doughboys on leave or passing through the city. It served meals, offered tours, and gave soldiers and sailors a place to rest or write home. It had a dormitory with more than 200 beds, as well as a prophylactic station. The Eagle Hut attracted some notable personalities. The noted American Shakespearean actor E. H. Sothern volunteered his time there. Even King George paid a visit. "The King's visit, of course, created immediate interest among the sons of the free and the brave," Sothern wrote of the event:

> One of them approached the monarch and held out his hand.
> "Hello King!" said he.
> King George took the proffered paw and exchanged compliments with the soldier-boy.

After the war, American shipping magnate Irving T. Bush, whose Brooklyn port facilities helped transport soldiers to Europe (see Chapter 4), built a trade center on the site of the Eagle Hut and dedicated it to Anglo-American cooperation. Included on the façade of Bush House at the foot of Kingsway is a small tablet commemorating the Eagle Hut. Thousands now rush past it every day and never notice it. For officers in London, the YMCA built the "Washington Inn" in the middle St. James Square, and there was also the American Officers Inn at 5 Cavendish Square. "By the use of a huge knocker on the door you can gain admittance," wrote Red Cross volunteer Isabel Anderson of the Cavendish Square Inn, and once inside she recalled that the officer found himself "in the midst of an atmosphere of cordiality . . . with an open fireplace, large, deep chairs, a table, and a telephone exchange board with a pretty London girl operating it."

The YMCA had several facilities in Paris too. "Paris, it seemed, could hardly be forbidden to the Army," observed YMCA volunteer Katherine Mayo. American soldiers "would one day feel themselves sadly aggrieved," she wrote, "if all their sojourn in France should pass without a glimpse of the enchanted city." The first YMCA facility opened in 1917 at 31 avenue Montaigne—barely a block from avenue des Champs-Élysées—a building that soon became the headquarters of the American YMCA in France. It proved inadequate, and the Y leased several Parisian hotels for Doughboy rest and relaxation. Enlisted men met at the Hotel Pavillon (38 rue de l'Echequier). An officers' facility opened at the Hotel Richmond (11 rue de Helder), run by Mrs. Theodore Roosevelt Jr., whose husband was on duty with the 1st Division. Conditions at the Richmond were crowded. Lieutenant Lee Levenger, a Jewish chaplain, arrived at the Hotel Richmond with a lieutenant colonel he met on the train to Paris. "We found only one room available with a double bed," Levenger recalled, "so for the first time in my life I had the honor of sleeping with a lieutenant colonel," an experience he found unpleasant since his bedmate had "a slight attack of the 'flu.'" To relieve the congestion, the Mrs. Roosevelt and her associates developed a program to have officers to stay in French homes around the city. Sightseeing tours introduced the City of Light to thousands of young Americans who might not otherwise have seen it. The YMCA offered generalized tours (on foot, by truck, or by boat) as well as special interest ones. According to *Summary of World War Work of the American Y.M.C.A.*, such excursions included "places made familiar by the novels of Victor Hugo," and one "through the sewers of Paris, designed particularly for engineers."

Paris in Wartime

Though Pershing located his headquarters at Chaumont, many Americans spent the war in Paris. Thousands of quartermaster troops operated warehouses across the city, for example. *Stars & Stripes*, the famed military newspaper, had offices at 1 rue des Italiens before moving to 32 rue Taitbout by the end of the war. The Air Service kept its headquarters at 45 avenue Montaigne, not far from the YMCA. The General Purchasing Board under Charles Dawes moved in and out of several locations in Paris, including an office building at 3 rue de Berri, the Hotel Méditerranée at 98 quai de la Rapée, and the Élysées Palace Hotel at 103 avenue des Champs-Élysées, where the German spy Mata Hari was arrested in February 1917. Dawes's work was critical to the American war effort. Since the U.S. was unable to manufacture enough aircraft, artillery, and machine guns to meet the needs of the AEF, Dawes had to purchase those items from the Allies. Foodstuffs, horses, and countless other items were also acquired overseas. By the end of the war, Dawes had purchased 10,200,000 tons of goods overseas. The American Red Cross made its headquarters across the street from the Louvre at the Hotel Regina (2 place des Pyramides). In 1919, representatives from the Red Cross organizations of Britain, France, Italy, Japan, and the United States gathered at the Hotel Regina and founded what is now the International Red Cross. A plaque on the wall near the hotel entrance commemorates the occasion.

Paris was also a great hospital center. In addition to the American Hospital in Paris (see Chapter 1), the Red Cross administered several other hospitals in Paris. Hospital No. 2 took over a clinic building at 6 rue Picinni. Hospital No. 5 set up buildings on the Auteuil Hippodrome in the Bois de Boulogne, and Hospital No. 9 was the building of a Turkish bath at 32 boulevard des Batignolles. The AEF had several hospitals in Paris as well, including Base Hospital 57 at the Lycée Montaigne at 17 rue Auguste Comte, across the street from the Luxembourg Gardens. With the Battle of Cantigny and the fight on the Marne in the summer of 1918, these hospitals were filled to capacity. The influenza epidemic filled them further. The doctors, nurses, and enlisted technicians saved many lives, but could not save them all.

In 1917, the U.S. Army Graves Registration Service began burying the American dead from the Paris area below the walls of the Fortresse du Mont-Valérien, on a hillside overlooking the city. Located in the suburb of Suresnes, 10 kilometers west of Notre Dame Cathedral, Mont-Valérien had been the home of French army installations since Napoleonic times, and was a key link in the chain of fortifications surrounding the city. During the war, American searchlight operators trained there with their French counterparts. As the war dragged on, the American cemetery at

Mont-Valérien grew, receiving victims of accidents and influenza, as well as those who died of battle wounds in nearby hospitals. After the war, the site became the Suresnes American Cemetery. President Wilson dedicated the cemetery on Memorial Day 1919 while in France for the Versailles Treaty negotiations, and the dead from AEF cemeteries across the SOS were brought to Suresnes for permanent interment. New York architect Charles A. Platt designed the chapel, and French landscape architect Jacques Greber laid out the grounds. Their work was completed in 1932. After World War II, the remains of twenty-four unidentified American GIs from that conflict were buried with their Doughboy predecessors at Suresnes, making it one of the few U.S. military cemeteries overseas holding the remains of soldiers from both wars. To acknowledge the cemetery's dual-war purpose, the American Battle Monuments Commission (ABMC) added loggias and memorial rooms to the chapel—one for each conflict—in the 1950s. Platt's sons, William and Geoffrey, designed the additions.

The cemetery is located on boulevard Washington. Commuter trains from the Gare Saint-Lazare make frequent stops at the Gare de Suresnes-Mont-Valérien, just below the hill. From the gilded iron gates at the entrance, a tree-lined mall leads up to the chapel. The graves stretch out on either side of the mall. The Paris skyline, including the iconic Eiffel Tower, is clearly visible from many portions of the graves area. As in all cemeteries maintained by the ABMC, the headstones give the deceased's name, unit, and date of death. Inspecting the unit designations here, one will note the unusually large number of dead who came not from combat arms, but support units like quarter-master, transportation, and various labor battalions—a testament to the sacrifices of SOS personnel. Numerous civilians are also buried

here. Those who worked for the Red Cross, YMCA, and other service organizations were just as susceptible to influenza as the soldiers. Civilians experienced the psychological strains of war as well. Indeed, this cemetery, with its disproportionate number of noncombatants, tells one of the most tragic stories of the First World War. Twin sisters Dorothea and Gladys Cromwell were Red Cross workers from New York who had served at the front near Verdun, endur-ing numerous air raids and the bloody sights and smells of

Suresnes American Cemetery, outside Paris, France.

frontline hospitals. The painful memories they carried in their heads were apparently too much to bear. On January 19, 1919, the sisters departed from Bordeaux on the ship *La Lorraine*, but they would never make it back to America. Shortly after shoving off on that dark and murky night, the sisters left suicide notes in their cabin, made their way to the deck, and jumped over the rail, plunging to their deaths in the Garonne River. The Cromwell sisters are buried side by side at Suresnes, in Plot B, Row 18, Graves 22 and 23.

The chapel, constructed of French limestone, has the appearance of an ancient Greek temple. (Richard Platt, the architect, was a leading light in the American Renaissance movement, which drew heavily on classical influences.) Inside is an altar made of dark Italian marble, and behind it a colorful mosaic by New York artist Barry Faulkner, depicting an Angel of Victory in flight. On the walls of the chapel interior are four bronze plaques, memorializing the names of 974 Americans who were lost or buried at sea—mainly in French waters. The loggias branch out from either side of the chapel interior; the one for the First World War is to the left. In keeping with the symmetry of the chapel, each loggia and memorial room is nearly identical. On the back wall of each loggia is a marble relief sculpture of a group of soldiers bearing an empty funeral bier, each by New York sculptor Lewis Iselin. The World War I memorial room contains a sculpture made of Carrara marble of a female figure with hands clasped as if in prayer, entitled "Remembrance" by New York artist John Gregory. The World War II memorial room holds a similar marble piece, this one entitled "Memory," by Lewis Iselin.

To commemorate the vital work of the Services of Supply, the ABMC dedicated a memorial fountain in central Tours in 1932. The memorial is on avenue André Malraux, overlooking the Loire River. The Pont Wilson, named in honor of the wartime American president, is just 200 meters to the west. At the base of the fountain are the coats of arms of French cities with a substantial wartime American presence, including Saint-Nazaire, Brest, Bordeaux, Nevers, Is-sur-Tille, and Tours itself, where the SOS made it headquarters. Rising from the fountain is a column with four classical female figures representing the four main categories of SOS

Tours American Monument, dedicated to the Services of Supply.

activities—administration, construction, distribution, and procurement. Capping the column is a gilded statue of a Native American with an eagle perched on his upraised forearm. The fighting man remained the central figure in the drama of the Great War, but the industrialization of war required increasing numbers of engineers and technicians, and mass armies needed their own army of support personnel to keep them fed, clothed, and battle worthy. The men and women of the SOS earned their service stripes, too.

CHAPTER 10:
AFRICAN AMERICAN TROOPS

Though President Wilson proclaimed that American participation in World War I would make the world "safe for democracy," some of the soldiers serving in his great crusade were systematically denied democracy at home. "I'd never heard of democracy before," observed African American World War I veteran Tela Burt. "I never knew what the hell I was fighting for." The early twentieth century was a time of bitter and entrenched racism in America. In 1917, slavery had been abolished just fifty-two years before, and many Americans—black and white—could still remember it vividly. The infamous Supreme Court case *Plessy v. Ferguson*, permitting Jim Crow racial segregation in the South, was just twenty-one years old that year. For African Americans in the South, poverty was widespread and lynchings occurred with appalling regularity. Those who migrated to the North did not find the racial climate much better. There they experienced *de facto* rather than *de jure* segregation in housing, as well as employment discrimination, and poverty was still the rule. And yet most African Americans embraced the war effort. Like other Americans, blacks were caught up in the patriotic fervor of the war years. But for African Americans the war meant even more. Fighting for democracy overseas, many fervently hoped, would lead to real democracy at home.

African American military history is long and distinguished. Since the days of the American Revolution, blacks had fought and died for the United States. By the end of the Civil War, roughly 10 percent of the U.S. Army was African American, serving in segregated regiments under the command of white officers. After the war, the army authorized four regiments of black soldiers (two infantry and two cavalry), which fought with distinction in the Indian Wars of the West. Likening the tenacity with which African American soldiers fought to bison, Native Americans on the Great Plains called them "Buffalo Soldiers," a term African American soldiers readily embraced. By the end of the nineteenth century, a few African Americans had reached the officer ranks, and a handful had even graduated from West Point. After the conclusion of the Indian

Wars, Buffalo Soldiers also took part in the colonial conflicts in the Philippines and the Caribbean, as well as the Mexican expedition of 1916–1917.

In addition to the regular army, a handful of states and the District of Columbia maintained segregated National Guard units. Of the southern states, only Tennessee allowed African Americans to serve. Before World War I broke out in 1914, the 8th Illinois Infantry was the only African American National Guard unit of regimental size, though Connecticut, Maryland, Massachusetts, and Ohio had segregated battalions and companies. New York state authorized an African American regiment in 1913, but the 15th New York Infantry did not really get off the ground until 1916. Its first commander was Colonel William Hayward, a wealthy and well-connected lawyer and civil rights supporter. Recruitment for the Harlem-based regiment was slow until Hayward convinced the noted bandleader James Reese Europe to sign up. Commissioned a lieutenant, Europe envisioned an unconventional regimental band that would play martial music in the emerging style of jazz. With Hayward's full backing, Europe recruited hundreds of talented musicians for the regiment. He traveled as far as Puerto Rico to find the saxophonists, clarinetists, and other woodwind players that would give the band just the right sound.

American entry into the war in 1917 sparked debate about Black America's place in the war effort. The army was not sure it wanted any more black troops. Despite plenty of historical evidence to the contrary, many still believed that African Americans would not make good fighters. Modern war was different than past wars, skeptics argued, believing that African Americans would not grasp its technological complexities. Some went so far as to claim that blacks did not have adequate night vision or that their noses would not fit properly in gas masks. The war divided African Americans themselves. Many civil rights leaders thought that blacks had no stake in it, but others saw opportunities. W. E. B. DuBois of the National Association for the Advancement of Colored People hoped that black participation in the struggle to make the world "safe for democracy" would lead to civil rights reform. DuBois had long been an advocate for full and immediate racial equality, but in a controversial 1918 essay he urged African Americans to "forget our special grievances and close ranks with our white fellow citizens and the allied nations that are fighting for democracy." Critics charged that DuBois had caved in to the superpatriotic pressures of the day, or that he was angling for a wartime position. Others saw merit in his views. White Southerners also had conflicted views about African Americans in uniform. DuBois's vision of military service leading to equal rights was anathema to most southern whites, and the thought of armed black men filled them with terror. Wealthy landowners also feared that African Americans' departure to the war would deprive them of workers. On the other hand, exempting African Americans from service meant that white Southerners would bear a disproportionate burden of the fighting, and as the war began to drain southern communities of young white men, attitudes about black service softened.

Ultimately the army could not ignore the significance of African American manpower, but from the beginning it made a concerted effort to marginalize black participation in the Great War. Take, for example, the case of Lieutenant Colonel Charles Young, the army's highest-ranking African American officer. Born in Kentucky in 1864, Young was a West Point graduate with a long and exemplary record, including time as superintendent of Yosemite National Park, professor of military science at Wilberforce University in Ohio, and distinguished combat service in Mexico. Young hoped the Great War would lead to his promotion to full colonel and to command of an African American brigade in France. His record was unassailable, but in June 1917 army physicians claimed that he had high blood pressure, sclerotic arteries, kidney problems, and a host of other ailments that limited his "ability to do active field service requiring physical stress and involving endurance." Young thought the conclusion bogus, and to prove it he traveled on horse-back 497 miles from his home in Wilberforce to Washington, D.C., sometimes enduring the sting of racism when he tried to check into hotels along the way. Unimpressed, the army promoted him to full colonel and placed him on the retired list. In November 1918—just days before the armistice—the army recalled Young and sent him to Camp Grant, Illinois, where he commanded a battalion of African American trainees. Though the army was in desperate need of capable and experienced officers, it went out of its way to deny Young any meaningful role. Today Young is a revered figure in both army and civil rights circles, and there are several memorials to his life and service, most notably in his adopted home state of Ohio. At the corner of Prospect Avenue and Prospect Road in Cleveland, a black granite column with an unfinished top outlines his extensive service to the nation. In 2013, President Barack Obama declared Young's home at 1120 U.S. Route 42 East in Wilberforce to be the Charles Young Buffalo Soldiers National Monument. Currently under development, it is not yet open to the public.

The Camp Logan Riot and Its Aftermath

Soon after the United States declared war, a terrible incident occurred in Houston that further soured the army on African American soldiers. In July 1917, the army began construction on Camp Logan (see Chapter 3), a training camp for the Illinois National

Guard, on the northwest edge of the city. To guard the site, the army transferred the Third Battalion of the 24th Infantry Regiment from Columbus, New Mexico, to Houston. The 654 black soldiers and eight white officers of the battalion bivouacked about a mile east of Camp Logan, north and west of the present-day intersection of Washington Avenue and Reinerman Street. Almost immediately, Houston simmered with racial tensions. Local whites insisted that African American soldiers abide by the city's segregation laws, even while in uniform. To make matters worse, white workers taunted the soldiers charged with protecting them, and local police harassed them when not on duty. Around noon on the exceptionally hot day of August 23, Private Alonzo Edwards of Company L witnessed a white police officer beating a black woman in the city's historically black Fourth Ward. Edwards intervened, and police arrested him. When an African American military policeman, Corporal Charles Baltimore, queried the officers about the incident, one of them hit him over the head with his pistol and then started shooting. Baltimore fled, but was quickly captured and arrested as well.

Word of the arrests soon reached the encampment on Washington Avenue, but in the excitement and tension of the moment it was erroneously reported that Baltimore was dead. Hoping to diffuse the situation, white officers extracted from the Houston police a promise to suspend the offending officer, but the soldiers bivouacking near Camp Logan were not mollified. That evening, fearing trouble, the officers began collecting all the battalion's weapons and ammunition, but as the collection was taking place, one soldier cried out: "The white mob is coming!" It was not true, but the soldiers grabbed their rifles and started firing. The white officers were unable to bring their men under control, and after half an hour a group of about 100 soldiers left the camp and marched toward the police station at the corner of Capitol and Bagby in downtown Houston to get their revenge. "To hell with going to France," one reportedly yelled. "Get to work right here." They marched down Washington Avenue, turned south on Brunner Avenue (today's Shepherd Drive), crossed Buffalo Bayou, and then headed east on San Felipe Road (now West Dallas Street), shooting and bayoneting the police officers and white citizens they encountered. At the corner of San Felipe and Heiner Street, the mutineers accidentally killed an Illinois National Guard officer sent in to quell the disturbance, mistaking him for a policeman. At this point the mob began quarreling and dispersed. Some headed back to camp. Some hid out in the homes of sympathetic residents of the Fourth Ward, only to be captured the next day. In all, the mutineers killed sixteen people, including four policemen. As for the soldiers, four died in the incident; two of them were shot accidentally by their fellow soldiers, and one committed suicide. The army whisked the battalion out of Houston within days, and in the following months 110 soldiers were court-martialed. Nineteen were hanged. The Camp Logan site is now Memorial Park (see Chapter 3). The marker for the camp, at the corner of Arnot and Haskell, mentions the tragic events of August 23, 1917. The area of the mutineers' rampage is now quiet and residential. A housing development occupies the site of the 24th Infantry's encampment.

In the aftermath of Houston, southern states asked, begged, and demanded that the government not station African American troops at camps within their borders. Secretary of War Newton Baker refused to cave in to this specific demand, but the army went to great lengths to address such fears and impose strict controls on African Americans in the ranks. Black recruits were spread far and wide across the country in order to avoid concentrating too many in one place. The army's policy was that African Americans could not make up more than 30 percent of personnel at any one post. The practice of having segregated black units led by white officers was never questioned. These officers were disproportionately white Southerners (based on the fiction that they understood African Americans better than Northerners), and were often supremely racist. The African American regiments of the regular army were not brought together into a segregated unit as Colonel Young and many others had hoped, but rather were dispersed and assigned duties far away from France. The 25th Infantry Regiment spent the war at Schofield Barracks, twenty miles northwest of Honolulu, Hawaii—a nice place, to be sure, but far from the glories of the European battlefields. The 9th Cavalry Regiment was halfway around the world at Camp Stotsenburg in the Philippines.

Two Buffalo Soldier regiments patrolled the Mexican border. In addition to the continuing revolutionary situation in Mexico, America feared that Germany could use Mexico as a base for espionage and sabotage. The 24th Infantry Regiment stayed at Camp Furlong in Columbus, New Mexico, throughout the war. The 10th Cavalry Regiment was at Fort Huachuca, Arizona, when the war began. In fact, the camp commander in 1914 was none other than Colonel Charles Young. The 10th Cavalry also stayed put, as Fort Huachuca expanded in the face of the ongoing border troubles. Fort Huachuca is still an important U.S. Army post, and probably no installation is more closely associated with the Buffalo Soldier. From the arrival of the 10th Cavalry in 1913 to the end of World War II, Fort Huachuca was home to more African American soldiers than any other installation. The Fort Huachuca Museum, housed in an 1892 officers' quarters, contains several exhibits about African Americans and the army, and devotes a considerable amount of space to the 10th Cavalry and the border troubles during World War I. From the museum, a walking path leads through the North Parade Field to the Buffalo

Barracks at Fort Huachuca, Arizona where the African American 10th Cavalry Regiment spent the Great War.

Soldier Legacy Plaza. Along the path are interpretive panels that point out some of the post's historic sites. One highlights a row of two-story barracks buildings along the west side of the parade ground. Completed in 1916, these barracks were home to the 10th Cavalry during the Great War. At the Buffalo Soldier Legacy Plaza stands a sculpture of a dismounted African American cavalryman from the Old West—rifle in one hand, saddle in the other—dedicated to all the African Americans who served at Fort Huachuca, including the Doughboys of World War I.

The Battle of Ambos Nogales

The U.S-Mexican border was a tense and dangerous place during the war years, and the 10th Cavalry in Arizona even saw a little action. The twin cities of Nogales face each other across the border, one on the Arizona side and the other in the Mexican state of Sonora. No fence or wall marked the boundary in "Ambos Nogales"—or "both Nogales," as the combined cities are sometimes called. There was just a dusty road called International Street, and each nation patrolled its own side of the thoroughfare. The communities had long been intimately connected, but U.S. entry into the Great War altered established patterns of behavior. Locals were in the habit of making frequent trips back and forth across the border, but in 1917 the Americans began to restrict crossings. Revolutionary turmoil in Mexico created food shortages on the already-impoverished Sonoran side, but U.S. wartime economic controls limited the amounts and kinds of foodstuffs Mexican nationals could take with them back into Mexico, resulting in "food runners" smuggling items across the border. American intelligence also heard disturbing reports of Germans on the Sonora side aiding the Mexican army, digging trenches on the hills above the town, and urging a strike across the border. The demeaning treatment American officials meted out to Mexicans crossing the border only made tensions worse. During this time of increasing anxieties, companies of the all-white 35th Infantry Regiment patrolled the American side of International Street. A detachment of 10th Cavalry, stationed at Camp Little half a mile north of the border on the main road out of town (see Chapter 1), backed them up.

On the afternoon of August 27, 1918, shooting broke out on International Street when a Mexican national crossed the border without having U.S. customs inspect a package he was carrying. An American soldier was wounded and two Mexican customs officials were killed. Gunfire then erupted from buildings on both sides of the border, as soldiers and local civilians joined the fray. The 10th Cavalry at Camp Little, under the command of Lieutenant Colonel Frederick Herman, rushed to the scene. Local civilians often transported the soldiers to the border in their own private vehicles. When he arrived, Herman found fire coming in from "a sharp knoll or hill" across the border, as well as from "the buildings, alleyways, and doorways of the houses on the Mexican side." He ordered his men to cross the border on foot, clear the buildings and streets, and seize the two hills on either side of the Sonoran half of the city. The Buffalo Soldiers moved through the streets "promptly and in a most creditable manner," as described in the *History of the Tenth Cavalry*. The streets of Nogales, Sonora, were not unknown to some of the Doughboys. When some 10th Cavalry men entered a bordello, one of the ladies working there reportedly exclaimed, "Sergeant Jackson! We are all glad to see you!" As the Americans pressed into his city, the mayor of Nogales, Felix Peñaloza, ran through the streets with a white flag, but was killed by a shot coming from the Arizona side of the border. Accounts differ as to whether the Americans had completed their seizure of the heights above the town, but by 8:00 PM a ceasefire had been arranged, ending the bloodshed. When it was all over seven Americans were dead (five soldiers and two civilians) and twenty-five wounded. Mexico reported fifteen dead, though some

Nogales, Mexico as seen from the Arizona side of the border. The so-called "Battle of Ambos Nogales" was fought mainly in the area between the two hills. The present-day border fence appears in the lower portion of the photograph.

believe the number may have been much higher. The existence of Germans on the Sonoran side of the border has never been proven.

Several century-old buildings remain in Ambos Nogales, including the old city hall and jail on the Arizona side at 136 North Grand Avenue. That 1914 structure is now home to the Pimeria Alta Historical Museum, which includes exhibits about the Buffalo Soldiers and the 1918 engagement. But in general, Nogales today looks very different than it did when its streets were a battlefield. The steel border fence now looms over International Street. Nogales is one of the busiest crossings on the U.S.-Mexican border today, with a complex of customs buildings controlling access between the two nations. The Battle of Ambos Nogales, as the incident is sometimes called, was in fact no more than a skirmish, and is little known outside of the area. There are a few memorials of the fight south of the border. A monument to the Mexican dead stands near the intersection of Adolfo Lopez Mateos and Pierson in Nogales, Sonora, less than 500 meters from the border crossing station. A small plaque on Adolfo Ruiz Cortina—just two blocks from the border—marks the spot where Mayor Peñaloza was killed. In 1961, the Mexican government declared Nogales a "heroic" city for its fight with the Americans in 1918. Not a single memorial exists on the Arizona side. The small monument at the present-day city hall of Nogales, Arizona, marking the spot of Camp Little does not even mention the events of August 27, 1918.

Serving a Democracy That Didn't Serve Them

Stung by criticism of the army's racial policies, Secretary Baker took steps to ensure African Americans a place in the war effort. He assigned Emmett J. Scott, the former secretary and confidant of the late civil rights leader Booker T. Washington, to be his special advisor on race relations, and authorized the creation of two new black combat divisions. Draftees made up the 92nd Division. Harkening back to the valorous service of the African American regiments during the Indian Wars, the 92nd took the nickname "Buffalo Soldiers" and adopted a shoulder patch with a buffalo on it. The 93rd Division was composed mainly of National Guard troops. The 15th New York Infantry became the 369th Infantry Regiment, and the 8th Illinois Infantry became the 370th Infantry Regiment. Draftees from the Carolinas filled the ranks of the 371st Infantry Regiment, while the 372nd Infantry Regiment was composed of National Guard regiments from various states and the District of Columbia.

Civil rights groups lauded the formation of these regiments, but the army seemed to guide them down the road to failure. Given the policy of dispersing African American troops, the 92nd Division could not train together in the same place, inhibiting unit cohesion. The division maintained its headquarters at Camp Funston during the training process, but elements of it trained in at least seven different places. The 93rd was really a division in name only. It had no artillery or support units. Indeed, through its entire existence, the 93rd Division was never together in the same place at the same time, and was referred to in official records as a "provisional" division.

Civil rights activists argued that black officers should lead black soldiers into battle. Once again, the army addressed their concerns, but did so in a way that undermined the divisions. In June 1917, 1,250 African American men (including 250 enlisted men from regular army regiments) began their training at a segregated officer candidate school at Fort Des Moines, Iowa. Problems emerged from the start. Although thousands of black college students across the country had expressed their desire to serve, admission to Fort Des Moines was limited to men ages twenty-five to forty-four, thus eliminating many promising younger men. While white officer candidate schools required a college education, at Des Moines a high school diploma was sufficient. The commandant was Colonel Charles C. Ballou, a white officer who had once served with the 24th Infantry Regiment. Perhaps more liberal on racial matters than most officers, Ballou was nevertheless an ardent segregationist and dubious of racial equality. In public he spoke well of the candidates, but in private Ballou frequently expressed his belief that African Americans lacked the character and intelligence to lead men into battle. Ballou's low expectations turned the training into a farce. Some candidates complained that commissions went to those who showed deference to whites, while more qualified men were passed over. Barely literate regular army enlisted men, others charged, were favored over the college-educated. "Commissions were often awarded to those who were more likely to fail than succeed," wrote William Colson and A.B. Nutt, graduates of the Des Moines program who penned a scathing critique of the army's treatment of African American officers after the war. One man, they claimed, got a commission "by singing plantation songs."

The school graduated just one class of 639 men, and closed in October 1917. During World War II, Fort Des Moines was a training center for female officers. The fort, at the corner of East Army Post and Chaffee Roads on the south side of the city, is no longer an active military installation, though its buildings are visible from the street. On the grounds is the Fort Des Moines Museum, a small facility dedicated to the installation's big place in the social history of the U.S. military. The graduates went on to serve in the 92nd Division as junior officers. Ballou was promoted to general and given command of that division. Very few other African Americans became officers. Fort Des Moines was also home to the

Colored Medical Officer's Camp, which commissioned about 100 dentists and physicians. A tiny handful of African Americans were later admitted to the same officer candidate schools as whites, and several traditionally black colleges founded training detachments to prepare others. Aside from that, there would be no more black officers. Once commissioned, these men faced daunting challenges. White soldiers often refused to salute them, and their white officers seldom forced them to do so. Indeed, white officers could be just as disrespectful, and rarely viewed their black colleagues as equals. W. E. B. DuBois was offered a commission to serve on an army intelligence board, but his assertive views on racial equality made some on the board uncomfortable. Like Colonel Young, the results of his physical exam gave the army a convenient excuse to deny him the opportunity to serve.

Combat soldiers made up just a small percentage of all black troops. Of the 380,000 African Americans who saw military service in World War I, 89 percent were assigned to noncombat labor units. The army needed all kinds of things done—from digging ditches to erecting buildings—and assigned African American troops to do them. Laborers typically received only about one month of training, learning little more than how to salute and wear the uniform, before shipping out for France. Service troops were the last to get uniforms. They were also last in line for weapons, and many got no weapons training at all. The majority of labor units went overseas, but thousands of black labor troops never left the United States. Indeed, many labor units were organized, trained, and put to work all at the same facility. The massive expansion of military posts in the United States during the war depended on these laborers, who were barely treated as soldiers at all. African American labor troops were a prominent part of the Newport News Port of Embarkation in Virginia (see Chapter 4). A portion of Camp Hill, on the James River about two miles north of the docks, was dedicated to training stevedore and labor battalions bound for Europe, as well as housing those who worked the Virginia docks. In August 1918, the African American labor troops got their own facility adjacent to Camp Hill. Camp Alexander was named in honor of Lieutenant John H. Alexander, the second black graduate of West Point. By November 1918, the camp had hosted 50,000 African American stevedores and labor troops. A Virginia historical marker commemorating Camp Alexander stands near the intersection of Hilton Boulevard and Jefferson Avenue. The camp extended from Jefferson eastward to Warwick Boulevard. A marker for Camp Hill lies in Huntington Heights Square, where Huntington Avenue splits off from Warwick Boulevard.

Life for African American soldiers stateside—whether in training or as their permanent station—was usually unpleasant. Posts were strictly segregated, and the living quarters for black troops often left much to be desired. The problem was especially acute in colder regions. "The climate of the North proved to be the source of much suffering," recalled Emmett Scott, "on account of its deadly effect upon colored soldiers bred and born amid the magnolia blossoms and in the balmy atmosphere of the 'sunny South.'" Winter winds whipped through tents or the slats between the wall-boards of hastily built barracks, and overcrowding spread disease. Black soldiers at Camp Hill, Virginia, had an unusually high death rate due to disease, and some stevedores reportedly even froze to death in their quarters during the harsh winter of 1917–1918. African Americans who found themselves in proscribed areas on post without permission were likely to face verbal and physical harassment from white soldiers, and then a punishment from their commanding officer for crossing the color line. Recreation was usually segregated as well. The Red Cross, YMCA, and other service organizations operated separate (and usually unequal) facilities for black troops, staffed by African American volunteers. Many posts had no recreational facilities for the black soldier at all. Places like the YMCA were nevertheless a godsend to the African American soldiers, offering not just a respite from the drudgery of military life, but also a haven from the stinging racism they faced daily. Many YMCA huts offered classes on reading and writing to the large number of illiterates. In the fiercely patriotic time, many of the classroom readings focused on the blessings of American democracy, even though African Americans rarely experienced it themselves. As historian Nina Mjagkij observed, "the YMCA helped to raise the political awareness of black men and their expectations for civil rights after the war."

Things were not much better off the post. Northern cities and towns were little more hospitable to African American soldiers than the segregated South. Though Jim Crow was not official policy up North, black soldiers still found themselves denied service in shops and restaurants in town. Those who protested such treatment found little support from the army. In Manhattan, Kansas, a theater manager turned away a sergeant with the 92nd Division at Camp Funston, arguing that his presence would disturb white patrons. The indignant soldier took his case to the army, but his protestations did not necessarily have the desired result. General Ballou, the division commander, issued to his troops Bulletin 35, which became an infamous example of army institutional racism. The general conceded that the soldier was "strictly within his legal rights in this matter," and indeed the theater manager was fined $10 for violating the state's antidiscrimination laws. But Ballou also admonished the soldier, arguing that he was "guilty of the GREATER wrong [of] doing ANYTHING, NO MATTER HOW LEGALLY CORRECT, that will provoke race animosity." He told the "colored members" of the division to "refrain from going where their presence will be resented," and further warned, "White men made the division, and they can break it just as easily if it becomes a trouble maker."

In the South, Jim Crow made no exceptions for wartime. For many Northern blacks, army service was their first exposure to legally segregated world of the South. African American combat troops faced particular hostility. The 8th Illinois Infantry Regiment, soon to become the 370th Infantry Regiment, trained with other Illinois National Guard units at Camp Logan, Texas—the site of the bitter 1917 racial disturbance. "At several places en route to Houston from Illinois they were jeered at along the way," reported Emmett Scott, "stoned in one or two places, and a riot was barely averted at a way station in Texas." After their arrival, the Illinoisans immediately sensed the racial tension bubbling across the city. Captain Charles Braddan, the regimental chaplain, noted the starkly different reactions of the local populace to the sight of African American troops during a parade through Houston. "The black population that had choked the streets to see their boys gasped with admiration," he wrote, "held their breath with wonder, then opened their mouths with pride and yelled 'Atta Boy, now let these white folks start something.'" He also noted "not a handclap from the whites, who regarded us with sullen silence." Fortunately, the regiment's time in Houston passed without incident. Indeed, one advantage to service in the South was the warm support of the local African American community. "Our stay in Houston . . . was one of the most pleasant of the entire period of our enforced absence from our home towns," wrote Braddan, "for the Negro population tried to outdo each other in making us welcome and many were the men of the regiment who fell pierced by the arrow of that Little Cherub, Cupid."

The only African American unit that experienced any significant trouble was the 15th New York Infantry, which trained with the other Empire State regiments at Camp Wadsworth near Spartanburg, South Carolina. White South Carolinians welcomed the white New Yorkers, but news that African Americans would also be coming generated a firestorm of angry denunciations. A spokesman for the Spartanburg Chamber of Commerce argued that "it is a great mistake to send Northern negroes down here, for they do not understand our attitude," and declared that "if any of those colored soldiers go into any of our soda stores and ask to be served they'll be knocked down." Spartanburg's mayor, J. F. Floyd, referenced "the trouble a couple of weeks ago in Houston," and stated that the presence of the 15th New York was "like waving a red flag in the face of a bull." When the 15th New York arrived in October 1917, Spartanburg seethed with racial tension. Hayward implored his men to exercise restraint in the face of racial taunting, which was omnipresent. The black New Yorkers awoke on more than one occasion to find a sign affixed to their barracks stating "No Niggers Allowed." A Harvard-educated black officer was forced off a streetcar even after having paid for a ticket. An enlisted man was attacked by a group of whites for having the temerity to use the sidewalk, which under Jim Crow was for whites only. The victim of the assault followed Hayward's advice and did not fight back, but—in a rarity for World War I racial incidents—a small group of white New York soldiers stuck up for their black comrade and roughed up the attackers.

In the face of all this, the 15th New York Infantry showed remarkable patience and discipline, but in some cases violence was barely averted. One day two men were missing from roll call, and a rumor circulated through the camp that local police had lynched them. Outraged, a small band of 15th New York soldiers began an armed march into Spartanburg to "shoot up the town." Catching wind of the situation, Colonel Hayward raced toward Spartanburg "to save the regiment from disgrace." He found the group on the main road into town and managed to diffuse the situation. The two missing men later turned up safe and sound. "That town was, for half an hour or more, just balancing between tragedy and normality," Hayward later recalled. Another incident involved Sergeant Noble Sissle, the drum major of the regimental band (and later a noted jazz artist). Sissle walked into the Sphinx Hotel in downtown Spartanburg to buy a newspaper. The lobby was filled with plenty of other New York soldiers enjoying a little time away from the post, though Sissle was the only African American. After making his purchase, the hotel owner approached Sissle, struck him in the head, and yelled: "Say, nigger, don't you know enough to take your hat off?" Sissle pointed out that he was a United States soldier and that the hat he just knocked to the floor was government property. "Damn you and the government too," responded the proprietor, who continued yelling and kicking Sissle. Once again, the white New York soldiers defended their black comrade, doing so now in the hotel as they began to threaten the proprietor. The renewal of the Civil War seemed to brewing. Learning of the commotion, Lieutenant James Reese Europe—who was standing outside not far away—entered the lobby, called the soldiers to attention, and ordered them all out of the hotel. Shocked by the sight of a black man exercising his authority, the proprietor then began to curse at Europe, who turned his back and walked away. A South Carolina historical marker commemorates the Camp Wadsworth on Willis Road (State Highway 42-686) near the intersection with Ravines Lane, in front of an athletic club. It does not mention the 15th New York Infantry. However, not far away, at the busy intersection of East Blackstock Road and W.O. Ezell Boulevard, is another marker specifically dedicated to the New Yorkers, one that acknowledges the racial tensions in Spartanburg during the war.

Musical and Military Glory—and Homegrown Discrimination—in Europe

Both incidents were hushed up, but not long afterward the 15th New York Infantry received orders to sail for France—despite having just two weeks of training at Camp Wadsworth. It was clear that the army simply wanted to get the regiment out of South Carolina as soon as possible. When they sailed from Hoboken in December 1917, the regiment had not yet been officially accepted for federal service. The 15th New York was the only unit in the U.S. Army to go overseas under the flag of its home state. The first elements stepped off the boat in France on New Year's Eve, and the rest followed shortly thereafter. The regiment gathered in Saint-Nazaire, where it was put to work on construction projects and offloading ships. Arriving white soldiers received such details, too, but given the army's attitudes about African Americans in combat many feared that the labor detail would be made permanent. The well-connected officers of the 15th New York went to work to get the regiment a combat assignment.

Then something quite fortuitous happened. Jim Europe's reputation preceded him, and word spread that his unique regimental band was in France. In February 1918, the band received orders to proceed to the AEF leave center at Aix-les-Bains to entertain the soldiers there. The train ride took three days, and the band played numerous gigs in along the way, changing the face of popular music forever. The first stop was Nantes, fifty kilometers east of Saint-Nazaire. Their first performance was an informal one on place Graslin in front of the city's opera house. The classical columns of opera house façade stood in stark contrast to the modern sounds of jazz being played before it. The French had never heard these kinds of syncopated rhythms, or familiar instruments making such unfamiliar sounds, and the crowd was electrified. Arthur Little, a white regimental officer, wrote that the "entire plaza was crowded with an audience which maintained silence during the playing of a number—and then made up for lost time, by wild applause." The band then played inside the opera house. "The audience sat patiently," Noble Sissle remembered, until it "could stand it no longer, the 'jazz germ' hit them and it seemed to find the vital spot loosening all muscles and causing what is known in America as an 'eagle rocking it.'" The place Graslin in Nantes may well be considered the birthplace of jazz in France. After its arrival in Aix-les-Bains, the band made an even bigger splash. It played mainly in the theater of the casino, but gave many other concerts in Aix-les-Bains and surrounding towns for both French and American audiences. During concerts, Doughboys sometimes climbed up on tables and shouted for more. French crowds went wild over Europe's unusual jazz version of *Le Marseillaise*. Their original two-week stay was doubled.

James Reese Europe (far left) and the 369th Infantry Regiment "Hell Fighters" Band. (Courtesy of the National Archives)

They were like rock stars of a later age, and their departure generated pandemonium rather like that which was to greet Elvis or the Beatles. A massive crowd of local women and children descended on the musicians at the rail station. "The band played its farewell," Little wrote, and "the crowd cheered without ceasing; women and children wept."

For the 15th New York, musical talent led to martial glory. General Pershing fought vigorously to maintain an independent American army and ensure that U.S. soldiers would not have to fight under a foreign flag, but his principled stand did not extend to African Americans. Pershing had no plans to integrate the now-famous Harlem men into the AEF command structure. When the regiment was finally federalized and redesignated the 369th Infantry Regiment, Pershing was happy to hand them off to the French. As Colonel Hayward told a French colleague, the U.S. Army "put the black orphan in a basket, set it on the doorstep, pulled the bell, and went away." In March 1918, the 369th Infantry moved to Champagne to begin its tutelage in the trenches, becoming part of the French 16th Division, Fourth French Army. The Americans began their initiation in an area known as the "Afrique Sector," located about fifty kilometers southeast of Reims on the edge of the Argonne Forest, where the French had stationed many of its African colonial troops. The area was the scene of some exceptionally bloody fighting in 1914 and 1915, but had remained quiet since then. Three years of infantry charges and artillery duels transformed the woods and farmlands of Champagne into an apocalyptic moonlike landscape. In a slew of villages behind the lines the men began their training. They wore American uniforms, but all their equipment was French. They used French rifles and gas masks. They wore French Adrian battle helmets with their stylish brim and ridge along the top. The Americans voiced numerous complaints about the skimpiness of French rations, but they did enjoy the wine—that is, until their American officers took it away and substituted it with extra sugar. The U.S. Army had effectively abandoned the 369th Infantry, but as historian Richard Slotkin put it, service with the French "was a liberation rather than an exile." The French did not share the white American view that blacks made poor fighters. Their experience in three years of war proved otherwise. Low expectations and inferior resources did not mar the training of the 369th Infantry. They were treated like soldiers and men.

By April 1918, the 369th Infantry moved into the trenches. Along with French mentors, they occupied a five-kilometer front south of the Tourbe River running from Ville-sur-Tourbe on the western end to the Aisne River on the east. On April 20, the French trainers withdrew, leaving the 369th alone to face the Germans. "We should have to sink or swim," recalled Arthur Little, who admitted frankly in his memoir, "I was frightened." For the most part the sector remained quiet, but there were of course the occasional trench raids. One evening, some French soldiers invited Lieutenant Europe to go along with them on a raid, an offer the bandleader accepted with trepidation. He was dressed in a French uniform, handed a small pistol, and headed up to no man's land with the raiding party. "I thought I was having a terrible nightmare and kept trying to wake up," Europe remembered, but he also "noticed how beautiful the night was. Every star seemed as bright as a shining silver light." The men slipped across no man's land, and upon reaching the German trench, French artillery opened up. "It looked and sounded like the 'Forty-Fourth' of July," recalled Europe. The raiders then plunged into the German trenches. After a few minutes a French officer sent up a green flare, signaling withdrawal. The raid "hardly took five minutes," Europe believed, "but it seemed like ages to me." The party scampered back to its own lines with some papers and German uniform parts (but no prisoners) as German artillery pounded their escape.

The Germans conducted their own raids, and one in the early morning hours of May 15 became the stuff of legend. On the far western end of the 369th sector was an area known as Montplaisir, a high ground between the Tourbe River and the Bois d'Hauzy north of the hamlet of Malmy. Observation posts detected the German raid and sounded the alarm. About twenty Germans descended on the outpost occupied by five Americans, among them Needham Roberts, a seventeen-year-old from Trenton, New Jersey, and

Henry Johnson, a porter for the New York Central Railroad from Albany, New York. The two men heard the Germans cutting the wire in front of their position, and sent hand grenades and rifle fire in their direction. German grenades quickly began to rain into their position, trapping three men in an underground bunker and wounding Roberts and Johnson. Unable to stand, Roberts bravely kept shooting as the Germans jumped into their outpost, but it was Johnson's actions that became legendary. Wounded in numerous places from head to toe, Johnson took on the German raiders in fierce hand-to-hand fighting. His rifle jammed, but Johnson used it as a club to fight off several Germans until the weapon broke apart. When Johnson saw three Germans carrying Roberts away, he charged them with his bolo knife in hand. One German took a chop to the head, slicing through his helmet and cracking open his skull. One ran away. The last German shot Johnson several times with his Luger, but Johnson lunged at him and plunged the knife into his guts. The surviving Germans gathered their wounded and dashed back to their lines. They took no prisoners, but the Germans gained one valuable piece of information from the raid—the men of the 369th Infantry Regiment could fight.

The incident became known as the "Battle of Henry Johnson," and was widely reported in the papers back home. France awarded Johnson the Croix de Guerre with Gold Palm, the first American soldier to receive that honor. Johnson's actions were a morale booster—not just for African Americans, but for all Americans—and should have put to rest suggestions that black soldiers could not fight. And yet, press reports of the incident were still filled with insulting racial stereotypes. The most noted journalist on hand was Irvin S. Cobb, a southern white humorist on assignment for the *Saturday Evening Post*. Cobb was known for his portrayals of southern blacks as being lazy and childlike, and his writings were laced with his own demeaning interpretations of black vernacular speech. Cobb wrote a story that he genuinely believed heaped praise upon the 369th Infantry, but he could not overcome his racial prejudices. For example, he quoted one soldier, whom he described as having "a complexion like the bottom of a coal mine and a smile like the sudden lifting of a piano lid," as telling him, "'Effen they'll jes gimme a razor an' a armload of bricks an' one half pint of bust-haid licker I kin go plum to Berlin.'" In Cobb's estimation, the men of the 369th "were apt to be mulattoes or to have light-brown complexions instead of clear black," suggesting that it was the influx of white blood that made them creditable soldiers. In the ultimate backhanded compliment, Cobb claimed that because of the 369th Infantry, after the war the word "n-i-g-g-e-r will merely be another way of spelling the word American." Even in their moments of triumph, African American soldiers were robbed of their dignity.

Many feel that Johnson and other African American soldiers were robbed of official recognition was well. Though Johnson received the Croix de Guerre from France, his own government did not decorate him—not even the Purple Heart was awarded to those wounded in combat. After the war Johnson returned to Albany and resumed his job with the railroad, but was never able to recover his health. He hit the bottle, and died alone and penniless in 1929. Johnson's case was heart-wrenching but hardly unique. African Americans and other minority soldiers frequently claimed that they were denied medals for valor or, due to discrimination, received decorations of lower prestige. Similar charges reemerged during World War II. Though Johnson never received proper government recognition during his lifetime, his case was not forgotten. Beginning in the 1980s, in the wake of the civil rights movement, the military reopened the cases of Johnson and many others. He posthumously received his Purple Heart in 1996, and the Distinguished Service Cross—the army's second highest decoration for valor—in 2003. Many feel that that is still not enough. A campaign is currently underway to upgrade his award to the Medal of Honor. There is a monument to the Battle of Henry Johnson,

Battle of Henry Johnson Memorial, Washington Park, Albany, New York.

but not at Montplaisir. Rather, it is located 4,000 miles away in the southeastern corner of Washington Park in Albany, New York. The granite base tells the story of Johnson, as well as that of the 369th Infantry, which earned the nickname "Harlem Hell Fighters" during the war. Capping the monument is a painted bronze bust of Johnson.

The 369th suffered many other casualties during its initiation into the world of the trenches, among them James Reese Europe, who took a hefty dose of gas. The regiment came off the line on July 4 and went to the rear for some training and a little rest, but it would not take long until its members were back in action. When they returned to the front, James Reese Europe would not be with them. While in the hospital recovering from the gas attack, Europe wrote a song about his experiences at the front. Entitled "On Patrol in No Man's Land," it evoked the emotions of being in combat and even featured percussionists simulating machine guns, grenades, falling shells, and gas alarms. After recovering from his wounds, Europe and the rest of the 369th Infantry Regiment Band went to Paris to help raise money for war relief. Their concert at the Thêâtre Champs-Elysèes (15 avenue Montaigne) electrified the

City of Light and made them an international sensation. "We had conquered Paris," Europe commented. While in Paris the band also began recording its music. "On Patrol in No Man's Land" became of the America's most popular songs during the Great War. Europe and the rest of his band spent the remainder of the war in Paris, giving concerts in hospitals and other venues to keep up morale, and mesmerizing the French with jazz. Europe returned from the war poised to become a jazz superstar, but he never got the chance. After a concert in Boston on May 9, 1919, a disgruntled band member stabbed Europe in the neck, killing him.

The remaining three regiments of the 93rd Division arrived in France in April 1918. Like the New Yorkers, these African American units were parceled out to the French, where they received French equipment, ate French rations, and were integrated into French divisions. The 171st and 172nd Infantry Regiments entered the trenches of Lorraine for training, and then joined the 369th in the French Fourth Army in Champagne (see Chapter 15). The 370th Infantry Regiment trained at Grandvillars in the Vosges Mountains. "The men were greatly chagrinned when they were ordered to turn in their American equipment and were issued French equipment instead," reported Chaplain Braddan of the 370th. "This man's army certainly doesn't want us, was heard on all sides." The Illinois men eventually saw action in Picardy, northeast of Paris (see Chapter 16). Only the Buffalo Soldiers of the 92nd Division would be under American command. They arrived early in the summer of 1918, and by August began their first stint on the front near Saint-Die in the Vosges Mountains.

African American soldiers had proven themselves on the battlefield, but the U.S. Army still stationed most of its black soldiers behind the front lines. Two hundred thousand black Doughboys served in least 136 distinct labor units in the AEF, mainly under the aegis of the Services of Supply. Most common was the Service Battalion. These troops performed a great variety of jobs, ranging from food service to forestry. It was often African American soldiers who gathered the dead from the battlefields and buried them in cemeteries. This was "the most ghastly and gruesome task in the A.E.F.," according to Charles Williams, an observer of African American soldier welfare for the Federal Council of Churches of Christ. Williams observed a mortuary detail near Romagne-sous-Montfaucon (at what is now the Meuse-Argonne American Cemetery), shortly after the armistice. "The nature of the work required that much of it be done after midnight when most of the men were asleep," he wrote. "One could hear the sound of the hammer and the tread of feet, and the lonely minor chord of the Negroes' song as they drove nails into the coffins."

Many men who served in "Colored Service Battalions" were attached to engineering units. Highways, railroads, warehouses, and other army construction projects were frequently built with African American hands. The fast-expanding army depended on the work of these men. "Great warehouses were built as well as barracks, cantonments and hospitals," noted the *History of the American Negro in the Great World War*. "Without these facilities the army would have been utterly useless. Negroes did the bulk of the work. They were an indispensable wheel in the machinery, without which all would have been chaos or inaction."

One of the most visible African American soldiers in the AEF was the denim-clad army stevedore who loaded and unloaded the ships in French ports like Brest, Saint-Nazaire, and Bassens. Working the docks involved long hours and backbreaking labor, and was often made more difficult because of poor equipment. Ely Green, an NCO in a stevedore company in Saint-Nazaire, implored his superiors in September 1918 to get rain gear and gloves for his men. Describing how his men handled cold steel and copper with bare hands, and frozen meat using socks for gloves, he told them "my men's hands are bleeding." When the gear finally arrived in November, he believed it was "the happiest day our men had in France except Armistice Day." The work was dangerous, too. Green recalled another incident where a hatch cover on a ship had accidentally closed on a man, cutting him in half. "His hips and legs lying on the deck," Green wrote, "the upper part of his body falling into the hatch."

African Americans were also commonly assigned to the "pioneer infantry," as were a good many white soldiers. Pioneers were armed labor troops with infantry training who worked near the front lines—often close enough to come under shellfire or air raids. In addition to jobs like road and rail construction, pioneer troops also did salvage work. The 805th Pioneer Infantry, an African American unit organized at Camp Funston, was assigned to clean up the battlefield after the Meuse-Argonne Offensive. "Over those hills and through those woods surrounding Briquenay not one salvageable thing was unfound, unseen, unmoved, from the smallest to the largest article used in war," according to the unit history. "Many burdensome loads were brought from places in the hills through almost impassable roads." Among the items the 805th cleaned up was unexploded ordnance. "On one occasion, after patiently and laboriously ridding the country for miles around of bombs and ammunition and collecting it in a specified place, the company was ordered to carry the entire collection back into the hills and blow it up."

These soldiers received little praise for their difficult and indispensible work. In fact, their white commanders and contemporaries often minimized their significance and denigrated them as men. General James Harbord, the head of the SOS, described the stevedore troops under his command as "cornfield darkies who never smelled salt water or knew that ships existed except in traditions of the old days of slavery when their Congo ancestors were shipped over in chains." In labor units, most NCOs and officers—and all of the high ranking ones—were whites who typically shared Harbord's attitudes. The ship that conveyed the 371st Infantry Regiment to France also carried a large contingent of African American labor troops. Chaplain Braddan was disgusted by their treatment. In a letter to his church back in Chicago, Bradden bitterly described them as a "Slave Battalion":

> Yes, slave, for no name better suits the conditions under which these noble patriots labored. They were called Labor Battalions, Engineers and Pioneers, but ask them how they were treated at home and abroad, when they were under the complete control of white non-coms, as well as line officers, not even a Negro Chaplain to offer words of advice and encouragement; ask them how they were cursed and damned and worked at high gear from morning until night, and if their story does not melt your heart then it's because you have one of stone.

Ely Green remembered an incident on the Saint-Nazaire docks where a guard bayoneted a stevedore for picking up a piece of candy from a broken shipping crate. The incident almost started a riot. Though Green tried to calm down his men, he was arrested for fomenting a mutiny, beaten severely, and put in the brig. There he witnessed numerous abuses against black soldiers. In one case, guards made one man who was "so sick he held his head with one hand and his stomach with the other" drink castor oil. "He drank it and began vomiting," Green recalled. "One of the guards slambed [sic] his gun butt in his back so hard I heard his back bones crack. He went to his knees and started to crawl away. The two guards helped him by kicking him down the corridor."

Like stateside posts, those overseas were separate and unequal, and African Americans were last in line for supplies and equipment. White soldiers usually stayed in wooden barracks, for example, while blacks were more likely to be housed in tents. Charles Williams visited some black forestry troops in southern France. "The woodcutters lived in floorless tents often surrounded by mud," he observed. "Many times the necessary clothing and boots could not be secured, and sometimes they were obliged to eat in the rain and snow." It was the same at the camp recreational facilities. In places with large concentrations of U.S. troops, the YMCA and other service organizations maintained separate facilities for black troops, sometimes staffed with African American volunteers. Where separate huts were not available, the quality of service for African Americans varied. "Some huts would permit colored men to come in and purchase supplies at the canteen, but would not let them sit down and write," wrote Addie Hunton and Kathryn Johnson, two African American

YMCA hostesses in Europe, "while others received them without any discrimination whatever." In many cases, African American soldiers were denied access to recreational facilities. The Knights of Columbus operated a tent at Romagne-sous-Montfaucon that was initially open to all soldiers, including the African American troops working in the cemetery. But when the camp commander imposed racial segregation on his post, the Knights turned the black soldiers away. Angered, black soldiers tore the tent down.

Military life may have been strenuous and repressive, but many African American soldiers found French society liberating. France was not racially segregated like the Jim Crow South, and many found it even more accepting than the Northern states. One soldier in the 372nd was elated to find that in Saint-Nazaire "the inhabitants were all of the true democratic spirit, catering alike to all." African American officers found the respect among the French that was lacking among white soldiers in their own army. "I am 'Billeted' (rooming) with one of the wealthiest French families in this quaint village," Chaplain Braddan reported to his church from Grandvillars. "Nothing is too good for me. The fact that I am 'Curate' of Le Regiment, The Priest of the Regiment, is my passport to every home." This acceptance of African Americans extended to dating and sexual relationships. Ely Green and a white soldier went to a farm near his camp to get milk when, as Green wrote, a "young girl put her arms around my waist jabbering French [and] looking into my face." The white soldier, from South Carolina, was appalled. The two men went to the farm again the next day, this time accompanied by another white soldier. When the girl hugged Green again, the South Carolinian pulled her away and announced that he had "brought a white man" for her. She was unimpressed, and Green recalled that "the girl held my hand" until he left. Green was taken off the milk detail. In America, nowhere was the color line drawn more starkly than with love and sex. In France, that line was greatly blurred.

The democratic treatment black soldiers received rankled many white Americans, who advised the French and British not to "spoil" African American soldiers. Relationships between African American men and European women caused no end of consternation. General Harbord lamented the fact that black troops "land in a country where no color line is drawn and white women of their stratum of society are willing to associate with them," and complained that "their letters as censored are full of their relations with white women." Falling victim to the stereotype of African Americans as being promiscuous and having unquenchable sexual desires, Harbord believed that this interracial wartime romance and sex would become "a promising problem for the South after the war." General Charles C. Ballou, commander of the 92nd Division, once reportedly referred to his own unit as the "rapist division." French society was hardly free of racial prejudice, of course. The existence of the vast French colonial empire alone suggested that racism infected the French mind as well. Nevertheless, the relative openness of French society was a breath of fresh air for African American soldiers. Experiencing a land that was not racially segregated, Ely Green was "glad to know that my dreams were really true." "I am hoping that when the War ends," reflected Chaplain Braddan, "the same spirit of manhood that prevails here will obtain over there."

Despite the sting of racism and the denigration of his work, the African American Doughboy soldiered on in the hope that his wartime service and sacrifices would lead to a better life back home. France gave him a vision of the democratic, unsegregated world he hoped to find at home after the war. The final campaigns of the Great War would give African American soldiers more chances to prove their value to the nation, but would the army take notice? The case of Eugene Bullard, a pilot in the Lafayette Escadrille, suggested that it might not. An African American man from Georgia, Bullard left the United States after the lynching of his father and made his way to France. In 1914 he enlisted in the French Foreign Legion, and after some time in the trenches he learned to fly and joined his fellow Americans in the Lafayette Escadrille. When the U.S. entered the war in 1917 most of the Escadrille flyers entered U.S. Army, but Bullard found his application for transfer denied. Despite his flying experience and combat record, racism kept Bullard from flying for the land of his birth. The army desperately needed pilots, too. World War I was the first major war in which air power played a critical role, but America lagged far behind European countries in military aviation. If the United States were to contribute fully to Allied victory, it would have to create an air force from almost nothing, and do so as fast as it raised its ground forces.

CHAPTER 11:
THE GREAT WAR IN THE AIR

In a war characterized by bloody murder in muddy trenches, the Great War in the air seemed somehow noble. In the popular mind, World War I aerial combat featured two skilled warriors fighting it out man to man, like jousting medieval knights. The air war seemed both to highlight the American individualist ethic and embrace the nation's love of technological prowess. These kinds of romantic notions seldom stand up to the withering analysis of the historian, and yet the air war continues to fascinate even the most critical observer. Flyers became the most romanticized figures of the war, such as Germany's Baron Manfred von Richthofen. Known popularly as the "Red Baron," von Richthofen flew a blood-red Fokker triplane and downed eighty Allied planes before being shot down himself in April 1918. When the United States entered the war, the Aviation Section of the Signal Corps—the branch of the army charged with aerial operations—had a mere 131 officers (only thirty-five of whom knew how to fly); 1,087 enlisted men; and just 280 planes, which were obsolete by European standards. When the war ended only eighteen months later, the U.S. Army Air Service—officially detached from the Signal Corps in May 1918—had 200,000 members, 50,000 of whom were overseas. The story of American aviation during the Great War features some of conflict's most interesting personalities—including an automobile racer, the son of a former president, an explorer, and one of the most influential military theorists in world history.

At the outset of the war, airplanes were used almost exclusively for reconnaissance, but that soon changed. Observation pilots encountering each other in the air took to shooting pistols and throwing hand grenades at each other. Soon planes were outfitted with machine guns, and "pursuit" planes emerged to shoot down enemy planes and balloons, or attack ground forces from the air. Pilots fought aerial engagements known as "dogfights" in order to gain air superiority over the trenches, and any flyer who shot down five enemy planes or observation balloons earned the title of "ace." In addition to using airplanes in tactical battlefield situations, all sides also began to use them strategically to bomb behind enemy lines. German dirigibles called Zeppelins bombed London for the first time in 1915, and by the end of the war Zeppelin raids had killed more than 500 Britons and injured another 13,000. The Allies responded in kind. General Hugh Trenchard, commander of British air forces, saw air superiority as key to winning the war. Beyond reconnaissance and tactical battlefield support, Trenchard believed that a systematic campaign of bombing deep behind enemy lines to destroy transportation, communications, and industry would sap Germany's will and ability to make war. By 1918, Trenchard's formations appeared over northern and western Germany with increasingly frequency, destroying what it could of German factories and railroads. As the war dragged on, wood and canvas bodies gave way to steel, making planes more durable under fire. Planes got bigger and faster too. Modern air power was born.

Though aviation made up only a tiny portion of the U.S. Army, it attracted some of its most talented young officers. One was Benjamin Foulois. Born to a French immigrant father and American mother in 1879, Foulois enlisted in the army during the Spanish-American War of 1898. He took to soldiering immediately, and in 1901 gained a field promotion to lieutenant after valorous combat service in the Philippines. In 1908 he attended the Signal School at Fort Leavenworth and wrote a thesis entitled *The Tactical and Strategical Value of Dirigible Balloons and Aerodynamical Flying Machines*. In it, he predicted that aircraft would replace the horse cavalry as the primary reconnaissance tool, and that "in all future warfare, we can expect to see engagements in the air between hostile aerial fleets." He furthermore noted that France and Germany had taken a great interest in aviation and claimed that the United States should do so too. "Our geographical position with respect to Europe has saved us from numerous difficulties in the past," he argued, "but it is hardly possible that we can expect to be unmolested in the future [given] such means of transport and communications as are available at the present day." The thesis landed him an assignment testing aircraft, working with the likes of Orville Wright. In 1914 he organized the 1st Aero Squadron, the first unit in the army devoted exclusively to flying, and in 1916 he flew the army's first reconnaissance mission in a hostile operation, during the Mexican border crisis (see Chapter 2).

Another important figure was William L. "Billy" Mitchell. Born in Nice, France, in December 1879, Mitchell was the son of a wealthy Milwaukee businessman. When the Spanish-American War broke out, Mitchell left his studies at Columbian (now George Washington) University to enlist in the 1st Wisconsin Infantry Regiment, but thanks to his father—then a U.S. Senator—he received an officer's commission and an assignment to the Signal

Corps. After the war Mitchell made the army his vocation, serving in Cuba, the Philippines, and Alaska. Mitchell was ambitious and brilliant—though he could also be impetuous and abrasive—and he quickly moved up through the army's command structure, even landing a spot on the General Staff at the tender age of thirty-two. Signal Corps duties introduced Mitchell to aviation, though he did not take to it immediately. It was the outbreak of World War I that first made him think seriously about the airplane as a tool of war, and after temporarily assuming command of the Aviation Section in 1916 following a scandal in that office, his interest grew into an obsession. He took flying lessons on his own time and his own dime, and finagled an appointment to serve as an aviation observer Europe. Arriving just days after congress declared war, Mitchell set up an office in Paris at 138 boulevard Haussmann and quickly made contact with top Allied air commanders. He was especially taken with Hugh Trenchard and his ideas about strategic air power. "His judgment inspired my immediate confidence," he wrote of his meeting with Trenchard, "as we became fast friends at once." On April 30, 1917, Mitchell flew as an observer on a French plane, and became the first member of the American military to fly over enemy territory during World War I.

The Air Service had plenty of talented people, but it faced numerous challenges getting off the ground. First and foremost, it needed airplanes. Though the United States was world's leading industrial power, there were only a dozen companies capable of manufacturing planes in the entire nation—and none on the mass scale necessary. Washington drew up grandiose plans and appropriated millions of dollars for aircraft construction during the war, but the effort mostly went nowhere. During World War I, American pilots on the Western Front flew almost exclusively in British, French, or Italian planes. The only American-built plane to see action in Europe was the DeHaviland DH-4, a British-designed plane with an American-designed Liberty engine, used for observation and day bombing. Nicknamed the "flaming coffin" for its tendency to catch on fire, only 1,200 of the American DH-4's ever made it to France. In all, the United States produced just 11,754 planes during the entire war, most of them noncombat training craft like the JN-4 "Curtiss Jenny" that stayed in the United States. The war nevertheless stimulated the growth of an American aviation industry that would one day make the United States an economic and military superpower. For example, a Seattle lumber baron named William E. Boeing took an interest in flying and in 1916 founded his own airplane company. The following year, the U.S. Navy placed an order for hydroplanes. The Boeing Airplane Company had its first contract. Boeing produced the Model C trainer in a large wooden building known as the "Red Barn" in an industrial area on the banks of the Duwamish River. The Red Barn is now part of the Boeing's Museum of Flight, two miles down the road from the original site. Exhibits in the Red Barn tell the story of early aviation and the founding of the Boeing Corporation, and the navy contract. The museum also devotes an entire gallery to World War I aviation.

Sprucing up the Nation's Air Power

Harnessing the nation's natural resources for aircraft production was another problem. Most planes were made of wood, and the Pacific Northwest had plenty of it, especially the Sitka spruce, which had the qualities of lightness and flexibility that aircraft engineers prized. However, bitter labor troubles plagued the region. Before 1917 Britain and France bought Northwestern spruce for their planes, but the Industrial Workers of the World (IWW), a radical union popular with the hard-pressed loggers, staged numerous strikes that made the wood supply unpredictable. After America joined the war, Uncle Sam was not about to tolerate such interruptions. In 1917, the U.S. Army created the Spruce Production Division (SPD) to take over the Northwest lumber industry and ensure a steady supply of wood. Nearly 30,000 soldiers spent the war in the forests of Washington and Oregon working in various facets of the lumber industry. The SPD also oversaw the work of 100,000 civilians. At first both workers and logging companies resented the SPD, but each soon found the arrangement beneficial. Under army supervision, civilian workers toiled under better and safer conditions, and achieved their longstanding demand of an eight-hour workday. Companies liked the steady supply of timber, as well as the SPD-sponsored Loyal Legion of Loggers and Lumbermen, a conservative alternative to the IWW.

The SPD made its headquarters on the fifth floor of the Yeon Building at 522 SW 5th Avenue in downtown Portland, Oregon, but its largest base was at Vancouver Barracks, just across the Columbia River in Vancouver, Washington, where the army constructed the world's largest lumber mill. At its peak of operations in 1918, the mill covered fifty acres, employed nearly 3,000 soldiers, and produced one million board feet of lumber each day. The site is now part of Fort Vancouver National Historic Site, which marks the location of a nineteenth-century British fur trade post and preserves the U.S. Army base that operated there from 1849 to 2011. No trace of the spruce mill survives, though interpretive panels indicate its location, and the Spruce Mill Trail crosses the field where the mill once stood. Just to the east of the mill site is Pearson Field, named for a World War I pilot named Alexander Pearson, who was killed in a 1924 test flight. Once a polo ground, the field saw its maiden flight in 1905, making it one of America's first airfields. Indeed, a 1918 wooden hangar still stands there. A civilian airport today, Pearson Field is one of the oldest continually operating airfields in the world. Overlooking the entire army post was Officer's Row, a collection of stately Victorian mansions. Those interested in World War I will note the Marshall House, which was the post commander's quarters. George C. Marshall, whose vast administrative skills helped win both world wars, was post commander here from 1936 to 1938.

In addition to the Vancouver Barracks mill, SPD "spruce squadrons" worked in 234 lumber camps scattered across the Pacific Northwest. Valuable stands of trees were often located in remote areas, so soldiers and civilian workers constructed railroads deep into the forests to get at them. Most of these railways were abandoned after the war and swallowed up by the forests, but travelers today can hike on the remnants of Spruce Production Division Railroad No. 1 on Washington's Olympic Peninsula. This was the most ambitious of all the forest railways, running thirty-six miles from Port Angeles southwest to Lake Pleasant, passing through portions of what is now Olympic National Park. Eight thousand workers, half of whom were soldiers, chopped down trees and leveled roadbeds in rugged territory and in all kinds of weather. Along the north shore of Lake Crescent, workers blasted two tunnels through the base of Pyramid Mountain, which rises up starkly from the lake. Despite such Herculean efforts, Spruce Railroad No. 1 was not completed until November 30, 1918—nineteen days after the war ended—and never delivered a single log to the army, though logging companies used it until the 1950s. SPD operations stopped within weeks of the armistice. Most "spruce soldiers" had their discharges in hand by the end of 1918, and logging corporations quickly snapped up army surplus equipment at bargain prices. In all, the SPD produced 79,366,508 board feet of spruce, as well as 59,906,684 board feet of fir, and 3,735,769 board feet of cedar, for a grand total of 143,008,961 board feet of lumber. Most of the lumber went to Great Britain (29 percent) and France (24 percent) for aircraft and ship construction. Only 37 percent went to American companies.

Today, the 9.9-mile Spruce Railroad Trail hugs the north

Spruce Production Division logging operations in Olympic National Park in Washington State. (Courtesy of the National Archives)

View of Crescent Lake from the Spruce Railroad Trail in Olympic National Park today.

shore of Lake Crescent in Olympic National Park, following a portion of the old Great War rail line. U.S. Highway 101 follows the south shore. Camp David Junior Road, off U.S. 101, gives the best access to the trail on the west end of the lake. The east trailhead is on East Beach Road, about two miles east of the intersection with U.S. 101. Much of the trail (especially on the west end) is now paved, and thanks to the grading work of army engineers a century ago, it is also remarkably level, making it one of the most widely accessible trails in the entire park. Construction on the remainder of the pathway—including the restoration of the railroad tunnels—is ongoing. The views along the Spruce Railroad Trail are so spectacularly scenic that one's thoughts will easily drift away from its wartime origins. Crescent Lake is renowned for its unusually clear turquoise waters, which can be mesmerizing. Frequent rains create the green riot of pine trees, ferns, and moss for which the temperate rainforests of the Northwest are famous. The rains also promote landslides—moss-covered rocks indicating older ones, bare rock showing recent events—highlighting the difficulties of building and maintaining the railroad. The Spruce Railroad Trail is part of a larger system called the Olympic Discovery Trail, which extends outside the park toward Port Angeles and also follows portions of the old World War I railway. Just east of Port Angeles, the Olympic Discovery Trail passes the mouth of Ennis Creek, where the army built a sawmill to handle the timber from the railroad. It was 70 percent complete when the war ended.

Training America's Finest to Fly

America not only lacked planes, but also the pilots to fly the planes and the crews to maintain them. After the U.S. Congress declared war, many members of the Lafayette Escadrille (see Chapter 1) changed uniforms and began flying for their home country, forming the core of the 103rd Aero Squadron. To get the Sammies into the skies as soon as possible, the Allies agreed to train American pilots and technicians themselves. Britain and France accepted more than 1,000 Americans into their own pilot training programs.

Throughout 1918, there were about 15,000 American aircraft mechanics in Britain at any given time, training with the British before being rotated to frontline units in France.

To produce its own qualified pilots, the army turned to Major Hiram Bingham III. A Yale history professor famous for his 1911 discovery of the Inca ruins at Machu Picchu in Peru, Bingham had become convinced by 1916 that war with Germany was inevitable, and looked for a way to contribute to the coming war effort. He readily admitted that his "personal experience with mules, South Americans, pack oxen, Indians, ruined Inca cities, and Andean highlands would be of little use in France," but after a conversation with a colleague about "the remarkable progress that aviation was making on the western front," he set his course for the skies. Bingham learned to fly at the age of forty-one and got his commission in the Connecticut National Guard converted into an appointment with the Signal Corps. Too old to fly in combat, he was determined to use his experience as an educator to help defeat the Germans. In May 1917, Bingham was part of a Signal Corps contingent that traveled to Canada to observe their training procedures. Soon after his return, he devised a three-stage training program for the U.S. pilots. First came a course of classroom instruction called "ground school." Those who passed the classes then entered "primary school," where candidates got their first chance to fly. If they survived that, they then went on to "advanced school" where they were assigned to one of three flying specialties—pursuit, observation, or bombing—and learned their deadly trade.

Thousands of adventurous young men were attracted to the danger and romance of the air. One was Congressman Fiorello La Guardia of New York. "I never saw such a collection of applicants," he wrote of his experience at the recruiting office in Washington in July 1917, "young cleancut college boys who had heard about flying but knew nothing about it; acrobats and tumblers who thought that because they were good on a tightrope or trapeze, they would be able to fly; and a large miscellaneous group of boys without the necessary educational background who were eager to get to war, and the quicker the better." Bingham's program had the rigor of an Ivy League graduate school. Of the 40,000 who applied for pilot training, only 22,000 were accepted. Several major universities hosted the schools, from the University of California at Berkeley to the Massachusetts Institute of Technology. Ivy League schools—Columbia, Cornell, and Princeton—were disproportionately represented. Volunteers enlisted in the army like any other recruit. The eight-to-twelve-week program of study included classes on topics like aerodynamics, engineering, and meteorology, taught by university faculty members. Students also received instruction on aerial combat tactics and got hands-on experience with weapons and engines. Bingham remembered that

SIDEBAR 2—STATESIDE FLYING FIELDS

FLYING FIELD	NEAREST CITY	GPS COORDINATES
Bolling	Washington, DC	N 38.84443 W 77.01653
Brooks	San Antonio, TX	N 29.35171 W 98.44844
Call	Wichita Falls, TX	N 33.87132 W 98.54150
Carlstrom	Arcadia, FL	N 27.13833 W 81.80278
Chandler	Essington, PA	N 39.86056 W 75.30000
Chanute	Rantoul, IL	N 40.29417 W 88.14306
Chapman	Miami, FL	N 25.63944 W 80.29222
Dorr	Arcadia, FL	N 27.20722 W 81.67000
Eberts	Lonoke, AR	N 34.79528 W 91.91917
Ellington	Houston, TX	N 29.60722 W 95.16389
Gerstner	Lake Charles, LA	N 30.11861 W 93.08000
Godman	Fort Knox, KY	N 37.90694 W 85.97222
Hazelhurst (Roosevelt)	Garden City, NY	N 40.74194 W 73.59889
Kelly	San Antonio, TX	N 29.38028 W 98.58431
Langley	Hampton, VA	N 37.08306 W 76.35917
Love	Dallas, TX	N 32.84889 W 96.85056
March	Riverside, CA	N 33.88944 W 117.25889
Mather	Sacramento, CA	N 38.55833 W 121.30000
McCook	Dayton, OH	N 39.77583 W 84.19083
Mitchel	Garden City, NY	N 40.72556 W 73.59500
Park	Millington, TN	N 35.35417 W 89.86861
Payne	West Point, MS	N 33.66556 W 88.63250
Penn	Austin, TX	N 30.22716 W 97.75958
McCook	Dayton, OH	N 39.77583 W 84.19083
Post	Lawton, OK	N 34.64879 W 98.40228
Rich	Waco, TX	N 31.54583 W 97.18778
Rockwell	Coronado, CA	N 32.69778 W 117.21306
Scott	Belleville, IL	N 38.54056 W 89.85306
Selfridge	Mt. Clemens, MI	N 42.62083 W 82.83917
Souther	Americus, GA	N 32.11139 W 84.18694
Taliaferro 1 (Hicks)	Saginaw, TX	N 32.93083 W 97.41167
Taliaferro 2 (Barron)	Fort Worth, TX	N 32.62556 W 97.30472
Taliaferro 3 (Carruthers)	Benbrook, TX	N 32.67806 W 97.46000
Taylor	Montgomery, AL	N 32.30389 W 86.12167
Wright	Dayton, OH	N 39.79467 W 84.08785

British observers were favorably impressed with the schools. "Perhaps they were trying to flatter us," he surmised, "but remembering that British officers have very poor reputations as flatterers, we felt greatly encouraged." If the candidate completed ground school successfully he became an aviation cadet. Of the 22,000 admitted to ground school, 17,000 earned the chance to get into the cockpit.

Primary school lasted six to eight weeks. Since the Air Service had precious few experienced pilots, British and French fliers provided much of the instruction. At first cadets flew with instructors accompanying them, but as their skills grew they began to fly solo. Flight training could be very dangerous. The *Air Service Journal* told of a three-plane pile-up at Rockwell Field near San Diego. "Two of the planes met in a head-on collision by smashing into each other at top speed," the report stated. "A third plane entered the tangle and after a steep nose dive landed in the brush at the southern end of one of the fields. The pilots escaped with a slight shaking up." Not all cadets escaped such incidents with their lives—263 pilots died in training accidents during the war. When America first entered the war in 1917, the army had just three flying fields capable of training pilots—Hazelhurst Field on New York's Long Island, Chandler Field in Essington, Pennsylvania; and Rockwell Field near San Diego. It was not nearly enough. By the end of the year, the army had constructed fifteen more. Most were located in the South and West, where the weather permitted year-round flying. Construction continued into 1918. From coast to coast, runways suddenly appeared in farmers' fields and other such places as the Air Service scrambled to build places for their trainees to fly. By the armistice, the Air Service had thirty-two stateside flying fields. Airfields were usually named after men who died in plane crashes. March Field in California was named after Peyton C. March Jr.—son of U.S. Army Chief of Staff Peyton C. March—who died in a training accident in Texas. Cadets had to take care not to have a field named after them.

After acquiring forty to fifty hours of flying time, the cadet then took Reserve Military Aviator's test, which involved performing various feats of flying and navigation. If completed successfully, he received his officer's commission and his wings. In all, just 10,000 received that honor. Pilots were just the tip of the Air Service spear. Not everyone who went into the air was a pilot. Observation planes had a crew of two, a pilot and a specially trained observer whose job was to scan the ground and skies. Manned balloons hovered above the trenches to peek behind enemy lines. There were also thousands of support troops like mechanics, photography and radio technicians, supply personnel, and myriad others who never left the ground. Those who washed out of flight school often ended up in such supporting roles. Some soldiers felt that unscrupulous recruiters had lured them into the less glamorous jobs of the Air Service with the promise of flight. "All of us had enlisted voluntarily and with great eagerness in answer to the country's call for 'aviators,'" noted the anonymous author of the 639th Aero Squadron's history. "They told us we would be flying within a month." But after several months the author noted with a tone of resignation that "the signs pointed to anything but our training as pilots, as had been promised us upon enlistment." In the end, just five men in the unit had met the qualifications for flight training, the remainder having ended up as enlisted men on ground crews. In addition to airfields, scores of warehouses, repair shops, storage depots, and other such facilities cropped up during the war. By November 1918 there were more than 100 Air Service locations across the United States.

The largest Air Service facility was Kelly Field near San Antonio, Texas. Opened in March 1917, Kelly quickly became the most important Air Service training center. Recruits poured in, but the unprepared army did not have the facilities to house them, much less the staff to train them. By Christmas Day there were 37,000 enlisted men at Kelly but fewer than 500 officers. As the facility expanded, it hosted many different functions. It was a primary school for flying cadets. The army maintained its largest aircraft mechanics school there. There were also schools for supply and engineer officers, and a supply depot to boot. Several other airfields opened in the San Antonio area to absorb the overflow from Kelly. Brooks Field, which opened on the southeast side of San Antonio in December 1917, served as an instructor school. Stinson Field, the city's civilian airport located just west of Brooks Field, was also used for military pilot training. Camp John Wise, established in January 1918, trained observation balloon crews just north of the city limits near Fort Sam Houston. With its air bases and army posts, San Antonio was inundated with soldiers. A century later, San Antonio remains very much a military town. Anyone who has ever visited the city will undoubtedly recall the hoards of blue-clad young men and women milling around the famous Riverwalk—basic trainees from nearby Lackland Air Force Base. Kelly Air Force Base officially ceased to exist as the result of the 1995 base closures, but the grounds were simply absorbed into neighboring Lackland and thus the site remains in Air Force hands. Brooks Field is now Brooks Air Force Base, and Stinson Field has returned to civilian use. Only Camp John Wise is gone. The site, north of East Hildebrand Avenue and east of McCullough Avenue in the present-day suburb of Olmos Park, is today residential.

At some places, today's U.S. Air Force jets take off from the same runways that World War I aviators used a century ago. Scott Field in Illinois, for example, is now Scott Air Force Base, home of the Air Mobility Command. Minor Air Service installations sometimes evolved into important bases. Camp George Crook near Bellevue, Nebraska, home to a balloon training center, grew into Offutt Air

Force Base, today the headquarters of the U.S. Strategic Command. Over the past few decades, many air bases have been consolidated with the facilities of other armed services for more streamlined administration. What was once Bolling Field, located in the District of Columbia directly across the Potomac River from Reagan National Airport, is today known as the Joint Base Anacostia-Bolling, and houses air force, coast guard, and navy offices. The airfield itself is long gone. Langley Field in Hampton, Virginia, merged with Fort Eustis in 2010. Now Joint Base Langley-Eustis, it is home to the Air Combat Command. Ellington Field (Houston, Texas) and March Field (Riverside County, California) are today air reserve bases, and Selfridge Field north of Detroit is run by the Michigan Air National Guard. Rockwell Field near San Diego was turned over to the navy in 1939, and is now Naval Air Station North Island. As with army and navy bases, active air installations often have rigid security policies and travelers would be wise not to poke around them. A few host publicly accessible museums on or adjacent to the base, many of which enlighten visitors about Great War aviation history. Lackland Air Force Base in San Antonio hosts the USAF Airman Heritage Museum, commemorating the service of enlisted personnel, and March Air Force Base has the March Field Air Museum.

One former Great War flying field, in Dayton, Ohio, is today home to the world's largest air museum. As the hometown of the Wright Brothers, Dayton has an unrivaled place in aviation history. After their triumph at Kitty Hawk, the Wright Brothers returned to Dayton to improve their machines. They flew their new and improved aircraft at a place called Huffman Prairie, just east of the city. They opened a flying school there that trained several army pilots and developed their first military plane, which they sold to the army in 1909. In 1917, the army acquired Huffman Prairie, renamed it Wilbur Wright Field, and turned it into an important pilot training center. The army held on to the property after the war, and the facility evolved into Wright-Patterson Air Force Base. Today, the National Park Service maintains the Dayton Aviation Heritage National Historical Park, with a visitor center in downtown Dayton, to preserve some of the most sacred sites of early aviation, including Huffman Prairie. The prairie is located on the sprawling grounds of Wright-Patterson AFB, as is the National Museum of the U.S. Air Force, about a mile away from Huffman Prairie. The museum's Early Years Gallery contains specimens of nearly every kind of plane U.S. pilots flew in the Great War, as well as a good many German planes.

But at other stateside Great War airfields, military aviation is but a memory. Some did double duty during World War II, such as Dorr and Carlstrom fields near Arcadia, Florida, both of which now host correctional facilities. Concrete slabs and even a few buildings remain at the sites, but they date from World War II. Souther Field

Love Field, Dallas, Texas, 1918.

near Americus, Georgia, also came back into service in World War II, its grounds now a civilian airport and a college. A few stayed on active duty through the Cold War. Civilian planes today take off from the runways of the former Chanute Air Force Base (near Rantoul, Illinois), whose buildings host not only a wide range of civilian enterprises but also the Chanute Air Museum. Mather Field, near Sacramento, is now a civilian airport as well. Some fields went on to make history in other ways. In June 1918, the Army Balloon School opened at Ross Field near Arcadia, California, on the grounds of a racetrack. After the war Santa Anita Race Track became one of the world's premier horse racing venues, made famous by the exploits of the legendary horse Seabiscuit. It was also a gathering point for Japanese American internees during World War II before they were sent off to the infamous "Relocation Centers." Other flying fields just disappeared. The runways of Payne Field near West Point, Mississippi, have returned to farmland. Not a trace remains except some concrete slabs in a wooded area along Payne Field Road northeast of town.

New York's Long Island also had a slew of military airfields during the Great War. As early as 1911, the army began using the site of an old Spanish-American War mobilization camp on the Hempstead Plains near Garden City for aviation. Known as Hazelhurst Field—later renamed Roosevelt Field—it was one of just a handful of Signal Corps airfields operating before America entered the war. In 1918, on the plain south of the first airstrip, the army opened Aviation Field No. 2, later named Mitchel Field in honor of former New York City mayor and Air Service pilot John P. Mitchel, who died in a training accident that year. The Camp Mills embarkation camp was located adjacent to the airfields (see Chapter 4), and the soldiers there awaiting transportation to Europe often marveled at the aerial traffic. "There are over a hundred machines on the field," reported Martin Kimmel of the 41st Division, "and it is no strange or unusual sight to see 15 or twenty of them in the air at one time. They appear like a great flock of buzzards overhead and

the roar of their engines never ceases all day long." In 1927, Charles Lindbergh took off from Roosevelt Field for Paris on his famous first solo crossing of the Atlantic by air. During World War II, coastal defense planes took off from Roosevelt and Mitchel Fields, and the latter remained in the hands of the U.S. Air Force until 1961. The area of the airfields is now used for various retail and commercial purposes. Roosevelt Field lay just east of Roosevelt Field Mall, one of Long Island's most popular shopping centers. Mitchel Field is less than a mile south. On the grounds of the latter is the Cradle of Aviation Museum, housed in old military hangars. It depicts Long Island's illustrious aviation history, from ballooning to the Space Age, and contains several planes and exhibits covering the activities of Roosevelt and Mitchel Fields during World War I. A small plaque in the center of a traffic circle in front of the museum marks the site of Mitchel Field and pays tribute to its flyers and crews.

Texas has an unusually large number of former Great War airfields. Love Field in Dallas lives on as a public airport. Adjacent to it is the Frontiers of Flight Museum. Much of the museum focuses on commercial aviation, but it also dedicates a gallery to Love Field's World War I origins, and among the many machines hanging from its ceiling is a Curtiss Jenny. In some cases, fragments of air bases live on though the planes are long gone. The brick buildings at Austin's Penn Field, for example, were put to various industrial uses after the war. By the end of the twentieth century the buildings had been abandoned and the site was an eyesore, but in 2000 a group of local businessmen bought the site and converted it into an office complex. Although architects substantially altered them during the renovation, its century-old army buildings still stand, as does the old water tower. A small plaque on Building F, the former hangar, tells the site's history. In some cases, only the name of the field lives on. Call Field was located on the southwest side of Wichita Falls, Texas. The base ran along what is now Call Field Road, the runway just south of the road in the University Heights subdivision. Kickapoo

Airport, two miles west of the old airfield, once hosted the Call Field Museum. This museum featured a restored Curtiss Jenny and a stone monument to Call Field, listing the names of those who died there, that once stood at the intersection of Kemp Boulevard and Call Field Road. In 2014, the Curtiss Jenny, the monument, and the rest of the museum began moving into a new facility in the terminal of Wichita Falls Regional Airport. Some Texas World War I airfields have disappeared altogether. The grounds of Rich Field in Waco are now occupied by a high school and the Heart O' Texas Fairgrounds. There is no historical marker there.

Three airfields in the Fort Worth area, known collectively as Camp Taliaferro, highlight the cooperation between the American and Canadian governments during the war. Canadian pilots trained at flying fields near Fort Worth when harsh winters halted training in their home country. Hicks Field was located north of the city near the village of Saginaw. Carruthers Field was located to the southwest near Benbrook, and Barron Field was directly south of Fort Worth, near Everman. Of the three, only Hicks Field survives, serving as a public airport. The area of Barron Field, now part of the City of Fort Worth, is an industrial park, bounded by Everman Parkway, Oak Grove Road, and Forum Way. A historical marker just south of the intersection of Everman Parkway and Oak Grove Road stands in front of the field's ammunition building, its only surviving structure. Nothing at all remains of Carruthers Field. The runway ran east–west along what is today Mercedes Street in Benbrook, a quiet and unremarkable residential area.

Twenty-eight Britons and Canadians lost their lives at Camp Taliaferro, among them the noted ballroom dancer Vernon Castle. Born in Norwich, England, in 1887, Castle came to New York

Vernon Castle Memorial, Benbrook, Texas.

as a young man to pursue a career as an entertainer. There he met a New York dancer named Irene Foote, married her, and together they became America's hottest dancing couple in the years before the war, best known for popularizing the foxtrot. Among the bandleaders with whom the Castles worked was James Reese Europe, who served and fought with the 369th Infantry Regiment during the Great War and introduced jazz to France (see Chapter 10). When World War I broke out Vernon

Commonwealth War Graves Commission burial area in Greenwood Cemetery, Fort Worth, Texas.

Castle returned to England, joined the Royal Flying Corps, and flew more than 300 missions over the Western Front. He then came to North America to train pilots. While flying over the prairies near Benbrook on February 15, 1918, Castle swerved to avoid a collision with another plane. His machine stalled and it came crashing to the ground, killing him. Today, a memorial to Castle—a white pyramidal structure capped with a scale model of a Curtiss Jenny—stands near a water tower at the intersection of Vernon Castle Avenue and Cozby Street near the spot of the crash. Castle is buried at Woodlawn Cemetery in New York, but several other members of the Royal Flying Corps still lie in Texas soil. Under the shade of a live oak tree in Section 5 of Fort Worth's Greenwood Cemetery, the Commonwealth War Graves Commission maintains the final resting places of twelve members of the Royal Flying Corps, mostly Canadians. Eleven of them died in Texas during the war. One died in 1975, and had requested to be buried alongside his wartime comrades from Camp Taliaferro. Also buried there is the infant daughter of a Canadian instructor. In the center of the Commonwealth graves stands a memorial, listing those buried in Fort Worth, as well as those who died there but are buried elsewhere. Topping the list is the name Vernon Castle.

On to France for More Training—and War

By necessity, nearly all advanced training had to be done overseas. None of the planes that American pilots would actually fly into battle existed in the United States, and even if they did, there were few

Americans with enough experience flying them to provide competent instruction. So after completing primary school, pilots typically headed off to the AEF to complete their training. Most ended up at the 3rd Aviation Instruction Center in the countryside north of Issoudun, in central France. Located on a plateau south of the Cher River, Issoudun lay astride the main American communication lines across France. The level land and sparse population of the region made it a convenient place for the Americans to set up new airfields, which were spaced a few miles apart in order to avoid accidents. The sprawling complex eventually covered more than twelve square kilometers to the northwest of Issoudun, and included seven camps, eleven airfields, and two hospitals, mainly between the villages of Lizaray and Vatan. Hiram Bingham noted its jerry-rigged appearance. "The barracks were of various sizes and kinds," he noted, and "the shops were of different vintages. The hangars were a medley of canvas, steel, and imitation concrete." Throughout its existence the camp saw almost constant expansion, and over time took on a more orderly appearance. "To appreciate this flying city, it would have to be viewed from the air," recalled Lieutenant Colonel Harry Toulmin Jr.:

> When seen from an appreciable height, it lay spread out in symmetrical orderliness. . . . Above these fields, various types of training were going on, so that on a busy day with numerous planes aloft, it was a magnificent sight. The main field was composed of hangars, headquarters, buildings, shops, hospitals, stores, and recreation centers, with well laid out roads and communication facilities. It was a city in itself.

By November 1918, Issoudun was home to 7,500 Americans, and not only was it the largest U.S. air base in the AEF but also perhaps the largest airport in the world.

At Issoudun, each of the eleven flying fields served a specific phase in the training process. At Field 1, all American pilots—no matter the extent of their training—began with flightless French planes called Rouleurs, which the Americans nicknamed "Penguins." Some initially thought starting their training again from scratch humiliating, but they soon discovered that the French machines handled much differently that the Curtiss Jennies they flew back in the States. Once they mastered the Penguins, the trainees moved on to Field 2, where they got back into the air in a French Nieuport, first with an instructor and graduating to solo flights. Other fields were dedicated to such specialties as acrobatics, formation flying, and navigation. There was also plenty of classroom time as well. Disease took its toll, and Issoudun saw its fair share of accidents. A spot known as Field 13 was the base cemetery, where 171 men were buried by war's end. Most of the instructors at Issoudun were French, though as American pilots gained more experience they

SIDEBAR 3—IMPORTANT COMBAT AERODROMES (IN FRANCE)

AERODROME	NEAREST CITY	GPS COORDINATES
Amanty	Amanty, Lorraine	N 48.52694 E 5.59833
Autreville	Autreville-sur-le-Renne, Champagne-Ardenne	N 48.46083 E 5.82806
Belrain	Belrain, Lorraine	N 48.85278 E 5.30472
Coincy	Coincy, Picardy	N 49.15958 E 3.39633
Delouze	Delouze-Rosieres, Lorraine	N 48.57167 E 5.53417
Épiez	Épiez-sur-Meuse, Lorraine	N 48.54528 E 5.61944
Foucaucourt	Foucaucourt-sur-Thabas, Lorraine	N 48.99583 E 5.12139
Francheville	Mouroux, Île-de-France	N 48.85278 E 3.04222
Gengault	Toul, Lorraine	N 48.69806 E 5.91722
Gondreville	Gondreville, Lorraine	N 48.68389 E 5.96556
Julvécourt	Julvécourt, Lorraine	N 49.06361 E 5.18028
La Noblette	Mourmelon-le-Grand, Champagne-Ardenne	N 49.11583 E 4.39083
Luxeuil-les-Bains	Luxeuil-les-Bains, France-Comté	N 47.79056 E 6.37250
Maulan	Maulan, Lorraine	N 48.66583 E 5.25083
Ourches	Ourches-sur-Meuse, Lorraine	N 48.66306 E 5.68667
Rembercourt	Rembercourt-Sommaisne, Lorraine	N 48.91889 E 5.21278
Saints	Saints, Île-de-France	N 48.76487 E 3.05197
Touquin	Touquin, Île-de-France	N 48.72861 E 2.98806
Vaucouleurs	Vaucouleurs, Lorraine	N 48.62972 E 5.64917
Vavincourt	Vavincourt, Lorraine	N 48.81556 E 5.21222
Villeneuve-les-Vertus	Vertus, Champagne-Ardenne	N 48.93722 E 4.07176

took an increasing role in teaching.

As the training progressed, instructors evaluated the strengths and weaknesses of each candidate, and assigned them to become either a pursuit, observation, or bomber pilot. The glamour and the glory lay with pursuit. "Due to its exciting character, we found great difficulty in persuading young pilots to abandon their ambitions and learn to be good reconnaissance pilots," recalled Bingham. Americans gave life at Issoudun mixed reviews. Hamilton Coolidge found the French countryside charming. "The little country towns . . . are the most picturesque I have ever seen," he wrote in a letter home. "All the farm buildings are made of stone, and the tiled roofs often overgrown with moss. They looked as if they had been there since the beginning of time." The region's sparse population owed itself to its marginal clay soils, and when it rained the Issoudun airfields became a wet, sticky sea of mud. Another pilot, Charles Codman (who would serve as General Patton's aide-de-camp during World War II) described Issoudun as "a frozen sea of mud," and continued with a list of other complaints: "Wretched flying equipment. Broken necks. The flu. Hell of a place, Issoudun."

The 3rd Aviation Instruction Center at Issoudun closed within months of the armistice. The Air Service dismantled and sold off the buildings, and farmers resumed tilling the sticky clay soil. Those Americans buried in Field 13 were disinterred and returned to their families or reburied at the Suresnes and Saint-Mihiel American Military Cemeteries. Today one can drive through the countryside north and west of Issoudun and never know that the wheat fields they see once hosted thousands of pilots and planes. The only reminder of the site's role in aviation history is a modest memorial thirteen kilometers northwest of Issoudun on the D960 highway, near the hamlet of Vœu. The monument, a fifteen-foot-high cement obelisk, is located at the site of Field 13. On

Memorial to American fliers killed at Issoudun, France.

bronze plaques at its base are the names of the young Americans who died in the surrounding skies and fields. Looking off into the nearby fields, one can only imagine the barracks, hangars, and repair buildings that stood in the area a century ago, or the skies filled with buzzing biplanes. Six airfields were located within two kilometers of the monument. Field 3, where pilots began cross-country navigation and acrobatic training, was just across the road. Over the years the monument had fallen into disrepair, but thanks to the efforts of a local historian named Bernard Gagnepain, the monument was restored and rededicated in 2009.

From Issoudun, American pilots went off to other training bases in France to learn specific fighting skills. At France's *Ecole de Tir Aerien* (School of Aerial Gunnery) at Cazaux, sixty kilometers southwest of Bordeaux, American pursuit pilots learned to strike stationary and mobile targets from the air. The French Air Force still operates out of the base today. The U.S. Air Service opened its own gunnery school at Saint-Jean-de-Monts, on the Atlantic coast seventy kilometers south of Saint-Nazaire. Harry Toulmin thought the site "as uninviting a spot for flying as man ever looked upon," but engineers leveled the sand dunes and erected targets. Though desolate, "this location, sparsely settled, permitted uninterrupted firing in the air over land and sea," Toulmin wrote. "Targets could be towed over and on the sea, or left on the beach, and shooting at captive balloons could be carried out over land without fear of injuring the civilian population." The former gunnery range has returned to beachland, sprinkled now with campgrounds, resort homes, and other recreational venues. Avenue de Baisse and avenue de Becs (the D123 highway) run through the center of the old gunnery range. Those assigned to bombing went to Clermont-Ferrand. The former air base is now the city's municipal airport. Observation pilots and balloonists usually trained near artillery schools, such as le Valdehon, Camp de Souge, and Saint-Cyr Coëtquidan (see Chapter 6) to work with artillerists.

The Air Service established a network of construction, maintenance, and repair facilities to keep their pilots flying. Most of the planes the Americans flew were French, assembled in plants near Paris. At Orly Field, fifteen kilometers south of central Paris, the U.S. Air Service established an acceptance park where new planes were inspected and, if deemed serviceable, ferried on from there to a training field or a forward air depot. The Americans also used Orly as a storage base. After World War II, Orly became Paris's most important commercial airport, until Charles de Gaulle opened in the 1970s. It remains the second-busiest airport in France today. The most important forward depot was the 1st Air Depot at Colombey-les-Belles, in the American rear area twenty kilometers south of Toul. This depot supplied nearly every frontline squadron with everything it needed, from spare parts to gasoline to ammunition. Colombey-les-Belles also had repair facilities for damaged or malfunctioning planes. By the time of the armistice, more than 2,000 soldiers operated the complex. The depot was located just a kilometer west of the village, north of what is now the D4 highway. There is virtually no visible trace of the facility today. The largest Air

Service supply and repair facility was located safely out of range of German planes at Romorantin, adjacent to the massive SOS supply base at Gièvres (see Chapter 9). The Romorantin facility had three huge workshops. One was devoted to repairing the fuselages of damaged planes. Another was an engine shop. The third was an assembly hall for planes coming in from the United States. Shipped across the Atlantic in creates, the plane pieces were transported to Romorantin by train, assembled, and then dispatched to the front. Damaged planes usually came in by rail, but left from an airstrip next to the shops. The American-built workshops are long gone, but the French Air Force still uses the site today.

The command structure of the Air Service in the AEF was confused and ever changing. This was the case in part because air power had never played a major role in war before, and nobody quite knew how to fit it into the administrative system. The gigantic egos of Air Service officers further complicated the issue. Before leaving for Europe in May 1917, Pershing assigned Major Townsend F. Dodd as his aviation officer, but when Dodd arrived in France he found himself outranked by Lieutenant Colonel Billy Mitchell, who was already there, so Mitchell assumed the job. In September 1917, Pershing put Brigadier General William Kenly in charge of the Air Service in the AEF and placed Mitchell in command of combat forces at the front. Mitchell accepted the decision, claiming that it allowed him to focus on fighting, but was incensed when Benjamin Foulois, now a Brigadier General, arrived in France in November 1917 to replace Kenly. The rivalry between Mitchell and Foulois was bitter, intense, and personal. In his memoirs, Mitchell conceded that Foulois "meant well," but "was not at all conversant with conditions in Europe." He characterized the staff Foulois brought with him as an "incompetent lot" of "carpetbaggers," and complained that most "had never seen an airplane." Foulois, for his part, argued in his memoirs that Mitchell was unswervingly insubordinate and that while he dreamed of martial glory, he was "grossly incompetent" when it came to logistics and other practical matters necessary to make those dreams reality. "He had been in France eight months," Foulois complained, "but I could find no evidence of solid accomplishment that I could attribute to his efforts." Pershing grew annoyed with the constant infighting, and once complained that the Air Service had "a lot of good men running around in circles." To clean up the mess he appointed an old friend and West Point classmate, Brigadier General Mason Patrick, to replace Foulois in May 1918. Foulois became assistant chief of the Air Service under Patrick at Chaumont. Mitchell assumed control of aerial operations for the First Army, and eventually over all U.S. air combat operations.

For combat air forces, the basic unit of organization was a

squadron, containing about twenty-five planes each. Like infantry regiments and divisions, each squadron developed distinctive insignia, which its members painted on their planes. The famed 94th Aero Squadron, for example, drew up an insignia of Uncle Sam's red, white, and blue hat in a circle, and called itself the "hat in the ring" squadron. Squadrons then organized into groups of about four squadrons each. Some groups were organized into wings, composed of about five groups. Groups and wings were then assigned to an army, integrating them into the larger AEF command structure. Like ground forces, air units were first put along quiet sectors of the front so that they could get accustomed to the unusual world of real combat. The men of the 94th and 95th Aero Squadrons (which formed the core of the 1st Pursuit Group) arrived at Villeneuve-les-Vertus in February and March of 1918, but when they arrived they had no planes. When their planes finally arrived they had no machine guns. Commanders also discovered that many pilots had not yet had gunnery training, and sent them to Cazaux. In March, Major Raoul Lufbery, a veteran of the Lafayette Escadrille now in the U.S. Air Service, led a few patrols out of Villeneuve-les-Vertus, but aside from taking some German antiaircraft fire the green American flyers saw no significant action. When the Germans launched Operation Michael on March 21 (see Chapter 8), the 1st Pursuit Group pulled back to the Épiez Aerodrome, near Épiez-sur-Meuse, but by the first week of April the Americans had moved up toward the front again, based at the Gengault Aerodrome near Toul, likewise in northeastern France. It was at Toul that American pursuit pilots shot down their first Germans. On the morning of April 14, two German planes appeared over the aerodrome at Toul, and the Americans went up to meet them. Lieutenant Alan Winslow sent the first one crashing to the ground—the first American pilot to score a victory in a dogfight. Lieutenant Douglas Campbell got the other one. Campbell went on to become the first American to shoot down five enemy planes, achieving the status of "ace."

Observers also first got their feet wet in the Tour Sector. The I Corps Observation Group arrived at the Ourches Aerodrome in April 1918 to begin reconnoitering the Saint-Mihiel Salient. On April 11, the 1st Aero Squadron, the unit that flew the army's first combat sortie in U.S. history, over Mexico in 1916 (see Chapter 1), performed the first American reconnaissance mission of the war, between Seicheprey and Flirey. Throughout the month, the 1st Aero Squadron and the other units of the I Corps Observation Group began flying missions out of an airfield at Ourches in support of the 26th Division holding that sector. A typical patrol schedule involved four short-range reconnaissance patrols each day—at dawn, late morning, late afternoon, and at sundown. On occasion, the observers participated in special missions like artillery spotting, photographic missions, establishing liaison with infantry patrols, and even an occasional long-range patrol behind German lines. During the Battle of Seicheprey (see Chapter 7), the American observation planes attempted liaison with troops on the ground, but the Doughboys of the Yankee Division had not yet been trained on how to communicate with the planes.

The German offensives in the spring and summer of 1918 meant that American fliers, like their counterparts on the ground, were thrown into major operations before they were fully prepared. During the Second Battle of the Marne (see Chapter 8), the 1st Pursuit Group and the I Corps Observation Group moved from the Saint-Mihiel area to airfields closer to Paris, and took responsibility for a fifteen-kilometer segment of the front, from Château-Thierry to Courchamps. Observation planes flew out of the aerodrome at the tiny village of Francheville, northwest of Coulomniers, and tracked German movements as the front lines fluctuated. Pursuit squadrons flew out of aerodromes at Touquin and Saints. Hoping to break through to Paris, the Germans threw some of their best pilots into the fray, including Baron von Richthofen's old unit, the Flying Circus. Going up against Germany's best, the Americans took substantial casualties at first, but as they gained experience and began flying more maneuverable Spad airplanes, the Yanks gave as good as they got. As the Germans retreated, American airmen took over some of the German airfields, such as at Coincy, out of which the Flying Circus had flown just weeks before. By the time the Marne campaign wound down in early August, the 1st Pursuit Group had downed thirty-eight German planes while losing thirty-six of their own. The I Corps Observation Group lost eleven airmen.

The 1st Pursuit Group became America's most celebrated Air Service unit, and some of its members were household names. Perhaps no airman was more famous than Quentin Roosevelt. As the son of former President Theodore Roosevelt, Quentin came from one of America's most prominent and powerful families, and had grown up in the public eye. Born in 1897, he was just three years old when his father became president. Teddy Roosevelt was a major proponent of the preparedness movement, and three of his sons, including Quentin, attended the Plattsburg training camp (see Chapter 1). When war came to America, Quentin left his studies at Harvard to join the Air Service, training at Hazelhurst Field on Long Island before shipping out to France. Roosevelt was among the first to train at Issoudun, and was assigned to the 95th Aero Squadron, flying out of Touquin and Saints during the summer of 1918. Despite his famous father and his blue blood, Roosevelt was well liked by his colleagues. He claimed his first kill on July 10, but was shot down himself just days later. Flying behind German lines near Chamery on July 14, German pilots riddled Roosevelt's plane with bullets. He was struck in the head and killed instantly, and the plane came crashing to the ground. The Germans buried him near the crash site, fashioning a cross out tree saplings bound together with wire from his plane. The Roosevelt family requested that Quentin remain buried where he was killed. "We feel that where the

Quentin Roosevelt Memorial Fountain, Chamery, France.

tree falls, there let it lie," the grief-stricken president told the army, a statement that inspired many bereaved parents to keep their fallen sons and daughters in France. Soon after the war the Roosevelt family fenced in Quentin's gravesite and gave it a proper headstone. They also commissioned the renowned architect Paul Cret to design a memorial fountain in Chamery in Quentin's memory. In 1955, Quentin's body was reinterred at the Normandy American Cemetery above the D-Day beaches to be with his brother, Theodore Jr., who died in the Normandy campaign twenty-five years later. Cret's fountain still flows in the center of the tiny village, on rue Quentin Roosevelt (the D14 highway), and an unpaved road heading southeast of the village center leads to the young flyer's original burial site (GPS: N 49.19034 E 3.62442). Hazelhurst Field, where he had trained to be a pilot, was renamed Roosevelt Field in his honor.

No American flyer in World War I better fit the stereotype of the cocky pilot than Frank Luke Jr. Born in Phoenix, Arizona, in 1897, Luke was the youngest of nine children. The Phoenix of Luke's youth had much of the Old West about it—horses and hitching posts were still common sights on the streets—though it was also rapidly growing into Arizona's largest and most modern city. Young Frank enjoyed exploring the vast Arizona wilderness, sometimes camping and hunting for days at a time in the mountains or among the yucca and giant saguaro of the Sonoran Desert. At Phoenix Union High School he was popular with classmates, though teachers did not always appreciate his frequent pranks and defiance of authority. During the summers he worked the mines in the rough-and-tumble town of Ajo near the Mexican border. When the war came, Luke naturally gravitated toward the most daring and dangerous duty—the Air Service. He went to ground school at the University of Texas at Austin, and primary at Rockwell Field, California. Luke arrived at Issoudun in March 1918, where the flight instructors found him an extraordinarily talented flyer, but also hard to control. One commented that to call Luke reckless was "putting it mildly." After a stint ferrying planes out of Orly Field, Luke finally arrived on the Western Front on July 25, assigned to the 27th Aero

Squadron then at Saints. His braggadocio did not make him popular with his superiors or even his fellow pilots, but there was no question that he got results. On September 14 he downed two heavily defended German balloons, and then bagged three more the next day. On September 18 he downed two balloons and three German planes—all within ten minutes. No pilot had ever accomplished so much in such a short span of time. Brimming with self-confidence and indifferent to authority, Luke often broke formation on missions to hunt Germans on his own. One of the mechanics charged with fixing his badly damaged planes said Luke had "had more guts, more skill, and less sense than any man I ever saw."

Nicknamed the "Arizona Balloon Buster," Luke became a national hero, but recklessness finally caught up with him. On September 29 he took off from Rembercourt to knock out three German balloons near Dun-sur-Meuse. Luke got all of them, but

Frank Luke statue, Arizona State Capitol, Phoenix, Arizona.

as he began to fly back toward home base machine-gun fire from a nearby ridge known as the Côte Saint-Germain hit his plane. Severely wounded in the head and chest, Luke landed in a field near the village of Murvaux and tried to escape the German troops coming to capture him. He made it about 200 meters and probably got off a few shots at his would-be captors before he succumbed to his injuries. The defiant, uncontrollable Luke was awarded a posthumous Medal of Honor for his actions, the first flyer to receive it. Today a decorative cross of iron on a cement base, dedicated to Luke, stands along the D102 highway just west of Murvaux. The scene of Luke's death was in the field along Milly Creek just 600 meters north of the marker. Luke's home state paid tribute to him as well. A statue of Luke, looking as defiant as ever, caps the Great War memorial on the Arizona State Capitol grounds. A Spad XIII plane, like the one Luke flew, greets those who land at Terminal 3 Sky Harbor International Airport in Phoenix. Interpretive panels near the plane tell Luke's interesting life story. Luke Air Force Base, twenty miles northwest of downtown Phoenix, is yet another tribute to the Arizona Balloon Buster. In all, Frank Luke racked up eighteen kills during the Great War. Fellow pursuit pilot Eddie Rickenbacker called him "the most daring aviator and greatest fighter pilot of the entire war." Even the "dreaded Richthofen," Rickenbacker believed, could not compare to Luke.

That was high praise indeed, since one of the few American pilots with more kills than Luke was Rickenbacker himself. Born in Columbus, Ohio, in 1890, Rickenbacker was a racecar driver before the war, and had already gained fame at such hallowed raceways as Indianapolis and Daytona Beach. That need for speed led him to apply for the Air Service when the war broke out. The army told Rickenbacker that he was too old to be a pilot, and since he had dropped out of high school lacked the educational background as well. However, his racing notoriety landed him a job as General Pershing's personal driver. In fact, Sergeant Rickenbacker was among the small party that sailed for Europe with Pershing in May 1917. As Pershing's driver he met many important people, among them Billy Mitchell, who intervened to get Rickenbacker flying. At Issoudun his flying talents became evident. After completing his training he was assigned to the 94th Aero Squadron, where his successes continued. On September 25, 1918, Rickenbacker downed six Germans in one day.

Rickenbacker ended the war with twenty-six kills, more than any other American flyer. Fast machines would continue to dominate his postwar life. Turning down various endorsement and film offers, Rickenbacker returned to Columbus and dove into business, most notably founding the Rickenbacker Motor Company in 1920—it went bankrupt in 1927—and establishing a longtime association with Eastern Airlines. A civilian during World War II, Rickenbacker was on a tour of air bases in the South Pacific in 1942 when the B-17 he was on ran out of gas and ditched into the ocean. Rickenbacker and the others drifted in the vast Pacific for twenty-four days before finally being rescued. He died in Florida in 1973. The home Rickenbacker lived in from 1895 to 1922 (war years excepted, of course) still stands at 1334 Livingston Avenue in Columbus. Over the years the home fell into disrepair. It has since been declared a national historic landmark, preserved, and restored, though is not open to the public. However, one can visit a replica of the Rickenbacker home at Mott's Military Museum in the Columbus suburb of Groveport. The Rickenbacker family has provided the museum a wealth of memorabilia to display there, right down to his World War I footlocker. The main Columbus airport is also named in Rickenbacker's honor, and is not far from the museum in Groveport.

During the summer of 1918, more and more American air assets began to make their way from Issoudun and other training fields up to quiet sectors of the front. The 2nd Pursuit Group formed at Gengault Aerodrome near Toul. The 3rd Pursuit Group, which gathered at Vaucouleurs, contained the 103rd Aero Squadron with its contingent of Lafayette Escadrille veterans. America's fledgling bomber force also went into action that summer. Pershing saw air power mainly in terms of tactical support for ground forces, and the Air Service placed little emphasis on bombing behind enemy lines. Only one American bombing group, the 1st Day Bombardment Group, ever saw action. On June 12, 1918, the 96th Aero Squadron made its first bombing raid—on the railroad yards at Dommary-Baroncourt, thirty kilometers northeast of Verdun. The eight Breguet bombers, under the command of Major Harry Brown, endured stiff antiaircraft fire and German pursuit planes, but the Americans hit their target and returned without loss of life. That evening at their base near Amanty, the men of the bombardment group held a big party to celebrate. Not every raid went so well. On the stormy and overcast afternoon of July 10, Brown set off from Amanty with six planes to bomb the rail yards at Conflans, thirty kilometers west of Metz. It became the most embarrassing disaster in the history of the U.S. Air Service. On the way to Conflans, the bombers got lost in the thick clouds, and strong winds blew them off course. As fuel became low, Brown decided to land their planes, but did not realize how far off course he was. Brown and his men had unknowingly ended up in Koblenz, Germany, where they were promptly taken prisoner. The Germans sent Mitchell a message that read: "We thank you for the fine airplanes and equipment you sent us, but what will we do with the Major?" Mitchell was livid. He later wrote that the incident was "the worst exhibition of worthlessness that we have ever had at the front," and that Brown "was better off in Germany at that time than he would have been with us."

Pershing may have thought little about the strategic uses of air power, but with Mitchell it became an obsession. Like his friend and mentor Hugh Trenchard, Mitchell believed that bombing German factories and transportation hubs would inhibit the enemy's ability to make war. But Mitchell took the idea one step further. He envisioned mass formations of planes that would destroy Germany's economy and bomb it into submission. The American offensive at Saint-Mihiel in September 1918 gave Mitchell an opportunity to put his theories into practice, and when he did, he set in motion a military revolution that would change the face of warfare.

CHAPTER 12:
SAINT-MIHIEL

"I never saw General Pershing looking or feeling better," noted General Charles G. Dawes in his diary in August 1918, and since the two men had known each other since their days at the University of Nebraska in the 1890s that was saying something. The reason for Pershing's jauntiness, Dawes wrote, was because "he will soon strike with his field army." Ever since Pershing's arrival in France in June 1917, the Saint-Mihiel Salient—the German bulge into Allied lines south of Verdun—tempted him like a dangling piece of ripened fruit. For the better part of a year, American planners had been poring over maps of the area in preparation for an offensive that Pershing hoped would win the war. U.S. troops had served in quiet sectors along the salient for months to familiarize themselves with the region. By September 1918, the conditions were right to strike. Pershing now had his independent U.S. First Army, containing several battle-tested divisions, while Ludendorff's failed summer offensives left Germany substantially weakened. The rapidly changing situation on the Western Front forced Pershing to alter some of his expectations, but the Saint-Mihiel Offensive was nevertheless a significant moment in the history of the AEF. It was America's first major, independent offensive of the war. Thanks to two of Pershing's field commanders, Billy Mitchell and George S. Patton Jr., the Saint-Mihiel Offensive would become historically significant far beyond the amount of territory ultimately taken.

Pershing's original plan for the Saint-Mihiel Salient called for its reduction in 1918, followed by a decisive drive toward Metz in 1919. But with the Germans on the run, Pershing sped up his timetable, proposing to take both in one fell swoop. The Americans had been planning the Saint-Mihiel operation for so long that German intelligence had likely picked up some knowledge of U.S. intentions, and the movement of troops into the area was difficult to conceal, so complete operational secrecy was impossible. To throw the Germans off the trail, Pershing took a tip from General Pétain and created a diversion. In late August, he sent General Omar Bundy and a small staff on a secret mission to Belfort in Alsace to begin planning an offensive on the southern extreme of the Western Front. Bundy and his staff reconnoitered the front lines, and in a few days he sent

Pershing his assessment. "Now is the most propitious time for an attack," he advised, since "the country is now as dry perhaps as it ever gets, the enemy is weak, and conditions are otherwise favorable." But Pershing had no intention of striking in Alsace. Bundy was a decoy, though he didn't know it. Indeed, nobody on the mission knew its real purpose except its intelligence officer, Colonel Arthur Conger. American intelligence was well aware that Belfort was riddled with German spies, who would keep an eye on Bundy and report back to Germany. Conger even left bogus messages for German spies to find. The ruse worked. Within days of Bundy's arrival, panicked German civilians began to evacuate the area behind the lines, and troops moved in to repulse a potential American invasion.

But just as Pershing was about to pull the trigger on the Saint-Mihiel operation, Marshal Foch came to see him on with a new plan. Working off the suggestion of British Field Marshal Douglas Haig, Foch envisioned a "Grand Offensive" to finish off the Germans and win the war, and planned to strike on September 15. The Western Front from Belgium to Lorraine was one massive salient, Foch argued, that could be pinched off and reduced with powerful, coordinated attacks. American divisions were essential to the plan, but it was the way Foch proposed to use them that raised Pershing's ire. He asked Pershing to limit his Saint-Mihiel operation to the reduction of the salient only. The attack on Metz, he argued, would divert critical manpower and weaken the Grand Offensive. As for American troops, Foch wanted to transfer four or six divisions from U.S. First Army to the French Second Army, which would attack between the Meuse River and the Argonne Forest west of Verdun. To the west of the Argonne, Foch proposed the creation of a new U.S. field army of eight to ten divisions that would drive down the Aisne River, bracketed by the French Second Army on the right and the French Fourth Army on the left. Pershing immediately objected to splitting up American forces, and the diminishing of the Saint-Mihiel operation. "This virtually destroys the American army that we have been trying for so long to form," he complained. "Do you wish to take part in the battle?" asked an exasperated Foch. "Most assuredly," responded Pershing, "but as an American army and in no other way."

Pershing next met with Pétain, who effectively brokered a compromise. The Saint-Mihiel operation would go forward, with the limited objective of reducing the salient. Pershing would then position the U.S. First Army between the Meuse River and the Argonne Forest, and attack from there as part of the Grand Offensive, keeping American forces undivided. To give Pershing time to reposition his forces after Saint-Mihiel, Foch delayed the Grand Offensive until late September. Under the final timetable, the American First Army in the Meuse-Argonne and the French

Fourth Army to its left in Champagne would kick off the offensive on September 26. The British would attack Cambrai in northern France on September 27. An Allied force under the King of the Belgians would hit Flanders on September 28, and the British would strike again near Saint-Quentin the day after that. Pershing had once again successfully kept his independent American army intact, though planning and executing two major offensives in as many weeks was a nightmare for his staff. "This appalling proposition rather disturbed my equilibrium," wrote Colonel George C. Marshall, now the planning officer for the First Army. "I could not recall an incident in history where the fighting of one battle had been preceded by the plans for a later battle to be fought by the same army on a different front," he wrote. "The harder I thought the more confused I became." Marshall recalled that it was "the most trying mental ordeal experienced by me during the war," but he got right to work. "With a map spread out on the table and the line-up of divisions for battle in my hand, I started with the proposition that the only way to begin is to commence."

Pershing wanted an easy victory at Saint-Mihiel that would instill confidence in the Doughboys, give them the experience they would need to conduct larger operations, and garner respect for American forces among both the Germans and the Allies. Pershing had good reason to expect such a victory. The Germans had occupied the area since 1914, but ever since the end of the 1916 Verdun campaign it had been quiet. Like the Allies, the Germans defended the sector with inexperienced troops and exhausted divisions. The Germans maintained two defensive zones across the area. The Wilhelm defense zone covered the front of the salient, and was relatively weak. The Michel defense zone, part of the vaunted Hindenburg Line, ran diagonally behind the salient, giving the Germans a strongly fortified backstop. German commanders might well have been wise to pull back to the Hindenburg Line to shorten their front and conserve manpower and resources. Ultimately, they decided that blocking the French rail and communication lines justified keeping the salient, and with their control of the area's highlands, most notably the Butte de Montsec, they believed they could hold it with a minimum of soldiers.

Rather than take the formidable Montsec head on, Pershing opted to envelop it with a pincer movement. The main assault would come along the south face of the salient, from Marvoisin to Pont-à-Mousson. Two corps would administer the blow. On the eastern end of the line was I Corps, under General Hunter Liggett, which consisted of (left to right) the 2nd, 5th, 90th, and 82nd Divisions. The 2nd Division, with its contingent of U.S. Marines, had seen plenty of action already in the operations along the Marne that summer, most famously at Belleau Wood (see Chapter 8). The

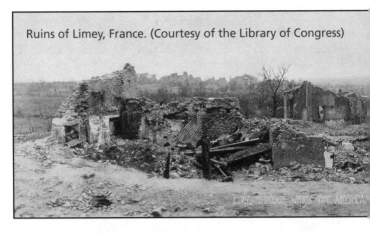

Ruins of Limey, France. (Courtesy of the Library of Congress)

5th "Red Diamond" Division had seen some action in the Aisne-Marne Offensive, but the remainder of the divisions in the corps had seen very little. I Corps was to press northward into the woodlands between Pont-à-Mousson and Thiaucourt, stopping at the Hindenburg Line. The 82nd Division would not participate in the first day's attack, but hold off until day two. To the west of Liggett's men was IV Corps under General Joseph Dickman, which would carry out the main thrust. Leading the way for Dickman would be the veteran 1st Division on the far left, which would drive toward Vigneulles. Supporting them on their right was another veteran outfit, the 42nd "Rainbow" Division. The rookie 89th "Middle West" Division, a draftee unit from the Great Plains and Southwestern states, was on the far right if the IV Corps area, sandwiched between the experienced 42nd and 2nd Divisions.

While Liggett and Dickman drove up from the south, the U.S. V Corps, an agglomeration of French and American units under General George Cameron, would attack the western face of the salient. Here the 26th "Yankee" Division had the starring role. Its assignment was to advance through the woodlands on the Heights of the Meuse and link up with the 1st Division at Vigneulles. The 4th "Ivy" Division was to stay in place on the first day of the attack, but on the second day would advance toward Fresnes-en-Woëvre and to the Hindenburg Line. While American forces hit the southern and western faces of the salient, the French II Colonial Corps was to engage the Germans at its nose near the city of Saint-Mihiel, holding German forces there in place while the Americans enveloped them. Montsec would then be surrounded, and the salient itself erased from the map of the Western Front. In all, Pershing had about 550,000 American troops at his disposal, along with about 110,000 French. In the week before the attack, thousands of men and tons of equipment clogged the roads behind the salient, getting into position for the assault. To prevent the Germans from detecting

them, much of the movement occurred at night. On the evening of September 11, 1918, as the Yanks prepared to attack, a steady, windblown rain began to fall.

Unbeknownst to American planners, the Germans had already decided to evacuate the salient and withdraw behind the Hindenburg Line. Indeed, preparations for the pullback were already underway when the American attack came. At 1:00 am on September 12, the First Army hit German lines with a terrific artillery barrage. The "quivering light" the barrage created was so bright, according to one history of the 1st Division, that one "might see to read" by it. The preparatory barrage then became a rolling barrage, and the infantrymen climbed out of their trenches and followed it. I and VI Corps jumped off at 5:00 AM, the French II Colonial Corps at 7:00 AM, and V Corps at 8:00 AM. From the beginning, it was apparent that the Americans were going to have a good day. German barbed wire entanglements, which worried American planners, were not nearly as formidable as feared. Some of the wire had been laid way back in 1914, and over the years had become rusty and brittle. The Doughboys passed through it with relative ease. German resistance sometimes lacked heart. Morale was low, and many of their divisions were of poor quality or had been chewed up in the campaigns of the previous summer and were there to rest. "The men are so embittered that they have no interest in anything," one German soldier in the salient wrote, "and they only want the war to end, no matter how." The appearance of American soldiers at their front was often an opportunity to surrender.

In the I Corps area, the 2nd and 5th Divisions did the heavy lifting. The 2nd Division attacked northward into Remenauville and advanced seven kilometers, liberating Thiaucourt and approaching the southern fringes of Jaulny on the first day of the battle. A memorial boulder on the D28 highway between Jaulny and Xammes marks the furthest point of their advance on that first day. Just to the east of the 2nd Division, the 5th "Red Diamond" Division advanced from the ruins of Regniéville and advanced roughly five kilometers, taking Viéville-en-Haye and part of a forest, the Bois Gérard, to the north of the village. Three memorial obelisks mark their advance. One stands at the intersection of the D3 and D75 highways, marking the trench line from which the division jumped off that morning. Another is on the east end of Viéville-en-Haye. An obelisk also marks the location of a brigade headquarters behind the lines. That one is on the D958 highway about a kilometer east of Limey. Over the next few days, I Corps continued north and slowed as it made contact with the Hindenburg Line. The villages of Remenauville and Regniéville, located right along the front lines, had already been pounded to rubble over years of war. Like scores of other small hamlets along the Western Front, they were not rebuilt. These *villages détruit* (destroyed villages) are still marked on road signs, but are no more than ruins. The church of Regniéville is located on the east side of the D3 highway, less than 100 meters south of the 5th Division obelisk. Remenauville's church is in the woods just north of the D75. When the war ended and the villagers returned to the area, the inhabitants of the ruined hamlets essentially moved in with their neighbors. Limey is officially known as Limey-Remenauville, and Thiaucourt is now Thiaucourt-Regniéville.

IV Corps also got off to a fast start. The attacking divisions all reached their day's objectives by midday, capturing thousands of guns and prisoners, and pressing on toward the next day's objectives. "It was like a moving picture battle," thought Father Duffy of the 42nd Division. "Tanks were crawling up along the muddy roads and khaki-colored figures could be seen about in ones and twos and fours along the edge of the woods and along the grassy plains." On the western face of the salient, the 26th "Yankee" Division also made excellent progress. Indeed, movement was so rapid on that first day that the 1st and 26th Divisions were ordered to continue attacking through the night and link up to encircle Montsec as soon as possible. During the night of September 12–13, the Yankee Division advanced in a column down an old straight Roman road through the forest known as the Grande Tranchée de Calonne—which one can still drive down today—encountering no opposition as it marched with fixed bayonets through the dark woods. "That march through the woods was never to be forgotten," recalled the 101st Machine Gun Battalion official history. "Footsteps were heard in the woods, showing the presence of the enemy on either side," though they did not strike. At 2:00 AM the Yankee Division entered Hattonchâtel, a small hilltop village above Vigneulles. Soon the Americans were in Vigneulles itself. The French residents were "beside themselves at seeing the Americans," according to the 101st Machine Gun history, and "hung out their proud little flags of France, which had been kept carefully concealed from enemy eyes all these years—waiting for just this glorious day." Before leaving, the Germans set fire to anything of military value, leaving scores of burning villages in their wake. The Americans found it a heartbreaking yet awesome spectacle. "Hattonchâtel and Vigneulles had both been set afire by the Germans," wrote Frank Sibley, a *Boston Globe* reporter with the Yankee Division. "Hattonchâtel in particular was a beautiful spectacle, because of its position on the point of the hills. And out in the plain of the Wœvre, the little towns could be seen burning for miles, dotting the dark landscape with little glowing spots."

After dawn, 1st Division patrols began to meet up with the men of the 26th Division holding Vigneulles. About 8:00 AM, the 101st Machine Gun Battalion was resting near a cemetery on the eastern fringe of Vigneulles when they heard "many hoof-beats approaching" and saw mounted cavalrymen in "tin derbies" from the 1st Division approaching them. Men on horseback were a "queer sight," according to those in the 101st Machine Gun Battalion, "and aroused much interest among those of us who had soldiered . . . on the Mexican Border." Two hours later, they saw another unexpected sight, a "whole brigade drawn up in combat formation" coming toward them on the plain to their southeast. A lieutenant set out across the field to investigate. "He could see the ground scouts out in front looking at him with suspicion and fingering their rifles in an unpleasant way," reported the battalion history:

> When he came within speaking distance he hailed a sergeant and two men, noting two service stripes on their sleeves. The Lieutenant asked what outfit it was and the sergeant replied,

Plan of Attack of First Army, September 12, 1918

"Foist Division, sir." When he looked at those clear-eyed, square-jawed, young Americans he was more than ever glad that he had not invited unfavorable attention from them. "Gee, Lieutenant, we didn't know whether you was Boche or American when you come across that field. . . . We was all ready to take this burg," said the doughboy.

With this meeting outside Vigneulles, VI and V Corps had effectively isolated Montsec and surrounded thousands of German soldiers. Some Germans sneaked through American lines and made it back to the Hindenburg Line to fight another day. Most put down their arms. Near a traffic circle where the D179 and D910 highways meet, a 1st Division monument now stands to commemorate the event.

American successes continued on the second day of the offensive. On September 13, the Rainbow Division reached the crossroads town of Saint-Benoît. The chateau on the northern fringe of the village, which served as a German army headquarters, now belonged to the Yanks. The first to move in was the 84th Infantry Brigade under General Douglas MacArthur. Despite the luxurious surroundings, everyone understood that the war was not far away. Colonel George Leach, one of MacArthur's subordinates, took an office in the upper floors of the building, and from his window "saw the famous Hindenburg Line for the first time." Leach recalled another incident at the chateau in which he dismounted his horse and had his orderly,

Ruins of the Château de Saint-Benoît, where General Douglas MacArthur once made his headquarters.

Sergeant Peterson, bring it into the barn. "A moment later a German shell went into the roof of the barn and I felt that was the last of Peterson and the horses." Leach was relieved to find that Peterson "had gone out the door on the other side and was safe." The Germans shelled the chateau repeatedly, and on September 24 destroyed it a massive barrage. The shells "tore up the thick masonry of the chateau as though it were chalk," observed the official history of "Alabama's Own" 167th Infantry Regiment. "All that remained of the ancient and proud Château de Saint-Benoît was a smoldering heap of stone and a jagged mass of walls with smoke-blackened, gaping window spaces. Its pink and blue draperies, and furniture similarly upholstered; its music-room; its old tapestries hanging in its stone hallway—all were gone." Travelers can still see the skeletal remains of the once-venerable chateau, which lie within sight of the D904 highway.

September 13 saw the last two American divisions go into action. The 4th "Ivy" Division joined the fray on the northwest corner of the battlefield, taking Manhuelles. A monument to the division now stands at the intersection of the D903 and D904 highways east of the village to mark their contribution to the battle. The 82nd "All American" Division also attacked. Late that afternoon they crossed no man's land and took the village of Norroy. After the stunning gains made during the first two days of the offensive, the fighting shifted to the Hindenburg Line, as the Americans established their new front and the Germans probed and harassed them. The Saint-Mihiel Offensive officially concluded on September 16, though fighting along the Hindenburg Line continued.

The Americans Get Serious about Tanks and Planes

Through the Saint-Mihiel Offensive lasted only a few days, it marked some very important firsts in the U.S. military experience. It was the debut of American tanks in combat, for example. Lieutenant Colonel George S. Patton Jr. had been developing his tank corps near Langres (see Chapter 7), and the open flat lands of the Woëvre Plain seemed like a good place to give them a try. Patton was excited as he moved his men and their 144 Renault tanks into position in support of IV Corps, anxious to prove the efficacy of American armor. "You must establish the fact that AMERICAN TANKS DO NOT SURRENDER," Patton told his men. Should the guns in one's vehicle fail, he told his tankers to "squash the enemy with your tracks." One battalion, under the command of Captain Serano Brett, was to lead the Big Red One, which had already staged an attack with tank support at Cantigny. Another battalion, under Captain Ranulf Compton, was to follow in support of the 42nd Division. French tanks supported the I Corps attack, and also supplemented Patton's armored forces.

Patton carefully reconnoitered the ground across which his tanks would attack. Heavy rains the night before the assault worried him, and rightly so. As soon as the operation commenced, many of the machines promptly got stuck in trenches and bogged down in the mud like wallowing hippos. Patton anxiously remained behind the lines at a command post in Seicheprey, but when the tank battalion supporting the 84th Brigade of the Rainbow Division faltered, he rushed to the battlefront with is prized pearl-handled revolver to remedy the situation. On a hill about halfway between the Bois de la Sonnard and the village of Essey, Patton encountered the brigade commander, Douglas MacArthur. As the two men talked, a German artillery barrage suddenly rained down on the vicinity. Nearby soldiers dove into shell holes for cover, but the two officers remained standing. "I think each one wanted to leave but each hated to say so," Patton wrote his wife a few days later, "so we let it come over us." Both men came from distinguished military families, were West Point graduates, and were notorious for their outsized egos, yet they had never before met. Each would become giants of American military history during World War II.

Now out in front of the infantry, Patton then made his way toward Essey and found his tankers reluctant to move into the village due to German shelling. He led the tanks into town on foot, but then the tankers refused to cross the bridge over the Rupt de Mad, fearing it booby-trapped. Patton "walked over the bridge in a cat-like manner," as he described it, proving it was safe, and the tanks rolled toward Pannes, a kilometer away. As his tanks once again slowed down outside Pannes, Patton climbed onto the top of one of the vehicles and led the Doughboys into town. After taking thirty Germans prisoner, the column moved on toward Beney, Patton back atop a tank leading the way. Somewhere between Pannes and Beney, Patton noticed that the paint on his tank began peeling away just below his knuckles, and realized that German machine guns had opened up on them. Brave but not stupid, Patton jumped off the tank and headed for the nearest shell hole. After he gathered enough tanks and infantry to make a creditable assault on Beney he did so, seizing some Germans artillery pieces and machine guns. Patton would have continued, but by late afternoon his tanks ran out of gas.

American armored operations on the first day of the Saint-Mihiel Offensive produced mixed results. Of Patton's 144 tanks, five were lost due to mechanical issues, forty got stuck in the mud and thirty ran out of gas. Only two were lost to German guns. Supply problems kept Patton from getting fuel the following day as well, but by September 14, a battalion of tanks was back in action, under Captain Brett. Prowling the countryside in the shadow of the Hindenburg Line, it broke up a German infantry battalion south of Jonville. "Fighting by themselves," wrote Patton biographer Stanley Hirshson of the operation, "American tankers had for the first time defeated German ground forces." For Patton, the Saint-Mihiel Offensive ended too soon, but he had shown that his hard work at Langres had paid off. American armored forces could be effective on the battlefield.

Patton's experiences at Saint-Mihiel also stimulated a great deal of thought in his mind about the best way to utilize tanks on the battlefield. Most commanders argued that they should be interspersed with the advancing infantry to give the ground soldiers fire support, but Patton had other ideas. Viewing tanks as the successors to the horse cavalry, he believed they would be most effective by penetrating enemy lines and creating havoc in rear areas. Historian Carlo D'Este argued that the Saint-Mihiel experience "sowed the seeds of what was to become a Patton trademark—the deep penetration." He was beginning to learn the trade that would make him one of the most brilliant armored commanders of World War II—if not of all time. Travelers today can follow in Patton's footsteps during the first-ever U.S. armored operation by following the D28A highway from Seicheprey to Saint-Baussant, the D28 from Saint-Baussant to Essey, and the D904 from Essey to Beney. The General George Patton Museum of Leadership at Fort Knox, Kentucky, which covers his life from childhood through World War II, is an alternative for those in the United States to learn more about one of America's most famous and controversial military figures.

The Saint-Mihiel Offensive was also an important moment in the history of U.S. aerial operations. With the creation of the First Army, Colonel Billy Mitchell became the head of its air forces. Mitchell estimated that the Germans might bring as many as 2,000 planes to bear against the American offensive, and requested every Allied plane that could possibly be spared. He got much of what he wanted. In addition to the growing number of American planes, Mitchell also got control of several French, Italian, and Portuguese squadrons. The British threw in some night bombers to boot. In all, Mitchell had nearly 1,500 planes at his disposal. Including ground crews, the number of men involved in Saint-Mihiel aerial operations reached 30,000. It was the largest concentration of air power ever assembled on the Western Front.

Mitchell's planning was thoughtful and thorough. In preparation for the offensive, his pursuit planes sealed off the front lines from Verdun to Nancy, protecting rear areas from German reconnaissance patrols. To further conceal the mass movement of planes, he had the pilots move their machines up to forward air bases at night. Allied reconnaissance of German positions went on at a feverous pitch, photographing nearly every square inch of the salient. Mitchell did some of the reconnaissance himself. Once the infantry was on the move, planes were to provide tactical support to infantry, spotting for artillery, reporting the movements of infantry units, and strafing German ground forces. But as an admirer of the British air commander General Hugh Trenchard (see Chapter 11), Mitchell also planned for the strategic use of air power, penetrating deep behind enemy lines to hinder the enemy's ability to fight back. He envisioned mass formations of hundreds of planes that would hit German aerodromes to keep their planes on the ground, destroy supply dumps to deny the Germans access to vital materials, and destroy roads and bridges to prevent reinforcement of the salient, or escape from it. All of these ideas had been employed before, but never on such a large scale. "It was the first time in history," Mitchell bragged in his memoirs, "in which an air force, cooperating with an army, was to act according to a broad strategical plan which contemplated not only facilitating the advance of the ground troops but spreading fear and consternation into the enemy's line of communication, his replacement system and the cities behind them which supplied our foe with the sinews of war."

September 12 dawned with low clouds, rain, and gusty winds. Mitchell's plans for mass aerial formations had to be shelved, but Allied planes nevertheless struck hard. Eddie Rickenbacker spotted a column of retreating Germans on the road between Saint-Mihiel and Vigneulles. "Dipping down at the head of the column I sprinkled a few bullets over the leading teams," he wrote:

> Horses fell right and left. One driver leaped from his seat and started running for the ditch. Half-way across the road he threw up his arms and rolled over upon his face. He had stepped full in front of my stream of machine-gun bullets! All down the line we continued our fire—now tilting our aeroplanes down for a short burst, then zooming back up for a little altitude in which to repeat the performance. The whole column was thrown into the wildest confusion. Horses plunged and broke away. Some were killed and fell in their tracks. Most of the drivers and gunners had taken to the trees before we reached them. Our little visit must have cost them an hour's delay.

Because of the poor weather, pilots had to fly low, exposing them to deadly ground fire. One observation plane from the 90th Aero Squadron, flying at an altitude of just fifty meters near Thiaucourt, took a machine gun bullet to the radiator, forcing it toward the ground. "So near were they to crashing behind the German lines," reported the squadron history, that "German Infantrymen ran in their direction, expecting the plane to crash in a shell hole." The pilot miraculously "brought the plane back into friendly territory, finally landing just behind the advancing American lines." By the end of the first day, Mitchell's planes had flown 390 sorties and dropped more than 14,000 pounds of bombs.

For the first two days of the campaign, American and French planes had almost complete control of the skies over the salient, and British bombers repeatedly hit important rail yards like those at Metz-Sablon. But as the weather cleared, German planes came up to challenge the Allies. While on patrol on September 14, Eddie Rickenbacker spotted four German Fokkers near the Lac de Madine. He climbed, got behind one of them, and "pressed my triggers and played my bullets straight into the pilot's seat." As his victim plummeted toward the earth, the other three wheeled around to engage him, and Rickenbacker immediately noticed the red color of the planes. It was the squadron of the late Baron von Richthofen, the famed Flying Circus. He "scarcely needed their color to tell me who they were," Rickenbacker wrote, "for the skill with which they all came about so suddenly convinced me that this was no place for me." After much deft maneuvering, he managed to escape the cream of Germany's pursuit pilots. Not even the Flying Circus could knock the Allied planes out of the skies. Despite their best efforts, the Germans could only get 243 planes into the Saint-Mihiel area—far below the number Mitchell had at his disposal. By September 16, Mitchell's men had flown 2,469 sorties and delivered 44,118 pounds of bombs to enemy targets.

Mitchell was proud of his accomplishments at Saint-Mihiel, but in his mind the campaign had not gone nearly far enough. He continued to develop his ideas about the employment of air power, sending mass formations of as many as 200 planes to soften up the Germans during the Meuse-Argonne Campaign (see Chapter 13). But Mitchell would never again have as many planes at his disposal as he had at Saint-Mihiel. After the war, Mitchell became assistant chief of the Air Service, and used that position vigorously to promote his views on air power. He argued for an air force independent of the army or the navy, and his claims for the efficacy of air power only grew bolder: the airplane would soon become the predominant weapon of war, he insisted. Mitchell argued that planes rendered battleships obsolete, for example, and to prove it he had airplanes attack several captured German battleships and other obsolete vessels in Chesapeake Bay in 1921 and again in 1923. The ships were sunk. Mitchell's theories did not sit well with many army and navy traditionalists, however, and his outspokenness and his abrasive personality only made matters worse. After a navy dirigible was lost in a storm in 1925, Mitchell charged the leadership of both services with "incompetency, criminal negligence, and almost treasonable administration of the national defense," and he further claimed that the Coolidge administration was covering it all up. Mitchell was demoted and court-martialed for insubordination in 1926. He resigned his commission, but spent the rest of his life promoting his views on air power. He died in 1936.

Billy Mitchell is today recognized as a military visionary. He, along with Hugh Trenchard and the Italian air commander Giulio Douhet, are considered the fathers of air power theory. Though Mitchell did not live to see it, during World War II the United States employed the long-range strategic bombing campaign he had envisioned, wreaking incredible destruction on Germany and Japan, though historians still fiercely debate its overall contribution to Allied victory. Indeed, the B-25 Mitchell bomber, used extensively in World War II, was named in Mitchell's honor. Congress awarded Mitchell a special posthumous Medal of Honor in 1946, and the National Security Act of 1947 created the U.S. Air Force, a separate branch of the military coequal with the army and navy, just as Mitchell had advocated. Some of the nation's premier aviation museums, like the National Museum of the U.S. Air Force near Dayton, Ohio, and the Smithsonian Air and Space Museum in Washington, feature exhibits about Mitchell's life and contributions to U.S. military history. His hometown of Milwaukee also remembers him. Meadowmere, the Mitchell family estate where Billy grew up, is in the suburb of West Allis. The mansion is now part of the Mitchell Manor Senior Living Community (5301 West Lincoln Avenue). At 57th and Hayes Streets in West Allis is a historical marker outlining Mitchell's contributions to air power. Travelers flying into Milwaukee land at General Mitchell International Airport, named in Billy's honor. In the main terminal building is a one-room museum called the Mitchell Gallery of Flight. Dedicated to Milwaukee's aviation history, it prominently features Mitchell. Among the items on display is the general's personal insignia from one of his World War I Spad planes. He is buried with other family members at Forest Home Cemetery on Milwaukee's South Side.

Remembering America's First Major Offensive

Today the Saint-Mihiel tourist office (on rue du Palais de Justice in the center of town) offers guided tours of the area battlefields and memorials. Though their excursions focus mainly on the places where the French soldiers fought—and one should not forget that the French tangled with the Germans here for years before the U.S. troops showed up—they also cover the region's American connections, and English-speaking guides are available. For those who wish to visit the Doughboy battlefields on their own, the place to begin is the Montsec American Memorial, built on the German gun position that had vexed the Allies for so long. The American Battle Monuments Commission completed it in 1932. The circular neoclassical colonnade, made of Euville limestone quarried nearby, was the brainchild of New York architect Egerton Swartwout. In the center of the colonnade is a bronze relief map of the Saint-Mihiel Salient, showing the woods, fields, and hills through which the Allies fought. Standing beside the map, one can look out between the columns to see the battlefield itself. The views from atop Montsec are indeed commanding. Gazing out toward Thiaucourt or Seicheprey, one can easily see why the Germans held onto it for so long and how difficult it was for French and American soldiers to operate beneath it. (Incidentally, the views of the monument from the plains below are equally impressive.) The names of some of the villages the Americans liberated during the Saint-Mihiel Offensive appear in the lintel above the columns, such as

View of the Montsec American Memorial. The hill gave the Germans a commanding position over Allied lines below until taken during the Saint-Mihiel Offensive.

Thiaucourt, Vigneulles, and Saint-Benoît. In addition to commemorating the reduction of the Saint-Mihiel Salient, the Montsec Memorial is also dedicated to those who fought in the Vosges Mountains and Alsace, mostly during training periods (see Chapter 7), as well as those who fought in the Woëvre Plain Offensive during the last days of the war (see Chapter 17). Montsec even had a small role in World War II. As U.S. forces swept into the area in 1944, the retreating Germans placed a machine-gun nest atop the prominence to slow the GI advance. On the morning of September 2, Americans forces hit Montsec with an artillery barrage, knocking out the Germans but also damaging the colonnade. The monument was repaired in 1948, and the story of its World War II connection is engraved into one interior column.

There are also several French memorials to the American soldiers who liberated the area from four years of German occupation. Lorraine pays tribute to the American soldier with a monument in Flirey. Dedicated in 1921, it features a bronze relief sculpture of two Doughboys in a triumphant pose, a German helmet at their feet. In the background is

Lorraine's tribute to the American Doughboy, Flirey, France.

Metz Cathedral, symbolizing the reunification of Lorraine after the war, and brass stars above the sculpture represent the states of the American union. Like many villages in the area, Flirey was utterly destroyed after four years of being on the front lines, but residents rebuilt their community adjacent to the ruins. A few remnants of old Flirey remain in the eastern portion of the village. A town with an even stronger American connection is Thiaucourt-Regniéville. Inscribed on the base of the village war memorial is the usual dedication to local boys killed in World War I, but a closer examination reveals more. The memorial features a bronze sculpture of a mustachioed French Poilu shaking hands with an American Doughboy. In his other hand, the American soldier is holding up a U.S. flag, the stars and stripes clearly evident. At the base of the monument a bas relief depicts the arrival of 2nd Division into the village on September 12, 1918. Honoring Thiaucourt-Regniéville's dead, the monument also pays tribute to its liberators. Not far away is the Musée de Costume Militaire (Museum of Military Costume), which holds a large collection of twentieth-century uniforms. Most are French and German, but the American soldier is well represented.

One kilometer west of Thiaucourt-Regniéville on the D3 highway is the Saint-Mihiel American Cemetery. It is the final resting place of 4,153 Americans, 117 of whom are unknown. The graves area is divided into four sections, with a linden-lined grassy mall separating them. In the center is a large sundial. A sculpture of an eagle, with distinctively squared shoulders and flat back, serves as the gnomon. To the west of the eagle at the far end of the mall is a sculpture by New York artist Paul Manship of a youthful-looking officer standing in front of a cross. To the west is a decorative urn. The buildings on the cemetery grounds are the work of New York architect Thomas Harlan Ellett. Just behind the gates along the highway at the north end of the grounds are the superintendent's office and visitor center. At the south end of the grounds is the memorial, a limestone peristyle with a circular colonnade in the center and two buildings on either side. In the center of the colonnade is granite sculpture of an ancient funeral vase. The building on the east end is the chapel. The interior features a brightly colored mosaic of a winged angel sheathing her sword. The building on the west end contains a map mosaic—just as brightly colored as the chapel—of U.S. military operations in the Saint-Mihiel region. Engraved on the walls are the names of 282 Doughboys whose bodies were never recovered or identified.

Among the soldiers buried at the Saint-Mihiel American Cemetery is Captain Oliver Cunningham. The only son of a wealthy Chicago businessman, the Yale graduate was a forward artillery observer in the 2nd Division. On September 17, 1918, Cunningham spent his twenty-fourth birthday in combat near Jaulny, a small village just north of Thiaucourt. That morning, German mortar fire

War memorial in Thiaucourt-Regniéville, France, which also pays tribute to the Americans who liberated the village from German occupation.

rained down on his position, killing him. Cunningham was buried in the Bois de Blainchant, a wooded area to the east of the village, near the spot where he fell. Later, his body was moved to the nearby American cemetery, but a small memorial in the woods still marks his original resting place. Though devastated by the loss of its son, the Cunningham family was determined to help rebuild the village where he had spent his final days. It helped finance the reconstruction of a new village hall and repair the bomb-damaged church. At

Saint-Mihiel American Cemetery, Thiaucourt-Regniéville, France.

the entrance to the church is a plaque (in French) stating that the church bells are dedicated to Captain Cunningham's memory.

The Cunninghams were not the only wealthy Americans to help rebuild the war-ravaged lands of the Saint-Mihiel Salient. When the Yankee Division entered the hilltop village of Hattonchâtel in the early morning hours of September 13, 1918, it found little more than a pile of flaming ruins. The following year Belle Skinner, the daughter of a silk manufacturer in Holyoke, Massachusetts, and an ardent Francophile, visited the village and was so heartbroken and horrified by the destruction she saw that she devoted her life to rebuilding it. Her reconstruction maintained the Hattonchâtel's prewar medieval appearance, yet gave it a modern water system. Particularly impressive was the rebuilding of the chateau at the peak of the hill overlooking the Woëvre Plain. With Skinner's financial backing, architect Henri Jacquelin incorporated the remnants of the old structure, parts of which dated to 860, but rebuilt the chateau in a fanciful neo-Renaissance style. Skinner lived in Hattonchâtel for a year to supervise the reconstruction, and in the end spent a million dollars rebuilding the village of barely 200 residents. Locals called her *marraine* (godmother) and the French government bestowed upon her membership in the Legion of Honor. When Skinner died in 1928, her brother William saw the project through to completion. Today the winding, narrow main street through Hattonchâtel is called rue Miss Skinner, and one can still amble through the medieval-looking village and see what Belle Skinner's philanthropy produced. The chateau is today a hotel and conference center. Two plaques at the entrance to the chateau tell the story of Skinner's generosity to Hattonchâtel and her affection for France.

Sculpture of a young officer by Paul Manship, Saint-Mihiel American Cemetery.

New Englanders not only liberated Hattonchâtel from German occupation, they also resurrected it.

The Saint-Mihiel Offensive gave the Americans—from its commanders down to the common foot soldier—the experience and the confidence to take on bigger challenges, and in the end Pershing got the quick and easy victory he sought. In fact, it was deceptively easy. The Germans troops the Doughboys faced in the Saint-Mihiel Sector were battered and broken and already planning to pull out. More than 16,000 surrendered.

Even under those conditions, the Germans nevertheless staged a fighting retreat that inflicted 7,000 casualties on the AEF in five days. Pershing saw Saint-Mihiel as validation of his open warfare tactics. But there was little time to celebrate. The Meuse-Argonne Offensive was scheduled to begin on September 26, where the First Army and its open warfare tactics would receive its biggest test yet.

CHAPTER 13:
MEUSE-ARGONNE

At 5:20 AM on September 26, 1918, Ray Johnson of the 37th Division stood in a trench near Avocourt. "The zero hour was approaching," he later wrote of the moment. "The doughboys gripped their rifles tightly. We machine-gunners looked carefully over the guns, testing their mechanism and making sure that the tripods were clamped and strapped tightly." The soldiers talked and checked their watches, and a few actually napped, while their artillery thundered in the distance, softening up the German positions. Johnson wondered "at the absolute coolness with which we spent those last minutes before the attack. Perhaps it was merely blissful, ignorance!" At precisely 5:30, Johnson's commanding officer gave the order to attack. His voice, the machine gunner remembered, "carried above that awful din as it had carried over the drillfields at Camp Sherman." The men climbed over the parapet and into no man's land. Johnson remembered, "as we started forward a great broad flare of red, white, and blue lit up the sky—America was striking!" It was the beginning of Foch's Grand Offensive, and American troops were among the first to jump off. The U.S. First Army called the operation the Meuse-Argonne Offensive. Leaders on both sides of the Western Front had speculated for years whether the American Doughboy would make a difference in the outcome of the Great War. The moment had finally arrived to see whether or not he would.

Of all the portions of the Western Front slated for action in Foch's Grand Offensive, the one assigned to the Americans was by far the most challenging. The eastern boundary was the Meuse River. Though the river protected the Americans on the right from a potential German ground assault, the Heights of the Meuse just across the river allowed the Germans ample opportunity to observe American movements and harass them with artillery. On the western edge was the Argonne Forest, a densely wooded highland cut with numerous ravines that would be difficult to attack through but would give the Germans ideal defensive positions. In between was thirty kilometers of rolling farmland punctuated with numerous woodlands. Standing in the path of the American advance through this bucolic landscape were several natural obstacles. One was the Butte de Montfaucon, just five kilometers behind the American lines. A lone promontory rising sharply above the surrounding countryside, it stood roughly halfway between the Meuse and the Argonne Forest. Nicknamed the "Little Gibraltar," Montfaucon gave the Germans an excellent observation post of the Allied lines in the region. Roughly ten kilometers further north were the even more formidable Romagne and Cunel Heights, rugged highlands standing directly in the path of the American advance. The Germans, having been in the area for several years, had prepared well-fortified defensive lines running east to west across the area. The most formidable of these lines was the Kreimhilde Stellung, a series of defensive works running across the length of the Romagne and Cunel Heights, which formed a portion of the Hindenburg Line. The area was so suited for defensive purposes that the Germans only stationed four divisions in the area, though more could be moved in quickly in an emergency.

Pershing's plan depended on two things: surprise and speed. In mid-September, French troops occupied the Meuse-Argonne front, along with two American divisions, the 33rd and 79th, which were there to do some time in a quiet sector. To prevent tipping off the Germans that something big was afoot, French forces were to remain on the line until the last minute, with the American troops replacing them under cover of darkness just hours before the attack was to begin. American officers reconnoitering the front in the days before the attack even wore French uniforms to avoid being spotted. Once the offensive began, Pershing believed his open warfare tactics would carry the day and ensure penetration deep behind German lines. He expected his men to reach the Romagne and Cunel Heights and pierce the Kreimhilde Stellung by the first day of the attack. Strongpoints like Montfaucon were to be bypassed and mopped up later. It was an ambitious plan. As historian Edward G. Lengel wrote, Pershing "devised an attack timetable fit for an army of supermen." Pétain warned that the plan was overly optimistic, and suggested that Montfaucon might not be taken until Christmas. But flush with success from the Saint-Mihiel Offensive, Pershing expected much the same in the Meuse-Argonne, and believed that the Doughboy's high morale and marksmanship would carry the day. There were other problems with Pershing's plans. It seems he gave little thought to the threat posed by the German positions on the Heights of the Meuse, believing Allied artillery would be enough to suppress the German guns. There were also questions about the readiness of his men. Because many of Pershing's best and most experienced divisions had just wrapped up the Saint-Mihiel Offensive, they would not be available for the initial Meuse-Argonne assault. Only three of the divisions had any real combat experience, and even those units were filled out with rookie replacements. Other divisions had been rushed through training that summer, and had seen frontline service only in quiet sectors.

Pershing directed the campaign from the town hall at Souilly, nineteen kilometers southwest of Verdun—the same place Pétain made his headquarters during the 1916 Verdun campaign. A plaque on the building's façade, placed by the American Battle Monuments Commission (ABMC), marks its place in U.S. military history. The First Army attack came from three corps of three divisions each. On the far right was III Corps under General Robert Bullard. The 33rd "Prairie" Division, a National Guard unit from Illinois, was to advance along and defend the west bank of the Meuse. The 80th "Blue Ridge" Division, made up of draftees from Pennsylvania, Virginia, and West Virginia, took the center of the III Corps area. To their left was the experienced 4th Division, made up of regular army soldiers. The "Ivy" Division had seen action in the Aisne-Marne offensive that summer, and elements of it had also fought at Saint-Mihiel. Their line of departure was in a swampy morass just south of Forges Creek, an area fought over bitterly during the 1916 Battle of Verdun. France's Mort Homme Memorial, honoring its soldiers lost fighting in the area, is nearby.

On the far left of the American sector was I Corps under General Hunter Liggett. The 77th Division, made up mainly of New York City men, was given the unenviable assignment of taking the Argonne Forest. The 28th Division, the Pennsylvania National Guard unit roughed up at Fismes that summer, was in the middle, tasked with taking the west bank of the Aire River. The rookie 35th Division, made up of National Guard troops from Kansas and Missouri, would take the east bank. To the left of I Corps was the French Fourth Army, as well as elements of the African American 92nd Division acting in a liaison capacity (see Chapter 15). Like III Corps, these troops also began the campaign in an area that had seen incredible devastation. For example, the 35th Division took up positions in the southern portion of the Butte de Vauquois, two kilometers east of Boureuilles. The French and Germans had fought bitterly over the hill for years, each tunneling under the other's trenches and blowing up tons of explosives, leaving the hilltop pock-marked with massive craters. A century later, the massive craters and remnants of the tunnels still scar the land, and from the air the Butte de Vauquois looks rather like a line of volcanoes. Near the crest of the hill today there is French war memorial and an orientation table pointing to key wartime sites. The view northward from it gives an excellent view of the Meuse-Argonne battlefield.

In the center of the American Line was V Corps, under General George Cameron. The Ohio guardsmen of the 37th Division were in the middle, flanked by the 79th Division (made up of draftees mainly from Pennsylvania and Maryland) on the right and the 91st Division (draftees from the Northwest) on their left. None of these divisions had any significant combat experience. The 79th Division

View of the Meuse-Argonne battlefield from the Butte de Vauquois. The Montfaucon American Monument appears in the distance in the upper left corner of the photograph.

was especially green. More than half the outfit's infantry and artillerymen had been in the army four months or less, and the division had never been to the front before taking up positions between Avocourt and Esnes-en-Argonne in mid-September to relieve the French 157th Division. The men of the 79th "looked upon the tenanting of the Avocourt-Malancourt Sector as part of the seasoning process," observed the division's official history:

> No one in the enlisted ranks dreamed that the Division, without previous 'blooding,' was to be one of the center divisions in the opening phase of the final drive of the World War. If the men heard rumors that they were destined to take Montfaucon they laughed at them. It would not be likely that a green division would be hurled at the strongest point in the whole German line.

Nevertheless, these inexperienced troops of V Corps were expected to hold the First Army center. In fact, the combat virgins of the 79th Division were assigned the task of taking the fortified Montfaucon, a job that would have been difficult even for an experienced division.

In the days leading up to the assault, the American troops filtered up to the front. All movements were conducted at night to avoid German observation planes, as well as to minimize the impact of the constant German artillery harassment. It was a chaotic scene. The dark and muddy roads leading up to the front were jammed with men and equipment getting into position. Artillery troops set up their guns, and the infantrymen spent their days concealed on farmsteads and in forested areas, or in the ruins of villages behind the front. "The days and nights of waiting in the forest had been under almost constant shell fire," reported the 35th Division's official history, "and there had not been a great deal of sleeping." Neuvilly-en-Argonne, not quite four kilometers behind the front line, hosted members if the 28th and 35th Divisions, and today a small monument on rue Maginot in that village stands in commemoration of their brief residence there. After dark on September 25, the Americans filtered into the frontline trenches to replace the French. As George Cooper of the 28th Division made his way up to the front, he remembered seeing some French troops who had just been relieved headed in the opposite direction. "As we passed them we would yell, 'Fini la guerre,'" he remembered, "and they would respond with the same expression and seemed ticked to death about it." Not all Poilus were so comforting. Giuseppe Romeo of the 91st Division recalled that the French troops he relieved insisted that "advance against [the] Boches was impossible."

America Attacks

The first Allied artillery hit positions far behind the German lines just before midnight. Then, at 2:30 AM on September 26, more than 2,700 artillery pieces began blasting away, unleashing what the Doughboys called the "million dollar barrage." "It seemed as tho all hell had been loosened," recalled Adolphus Graupner of the 91st Division. "The roar of the artillery was terrific and continuous. The horizon was illuminated by the flash of the guns and the bursting of star shells and flares. The lower edge of the sky was lit by a quivering light." At 5:30 AM, the Americans went over the top and surged forward under the cover of a rolling barrage, while the Germans launched countless signal flares, lighting up the sky like fireworks. When dawn came the battlefield was covered in a thick morning fog, but the artillery superfluously unleashed a smoke barrage, anyway, as ordered. The attackers groped their way forward. Kerr Rainsford of the 77th Division remembered feeling "adrift in a blind world of whiteness and noise, groping over something like the surface of the moon." German artillery soon came sailing in, and Americans began to fall. Through the mist, Ray Johnson could see his comrades being hit. They "would stagger, reel, and crumple in a heap; struck by a flying bit of shrapnel or a shell fragment," he wrote. Johnson found the sight "ugly, sickening, [and] unnerving, but our training and our 'keying up' overcame the nausea we could not help but feel."

III Corps proceeded well. By noon, the 33rd Division pushed through the Bois de Forges. The night before the attack, engineers had marked out pathways through the swamp with white tape and laid down duckboards. The Germans did not expect an attack through the swamp, and the Prairie Division's casualties were fairly light. They reached high ground above the banks of the Meuse, and dug in along a rail line (now abandoned) that parallels the present-day D123 highway to guard the First Army flank. The 4th "Ivy" Division had penetrated six kilometers, taking the village of Septsarges immediately east of Montfaucon, and moving into the woods of the same name north of the village by nightfall. Combat rookies experienced the surreal nature of war for the first time. Ashby Williams of the 80th Division saw several dead German soldiers. One, who "evidently died instantly, was lying on his right side," while another, "who had evidently lingered some time, had crawled up and put his arms around him. Who knows but they might have been buddies." He also saw two wounded Germans in a shell hole, "one a middle-aged man and the other a boy about 19." Williams thought it odd to find the boy "eating a piece of schwarzbrot."

General Liggett's I Corps also made impressive advances, though it did not meet Pershing's demanding first-day schedule. The 77th Division made slow progress through the Argonne Forest, but that was expected. Pershing anticipated that the 28th Division to its right would make more a more rapid advance across the open rolling hills of the Aire Valley, outflank the Germans in the forest, and force them to withdraw. The experienced Keystone Division did indeed make good progress. With support from 1st Tank Brigade under Lieutenant Colonel George S. Patton Jr., the Pennsylvanians advanced along the west bank of the Aire River, punched through the Wiesenschlencken Stellung—the first of the German defensive lines across the area—and took the western portion of Varennes-en-Argonne by midday. The Kansas-Missouri Division bypassed the Germans facing them atop the Butte de Vauquois and attacked in two columns on either side of it, each with the support of Patton's armor. At first things seemed to be going well for the inexperienced Midwesterners, but they were not. After the initial rolling barrage, artillery support petered out. In the dense morning fog, the advancing soldiers could not see more than a few feet in front of them, and as they advanced they unknowingly moved past many German machine-gun nests and other strongpoints. When the fog lifted at midmorning, the attackers suddenly found themselves exposed to German machine guns not only to their front, but in their rear areas as well. The Kansans of the 137th Infantry Regiment moved along the Aire toward Varennes-en-Argonne, but by midmorning had stalled outside the village under withering German fire from the Wiesenschlencken Stellung. By late morning, the 139th Infantry Regiment, which had just finished mopping up the Butte de Vauquois, arrived at Varennes-en-Argonne. Those reinforcements, along with a little help from the 28th Division on the other side of the river, allowed the 35th Division to move into the eastern half of Varennes-en-Argonne in the early afternoon. German resistance stiffened, and the shredded units of Doughboys could not advance much more than a kilometer or two north of Varennes-en-Argonne in the afternoon.

The Missourians of the 138th Infantry Regiment proceeded along the west bank of Buante Creek toward the village of Cheppy, roughly following the present-day D38 highway. Things got especially tough at a fork in the road just a few hundred meters southeast of the village—where today the D19 meets the D38. Though the creek was small and a bridge spanned it not far from the road junction, numerous machine-gun nests and concrete bunkers prevented the Doughboys from crossing the creek in force and seizing the village. For most, this was their baptism of fire. Some panicked. Many fought gallantly, and two received posthumous Medals of Honor for their actions. Captain Alexander Skinker led an automatic rifle crew in a brave but doomed assault on a German machine-gun nest. Private Nels Wold and another man knocked out four German machine-gun nests and took eleven prisoners. Wold was killed in an attempt to take a fifth gun nest. Despite such heroics, the 138th could not reach the village.

The arrival of Patton's tanks finally allowed the 138th to break through to Cheppy. Despite orders to remain at his command post in Neuvilly-en-Argonne, Patton could not resist the lure of battle and made his way to the front. As he approached the fork in the road outside Cheppy, Patton discovered that things were not going well. The sight of panic-stricken soldiers disgusted him. "None did a damn thing to kill Bosch," he complained. As for his tanks, Patton discovered that one of them had gotten stuck in a trench not far from the road junction, impeding the progress of the others. He organized a small group of soldiers to dig out the tank while German bullets whizzed by. "To hell with them," Patton was heard to utter, "they can't hit me." When one soldier refused to cooperate, Patton struck him on the head with a shovel. After freeing the tank, he organized a group of leaderless men in an assault against German positions. As Patton and his party reached the crest of a small hill they were met with a furious burst of machine-gun fire and hit the dirt. As Patton later told the story, he lay there momentarily thinking about his family's distinguished military history and thought, "it is time for another Patton to die." He sprang to his feet, waved his pistol in the air, and ran and toward the Germans yelling: "Who's with me?" It may have been brave and inspirational. It may have been inexcusably reckless. Of the six who followed him, five were killed. Charging toward the enemy, a bullet entered Patton's left thigh and exited "just at the crack of my bottom." His assistant, Private Joseph T. Angelo, pulled him into a shell hole, from which Patton continued to bark orders. For Patton, the First World War was over, but his contribution was significant. His tanks were on the move again, and at midday a combined tank and infantry assault crossed the creek and broke through the German lines, though as at Varennes-en-Argonne the offensive stalled in the afternoon.

At the crossroads south of Cheppy, where the 138th Infantry Regiment had fought so hard and lost so much, the State of Missouri erected a monument to its Great War dead. Completed in 1922, it is a statue of a female figure representing liberty, eyes looking upward, with a laurel wreath in her upraised right hand symbolizing victory. It stands atop a granite base with the Missouri state seal affixed. Pennsylvania remembers the terrible price her sons paid at nearby Varennes-en-Argonne. After the war, the Pennsylvania Battle Monuments Commission chose a bluff above the Aire on the west side of the town as the location of the Keystone State's memorial to all of its soldiers who fell in World War I. The memorial, designed by Thomas Atherton and Paul Cret and dedicated in 1927, is built upon the ruins of German fortifications. A tree-lined lawn runs northwest from the flagpoles on rue Louis XVI (the D946 highway), sandwiched between rue du Général Pershing and rue du Général Price (the latter named for the head of the Pennsylvania Battle Monuments Commission, William G. Price Jr., who also served as an artillery brigade commander of the 28th Division during the war). At the

bluff overlooking the Aire is a plaza with classical colonnades on two sides and a raised altar in the center. Barely a block east of the memorial is the Musée de l'Argonne on rue Louis XVI. In France, Varennes-en-Argonne is famous as the place where King Louis XVI was captured in his attempt to flee revolutionary France. (He would later have a date with the guillotine.) The museum certainly devotes time and space to this famous event, but it also covers the region's Great War experience, and America's role in it.

Missouri Monument near Cheppy, France.

Pershing's main headaches came from the V Corps, in the center of the First Army, which had the formidable and critical Montfaucon in its path. Two of the divisions in the corps, the 37th and the 91st, had made impressive gains that morning. Indeed, the 37th Division had come within a few hundred meters of Montfaucon by day's end, and the 91st Division had entered the village of Epinonville to the west before being driven from its rubble-clogged streets at dusk. But for the rookie 79th Division, which was assigned the task of taking Montfaucon itself and was accompanied by a few French tanks, trouble quickly emerged. Two infantry regiments, the 313th on the left and the 314th on the right, spearheaded the attack. As was the case across the front, artillery support was ineffective, and the Doughboys got lost in the thick morning fog, bypassing German strong points that later wreaked havoc in rear areas. Communications between the various elements of the 79th Division were particularly poor. The lead regiments soon lost contact with each other, as well as with divisional headquarters. Long lines of advancing soldiers quickly devolved into men î advancing in uncoordinated clumps. Some of these clumps fell well behind the frontline troops, and reserve troops advanced too quickly, causing the units to become jumbled and confused.

The 313th Infantry Regiment advanced through the Bois de Malancourt—or, perhaps more accurately, the stumps and shattered tree trunks of what had once been a forest, now thick with underbrush, shell holes, and vast quantities of broken barbed wire. By 9:00 AM it had passed through the woods and entered a clearing known as the Golfe de Malancourt just west of the village of Malancourt. As the morning fog dissipated and the Americans looked out over the fields, they saw a high ground known as Hill 282 to their right, and Bois de Cuisy in the distance ahead. The Germans occupied both in force. Their line across the area held numerous concrete pillboxes and machine-gun nests, which quickly rained lead down on the Americans. Following Pershing's dictates about open warfare, officers ordered charge after charge against the German positions, all ending in failure. Having little experience with machine guns, the Americans did not employ their own machine guns to good effect or eliminate those of the enemy very effectively. Few Americans had grenades, and even those who did had not been very well trained on how to use them. Artillery support was nonexistent. For five hours the Doughboys tried unsuccessfully to cross the Golfe, and hundreds died as a result. Finally, fearing that the U.S. 37th Division on their right would outflank them, the Germans withdrew in the early afternoon. By the end of the day, the 313th had reached the far end of the Bois de Cuisy, exhausted and unable to continue. They were well short of Montfaucon.

Meanwhile, the 314th Infantry advanced along the road that is today the D18 highway. They reached the village of Malancourt at 7:30 AM but failed to search the ruins adequately, leaving dangerous numbers of German troops behind them. From Malancourt they continued up a shallow valley toward a low ridge above the village, but like their comrades in the 313th Infantry were abruptly halted about 9:00 AM. The Germans had constructed a formidable line of defense on that ridgeline, anchored by a strong point known as Ouvrage du Démon (Strongpoint of the Devil), which was located on the west side of the D18 just above the turnoff to Cuisy. As the fog dissipated the Germans opened fire, unleashing "a hot fusillade which filled the air with snaps, cracks, and whines of flying lead," recalled infantryman Arthur Joel. "Heinie saw to it that the Yanks continued to hug the ground most of the afternoon." Unlike the Golfe of Malancourt, these Germans did not withdraw, and American attempts to break through yielded little new ground. The 314th was stopped dead in its tracks.

The divisions on either side, the 4th to the right and the 37th to the left, had advanced well beyond Malancourt and might have come to the aid of the 79th. Indeed, late in the day the 4th Division to the right of the 79th prepared to take the Nantillois, one kilometer north of Montfaucon. If successful, the seizure of the village would have cut German road access to the hilltop fortification, possibly leading to its envelopment or an enemy withdrawal. But Pershing gave strict orders to divisions to confine their operations to the zone specifically assigned to them and not stray into the territory of another. Few commanders dared to defy him, and higher-ups ultimately nixed the plan. As historian Edward M. Coffman noted, the situation "illustrates the effect of restrictive orders carried out inflexibly."

Driving the rural roads around Malancourt today, one sees little obvious evidence of the bitter fighting of 1918. Battlefields are once again dedicated to the peaceful pursuit of farming, and much of the area has been reforested. But a closer look can reveal signs of the Great War. To the east of the D18 is Hill ("Côte" in French) 304, a place that saw immense bloodletting between the French and Germans in 1916 and 1917. The 79th Division began its attack in the Meuse-Argonne Offensive just below the hill on its north side. The woods of Hill 304 contain French monuments to their fallen and still shelter shell holes and debris from years of savage fighting, very little of which involved the United States. One place of interest to Americans is a smashed cement German machine-gun bunker known as the Abri de Malancourt, about a kilometer south of that village on the D18. Decorated with steel helmets and capped with a cross, it is now a memorial to the Allied soldiers killed in the vicinity. The plaque affixed to it pays homage to French 69th Infantry Regiment, which suffered greatly in the region in 1916, as well as to their *frères* (brothers) in the American 79th Division, who permanently liberated Malancourt from the Germans on the first day of the Meuse-Argonne Offensive in 1918.

By the end of the first day's fighting, the Americans occupied the land on three sides of Montfaucon, but could not get past its powerful fortifications. The inability of the 79th Division to advance to Montfaucon was particularly devastating, slowing down the rest of the V Corps, as well as the III Corps on its right. All across the First Army front, the Americans were still far from the first-day objectives of the Romagne and Cunel Heights. Pershing was furious, and issued unambiguous orders to the First Army that evening. "The Commander-in-Chief commands that division commanders take forward positions and push troops energetically," he wrote, "and the corps and division commanders be relieved of whatever rank who fail to show energy." Pershing still believed that his open warfare tactics would carry the day, and expected his men to demonstrate that—whatever the cost.

Montfaucon

September 27 arrived with a chilly, heavy rain, making life for the Doughboy in the field even more miserable. Fields became oceans of mud, and soaked the soldiers on both sides down to the bone. Pershing still expected his men to advance. The 79th Division resumed its attack on Montfaucon in the early morning darkness. The Germans concluded that their position there was untenable and began to withdraw, but they nevertheless made the 79th Division pay dearly for every inch of ground. French tanks led the way for the 313th Infantry Regiment and other elements of the 79th Division as they fought their way across muddy fields and reached the base of Montfaucon. They spent the late morning clawing their way up the hill, braving German machine guns and grenades and rooting German troops out of their pillboxes or the ruins of the village. Fighting was often hand to hand—a task at which the Yanks excelled. "The hardest fight of all seemed to be centered in the grave-yard," recalled Charles DuPuy of the 311th Machine Gun Battalion, "where each mausoleum contained its machine-gun and crew." Montfaucon was a scene of "awful carnage," according to one account, with the "torn bodies of 313th Infantrymen, Germans, and horses, lying in piles amid rubble and wrecked caissons and carts."

The 37th Division moved in from the west. Ray Johnson and his comrades were in a shallow valley beneath Montfaucon when "suddenly hell broke loose from three sides." Some were "literally riddled with bullets" while "men running for cover toppled down in their tracks; others were stricken where they lay, by flying shrapnel and shell fragments; many more were blown to bits by direct hits from big shells or killed by concussion."

Montfaucon American Monument.

Montfaucon was in American hands by noon, though the problems were hardly over. Enemy troops still had to be rooted out of the honeycomb of underground bunkers on Montfaucon, and German artillery hit it with great ferocity and accuracy. Pershing demanded that the 79th Division continue its attack northward toward Nantillois, but the spent division could proceed no more than a kilometer toward that village before German artillery stopped it.

The Montfaucon American Memorial, a sixty-meter-high granite column capped with a female figure representing Liberty, now stands atop the Butte de Montfaucon to commemorate the sacrifices of the Doughboys and their French allies in the Meuse-Argonne region. The work of the American Battle Monuments Commission, it was designed by New York architect John Russell Pope and dedicated in 1937. The top of the Doric-style column serves as an observation platform. On one wall of the memorial's vestibule is a map, made of polished marble, depicting American movements in the campaign. On the opposite wall is a narrative of the campaign in English and French. From there, a flight of 234 steps leads up to the observation platform. There is no elevator, so one must hoof it, though there are several resting places along the way. The climb is worth the trouble. The observation platform provides a 360-degree bird's eye view of the Meuse-Argonne battlefield. Inlaid into the shelf of the observation deck are arrows pointing to the sites of important engagements, along with the distance to each in kilometers. Looking south one sees the First Army's line of departure on September 26, 1918, including the Butte de Vauquois. The Argonne Forest appears darkly to the west, and the Heights of the Meuse loom up in the east. The elusive Romagne and Cunel Heights appear to the north. From this vantage point, one can appreciate how formidable a barrier these obstacles were to the foot soldier. A more peaceful rural scene can hardly be imagined now, and it can be difficult to imagine the carnage that once enveloped this blood-soaked landscape. Surrounding the monument are the ruins of the old village of Montfaucon, including the skeleton of its old church. Interspersed with the village ruins are several German cement bunkers left over from the Great War, as well as an observation tower amid the ruins of the church.

View from atop the Montfaucon American Monument.

Locals still lovingly maintain the Montfaucon village cemetery on the hill not far from the American monument, but after the war the village itself was rebuilt just to the west at the base of the promontory. The new village remembers the Americans who liberated them from the Germans. The square in the center of town is place du Général Pershing. On the northeastern corner of the square is a small monument, flanked by French and American flags, dedicated to the "Sammies" of the Meuse-Argonne Offensive. Americans also helped rebuild the village.

Captain Harry S. Truman, 129th Field Artillery, 35th Division.

After the war, the state of Ohio erected a hospice, or almshouse, for the village. That gray stone building still stands at the southeastern edge of the main square. It bears an inscription, facing the square, noting that it is dedicated to the 37th Division (the Ohio National Guard), which took from the Germans the territory where the village now stands. American troops were to liberate the village once more, in 1944. A Sherman tank on place du Général Pershing commemorates that event.

The rest of the First Army also made gains on that second day, but not as great as those of the first day, and still well short of the Kreimhilde Stellung. The 35th Division tried all day to take the village of Charpentry, but a ridge running northeast from the village blocked its path. Running along the ridge was an old, straight Roman road (the present-day D998 highway) studded with machine guns and protected with endless coils of barbed wire. The division launched several assaults, aided with tank support, but the Germans guns stopped it cold. All that morning, the enemy's machine guns filled the air with lead, its artillery rained down on the area, and its planes attacked from above. From behind the lines, Pershing complained about the 35th Division "being stopped by machine gun nests here and there," and demanded yet another charge that afternoon. Divisional artillery, which had lagged behind the infantry, got into position to support the attack. Captain Harry S. Truman of the 129th Field Artillery spent the afternoon as a forward observer. Guiding shells onto German positions, Truman spotted a German artillery battery to the west of the Aire, in territory assigned to the 28th Division. Despite orders to divisions to restrict attacks to their own sectors, Truman called in the coordinates and the 35th Division's guns blew it up. Truman's commanding officer threatened to court-martial him, but the captain was unapologetic. "Go ahead!" he retorted, "I'll never pass up a chance like that." His superiors dropped the matter. At 5:20 PM, in a drizzling rain, the division launched another attack. Casualties were extremely heavy, but this time the Missourians broke through, taking Charpentry, the ridge, and the Roman road. The 91st "Wild West" Division began the second day along the banks of Baronvaux Creek, in a valley below the village of Epionville, from which it had been ejected the day before. Filled with mud and hit with German artillery fire, the Americans knew the place variously as "Death Valley" or "Dead Man's Gulch." Three times on September 27 they emerged from the gully and took the rubble that was Epionville, only to be driven out again. By the end of the day, they had gained not an inch of ground.

Pershing's Army Loses the Initiative

The third day, September 28, saw more meager yet hard-won gains. After enduring a night of heavy German shelling on Montfaucon, the 79th Division attacked northward toward Nantillois. The 315th Infantry Regiment, raised mainly in Philadelphia, took the village by 11:00 AM, but at the cost of 40 percent casualties. Its attack continued toward a high point about a kilometer north of the village identified on military maps as Hill 274, which was about to earn the nickname "Suicide Hill." From the crest of the hill, the Doughboys saw a forested area called the Bois des Ogons. The Kreimhilde Stellung, the main German defense line they were supposed to reach on the first day, lay just beyond it. Supported with French Renault tanks—but not artillery or aircraft—the regiment attacked from Hill 274 at 4:30. It was a disaster. Machine gun bullets ricocheted off the tanks and into the bodies of the advancing troops. One compared this gruesome phenomenon to a "carom shot on a pool table." German artillery methodically picked off one French tank after another. Surviving crewmembers abandoned their vehicles and ran for the rear, cursing the "fool" Americans for launching such a hopeless assault.

Despite losing their armor support, the Americans moved through the woods inch by bloody inch, knocking out enemy machine-gun nests. The battled their way to the northern edge of the woods and the German field hospital at Madeleine Farm, but pulled back as the Germans prepared to saturate them with artillery. After the barrage, the Americans launched another attack at 6:00 PM, but the results were the same. The Americans pulled back to the reverse slope of Hill 274 north of Nantillois, and the rainy night they spent there was perhaps the most disturbing yet. No food had reached the

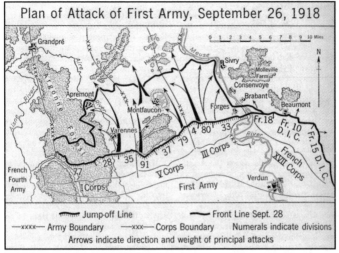

Plan of Attack of First Army, September 26, 1918

Jump-off Line ———— Front Line Sept. 28
—xxxx— Army Boundary —xxx— Corps Boundary Numerals indicate divisions
Arrows indicate direction and weight of principal attacks

front line, and the only water they got came from old gasoline cans still reeking and tasting of fuel. The men took cover in shell holes as German artillery pounded them, blasting many to eternity. "As the rain poured down on us," one account described, "so did the shells of the Boche." During lulls in the German shelling, the Doughboys could hear the moans and cries of their comrades wounded during that day's fighting, still laying in the fields and woods before them. But they were unable to come to their aid. "This is simply a living death," wrote Edward Davies from his mud-filled hole that night, "Hell can hold no terrors for me after this."

Today's Nantillois, a tiny village of fewer than 100 residents, is quiet and peaceful. Despite its diminutive size, Nantillois has several landmarks of interest to Americans. After the war, the veterans of the 315th Infantry Regiment raised funds for a village recreation hall, which was completed in 1930. Philadelphia mayor Harry A. Mackey, on hand for the dedication ceremony, noted the intimate and eternal connection between Nantillois and the City of Brotherly Love. "This ground on which you rebuilt your homes," he told the villagers, "was made sacred to us by the sacrifice of the flower of Philadelphia's youth." The building still stands at 9 La Grande rue. On its façade is a Lorraine Cross—the emblem of the 79th Division—and a dedication to the "glorious dead of the 315th Infantry." Next door, at 7 La Grande rue, is 14–18 Nantillois, a combination bed and breakfast and Great War museum. The focal point of the museum is its collection of wartime artifacts, from weaponry to the personal effects of the soldiers, which have been gleaned from the woods and fields in the area. The museum also offers battlefield walking tours. Sixty meters southwest of the 14–18 Nantillois museum, also on La Grande rue, is another Pennsylvania memorial, this one to the 80th "Blue Ridge" Division, which relieved the 79th (see Chapter 14).

It was much the same in other areas of the American front. Like the 79th Division, some divisions advanced toward the gates of the Kreimhilde Stellung only to be driven back. The Buckeyes of the 37th Division briefly occupied the village of Cierges. The 91st Division reached Gesnes before being forced out. "Hardest fighting yet," recorded Giuseppe Romeo in his diary, "and many of our boys were lost." The 35th Division was forced out of the Bois de Montrebeau between Exermont and Charpentry. The 28th Division took the village of Apremont and held it against fierce German counterattacks. Much has been written during the war of "the blood-soaked fields of France," stated the official history of the 28th Division, but the "officers who were at Apremont solemnly vouch for the fact that there was a time in that town when the water running in the gutters was bright red with blood. And not all of it was German blood." By the end of September 29, the AEF held a line running roughly from Apremont in the west to the Meuse River just south of Brieulles-sur-Meuse on the Meuse River to the east. "Raining had all the time and awful cold," wrote Romeo. "No raincoats or overcoats but plenty of ammunition."

But with each successive day, the American momentum slowed. The inability to crack the Kreimhilde Stellung, especially the delay around Montfaucon, bought the Germans time. The German commander in the region, General Max von Gallwitz, initially believed the attack in the Meuse-Argonne to be a feint, and expected an attack east of Verdun where the Saint-Mihiel campaign had just concluded. Surely the inexperienced divisions facing him could not be the main strike force, he surmised. But when von Gallwitz became convinced that the Meuse-Argonne was the main American thrust, he quickly brought in reinforcements. Even after Montfaucon was taken, the Germans still had commanding positions in the Argonne Forest and especially at the Heights of the Meuse. German artillery pounded the Americans, who could do little to stop it. American forces, at least according to some reports, also lacked air cover. Bad weather often kept planes grounded. Colonel Billy Mitchell, the First Army's air commander, focused on attacking German positions behind their lines, and insisted that German planes could not operate in force above American forces. The soldiers on the ground often insisted otherwise.

The First Army also had massive logistical problems. The muddy, shell-pocked roads behind the lines were jammed with military traffic. The problem was especially bad around Esnes, where the 4th and 79th Divisions used the same roads. On September 29, French Prime Minister George Clemenceau stopped in at Pershing's headquarters at Souilly and asked to be taken to Montfaucon. The prominence had bedeviled French troops during the Battle of Verdun, and he wanted to stand triumphantly on its slopes and pay tribute to the American soldiers who had finally taken it. The American commander demurred. "I felt real solicitude for his safety," Pershing later wrote, since Montfaucon was still "a prominent target for the enemy's artillery." Clemenceau insisted, and Pershing relented. The two men got into Clemenceau's limousine and headed up to the front, but they never reached their destination, and the reason had nothing to do with German artillery. Rather, the roads were impassibly clogged with traffic. There were artillery limbers, ambulances, and supply trucks, all of them intermixed with Doughboys standing around, smoking and talking. Clemenceau's driver honked his horn and the premier himself shouted in an effort to get traffic moving again, but to no avail. Clemenceau got out of his car and climbed a nearby hill to survey the problem, and from his vantage point saw traffic clogging the roads for kilometers ahead. Montfaucon was visible on the horizon, but tantalizingly out of reach. "He failed to reach Montfaucon and left rather disappointed," Pershing wrote, "thinking, no doubt, that our transportation was hopelessly swamped." Pershing was right. In fact, Clemenceau was incensed, and concluded that the Americans were not yet ready to sustain a major campaign. He was particularly critical of Pershing, and schemed to remove him from command.

In addition to the political headaches, snarled traffic also meant that frontline troops could not be supported properly. Artillery units—like Captain Truman's 129th Field Artillery—had great trouble moving up to the front and getting into the fight because of the traffic, denying the infantry critical battlefield support. In some cases, American troops used captured German guns since their own artillery was absent. The Doughboys were sometimes also unable to get adequate supplies of ammunition, forcing some to strip weapons and ammunition from their dead or wounded comrades in order to keep fighting. Food was yet another problem. Some went for days without sustenance, and some got so hungry they even took rations off of dead German soldiers. It was just as hard moving things to the rear, most tragically the wounded, who lay in fields and shell holes across the front. Many who might have been saved died for lack of medical attention.

Many soldiers had simply become exhausted. Days without food or sleep, living in the mud under constant shelling or machine-gun fire, took a physical and psychological toll on the Doughboy. Thousands of "stragglers" lingered behind their frontline comrades. Some had been separated from their units in the confusion of combat. Others set out on desperate searches for food and water. Untold numbers simply hid out in dugouts, old shell holes, ruined villages, and woodlands behind the lines to avoid the fighting. Patrols combed through rear areas to round up the stragglers, get them back

Traffic jam at Esnes-en-Argonne, France. (Courtesy of the National Archives)

to their units, or have them face disciplinary action. To top it all off, influenza and other diseases left thousands unable to fight.

Pershing continued to believe that lack of aggressiveness and fighting spirit were the reasons for the delays. He paid several visits to corps and divisional headquarters, haranguing their officers to be more aggressive. Soldiers who would not fight, he believed, should be court-martialed and shot for cowardice. But Pershing's threats and exhortations could not propel his army forward, and just five days into the campaign he had to hit the reset button. Except for the 77th Division, which continued its long slow drive through the Argonne Forest, the First Army temporarily halted offensive operations on September 30 and went onto the defense. American forces had penetrated ten kilometers into German-held territory, but casualties were high. According to official counts, the campaign for Montfaucon cost the 79th Division 3,591 casualties, a figure that historian Edward Lengel contends is "almost certainly an understatement." The Wild West Division took 4,700 dead and wounded. And despite the bloodshed, the First Army was behind schedule. The Meuse-Argonne Offensive was not going to be the quick and easy victory that the Americans had experienced at Saint-Mihiel.

CHAPTER 14:
HEROISM IN THE ARGONNE

By the first week of October 1918, the Allies had the Germans on the run. In Picardy, the British had blown a hole through the Hindenburg Line and were closing in on the Belgian border. In Flanders, a multi-national force had flushed the Germans from Ypres and was driving toward Brussels. But on some parts of the Western Front the Germans held on, and one of those places was the Meuse-Argonne region. Pershing's open warfare tactics had failed to break through and resulted in exceptionally heavy casualties. Questions about American readiness and Pershing's competence—subdued since the successful days of the Saint-Mihiel Offensive just weeks before—quickly resurfaced. But few questioned the raw fighting abilities of the Doughboy. In fact, in the darkness of the Argonne Forest, at this lowest point in the fortunes of the AEF, came some of the best examples of the fighting prowess of the American soldier. Two men in particular—Charles Whittlesey and Alvin C. York—would emerge from the Argonne Forest national heroes and household names.

After halting offensive operations on September 30, Pershing replaced some of his exhausted divisions and tweaked his battle plan. General Robert Bullard's III Corps was to continue its drive along the west bank of the Meuse. While the 33rd Division stayed put to guard the riverbank from any possible German attack into the corps flank, the 4th "Ivy" Division was to lead the charge north into the Cunel Heights between Cunel and Brieulles-sur-Meuse. To support them, Bullard repositioned the 80th "Blue Ridge" Division to Nantillois to support the 4th Division on its left. The Blue Ridge Division's task was to take the Bois des Ogons, which the 79th Division had been unable to do in September. The road that is today the D15 highway marks the western boundary of the III Corps zone. General George Cameron's V Corps, facing the Romagne Heights, was completely reconstituted and now consisted of two veteran divisions. The 3rd Division, which earned the nickname "Rock of the Marne" for its brilliant defense at Château-Thierry the previous summer, took up positions below Cierges. The 32nd Division, which the French nicknamed *Les Terribles* for its tenacity

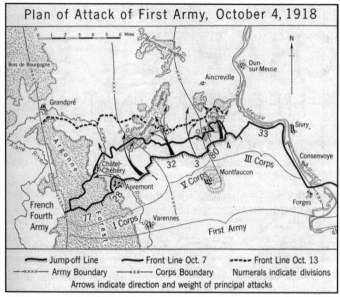

Plan of Attack of First Army, October 4, 1918

Jump-off Line   Front Line Oct. 7   Front Line Oct. 13
Army Boundary   Corps Boundary   Numerals indicate divisions
Arrows indicate direction and weight of principal attacks

in the Aisne-Marne Offensive, was to their left. Each faced open farmlands punctuated with numerous hills and wooded lots containing impressive German defensive positions. In General Hunter Liggett's I Corps, the 77th and 28th Divisions remained on the line, but the 1st Division, a veteran outfit that Pershing considered the best combat unit in the AEF, replaced the shattered 35th Division. Pershing hoped the experience and skill of the Big Red One would propel I Corps forward, completing the capture of the Aire Valley and forcing the Germans from the Argonne Forest.

The First Army resumed the offensive on October 4. The Americans moved back over ground captured but given up just a week before, but progress was still slow and difficult. The 4th "Ivy" Division attacked northward from the Bois de Brieulles, crossing the Nantillois-Brieulles Road (present-day D164 highway) into the rugged Bois de Fays. Despite taking terrible casualties, the Ivy Division entered the woods and pierced the leading edge of the Kreimhilde Stellung. It even reached the Cunel-Brieulles Road (now the D123 highway), but a strong German counterattack drove it back into the Bois de Fays. By the end of the day the Americans held most of the Bois de Fays—and a sliver of the Kreimhilde Stellung. Today a 4th Division monument is located on the D164 about a kilometer outside of Brieulles-sur-Meuse. From there, looking northeast, the Bois de Fays appears on the horizon.

The 80th Division advanced from Nantillois toward the Bois des Ogons. The fight for those woods on October 4 was, if anything, even tougher than it was for the 79th Division the previous week. The Blue Ridge Boys traversed Hill 274 and headed for the woods, but they were met with an intense dose of gas, machine-gun fire, and artillery. They were unable to take and hold the woods that day. The attack resumed the next morning, and the daytime attacks were as fruitless as the day before, but a final assault at 6:00 PM finally broke through. When darkness fell on October 5, the 80th Division controlled most of the Bois des Ogons. The following day it pushed on and reached the northern edge

Pennsylvania's memorial to the 80th Division, Nantillois, France.

of the woods, just shy of the German field hospital at Madeleine Farm. The 80th Division's headquarters during the attack on the Bois des Ogons were located at Nantillois, and that little village assumed a special place in the hearts of the division's veterans. In 1925, the Pennsylvania Battle Monuments Commission dedicated a memorial fountain in Nantillois to the 80th Division, a substantial part of which hailed from the Keystone State. The limestone fountain, designed by Thomas Atherton and Paul Cret, is embedded into a red brick wall at the intersection of La Grande rue and the route de Brieulles. The fountain is no longer functional. Junipers now grow where water once flowed, but the Pennsylvania state seal and the dedication to the "heroic service and notable achievements" of the 80th Division still pay tribute to those who fought and died in the area. The fountain is just sixty meters from the 14–18 Nantillois museum (see Chapter 13). The Bois des Ogons today seem as quiet and peaceful as all the other forests in the area. A German war cemetery at its northern edge, within sight of Madeleine Farm, is the only reminder of its war-torn past.

V Corps, in the center of the First Army, did not have it any easier. From its line of departure between Nantillois and Cierges— the one-lane rural road between the two hamlets roughly marks their starting line—the 3rd Division measured its gains on October 4 in mere meters. On October 5, the division took a wooded highland known as Hill 250, just to the west of the Bois des Ogons, and linked up with the 80th Division there, but the Germans still held several key positions in the American zone of advance. The crest of the bald hilltop slightly to the northwest of Hill 250, known as Hill 253, remained in German hands, though Doughboys held its southern base. The Germans also controlled the Bois de Cunel immediately north of Hill 250 and across the road from Madeleine Farm. On the V Corps's left, the 32nd Division reached the outskirts of Gesnes on October 4 but could not move into the village itself. It took the village the following day, but the Germans still held the heights to the north and subjected the Americans to a relentless rain of artillery. Paul Schmidt remembered that when the Germans were done, "all that was left was a heap of broken stone." Unsettling as the barrage was, Schmidt recalled an even more disturbing scene near Gesnes. "The bodies of about fifty dead American soldiers furnished mute and tragic testimony of the advance and retreat of American troops who had been here before us," he wrote in his memoir. "These corpses were men of the 91st Division, and from appearances had been laying on the field for at least a week." It was much the same in the I Corps area to the west. The 1st Division stepped off from the heights south of Exermont. The men of the Big Red One, veterans of the fights at Cantigny and Soissons, found the Meuse-Argonne Offensive their toughest battle yet. They took the Exermont and reached the outskirts of Fléville on the first day. The second day they captured the high ground north of Exermont known as the Bois de Montrefagne, but Fléville remained agonizingly out of reach.

But after just two days of modest gains, German counterattacks and effectively placed defensive positions had stopped the Americans dead in their tracks. After October 6, each side pummeled the other with machine guns and gas, but the front lines barely budged.

The experience of the 3rd Division typified that of most divisions on the line. Just after midnight on October 7, the Rock of the Marne made several attempts to cross the valley between Hill 250 and the Bois de Cunel. The Germans sent up flares and raked the valley with fire each time they discovered the Americans. None of the U.S. attacks succeeded. Also that morning, Private John L. Barkley was sent into no man's land on the ridge connecting Hills 250 and 253 on a mission to gather intelligence on German activities. Linked to headquarters by telephone wire, Barkley found

Madeleine Farm.

a shell hole in the early morning darkness and settled in, despite the smell of the decomposing bodies scattered around his position. After daybreak Barkley detected the massing of German troops in the Bois de Cunel, and phoned in the informa-tion. Early that afternoon the Germans laid down an artillery barrage on American positions, and then, under the cover of a smoke screen, began shifting troops from the Bois de Cunel to Hill 253 in preparation for an attack on the American troops holding the south slope of the hill. Barkley used the screen to take up a new position nearby in a ruined French tank. There he found an abandoned German machine gun, mounted it on the tank, and fired into the Germans crossing the open field between the Bois de Cunel and Hill 253, breaking up the counterattack. German artillery hit Barkley's tank, but miraculously he survived, using his machine gun to break up another counterattack. For his bravery and quick thinking, Barkley received the Medal of Honor. The site of the failed nighttime attacks and Barkley's heroics is visible today looking west from the D15 highway just a few hundred meters south of Madeleine Farm.

The Saga of the Lost Battalion

Meanwhile, a dangerous situation developed in the Argonne Forest with the potential of dealing a catastrophic blow to the morale of the American First Army, and indeed the entire American nation. Pershing's temporary pause in operations on September 30 did not apply to the 77th "Liberty" Division, which was slogging its way through the Argonne Forest. German artillery from the forest wreaked havoc on I Corps and had to be eliminated. Progress through the thick woodland was painfully slow, but by October 1 the Americans had gotten within a few kilometers of Charlevaux Creek and the Charlevaux Mill Road (present-day D66), which ran beneath a bluff on the north side of the creek. By seizing the road, the Americans would cut an important German communication line, but doing so would not be easy. About one kilometer south of the road was a German defensive line known as the Giselher Stellung. The Doughboys of the 77th Division attempted to pierce that line on October 1. They took heavy casualties and failed.

On October 2 they tried again. The 154th Brigade, made up of the 307th and 308th Infantry Regiments, held the far left segment of the American line, with the French Fourth Army on their left. According to the plan, the brigade would attack in conjunction with the French and take the Charlevaux Mill Road, as well as the bluff above. They stepped off at 7:00 AM. Fighting raged all morning and the Allies were unable to gain any ground, but by midday the 1st Battalion of the 308th Infantry found a gap in the German line, running through a ravine a few hundred meters south of Charlevaux Mill near a point known as Hill 198. The battalion commander was Major Charles Whittlesey, a Wisconsin-born New York lawyer. Whittlesey led most of his battalion through the gap. Elements of the 2nd Battalion under Captain George McMurtry, a veteran of Teddy Roosevelt's Rough Riders in the Spanish-American War, also made it through. Whittlesey established message runner posts along his route to keep up communications with brigade headquarters, and led his men toward the Charlevaux Road. The Americans crossed the creek, but heavy German resistance from the bluff above prevented them from crossing the road. Whittlesey had orders not to retreat, and well aware of the pressure from Pershing on down to move forward, he dared not disobey. Besides, he fully expected that other Allied troops would soon join him. In fact, Whittlesey was told that French forces on his left had already crossed the Charlevaux Road. The major ordered his men to dig in. They established a defensive perimeter, roughly 300 meters long and 100 meters wide, on the heavily wooded hillside between the creek and the road, and waited to link up with the other units. This position became known as "the Pocket."

Unfortunately, none of the other Allied forces got through. The French troops Whittlesey thought were on his left had in fact withdrawn in the face of strong German resistance. The composite battalion was all alone about one kilometer behind German lines. Whittlesey sent a message to his commander, Brigadier General Evan Johnson, outlining his position and situation. Johnson received it about dusk, and ordered a risky nighttime operation to exploit the breakthrough and link up with Whittlesey's men. The operation failed. Attacking troops blundered around in the dark. Only one company from the 307th Infantry Regiment got through, and rather than being rescuers its troops also became stuck behind enemy lines. On the morning of October 3, the Germans severed Whittlesey's communication line and fixed the gap in the Giselher Stellung. The battalion was now entirely cut off. It had a day's worth of food and meager medical supplies. Ammunition supplies were adequate, but would not last forever. A supply of carrier pigeons was the only way they could get messages out, and there was no way for them to receive any communications. Relief would have to come soon. On October 3 Whittlesey tried twice to break out of the Pocket, but the Germans rebuffed each attempt. That day the Germans began infantry assaults against the Pocket, and kept it under almost constant fire. The 60–70 percent grade of the bluff prevented direct German machine-gun fire from the north, though hand grenades and high-trajectory trench mortars from that direction proved deadly. The bluff on the south bank of Charlevaux Creek gave the Germans more direct lines of fire. Snipers abounded in the woods. Whittlesey and his men took fire from all directions.

Each day brought more misery for the Americans. Food quickly ran out. The only supply of water came from Charlevaux Creek, but the Germans shot at anyone trying to fill his canteen. The creek bed was soon littered with bodies, and the water ran red with blood. Casualties mounted and medical supplies were exhausted. Wounded men groaned in agony and the dead could not be buried, filling the air with the stench of death. The Germans attacked relentlessly. Each assault was beaten back, but also diminished the ammunition supply. With each attack, Whittlesey's men burrowed deeper and deeper into the earth, and the hillside began to resemble a prairie dog town. The Liberty Division tried numerous times to break through the

Giselher Stellung to reach Whittlesey, launching infantry assaults and artillery barrages. One barrage on October 4 mistakenly landed inside the Pocket. Down to his last pigeon, a bird named Cher Ami, Whittlesey desperately tried to halt the friendly fire and wrote one last note to division headquarters. "Our own artillery is dropping a barrage directly on us," he told them. "For heaven's sake, stop it." Cher Ami was released, but she promptly perched on a branch in a nearby tree. After shouting and throwing rocks and sticks at her, one soldier climbed the tree and shook its branches. The bird finally took off, arriving at headquarters twenty minutes later, suffering the loss of a leg and an eye, as well as other wounds. By the time Cher Ami arrived, the artillery had already adjusted its aim. American planes tried to drop supplies into the Pocket, but they had trouble finding Whittlesey's men through the dense forest canopy. Not one of the parcels landed inside the Pocket, and several airmen were killed in the attempts. German soldiers taunted the Americans as they ate the food intended for them.

The press learned of the situation, and promptly dubbed the trapped soldiers the "Lost Battalion." As the folks back home grew transfixed over the plight of Whittlesey and his men, the pressure to rescue them only grew more intense. On October 7, Pershing expanded the American offensive. The French XVII Corps, under Pershing's command, crossed the Meuse and began an assault on the Heights of the Meuse. Among the units comprising the French XVII Corps were the American 29th and 33rd Divisions. At the same time, Liggett's I Corps attacked west into the Argonne Forest, north of the Lost Battalion's position. The Pennsylvanians of the 28th Division took the village of Châtel-Chéhéry and the hills just to the west of it. The 82nd "All American" Division was brought

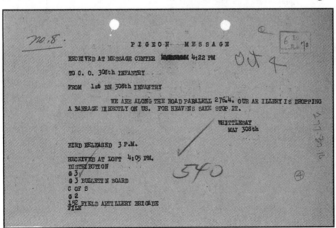

Transcription of message that Major Charles Whittlesey sent from "the Pocket," October 4, 1918, delivered by the famous pigeon Cher Ami. (Courtesy of the National Archives)

up from the corps reserve to supplement the 28th Division. This division had seen just a bit of action near Saint-Mihiel, but was essentially green. The All Americans made many rookie mistakes and took heavy casualties, but by the end of the day they moved up to the hills just north of Châtel-Chéhéry. Pershing hoped that expanding the battlefront would stretch out German lines, force the Germans to disperse their forces, and accentuate America's manpower advantage. Taking the Argonne Forest and the Heights of the Meuse would also knock out the heavy artillery guns there that had caused such havoc with the First Army in between. Liggett's incursion into the Argonne might also hasten the German withdrawal from the Argonne and relieve the Lost Battalion.

After nearly a week, the Lost Battalion drama reached a breaking point. Whittlesey steadfastly refused to surrender, but some under his command began to talk about it. Others grew so desperate that they tried to break out on their own in search of food or rescue. As for the Germans, their position in the Argonne had grown increasingly untenable. The advance of the Fourth French army to the west, especially the U.S. 2nd Division's taking of Blanc Mont Ridge (see Chapter 15), posed a serious threat to the German position in

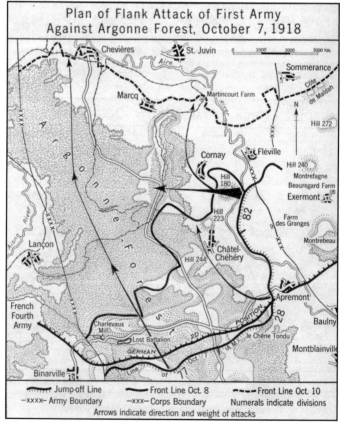

Plan of Flank Attack of First Army Against Argonne Forest, October 7, 1918

Jump-off Line — Front Line Oct. 8 — Front Line Oct. 10
-xxxx- Army Boundary   -xxx- Corps Boundary   Numerals indicate divisions
Arrows indicate direction and weight of attacks

the Argonne. Liggett's push into the eastern Argonne on October 7 only added to the Germans' dilemma. Their commanders prepared to pull out, but hoped to finish off the Lost Battalion before they did, bringing in flamethrowers and elite storm troopers to do the job. On October 7, the Germans gave Whittlesey a surrender ultimatum, delivered by a Doughboy they had captured while he was searching for an airdropped food parcel. Whittlesey ignored the demands, and prepared for yet another assault, which came about 5:00 PM. This one was also beaten back—but barely. The Pocket could probably not withstand another attack, but it would not have to. The Germans withdrew, and just after 7:00 PM advancing Liberty Division soldiers reached the Pocket. They found a group of bearded and bloodied men so weary they could barely celebrate. Of the nearly 700 Americans who went into the Charlevaux Ravine with Whittlesey, only 338 came out alive—the rest had been killed or captured. Most of the survivors had been physically wounded. The psychological impact of their ordeal can only be surmised.

The saga of the Lost Battalion was one of the most celebrated episodes of the war. In the end, it became a story of American heroism and perseverance. General Pershing considered it one of the most important events of the entire American war effort. Promoted to Lieutenant Colonel, Whittlesey was a national hero. He, McMurtry, and five others—including two pilots killed trying to drop supplies into the Pocket—received the Medal of Honor for their actions. The pigeon Cher Ami became the most celebrated American military fowl since Old Abe the War Eagle of Civil War fame.

The Pocket of the Lost Battalion is located about two kilometers east of Binarville on the D66 highway. (For those coming from Apremont, take the D442. It becomes the D66 upon crossing into the Department of Champagne-Ardenne.) The site is easy to miss. On the south side of the road stands a rectangular stone marker no more than a meter tall reading, "Lost Battalion," with an arrow pointing down the hill, indicating the location of the Pocket. From the marker one can descend the hill, though the steep grade and frequent mud makes it rather challenging. For those who scramble down the bluff, the remnants of the Lost Division foxholes are still evident, though filled in by years of erosion. Sadly, souvenir hunting and logging activities have altered the site, but it is still a moving experience to stand where this tough and determined bunch of Doughboys put up their heroic defense. Deeper into the woods, on the high ground to the south of Charlevaux Creek, are the remnants of the Giselher Stellung, through which the Lost Battalion fought. About half a kilometer west of the Pocket, near the banks of the Charlevaux Mill pond (the mill itself is long gone) is Binarville's memorial to the Lost Battalion, dedicated on October 7, 2008—the ninetieth anniversary of the Lost Battalion's rescue. Flanked by

Marker on the D66 highway east of Binarville, France, marking the site of "the Pocket" of the Lost Battalion.

French and American flags, the limestone memorial includes a carving of the famous pigeon Cher Ami standing atop a pile of U.S. combat helmets. Nearby is a panel in English and French telling the story of the Lost Battalion.

There are no Lost Battalion monuments in the United States. A memorial grove in New York's Central Park was dedicated to the 307th Infantry Regiment after the war, on the east side near the 72nd Street entrance. Each tree is dedicated to a specific company in the regiment, identified by a small brass plaque at its base. Sadly, many of the trees have succumbed to the ages, leaving only the plaques. Only Company K of this regiment was part of the Lost Battalion. The famous bird Cher Ami was stuffed after the war, and is now at the Smithsonian's National Museum of American History in Washington.

From Rowdy Mountain Boy to Pacifist to War Hero—the Incredible Life of Alvin York

The effort to free the Lost Battalion led indirectly to perhaps the most famous event of the American World War I experience—the battlefield exploits of Alvin C. York. York was born December 13, 1887, in the tiny hamlet of Pall Mall in Fentress County, Tennessee. Tucked away in the Cumberland Mountains at the upper reaches of the Wolf River, Pall Mall was poor and isolated. The nearest railroad was ten miles away at Jamestown, the county seat. Schools were few and far between, and not many children had the luxury of attending them anyway. Their hands were needed on the farm. The bottomlands along the Wolf River were fertile, but most residents scratched out a living on less productive soils farther away from the river. Such was the plight of the York family. Alvin was the third of eleven children born to William and Mary York. The family lived in a log cabin at the base of a hill not far from the local cemetery. "It was built out of hewn logs," York remembered of his birthplace and childhood home. "The logs were chinked with clay and sticks. The inside was pasted with newspapers and colored magazine covers." William York supplemented his farming with a blacksmith shop, and as a boy Alvin helped out with both. Work left little time for school, and Alvin never got beyond the third grade. In the mountains, hunting was often done for sustenance rather than for sport, but for

William York it was a passion. He sometimes disappeared into the woods for days in search of game. He taught his sons to hunt and shoot, and demanded they do it, too. As Alvin recalled, his father "threatened to muss me up right smart if I failed to bring down a squirrel with the first shot or hit a turkey in the body instead of taking its head off."

William York died in 1911, making Alvin the head of the household. He continued to farm and work in the blacksmith shop, and dreamed of getting his hands on some

Sergeant Alvin C. York. (Courtesy of the Library of Congress)

good bottomlands, but took other odd jobs to supplement the family's meager income. One summer, for example, he joined a road construction crew building what is today U.S. Highway 127, which runs through Pall Mall. Shooting competitions, regular events in the Tennessee mountains, offered other opportunities to provide for the family. Turkey shoots were popular. In these contests, a turkey was tethered behind a log so that only its bobbing head and neck showed. The first contestant to shoot off the turkey's head got the meat. York won many such competitions, as well as others with monetary prizes, and he was known as the best shot in the Wolf River Valley. There was a darker side to his reputation as well. York was fond of gunplay, fistfights, gambling, and moonshine whiskey. In one incident, a drunken York noticed some turkeys on a fence and wanted to see how many he could shoot. He hit all of them, but the farmer who owned the birds was not pleased and hauled York into court. "I was wild and bad for five or six years," York recalled, but he resolved in his heart to change. For one thing, he fell in love with a girl named Gracie Williams, but her family disapproved of York's rowdy reputation. He also found religion. In 1915, York joined a small fundamentalist denomination known as the Church of Christ in Christian Union, an offshoot of Methodism, which eschewed politics and stressed piety and the personal exploration of faith through Bible study. In his own reading of scripture, York found injunctions against violence that helped him end his aggressive ways. He also gave up drinking and gambling, and even tobacco. "When I quit, I quit it all," he explained.

When America entered World War I, York filed an application to be a conscientious objector, but since his church was not expressly

The sandstone bluff known as the "Yellow Doors," where York prayed for guidance before going to war.

pacifist it was denied. He was drafted and sent to Camp Gordon, Georgia, in November 1917. It was the first time he had seen the wider world, and he was shocked. "They put me by some Greeks and Italians to sleep," he wrote in his diary. "I couldn't understand them, and they couldn't understand me, and I was the home sickest boy you have ever seen." York was amazed at how poorly the "boys from the big cities" handled guns. "They would not only miss the targets," he wrote incredulously, "they would also miss the hills on which the targets were placed." Whether or not he would have to shoot any Germans still weighed heavily on his mind. After being assigned to an infantry company in the 82nd Division, York took his moral concerns about killing to his superiors. Major George Edward Buxton, his battalion commander, was a devout Christian with no compunctions about fighting. He spoke with York for hours, explaining how he believed military service to be compatible with faith. Buxton then gave York ten days leave to go home and think it over. If, upon returning to camp, he still believed that war was immoral, Buxton promised him a noncombat assignment. York went home and discussed his options with his family and his pastor. He also went off to a sandstone bluff known as the Yellow Doors, located in the hills just east of Pall Mall, where he spent nearly two days in prayer. He returned resolved to serve and fight, believing God approved and would protect him from harm. Some in his church were disappointed, but York was unmoved. "If some feller was to come along and bust into your house and mistreat your wife and murder your children," he asked his critics, "you'd just stand for it? You wouldn't fight?"

In the early morning hours of October 8, 1918, the 82nd Division moved into the woods and hills of the Argonne Forest just northwest of Châtel-Chéhéry. The 328th Infantry Regiment, which occupied a prominence known as Hill 223, was on the far southern edge of the division's zone of operations, and Company G—York's unit—was in the second wave of the assault. As the All-American Division advanced west across a valley toward German positions on the Champrocher Ridge, German machine guns opened up on it. York watched as his comrades in front fell "like the long grass before the mowing machine at home," and he dropped into the high grass. The platoon sergeant, Bernard Early, took a group of seventeen men—York among them—to outflank some of the guns and silence them. They crawled to their left through the grass, crossed over a wooded ridge, and got behind some of the machine-gun nests. A small group of German medics spotted them and dashed away as fast as they could. Early's men followed the medics, who inadvertently led them to a small shack occupied by some unsuspecting and mostly unarmed German troops from the 210th Landwehr Infantry, under the command of Lieutenant Paul Vollmer. The Americans charged. Stunned to find U.S. troops behind their lines and unable to do much about it, Vollmer and his men promptly threw up their hands. However, the machine-gunners of the 120th Landwehr, posted on a nearby ridge, saw what was happening. First shouting a warning to their comrades, the German gunners opened on the Americans. Sergeant Early was badly wounded. Several in the party were killed.

It was at this point that Corporal York's heroics began. He dove for cover, and found himself downhill from the machine-gunners, about twenty-five meters away. He noticed that due to the angle of the hill, the Germans could not see him without exposing their heads. York took his rifle, and whenever a German soldier's head appeared, he pulled the trigger and "jes teched him off"—much like a turkey shoot back in Pall Mall. After taking several casualties this way, six Germans on the hill got up and charged at York, firing away and with fixed bayonets. York now pulled out his .45 pistol and shot every one of them. He picked off the men in the rear first, so those in front of the charge did not know their numbers were diminishing. "That's the way we shoot turkeys at home," he explained. "I guess I jes naturally did it." Vollmer now offered to surrender. He blew a whistle, the firing stopped, and gray-clad German soldiers filed down the hill. One prisoner lobbed a grenade at York. It missed, and York shot him. The American party had been reduced to seven effective members, but they now had several dozen prisoners. York told Vollmer that there were "a-plenty" more Americans nearby, and the German officer bought the lie. Using his backwoods sense of direction, York led the bizarre procession back toward American lines. Vollmer led, with York and his .45 directly behind him. Encountering other German units along the way, Vollmer urged them to surrender as well. By the time York and his men got back to American lines, they had killed twenty-five German soldiers, knocked out thirty-five machine guns, and collected 132 prisoners. "I hear you have captured the whole damned German army," York's astonished brigade commander said to him afterward. York was promoted to sergeant and received the Distinguished Service Cross. In 1919, he was awarded the Medal of Honor. France awarded him the Croix de Guerre, and Marshall Foch told him: "What you did was the greatest thing accomplished by any private soldier in all of the armies of Europe."

A monument to Sergeant York, consisting of a granite base with a plaque describing his deeds, stands in front of the mayor's office in Châtel-Chéhéry today. Just a few hundred meters north of this monument, a road splits off to the west, providing access to the scene of the fight, though exactly where York performed his superhuman feat is the subject of fierce debate. The exact spot was never recorded. Lamenting that fact, an organization called the Sergeant York Discovery Expedition (SYDE) began research into the question. Its members scoured the forest for clues, and in 2006 found a location fitting the descriptions of the event. There they found .45 casings and German military insignia. This spot, they concluded, was where York made his stand against the bayonet attack. SYDE then developed a hiking trail to guide visitors along the route of York's party, and constructed a monument near the location of York's famous stand. Thanks to SYDE, travelers today can enjoy a nice walk through the Argonne Forest, but are they really walking in York's footsteps? The Sergeant York Project (SYP) says no. This group, composed of several academic experts and led by Dr. Thomas J. Nolan of Middle Tennessee State University, conducted its own field research. Nolan argues that the bayonet charge actually happened at a different unmarked site in the woods 500 meters to the south of the SYDE location. The SYP also found .45 casings and a host of other artifacts consistent with descriptions of the event. In addition, it believes it has found the original gravesites of the men killed in the firefight—the dead were initially buried where they fell, and were later exhumed and reinterred in the United States or at the Meuse-Argonne American Cemetery—providing further corroborating evidence of the legitimacy of the SYP site. Visitors to Châtel-Chéhéry who want to see where York made his legendary stand will have to do some reading, weigh the evidence, and come to their own conclusions.

"York marched out of the Argonne Forest and into the annals of American legend," wrote his biographer, David D. Lee. His story was not widely known until an article about him appeared in an April 1919 edition of the *Saturday Evening Post*. The story of the humble mountain man's triumph over the impersonal slaughter of modern war captivated the nation. "York seemed to be a reincarnation of pioneer America in the midst of the twentieth century," Lee explained. "His old-fashioned values emphasizing family and church were quaint but appealing to an urban nation insecure about its newfound sophistication." His arrival in New York in May 1919 was the occasion of great fanfare. The Tennessee Society in New York put him up in the Waldorf Astoria Hotel. He was whisked to Washington, where he met his congressman, Cordell Hull (later Secretary of State under Franklin D. Roosevelt) and got a tour of the White House. York was honored, but not especially interested. He wanted to go home. Within a week of his return to Pall Mall he married his sweetheart, Gracie Williams.

After the war, York lived by his values of humility and Christian charity. He consistently refused to cash in on his celebrity, despite many offers, believing it wrong to profit from his military deeds. He did accept one gift. Soon after his return the Pall Mall, the Rotary Club presented York with a prime bottomland farm along the banks of the Wolf River. In addition to farming, York operated a general store across the road beginning in 1925, and acquired a nearby grist-mill in 1943. But York also felt a higher calling and dedicated his life to improving conditions in the Tennessee mountains. Self-conscious about his own lack of schooling ("I ain't had much larnin' myself," he once said), he used his fame to raise money to build a technical high school, and used his political connections to garner state aid for it. The final result was the York Agricultural Institute, which opened in Jamestown, Tennessee, in December 1929. He also wanted to promote his Christian faith. In 1940, he finally allowed Hollywood to tell his story. The resulting film, *Sergeant York*, was one of the top-grossing films of 1941. Gary Cooper, who portrayed York, won the Oscar for best actor. York plowed the lion's share of his profits from the film into building a Bible school in Pall Mall, which opened in 1942. York's life was simultaneously filled with frustration. Financial problems plagued him. York was grateful for his new farm, for example, but in the agricultural depression of the 1920s he had trouble paying the bills. The national publicity surrounding his money woes led to a wave of donations that saved his farm, but York found the entire affair humiliating. Some of his disappointments were related to his achievements. He quarreled constantly with the administrators of the York Institute, and in 1936 was forced out of the operations of the school that bore his name. His cherished Bible school was forced to close within months.

The state of Tennessee honors its most famous Doughboy in many ways. A statue of York stands at the southeast corner of the State Capitol grounds in Nashville, and the Tennessee State Museum nearby exhibits some of his memorabilia. Tennessee also maintains the Alvin C. York State Historic Park in Pall Mall. The park itself consists mainly of York's farm and gristmill, but there "a-plenty" of other York sites nearby. The York General Store on U.S. 127 is the place to begin exploring Sergeant York's world. It is the very same one the famous soldier operated. Today the store sells a wealth of Sergeant York souvenirs rather than farm provisions, and it serves as a park welcome center. From the store, travelers can pick up a driving tour map of the area put together by the Sergeant York Patriotic Foundation. Many sites are within walking distance of the store. York's gristmill lies just across the river. His farm and the house in which Alvin and Gracie raised their family is across the highway. The house, built in 1922, has been left largely as it was when York passed away in 1964. Inside is a wealth of memorabilia from his wartime service and postwar activities. Surrounding the home are the rich bottomlands he received after World War I, still filled with crops each summer. A half-mile-long hiking trail leads from the home, passing through his fields and along the shady banks of the Wolf River, to the Wolf River Methodist Church, where York discovered his faith in 1915. Less than a quarter of a mile northwest of the church, on the north side of the road just past Tater Hill Road, is the site of York's birth. The log cabin is long gone, and the homestead site has been swallowed up by the woods. Just a little farther up the road, tucked away in the woods on the south side of the road, are the remains of York's unsuccessful Bible school. Across the road from the Methodist church is the Wolf River Cemetery, where York is buried. Alvin and Gracie's final resting place is easily the most prominent grave on the grounds. From the gravesite one can look out to the east and see the Yellow Doors—the sandstone bluff at which York prayed so fervently before deciding to go to war.

A little farther afield are still more Sergeant York sites. The Yellow Doors are now part of Pogue Creek Natural Area, administered by the Tennessee Department of Environment and Conservation, and popular with hikers. The York Agricultural Institute in Jamestown is now known as the Alvin C. York Institute, a public high school. York actively participated in building the school, located at 710 North Main Street, using his own hands to dig ditches and lay bricks. While York avoided talking about his experiences in the Argonne Forest, he loved to talk about his school. Even after he was forced out of its daily operations, he considered it one of his great-

The York General Store in Pall Mall, Tennessee, which serves as the welcome center for the Alvin C. York State Historic Park.

est achievements. The school has expanded greatly since the 1920s, so much so that the original building is no longer in use. The structure was nearly demolished, but thanks to the intercession of the Sergeant York Patriotic Foundation it has been saved. The building was listed on the National Register of Historic Places in 2008, and the foundation is renovating it with plans to convert it into a museum, archives, and educational center.

All of these sites are located along U.S. Highway 127, which is known locally as the Alvin C. York Highway—the very road York helped construct before the war. Pall Mall has hardly been immune to the forces of change, but it is not hard to imagine what it

Sergeant York's grave, Pall Mall, Tennessee.

was like a century ago. Harkening back to former times, Alvin C. York State Historical Park sponsors a black-powder shooting contest each spring. Indeed, any visitor to Pall Mall today is likely to meet a relative of the World War I hero. Many serve as guides to the home. Some might be sitting on the bench outside York General Store shooting the breeze with their neighbors or with visitors. They often have interesting personal stories to tell about their famous relative.

The Hard Road toward the Kreimhilde Stellung

Despite the heroics of men like Whittlesey and York, the progress of the First Army remained painfully slow. On October 9, 1918, after several days of no significant forward motion, V Corps surged forward and made some modest but important gains. The 3rd Division broke through to take the Bois de Cunel, Madeleine Farm, and the crest of Hill 253. From there it fought its way across Moussin Creek, crossing the Kreimhilde Stellung, and up to the hills just east of Romagne-sous-Montfaucon. Some patrols even entered the village itself, but the Germans pushed them back to a portion of the Kreimhilde Stellung called the Mamelle Trench, on a high ground just a few hundred meters southeast of Romagne-sous-Montfaucon. The 32nd Division was also on the move that day. The division pushed up to the Transvaal Farm, where it reached the southern edge of the Côte Dame Marie, a steep ridge forming a hook in the Romagne Heights. *Les Terribles* ascended the slopes of the Côte Dame Marie and entered the Romagne Heights, but they too were pushed back to Transvaal Farm and the Mamelle Trench. In the I Corps sector on that same day, October 9, the 16th Infantry Regiment of the 1st Division finally liberated Fléville after fierce fighting. Today in front of the Fléville town hall is a memorial to the 16th Infantry Regiment, placed there by its veterans in 1999. As the memorial states, the regiment incorporated the blue-and-white shield of Fléville's coat of arms into its regimental insignia, which it still uses to this day.

A general First Army push began on October 10 that lasted two days. The 4th and 80th Divisions took the Bois de Malaumont east of Cunel on the first day, and on the second day the Ivy Division carved out a foothold in the Bois de Forêt to the north. The 3rd Division surged out of the Bois de Cunel toward the village of Cunel, but was halted just short of the village itself. On the far west, the Big Red One began to press up against the western edge of the Romagne Heights. Pershing called for a pause in the offensive on October 12 to consolidate his gains and bring up some fresh divisions. It had been a big week for the Americans. They were now at the very gates of the Kreimhilde Stellung, and in a few places even held small portions of it. But they paid a very heavy price to get there. In one week, the 1st Division lost 1,790 killed and 7,126 wounded—far more than they lost in the Saint-Mihiel Offensive the month before. A 1st Division monument stands at the intersection of the D54 and D964 highways southeast of Saint-Juvin.

The entire zone south of the Kreimhilde Stellung became one massive killing zone. Nearly every hill and hollow, field and forest, was the scene of some bloody and desperate fighting. The enormous casualties took their toll on the divisions at the front. "We just kept on . . . getting replacements every day," remembered Ray Fuller of the 32nd Division, who had been with the division since Camp MacArthur. "You didn't know a third of the people in a company." It had now been more than two weeks since the Meuse-Argonne Offensive had begun, and the First Army had still not reached the goal Pershing had set for it on the first day. For Pershing, the pressure on him to break through the Kreimhilde Stellung mounted every day.

CHAPTER 15:
CHAMPAGNE

One of the many incongruities of the First World War was the fact that its mechanical slaughter played out across the backdrop of the picturesque French countryside. Nowhere was this more evident than in Champagne. The region is known for its distinctive sparking wine, a staple at weddings, New Years, and other celebrations of life. Today's tourists flock to Champagne for its wine tastings blissfully unaware of its blood-drenched past. When American troops arrived there in 1918 to fight alongside their French allies, they saw a landscape of astonishing destruction and impersonal death. Moving his men up to the Champagne Front in the fall of 1918, General John A. Lejeune of the U.S. Marines, commander of the U.S. 2nd Division, passed a spot called Navarin Farm. The land "had been shelled, and bombed and mined so frequently that it had lost all semblance of its former self," he wrote. He noticed that "not a tree was left standing anywhere," but that was just the beginning of the horrors:

> The debris of battle was still lying about—broken cannon and machine guns, rifles, bayonets, helmets, parts of uniforms, articles of military equipment, and partly buried horses; most grewsome [sic] of all, fragments of human bodies were often found. Arms and legs thrust out of the torn soil, and unrecognizable, long-buried human faces, thrown up to the surface of the ground by exploding shells, were frequently visible. The fearsome odors of the battlefield, too, were always present.

The roughly 70,000 Americans who fought in Champagne were an unusual mix that included National Guard troops from across the United States, African American regiments under French command, and a contingent of U.S. Marines. Their ranks were not large, but their victories—military and social—were among the most important of the war.

The countryside of Champagne consists of open, rolling farmland, occasionally punctuated with woodlands and hills. During World War I, the front lines in Champagne ran east–west between Reims and the Argonne Forest. Some of the Great War's bloodiest fighting occurred along this front in 1914 and 1915, but afterward it stabilized and became a relatively quiet sector. By 1918, the Champagne

Front was the responsibility of the French Fourth Army, under General Henri Gouraud. A career military man, Gouraud spent much of his early service overseas in various French colonies in Africa. In 1915 he commanded a French force at the Dardanelles in Turkey, and lost his right arm in the fighting. He assumed command of the Fourth Army in December 1915, and with the exception of a brief tour of duty in Morocco, remained there for the rest of the war. The feisty, one-armed general inspired great admiration in his men and earned the nickname "The Lion on Champagne." Those Americans serving under Gouraud found him an inspirational figure as well. General Lejeune described him as a "striking man" who was "tall, erect, with heavy dark brown beard and hair, and a complexion burnt dark by the blazing sun of Africa." The first American troops in Champagne were the men of the 369th Infantry Regiment, an African American unit that Pershing turned over to the French. The regiment received its introduction to the trenches that spring, and had already seen some action, most notably the so-called "Battle of Henry Johnson" in May 1918 (see Chapter 10).

Germany's offensives in the spring and summer of 1918 did not immediately have a major impact in Champagne. But with Ludendorff's July *Friedensturm* (Peace Offensive), in which he planned to encircle the critical transportation center of Reims in preparation for a drive on Paris, the heavy fighting shifted eastward into Champagne. Since intelligence had learned of Ludendorff's plans ahead of time, French commanders had time to prepare. General Philippe Pétain, the commander-in-chief of the French armies, had Gouraud organize his defenses in depth. In the event of a major attack, according to Pétain's plan, most soldiers in the frontline trenches would pull back to preprepared intermediate positions between the first and second trench lines. The Germans, he argued, would concentrate their fire on frontline trenches, which would be only lightly occupied. Those soldiers remaining in the first line trenches would man what were dubbed "sacrifice posts." Their job was to send information about the movement of German troops to the rear—either by telephone or signal flares—and slow down the German advance as best they could. Other sacrifice posts, like machine-gun nests and antitank positions, would be scattered like islands across the zone between the first and the intermediate positions, further impeding German forces. Serving in a sacrifice post was tantamount to a suicide mission, yet most who did so volunteered. The intermediate positions, about three kilometers behind the frontline, would then form the main line of resistance. Weakened by their push through the sacrifice posts, Pétain believed, the Germans would be unable to break the intermediate line. Should the intermediate positions fail, the secondary line of trenches, two to three kilometers behind the intermediate positions, would serve as a backstop.

Blunting the German offensive required not just a sound plan, but soldiers, and American troops factored into Pétain's calculations. The 369th Infantry Regiment was placed in the second line backstop near Laval-sur-Tourbe. In addition to the 369th, Pétain and Gouraud also had the services of the 42nd "Rainbow" Division, which had recently completed its initiation to frontline life in the Vosges Mountains. The division, composed of National Guard regiments from various states, arrived in Champagne on July 5, 1918. Several companies and battalions of Americans were placed in the intermediate line interspersed with French units between Aubérive and Perthes-lès-Hurlus. In addition, the Rainbow Division's 83rd and 84th Brigades made up the secondary line backstop between Aubérive and Perthes-lès-Hurlus. Brave Americans also volunteered to serve in sacrifice posts. One was Hamilton Fish, a white officer in Company K of the 369th Infantry Regiment. "I do not believe there is any chance of us surviving the first push," he told his parents in what must have been a difficult letter to write, but added: "I am proud to be trusted with such a post of honor and have the greatest confidence in my own men to do their duty to the end." In the days before the German offensive, Gouraud visited his soldiers at the front and provided his tried and true inspirational leadership. "A defensive battle was never engaged in under more favorable conditions," he assured his Franco-American forces. When the attack came, Gouraud implored: "Kill them, kill them in abundance, until they have had enough."

As German infantry forces massed for the attack on July 14, Allied artillery hit them hard. German artillery began its preparatory barrage just after midnight, but concentrated its fire on the lightly held Allied front line, as expected. The intermediate line remained largely untouched. German infantry stepped off at 3:50 AM. Pétain's plan worked flawlessly. The sacrifice posts gave warning of German movements, and they delayed the enemy advance. The Germans took the first trench line, but the real hard fighting took place along the intermediate line, and nowhere did the Germans penetrate it. Repeated attacks came throughout the day on July 15, but none broke through. There were more attacks the following day, but the results were the same. "It is a hard day for the enemy," Gouraud told the Fourth Army on July 16. "It is a beautiful day for France." Hamilton Fish miraculously survived the fighting in the sacrifice post, though several of his men were killed. "My helmet was hit with shrapnel," he wrote afterward, and "I had a few other close scrapes."

The Rainbow Division soldiers in the intermediate positions acquitted themselves well in the battle. Elements of the 165th Infantry Regiment (New York National Guard) held off the Germans from positions on either side of the D931 highway near its intersection with the D21 at Esperance Farm. Doughboys from the 166th Infantry Regiment (Ohio National Guard) successfully defended Saint-Hilaire-le-Grand from positions along an old Roman roadway (now part of farm fields and no longer clearly evident) just north of the village. The remains of a concrete bunker on the D977 highway just north of Souain mark the spot where portions of the 167th Infantry Regiment (Alabama National Guard) experienced particularly brutal, hand-to-hand fighting. Here too the Americans held their ground. "They cleaned up on the enemy," wrote Elmer Sherwood of the 150th Field Artillery in his diary, referring to the 167th Infantry, "but it is no surprise to any of us, because they are a wild bunch, not knowing what fear is." The Rainbow Division was pulled from the line on July 19 and moved west to fight in the Aisne-Marne Offensive. There are several French military cemeteries in the area and numerous war memorials sprinkled across the fields, but none dedicated specifically to the 42nd Division. There is a reminder of the U.S. military presence related to World War II. The D931 highway forms part of the Voie de Liberté—a memorial highway stretching across France marking the route of General George S. Patton Jr. into eastern France in the fall of 1944.

Camp de Suippes, a French military reservation just to the east of Souain, also contains some areas of interest to Americans. Companies of the 168th Infantry Regiment (Iowa National Guard) held a wooded area between Souain and the hamlet of Perthes-lès-Hurlus, which was destroyed during the war and never rebuilt. Perthes-lès-Hurlus was one of five *villages detruit* (destroyed villages) on the grounds of the reservation, along with Hurlus, Mesnil-les-Hurlus, Ripont, and Tahure. After the war Perthes-lès-Hurlus merged with Souain, and the village is now known by the unwieldy name of Souain-Perthes-lès-Hurlus. The reservation also contains the Cimitère National de Lègion Etrangére (National Cemetery of the Foreign Legion), which has its origins with a prominent American family. Henry Farnsworth, a Harvard-educated American writer serving in the French Foreign Legion, was killed in the area on September 28, 1915. In 1920, the Farnsworth family built a memorial to Henry and his comrades. Visiting the cemetery is difficult. The reservation grounds are normally closed to the public. However, each September the French military—in association with the Centre d'interprétation de Suippes, a war museum in the town of Suippes—grants limited access to the grounds so that the public can visit the memorials and the remnants of the villages.

To the east of the Rainbow Division was the 369th Infantry Regiment, which held a secondary line of trenches. "There was nothing for the infantrymen to do," wrote Arthur Little, "but lie down in the trenches and keep under cover." But the German artillery was fearsome, and the Americans were hardly taking it easy. Napoleon Marshall described the barrage as "myriads of hell furies madly shrieking midst reverberating thunder trebeled above its wonted noise." The "very earth [was] trembling as with an earthquake," he remembered, and "heavy smoke shut out the sky." Indeed, the 369th took some casualties in the barrage. But Pétain and Gouraud's elastic defenses held, and that is when the 369th joined the action as part of the counteroffensive. On the night of July 17, the regiment moved up in the darkness to the front, marching north along the present-day D66 highway through the villages of Laval, Wargemoulin, and Minaucourt. They joined the French 161st Division, and took up positions north of Minaucourt along the Marson Road, near the ruined Beauséjour Farm, west of Ville-sur-Tourbe. On July 18 they attacked—the regiment's first frontal assault. It was terribly bloody business. Corporal Horace Pippin of Company K remembered feeling "sad and mad all at the same time" at the sight of his dead comrades, but he and the others pressed on. They advanced two kilometers and retook the original front line.

The New Yorkers of the 369th spent the better part of the next six weeks fighting in the area between the Butte de Mesnil and the Main de Massiges. From mid-July through early September, the regiment experienced some of the very worst that World War I had to offer. Smoke, fire, and poison gas filled the muddy shell holes, through which the soldiers patrolled and fought. During those bloody summer battles, the Germans began to refer to the 369th Infantry Regiment as the "hell fighters." The nickname stuck, and the regiment would be forever after known as the "Harlem Hell Fighters." Much of the area where the Hell Fighters won their nickname, like Beauséjour Farm, is part of the Camp de Suippes military reserve and normally off-limits to the public. Some Hell Fighter battlefields are still accessible. One can still trace their July 17–18 march to the front along the D66, for example. Portions of the regiment's line of departure for the advance on July 18 were along the Marson Road just north of Minaucourt, near the Pont du Marson and the nearby French military cemetery, stretching westward into the military reservation.

The Glory and the Tragedy of the African American Combat Experience

For Foch's Grand Offensive in September, Gouraud's Fourth Army attacked on September 26 in conjunction with Pershing's U.S. First Army on his right. By this time, the 369th Infantry Regiment had been fully integrated into the French 161st Division. Joining the Harlem Hell Fighters in the French Fourth Army were two of the three other regiments that composed the U.S. 93rd Division, the 171st and 172nd Infantry Regiments, which became part of the

French 157th Division. The 157th was known as the "Red Hand" division because of its emblem of a blood-drenched hand. In fact, the 93rd Division planned to use the red hand for its own divisional emblem, but the army brass thought that African Americans using such a violent image was too provocative, and forced them to reconsider. Instead, the division adopted the image of a French helmet—symbolizing how these American soldiers had to fight under the French flag and not their own. In addition to those fighting under French command, the "Buffalo Soldiers" of the 92nd Division entered the fight at the far western edge of the American First Army. From a purely military standpoint, the role of the African American regiments in Champagne was not pivotal to the overall course of the war, but as historian Edward M. Coffman pointed out, their participation "had broader social significance than the military effort of all the other American units." Their experiences were also remarkably different. One would become the most maligned fighting unit in the U.S. Army. The others would amass a remarkable record of combat effectiveness that could not be ignored.

Clinging to the belief that African American soldiers were incapable of battlefield prowess, American commanders were reluctant to put General Charles C. Ballou's 92nd Division into action at all. Just days before the start of the Meuse-Argonne Offensive in September 1918, the 368th Infantry Regiment and two machine gun companies were finally selected to participate in the campaign, while the rest of the division was held in reserve. They took up positions along a two-kilometer segment of the front on the edge of the Argonne Forest, from Vienne-le-Château to Le Harazée, on the far western edge of the American sector. To their right was the U.S. 77th Division, and to the left was the French Fourth Army. One of their tasks was to maintain contact with the French and serve as a bridge between French and American sectors. In the attack, their objective was the village of Binarville, four kilometers north of the departure line. The assignment was a tough one. German troops had occupied the area for years. The thickly wooded landscape was strewn with plenty of barbed wire, laced with trenches, and dotted with tunnels. The regimental commander placed just one of his three battalions along the two-kilometer-long front, putting one in reserve and turning the other over to the French. That left fewer than one thousand men across a broad front and a challenging combat environment.

The Buffalo Soldiers stepped off with the rest of the American First Army on September 26. At first they advanced as expected, facing little opposition from the retreating Germans. But problems soon emerged. The battalion commander began to lose contact with his men as they became disoriented in the dense and foggy woods. Artillery support was virtually nonexistent, and the soldiers were not provided with the heavy wire cutters necessary to slice through the

German entanglements. When German resistance stiffened in the Moreau Valley about a kilometer north of the departure line, chaos ensued and most of the battalion withdrew. The attack resumed the following day, this time with two battalions, but the results were largely the same. The third day saw all three battalions in action, along with French reinforcements and even a little artillery support, but the regiment was still unable to penetrate the German lines. Finally, on the fourth day, September 29, the First Battalion under Major John Merrill reached Binarville. The Buffalo Soldiers were taken off the line on October 1.

The Buffalo Soldier battlefield today remains a densely wooded area that is now part of various forest preserves. Most of the fighting took place along the D63 highway and in the woods to the east of the road. The 368th Infantry's line of departure on September 26 lies roughly a kilometer north of the Biesme River. For travelers on the D63, the one-time line is no more than a few hundred meters north of a French military cemetery. Driving or hiking in the area today, it's not difficult to understand the problems the Buffalo Soldiers faced in advancing across this rugged landscape. In the Moreau Valley, that appreciation only grows. Remnants of German trenches and other fortifications remain in the woods of the Moreau Valley. At Camp Moreau, located along the banks of the Moreau Creek at its intersection with the D63, military enthusiasts have restored an old German camp. Open to the public only very limited hours in the summer, it contains restored trenches, bunkers, and even shower and laundry facilities. Camp Moreau makes no mention of the Buffalo Soldiers, though a visit does give the traveler an idea of some of the problems they were up against.

The 368th Infantry's troubles in taking the village only further diminished the already low expectations many U.S. commanders had for African Americans soldiers in combat. The judgment against African American officers was especially harsh. The white officers in the division almost unanimously blamed their black colleagues for its failures, arguing that they lacked bravery and initiative, and could not control their men. Such criticisms came right from the top. "It is probable that philanthropic considerations, or at any rate considerations not purely military, influenced decisions regarding the use of negro officers," General Ballou later remarked. "No good came, or could come, to the colored race from imposing on it responsibilities and burdens it could not creditably sustain." The experiment with black officers, he argued, "was unfair to the race and unfair to the handful of white officers whose reputation was bound up with the achievements of colored troops." In the latter comment, Ballou may well have been referring to himself. His own reputation was seriously tarnished by the failure at Binarville, and his bitterness sometimes boiled over. He viciously excoriated the

African American officers in front of the division's enlisted men. After Binarville, Ballou removed thirty black officers from command, but some enraged white commanders demanded even more. Five were court-martialed for cowardice—all but one of whom were sentenced to death by firing squad, though cooler heads eventually prevailed and the sentences were never carried out.

African American officers defended themselves. Writing after the war in *The Messenger*, William Colson and A.B. Nutt, junior officers in the 92nd Division, readily admitted that the division had failed but argued that white officers—indeed the entire white army establishment—was to blame. They argued that black officers were systematically denied the opportunity to succeed. They pointed out that black officers were not admitted to advanced training schools, like those at Langres (see Chapter 7), limiting their effectiveness. White officers and NCOs were mainly southern racists, they argued, whose "sole charge . . . was to make the life of the Negro soldier unendurable." Colson and Nutt concluded that "the Negro division was the object of special victimization, superimposed upon its sacrifice," and that "the 368th Infantry was sent 'over the top' for the avowed purpose of demonstrating a failure." After a century, it seems clear that Colson and Nutt made the better argument. Commanders from the very top deprived the Buffalo Soldiers of dignity and respect. Lacking the training, confidence, and *espirit de corps* soldiers need to fight, not to mention adequate leadership and equipment, it is little wonder the division performed poorly. It was indeed a self-fulfilling prophecy.

While the 92nd Division struggled near Binarville, three of the four regiments that made up the 93rd Division were amassing a stellar combat record just ten kilometers to the northwest. Unlike their counterparts under in the 92nd Division under U.S. command, the men of the 93rd Division under the French were adequately equipped, properly led, and treated with dignity. Given the opportunity to fight as equals, these men wrote themselves into the annals of U.S. military history in boldface type. Though attached to different French divisions, the regiments all fought in the same vicinity, near the village of Sechault. The 369th Infantry Regiment was the first to enter the fight. It began that first day in the second wave of the attack, but when a gap opened up between two French units, the Hell Fighters stepped in to fill it. They crossed the Dormoise River and took the ruins of Ripont (one of the destroyed villages on the Suippes military reservation). On September 27 they captured Fontaine-en-Dormoise, and began their fight up the strategic high ground southwest of Sechault known as the Bellevue Signal Ridge. The Germans stoutly defended their ground. In the face of machine guns, artillery, and poison gas, the 369th Infantry slowly made its way across muddy fields pockmarked with countless shell holes. "I were in some shell holes that were smokeing [sic]," one Hell Fighter wrote of the experience, "and they were hot." By the end of the day on September 28, the 369th Infantry had gained a foothold on the eastern side of the ridge.

At the same time just to the west, the 371st and 372nd Infantry Regiments also entered the fight for the Bellevue Signal Ridge. The African American soldiers of the Red Hand Division faced equally difficult conditions. The area was laced with trenches, from which the Germans put up determined resistance. One particularly dastardly incident took place atop a promontory known as Hill 188. As the 371st Infantry pressed its attack, German troops came out of their trenches, hands held high, as if to surrender. When U.S. troops came out to accept the apparent capitulation, the Germans jumped back into their positions and blasted the exposed Americans with withering machine-gun and mortar fire. After a day of bitter fighting such as this, the Americans had only advanced a few hundred meters, but those meters were important ones. Despite the German treachery, the 93rd Division took Hill 188, and had even moved off the ridge and occupied Bussy Farm in the vale just below. The Allies now had a commanding position above Sechault.

But there was little time to celebrate the victory or mourn the dead. The assault continued on September 29. The 369th Infantry completed the seizure of the Bellevue Signal Ridge, approached the low hill southeast of Sechault known as Mont Cuvelet, and pressed on toward the village itself. From its position atop the ridge, the 371st continued northward and captured the hamlets of Ardeuil and Montfauxelles, while the 372nd moved out into the flat open lands between Ardeuil and Sechault. Patrols from the 372nd had even entered Sechault, but were unable to hold the town. Later that day, however, the Hell Fighters moved into the village from the south. German machine-gunners and snipers lingered in the ruins of the village, and were cleared out only after bitter house-to-house fighting. The following day, September 30, the 369th continued its attack to the north and east of Sechault, moving into the area now occupied by a French Air Force base, before being relieved on October 1. Also on September 30th, the 372nd was withdrawn to the Bellevue Signal Ridge, but the 371st pressed on along a rail line (now abandoned and occupied by a road) and captured Trières Farm on the east side of the D982 highway. On October 1, the refreshed 372nd took over for the 371st at Trières Farm and advanced north toward Monthois. About a kilometer before entering the town, German enfilade fire from the woods and hills just to the southwest raked the Americans. They staunchly held their ground, even in the face of a determined German counterattack on October 5, and hung on until relieved two days later.

Casualties were heavy, and many soldiers were decorated for their bravery under fire. Two received the Medal of Honor. One was a First Lieutenant George S. Robb, a white officer in the 369th Infantry Regiment. On September 29th, the Kansas native was severely wounded by German machine gun fire in the battle for Sechault. Ordered to the rear for medical attention, he escaped the hospital and was back in the village leading his men within an hour. Early that next morning he was wounded again, and in the afternoon wounded a third time by a shell that killed his commanding officer and two others. None of this deterred Robb, who assumed command of the company and led it out of the village. This white Hell Fighter survived his wounds and received the Medal of Honor in 1919. In 2011, Robb's alma mater, Park University in Parkville, Missouri, installed a small interpretive panel and flagpole in Robb's honor outside the

Grave of Corporal Freddie Stowers, Meuse-Argonne American Cemetery, Romagne-sous-Montfaucon, France.

Thompson Commons Student Center on their campus.

The other was Corporal Freddie Stowers of the 371st Infantry Regiment. The grandson of a slave, Stowers was born in Sandy Springs, South Carolina, in 1896 and drafted in 1917. On September 28, Stowers's company was leading the assault on Hill 188 when the Germans staged their fake surrender. Half of the company's men were killed or wounded in the incident, including its lieutenant and NCOs. Corporal Stowers assumed the mantle of command and led the company on. The men took heavy casualties, but destroyed a machine gun nest and occupied the first line of German trenches. Stowers then led his men toward the second line. Crawling through the mud toward the enemy, Stowers was hit by machine-gun fire, but he continued to press forward and urged his men on until he finally succumbed to his wounds. His sacrifice and heroism inspired his comrades to keep up the attack that successfully pushed the Germans off the hill. Stowers's commanding officer filed papers recommending him for the Medal of Honor, but nothing ever happened. After reopening the case in the 1980s, the army found what it called the "misplaced" paperwork. On April 24, 1991, President George H. W. Bush presented Stowers's two surviving sisters with the Medal of Honor he had earned seventy-three years earlier. Corporal Stowers is buried in the Meuse-Argonne American Cemetery. The South Carolina Confederate Relic Room and Military Museum in Columbia and the Anderson County Museum in Anderson, South Carolina (just nine miles from the place of Stowers' birth), keep Stowers's memory alive with exhibits about his accomplishments.

Monuments to each of the three 93rd Division regiments stand in the countryside around Sechault today. On the west side of the village, at the intersection of the D982 and the D6 highways, is a small park with an informational panel about the American regiments that fought in the area. Next to it stands a black granite obelisk dedicated to the 369th Harlem Hell Fighters. An identical monument stands at the corner of 5th Avenue and East 142nd Street in Harlem. Across the street is the 369th Regiment Armory, built for the Hell Fighters after the war and still an active New York National Guard installation. For many years the armory hosted 369th Historical Society Museum, but in 2014 renovations forced the museum to close temporarily, and the site of the new museum has yet to be settled.

Roughly two kilometers north of Sechault on the east side of the D982 is another obelisk, marking the farthest advance of the 372nd Infantry Regiment. Two kilometers to the southwest of Sechault is the most interesting—and remote—of the three. The 371st Infantry Regiment memorial is located atop Hill 188, where the regiment fought so valiantly and where Corporal Stowers performed his extraordinary deeds. The monument itself is in a field at the crest of the hill. Finding it is not easy. There is no road access, and to reach it one must traipse through the countryside fought over so bitterly a century ago. Fortunately, the informational panel in the park outside Sechault provides directions to the memorial. Travelers who make the effort to visit the site will be rewarded. The monument contains the names of the officers and men from the unit who were killed in the area. Much of the monument's top has been shorn off, hit by an artillery shell during the German invasion of France in World War II. In the nearby woods, remnants of the German trenches remain. Looking north from the memorial, the fields of Bussy Farm can be seen in the picturesque valley off to the right, and off in the distance is the plain across

Harlem Hell Fighter Memorial, Sechault, France. An identical marker also stands in Harlem, New York.

which the 93rd Division advanced during those critical days of the Great War.

The U.S. Marines Play a Starring Role in Yet Another Critical Victory

The African American men of the 92nd and 93rd Divisions were not the only Doughboys fighting in Champagne during the Grand Offensive. Though the Allied high command berated Pershing for not advancing fast enough in the Meuse-Argonne Sector, the Fourth French Army to its left was moving even more slowly. Holding up the advance in Champagne was a German strongpoint on Blanc Mont Ridge, five kilometers north of Sommepy. The gently sloping limestone massif was the highest ground between the Py and Aisne Rivers, commanding a huge swath of French countryside. The Germans recognized its significance when they arrived in 1914 and heavily fortified the ridgeline. French attempts to retake the ridge over the years had all ended in failure, and during the September 1918 campaign the Germans were once again able to blunt French advances. Frustrated, Marshall Foch asked Pershing to loan him two U.S. divisions to help take Blanc Mont Ridge. Pershing turned over the army-marine hybrid and battle-tested 2nd Division, under the command of United States Marine Corps General John A. Lejeune, and the 36th Division, an untested National Guard unit from Texas.

Gouraud held the Texans in reserve, but put the 2nd Division on the front lines as soon as he could. The division set up headquarters in Sommepy and went right to work. The marine brigade took up positions just north of the village on October 2, and immediately began wrestling ground away from the Germans to gain a favorable position for an attack on the ridge. By the end of the day, they reached a point indicated by a 2nd Division boulder on the west side of the present-day D320 highway. An army infantry brigade assumed positions about two kilometers northwest of the village, just south of the D977 highway. The infantry assault, with tank support, began and 5:50 AM on October 3. Marine William Carter remembered "passing over the bodies of French soldiers who had fallen five days earlier in a similar attempt." Carter also remembered that the marines caught a German sniper who had shot and killed an unarmed Red Cross man. "He was surrounded, dragged from his hole, bound to the wire entanglements, and a volley of hot lead registered his last intolerable act." In the end, the Americans made it look easy. What the French had not been able to do for years, the 2nd Division had done by lunchtime. Within three hours of stepping off, Doughboys had reached Hill 210 at the top of Blanc Mont Ridge. "An exciting hand-to-hand fight took place when we came across a mass of Germans in a trench," wrote Carter of his arrival at the crest of the ridge, but the marine and infantry brigades quickly took the most strategic portion of the ridgeline into their possession.

But the battle was far from over. The French divisions on either side of the Doughboys had been unable to advance, creating a vulnerable salient in the Allied front. The Germans hammered away at the exposed flanks, but the American lines held. Indeed, on the afternoon of October 3 the Americans pushed into the countryside northwest of Hill 210 toward the village of Saint-Etienne-à-Arnes, but were unable to reach the village itself. By the end of the day on October 3, German commanders—seeing the Americans firmly in control of the strategic heights—decided to withdraw behind the Aisne River. It would be a fighting withdrawal, however, and the Germans made the Americans pay dearly for the ground they took. The fighting on October 4, according to one account, was of "exceptional severity." The Doughboys were unable to take much new ground, and the French troops on either side were still unable to advance. On October 5, the marines cleared the western slope of Mont Blanc Ridge, paving the way for French gains on their left. French troops were able to move even further on October 6. By October 7 the 2nd Division had undisputed control of Mont Blanc Ridge, and elements of the 36th Division began the relief of the 2nd Division. A memorial boulder at the intersection of the D23 and D41 highways in Saint-Etienne-à-Arnes marks the farthest extent of the 2nd Division in Champagne. The division was transferred back to the U.S. First Army and prepared to participate in the Meuse-Argonne Offensive, but the Texans of the 36th Division stayed in Champagne and picked up where the 2nd Division left off, taking Saint-Etienne-à-Arnes and chasing the Germans to the Aisne. Their advance roughly followed a line to the west of the present-day D977, taking the villages of Machault, Leffincourt, Dricourt, and Vaux-Champagne. They reached Attigny and the Aisne River by October 28.

The American Battle Monument Commission's Sommepy American Monument now stands at Hill 210 at the center of Blanc Mont Ridge. Designed by Arthur Loomis Harmon of New York, whose body of work included the Empire State Building, it is a square limestone tower, with each of the four sides representing one of the U.S. Divisions that fought

Sommepy American Monument on Blanc Mont Ridge.

Remnants of German trenches at the Sommepy American Monument on Blanc Mont Ridge.

in the area. On the north face is an eagle in Art Deco style with a dedication inscribed below. Etched into the stone on the tower's other faces are the names of each division, its emblem, and a list of the important engagements it fought in the area. Since the 92nd Division was not formally part of the French Fourth Army, it is not included on the monument. The memorial is also an observation tower. In the vestibule leading to the stairs, there is a description of the Champagne battles in both English and French. From the top, the Champagne battlefields are clearly evident. Directional arrows point to important spots, such as Sechault and Saint-Hilaire. Sommepy and Camp de Suippes are easily seen to the south. Looking north are the lands the 36th Division liberated afterward. The wooded grounds surrounding the monument still have remnants of the German trenches that the 2nd Division took on October 3, 1918.

Five kilometers south of the monument on the D32 highway is the village of Sommepy, which also has sites of interest to Americans. On the hill below the church along rue de la Chaussée is a 2nd Division memorial boulder, commemorating the division's initial entry into the village. Just meters away, proud marines placed another stone marker to the 5th and 6th Marine Regiments. The hillside also contains some remnants of German bunkers and fortifications, some which the Americans utilized when they took over the town, as well as small memorials to all five of the *villages detruit* in the Camp de Suippes military reservation. One of those villages, Tahure, merged with Sommepy after the war to create present-day Sommepy-Tahure. Sommepy came close to being irrevocably destroyed itself. Located just inside German lines for much of the war, artillery pounded it into a pile of rubble. Not a singe building emerged undamaged. As in many other places across rural France where Doughboys once fought, philanthropic Americans helped rebuild the village after the war. A French army officer named Andre L'Huillier, a Sommepy native, traveled the United States to raise funds for French postwar reconstruction. His appearance at Harvard University inspired a group of alumni from that institution to offer their services to rebuild L'Huillier's hometown. The resulting "Sommepy Fund" financed the construction of—among other things—a combination town hall and school, which still serves as the municipal building in that village today. Inside is the Musée Memorial Franco-Américain. In it are exhibits about the area's Great War history, including the world of the American fighting man. The beautifully decorated walls of the museum contain dedications to the local dead, the Doughboys who liberated their village, and the Americans who helped rebuild it. The museum is open by appointment only.

France honors its war dead from the Champagne battles in numerous ways. Monuments and military cemeteries appear across the landscape with heartrending frequency. The most grand of them all is the Monument aux Morts des Armées de Champagne, on the flat plain between Sommepy and Souain. A pyramid with a flattened top, this monument is both a memorial to the war dead as well as the final resting place for the bones of 10,000 French soldiers who died in the region between 1914 and 1918.

Thousands more, whose bodies were never recovered, still lie in eternal rest below the fields all across Champagne. The location was once a peaceful rural spot known as Navarin Farm, but when the war came it became the German frontline and one of the most violent places on the Western Front. The French built their memorial atop the

Monument aux Morts des Armées de Champagne, north of Souain, France.

German trenches, the remnants of which can still be seen in the surrounding fields. General Gouraud spearheaded the effort to build it, raising money all across France. The monument's cornerstone—a remnant from the ruined church in Souain—was laid in November 1923, with the monument completed in September of the following year. Inside is a chapel in which the family members of the missing have placed plaques in memory of their lost loved ones. Also interred there is General Gouraud himself, who requested that after his death he be laid to rest with the French soldiers who fought and died for him.

Capping the monument is a massive statue of three soldiers. The figure in the center is a Poilu about to lob a grenade. The one on the left is holding a rifle, slightly crouched, as if ready to charge. The soldier on the right is an American, easily identifiable by his "tin derby" helmet, carrying a machine gun and ammunition case. The sculptor, Maxime Real del Sarte, was a French war veteran who lost an arm in battle in 1916. He created each figure in the likeness of an actual person. The figure in the center was based on General

Gouraud. The infantryman on the left is modeled on the sculptor's brother, who was killed in the war. The face of the American is meant to resemble Quentin Roosevelt, the son of President Theodore Roosevelt, a pilot killed northeast of Paris in July 1918 (see Chapter 11). Engraved on the face of the pedestal on which the sculpture stands are the names of the units that served in the French Fourth Army. Eighty-five French infantry divisions are listed, as are various colonial ones. Cavalry, artillery, and aerial units also appear, as do two Russian brigades, a Czechoslovakian one, and a Polish regiment that fought on the Allied side. The four "Divisions Américaines" are honored as well.

The men of the 2nd Division had achieved one of the most important Allied victories of the war. It not only undermined the German position in Champagne, but also paved the way for American advances in the neighboring Meuse-Argonne region. Pétain reportedly commented that the 2nd Division's seizure of Blanc Mont Ridge was "the greatest single achievement of the 1918 campaign." Sadly, the contributions of those Americans fighting in Champagne went largely unnoticed by the folks back home. In the fall of 1918, the eyes of the nation were fixed on the U.S. First Army and its fight in the Meuse-Argonne. The African American soldiers of the 93rd Division provided still more proof that they could play an important role in an Allied victory. That too went unnoticed, though the travails of the 92nd Division did not. The Americans in Champagne were not the only ones participating in the Grand Offensive under foreign command. Farther afield, from Flanders to the Veneto of Italy, Doughboys were also pushing the Central Powers back.

CHAPTER 16:
FARTHER AFIELD

Ever since the United States entered the Great War in April 1917, Britain and France schemed to tap into America's vast manpower pool to augment their own depleted armies. Even the Italians wanted a share. In September 1918, the Italian commander-in-chief, General Armando Diaz, stopped in to see Pershing at Chaumont. It began as a friendly chat, "but in the course of our conversation," Pershing recalled, "it developed that the real purpose of his visit was to ask for American troops." Diaz wanted twenty divisions. "I showed no evidence of surprise," Pershing wrote, "having become quite accustomed to this sort of thing." Diaz apparently mistook his nonchalance for a "favorable sign," Pershing surmised, and promptly "raised the number to twenty-five." Pershing politely told Diaz that he had no troops to spare. Despite the enormous pressures on him, Pershing had masterfully created an independent American army in Europe, but he could not resist every Allied call for American troops. Doughboys appeared on the British front in northern France as early as 1917. Most returned to American command, but by the time of Foch's Grand Offensive in September 1918, there were still Americans fighting alongside the British Tommy. In fact, by the end of the war there were Americans on virtually every segment of the Western Front.

Within months of entering the war, American medical and engineering units arrived in Britain and the British-held areas of northern France. Some got up to the front right away. In August 1917, the U.S. Army's 11th Railway Engineers reached the front lines near Gouzeaucourt, fifteen kilometers southwest of Cambrai. Barely a kilometer from the German lines, they had the job of maintaining the railroads behind the front. A British officer advised the Yanks to "be well scattered to avoid attracting attention and reduce the number of serious casualties in case of shelling." It was good advice. On September 5, German shells came in along the tracks on the northeast edge of Gouzeaucourt—where the present-day D197 and D95 intersect—wounding two Americans. Those same tracks were the scene of an even bloodier episode two months later. On November 20, the British launched a surprise attack on German-held Cambrai. Charging infantry, accompanied by 380 tanks, tore through the Hindenburg Line and reached the outskirts of Cambrai. Unfortunately for the British, they could not hold their gains. On the morning of November 30, unarmed American engineers working on the line near Gouzeaucourt saw and heard the usual shelling in the distance, and thought little of it, but as the barrage got closer, intensified, and included gas, they realized that a German counteroffensive was underway. The Yanks joined their British counterparts and retreated to the west of the village with German troops fast on their heels. Some were caught behind German lines. One group took refuge in a dugout. When a party of German soldiers showed up, one American soldier who spoke German shouted from the darkness that they were wounded Germans. The ruse worked; the German soldiers pressed on. Others joined the British and Canadian troops digging in to halt the German advance, gathering weapons as best they could. By noon British infantry arrived to beat back the counteroffensive, and the armed American engineering troops were all too glad to help them. The engineers suffered six killed, thirteen wounded, and eleven taken prisoner. There is a British war cemetery in Gouzeaucourt today, but no marker to commemorate one of the first places American troops saw action in the Great War.

Other engineering units attached to the British saw some action. In February 1918, about 500 members of the 6th Engineers, a part of the 3rd Division, were sent to the British front east of Amiens for bridge construction projects near Péronne. When the Germans launched their Michael Offensive in Picardy on March 21 (see Chapter 8), the 6th Engineers dropped their shovels and picked up their guns. The Americans became part of "Carey's Force," named for their commander, General G.G.S. Carey. The eclectic mix of men included electricians, tunneling specialists, the students and staff of various training schools, some Canadian railway troops, and even 300 convalescent soldiers. Anyone who could fire a gun was put on the line. Carey hurriedly placed his men in the Amiens Defense Line—an old line of French trenches from an earlier phase of the war—just south of the Somme River about twenty kilometers east of Amiens. On March 27, the 6th Engineers took up positions in a segment of the line between Hamel and Warfusée-Abancourt (now known as Lamotte-Warfusée), running from the Bois de Tailloux south to the Amiens-Saint-Quentin Road (present-day D1029 highway). They fought off German attacks on March 29 and 30 successfully. The line bent in other places, but the American engineers held. They were withdrawn from the line on April 3 after suffering twenty-eight dead and fifty wounded. After the war, the citizens of Amiens placed memorial tablets on the pillars of the city's famous cathedral to honor the defenders of their city. Among them is one dedicated to the 6th Engineers, easily spotted by the American eagle with a red, white, and blue shield gracing the top of the tablet.

The British were grateful for these support troops, but what they really wanted was infantrymen. Since the earliest days of U.S. entry into the war, Britain proposed simply feeding American soldiers into their own regiments to get men into the trenches as quickly as possible. Pershing insisted on an independent American army, but under the terms of a January 1918 agreement (see Chapter 2), he agreed to give the British six raw U.S. divisions. According to the deal, the British would train them and use the Doughboys, but return them to American command if Pershing requested it. For AEF administrative purposes, those American units that served with the British comprised the U.S. II Corps, under the command of General George S. Read. Knowing of Britain's intense desire for fresh troops and fearful that its commanders might callously use inexperienced Doughboys as cannon fodder, Pershing insisted that those American troops training with the British not be put into combat "except in an emergency."

But the British worked assiduously to get the Americans into the fight as soon as possible. The 33rd "Prairie" Division, made up of Illinois National Guard troops, arrived at training camps near Amiens in June 1918. After less than a month it was attached to the Australian Corps and portions of it prepared to take part in an attack on the village of Hamel—just a few kilometers from where the 6th Engineers made their stand the previous spring. To promote American morale and a sense of Allied cooperation, General John Monash, the Australian commander, scheduled the attack for July 4 in honor of U.S. Independence Day. Just before the attack was to begin, Pershing insisted that the Americans be withdrawn, but the British gave him the runaround, and at 3:10 AM on July 4, a thousand U.S. troops from various companies of the 131st and 132nd Infantry Regiments stepped off with the "Diggers," as Australian troops were called. The 131st Infantry fought its way through the village of Hamel. Their counterparts in the 132nd Infantry pressed through the Bois des Vaire, about one kilometer to the south. The attack had the limited objective of some high ground just east of Hamel. Monash effectively meshed infantry, tanks, and aircraft, and though the battle was small in scale many military historians see it as a masterpiece of combined arms fighting. The entire operation lasted just ninety-three minutes, and was a smashing success. Though inexperienced, the Americans fought gallantly. "The Hamel attack taught us many things," according to Samuel Davis of the 131st Infantry Regiment, "and we owe much to the Australian soldiers who gave us confidence and experience in the war game." Pershing demanded that the British never pull such a stunt again, though he proudly wrote in his memoirs that "the behavior of our troops in this operation was splendid."

Today the Australian Corps Memorial Park occupies the high ground east of Hamel to commemorate the short but significant victory. Three curved granite walls, 4.5 meters high, stand on the crest of the hill. A large bronze Australian Imperial Service emblem is affixed to the center wall. Flanking it are the words of French Prime Minister George Clemenceau praising the Diggers—one inscription in French and the other in English. Behind the walls are the flags of the nations participating in the operation. The Australian flag is in the center. The others are the British, Canadian, French, and—on the far left—the American flag. Remnants of the German trenches captured that day survive near the memorial, and the walkway leading to it is lined with twenty interpretive panels describing the Battle of Hamel. Two are dedicated to the American participation. One gives the general context of the U.S. participation. The other is dedicated to Corporal Thomas Pope, who received the Medal of Honor for his actions at Hamel. When his advance was stopped by a German machine-gun nest, the Chicago native charged the nest by himself, shot or bayoneted the crew, and singlehandedly held the position until his fellows could make their way forward. Pope was the first in the U.S. Army to receive the Medal of Honor, and the British decorated him as well. King George V personally presented him with the Distinguished Service Medal.

The Americans of the II Corps saw a little more action along the Somme later that summer. On August 8, 1918, the British launched a major offensive in the area, sometimes referred to as the Battle of Amiens, to push the Germans back to the Hindenburg Line. The Prairie Division, now attached to the British 58th Division, fought near Chipilly on the north bank of the Somme. Jumping off from the Bois Malard just to the northwest of the village on the evening of August 9, it took the northern edge of the Chipilly Ridge overlooking the Somme, and moved into the Gressaire Wood. The following day it took the rest of the Gressaire Wood, crossing what is now the D1 highway and moving into the Bois Fosse between Bray-sur-Somme and Morlancourt. On August 13 the Illinois men joined the Australians in a successful assault on the high ground above the Somme southeast of Etinehem. The 80th "Blue Ridge" Division, a National Army unit raised in the Appalachian region from Pennsylvania to Virginia, also got a taste of frontline life during the Battle of Amiens. Four infantry regiments served at widely scattered positions along the front between Albert and Arras. Northernmost was the 320th Infantry Regiment, serving south of Boisleaux-Saint-Marc. The 319th Infantry was just to the south, on the eastern fringe of the village of Ayette. Southernmost was the 318th Infantry, which held the eastern edge of the Bois d'Aveluy south of Mesnil-Martinsart. The Battle of Amiens raged to the south of Albert while the 80th Division was on the line, and its soldiers mostly saw little more than some trench raids, although the 317th Infantry actually advanced. In the line with a division of New Zealanders east of Hèbuterne, the Allied soldiers watched as the Germans in their sector pulled back to more defensible positions. The U.S.-New Zealand troops followed them, meeting minimal resistance, and set up new lines about three kilometers southeast of their original lines, just past the present-day D919 highway between Puisieux and Serre.

Americans on the Fields of Flanders

By the end of the summer, most of the American divisions training with the British had been released to American command, but two of them—the 27th and 30th—remained under British control. They were dispatched to the Flanders region of Belgium, specifically Ypres—or Ieper, as its Flemish-speaking residents call it. In July they entered secondary trenches between Ypres and Kemmel but by August they moved up to the front line. The 27th Division was a National Guard unit from New York under the command of General John F. O'Ryan. Nicknamed "O'Ryan's Roughnecks," the division held a kilometer-long section of the front north of Kemmel, with the village of Vierstraat at its front and Dikkebus (known in American accounts as Dickiebusch) to its rear. Immediately to its north was the 30th Division, which occupied a section of the line north and west of Voormezeele. A National Guard unit from Tennessee and the Carolinas, it was known as the "Hickory" Division in honor of Andrew Jackson, the tough nineteenth-century U.S. president who hailed from that region. Few places on the Western Front provided a better example of Allied cooperation, much less American national unity. On the muddy plans of Flanders, the descendants of Billy Yank and Johnny Reb fought together alongside those of John Bull. It was also one of the most devastated parts of the front. The landscape was a moonscape of shell holes, which, because of frequent rains and the low water table, were usually pools of stagnant water. Once-pleasant country roads were now torn up and lined with wreckage and tree stumps. When the Doughboys arrived, the situation near Ypres was relatively quiet, though there was still plenty of action. Trench raids and patrols of no man's land were daily facts of life. German control of Mount Kemmel (Kemmelberg to the locals), a hill just south of the American lines, made enemy artillery especially accurate and deadly. "The American divisions became rapidly veteranized," recalled Gerald Jacobson of the 27th Division.

The Americans positions were on the far northern edge of the Lys Salient, a giant bulge into Allied lines that stretched from Belgium into northern France, created by the German offensives in Operation Georgette from the previous April (see Chapter 7). On August 30, 1918, the British detected that the Germans were preparing to withdraw from the salient in order to shorten their lines. Being at the northern hinge of the salient, the German withdrawal in front of the U.S. lines would be a shallow one, but it gave the Yanks a chance to liberate a little piece of Belgium. Both divisions sent patrols into no man's land to learn more about German intentions. Sharp clashes broke out, indicating that the Germans planned to make a fighting withdrawal. When the Germans evacuated Mount Kemmel on August 31, British commanders ordered the 27th Division forward to the Vierstraat Ridge, a slight rise on the low Belgian landscape along which the N331 highway now runs. They met tough resistance, but by the end of the day they had fought their way to the crest of the ridge and took the village of Vierstraat. Beyond them in the eastern distance was the Wytschaete Ridge, little more than a kilometer away, where the Germans had set up their new line of defense. O'Ryan's Roughnecks headed for the Wytschaete Ridge the following day, but could make no major gains. Heavy enemy fire kept the Hickory Division in place on August 31, but on September 1 it jumped off as well, capturing Voormezeele and Lankhof Farm, on the banks of the Ypres-Comines Canal. The 27th Division made some more small gains on September 2, and both of the American units fought off German counterattacks, but as they bumped up against the new German defense line, forward movement became much more difficult. By September 4, both divisions had been taken off the line. During its time in Belgium, the 27th Division suffered 1,336 killed or wounded. The figure for the Hickory Division was 777.

In 1929, the American Battle Monuments Commission (ABMC) erected the Kemmel American Monument, located on the N331 highway less that a kilometer south of Vierstraat. Designed by Philadelphia architect George Howe, it consists of a rectangular block of white Rocheret limestone at the center of a small viewing terrace. Inscribed on the western face of the monument, facing the road, is a dedication to the U.S. troops who fought in

the surrounding fields. Below it a sculpture of a Doughboy combat helmet resting upon a wreath of laurel leaves. The dedication is repeated in French on the north side of the monument and in Flemish on the south, and on the monument's eastern face are the emblems of the 27th and 30th Divisions. The monument

Kemmel American Monument, Vierstraat, Belgium.

stands on land taken by the 27th Division on August 31, 1918. O'Ryan's Roughnecks approached the area from the fields to the west. Looking east from the terrace is the Wytschaete Ridge. It may look unimpressive compared to the hilly AEF battlefields of eastern France, but in the flat, open lands of Flanders it proved to be a formidable barrier. Mount Kemmel is just to the south. Today the area around Ypres is strewn with British memorials and cemeteries. From Ypres numerous battlefield tours in English are available. The American contribution to Allied success in the Ypres area was small. Many battlefield tours make little or no mention of it. Fortunately, the Kemmel American Monument ensures that the Yankee contribution is not forgotten.

Piercing the Hindenburg Line with the Tommy and the Digger

After Ypres, the British transferred the 27th and 30th Divisions to France to participate in Foch's Grand Offensive. The Yanks were redeployed to the area around Bellicourt, fourteen kilometers north of Saint-Quentin in Picardy. Bellicourt was a tough place to be. The Hindenburg Line, running north–south across the area, was particularly formidable. A dense agglomeration of bunkers, trenches, and barbed wire entanglements, the Hindenburg Line at Bellicourt was nearly a kilometer in width. The fortifications completely enveloped the village of Bony, three kilometers north of Bellicourt. Just behind the Hindenburg Line was the Saint-Quentin Canal, a great gash in the earth that provided the Germans with another defensive barrier. Northward from the tiny hamlet of Riqueval, near Bellicourt, the canal passed through a six-kilometer-long tunnel dating from the days of Napoleon Bonaparte. The high ground above the tunnel was a vulnerability in the German defenses, giving the Allies an avenue to breach the canal, but the Germans found a way to make it work to their advantage. The tunnel interior gave the Germans an underground haven from even the heaviest Allied artillery barrages, and they used it for barracks, medical facilities, storage, and a host of other purposes. Several more defensive lines lay behind the canal. The first was the Le Catelet Line, roughly a kilometer behind to the east. There was also a chain of defenses on the western approaches to the main Hindenburg Line. A multilayered outpost zone of still more trenches and entanglements, it stretched one to two kilometers to the west of the main line, making excellent defensive use of the hills and valleys.

The Americans became part of the British Fourth army under General Henry Rawlinson. Bellicourt fell under the operational authority of the Australian Corps under General Monash. According to Foch's master plan for the Grand Offensive, the British were to attack the Hindenburg Line near Saint-Quentin on September 29—four days after Pershing's First Army stepped off in the Meuse-Argonne region. In his battle plan, Monash picked the Americans to be his shock troops. Their objective was to breach the Le Catelet Line and establish a new line from Gouy to Nauroy. Later in the day, Australians would pass through their lines and continue the assault. The choice to use inexperienced American troops in the first wave may have been a questionable one, but Monash had a positive view of the Doughboy's fighting prowess. "The arrangement caused me no anxiety or difficulty," he recalled. When the Americans arrived, Australian and British troops were in the bloody process of seizing portions of the German outpost zone, struggling for the best ground from which to launch the Grand Offensive. The newly arrived Americans picked up where their Allies had left off. The 30th Division entered the line west of Bellicourt on September 24, relieving the 1st Australian Division. The 27th Division took up positions opposite Bony the following day, replacing the British 18th and 74th Divisions. Each entered a very hot section of line. Their relief of the Diggers and the Tommies was done under heavy fire, and the Yanks immediately found themselves fighting off German raids. The front line the Americans assumed basically ran along what is now the A26 expressway, known as the "Autoroute des Anglais."

In their first few days at Bellicourt the Americans made some meager gains, but they came at a very heavy cost. In the zone of the Hickory Division, the British had made noteworthy progress in breaching the German outpost zone, and the Americans were able to follow up on their successes. On September 26, the 30th Division took a patch of trees known as the Quarry Wood, southwest of Bellicourt. The amount of land taken was small, but it nearly completed the penetration of the outpost zone in the 30th Division's sector, providing the good ground necessary for the main assault. To their north, the New Yorkers had a much more difficult time. Here the British had made only modest inroads into the outpost zone. It would be up to the Americans to push the lines farther. On September 27, O'Ryan's Roughnecks jumped off headed for three objectives: the Quennemont Farm southeast of Bony, the Guillemont Farm northwest of that village, and a spot of high ground simply known as "the Knoll" on the northern edge of their sector. With the help of British tanks and artillery, the Doughboys reached all of these positions, but the Germans hit back hard and forced them to retreat. Nearly all of the officers who went over the top were killed or wounded, and the division had gained very little ground. On September 28, the depleted regiments on the line were relieved and fresh troops brought up. Ready or not, the time had come for the main operation.

The Americans attacked at dawn on the foggy and misty morning of September 29, 1918. Having already busted through most of the outpost line, the 30th Division overran the Hindenburg Line in short order, capturing Bellicourt and the southern entrance to the canal tunnel, advancing as far as Nauroy. Unfortunately, they had bypassed numerous German positions, and the second waves—including the Australians who passed through their lines around midday—met with heavier-than-expected resistance. The 27th advanced too, but much more slowly and with greater casualties. Not only did they have to push through the unconquered portions of the German outpost zone, but British artillery support was inadequate and most of the tanks accompanying them—including the U.S. Army's 301st Tank Battalion—quickly fell victim to land mines and antitank guns. The Australians who expected to pass through U.S. lines instead found themselves struggling with the Americans to break through. On the southern edge of the division's sector, the 108th Infantry Regiment took Quennemont Farm despite heavy casualties, and pressed up the road toward Bony. On the northern edge, the Knoll was finally taken as well. But in the center, Guillemont Farm still eluded O'Ryan's Roughnecks. All advances came with a very heavy cost. "Most of the divisional zone between the jump-off line and the tunnel thus became one vast maelstrom of violence," reported *American Armies and Battlefields in Europe*, a fact to which the Doughboys attested. "It was a slaughter," recalled one man, "machine-gun fire was thicker than flies in summer." Another described watching his comrades fall to German guns "like pins in a bowling alley." On September 29, the 107th Infantry Regiment lost 337 killed and 658 wounded. No single regiment in the U.S. Army suffered so many casualties in one day during the entire war than did the 107th outside Bony. Only in a few places was the 27th Division able to penetrate the Hindenburg Line before being pulled off the lines on September 30, though some Americans moved forward with the Australians and fought for a few more days.

The American II Corps, though it had shown its inexperience, had still done its job, punching a hole in the Hindenburg Line. Allied penetration at other points along the line, particularly the British capture of the Riqueval Bridge across the canal one kilometer to the south of the tunnel entrance, forced the Germans to withdraw from the area. The battered and bruised American divisions went into reserve. From the time it entered the lines near Bellicourt to October 2, the 27th Division saw 4,632 of its soldiers killed or wounded. The 30th Division figure was 3,136. After a short respite, the Hickory Division went back into action on October 6 at Montbrehain in pursuit of the Germans as they continued falling back toward Germany. Its line of advance was just to the south of the present-day D932 highway. In the subsequent days, the 30th Division liberated the villages of Brancourt-le-Grand, Prémont, Busigny, Vaux-Andigny Saint-Souplet, and Mazinghien from years of German occupation before being pulled off the line on October 19. The 27th Division joined in on October 17 just east of Saint-Souplet, reaching a point just south of Bazuel before it was pulled

The Riqueval Tunnel of the Saint-Quentin Canal, near Bellicourt, France.

from the line on October 21.

Among the numerous British and Australian cemeteries and monuments in Picardy is a small island of American ones around Bellicourt. After the war, the state of Tennessee placed three monuments— each a stone obelisk—in the path of the 30th Division to commemorate the sacrifices of its sons. The first—which stands along the D1004, just south of Bellicourt in Riqueval, at the roadside entrance to the canal tunnel—honors the Tennessee soldiers who captured the canal entrance from the Germans. From there, a path leads through a wooded area to the canal entrance. The canal is still in use today, mainly for recreational purposes. Another obelisk stands in the northern part of Brancourt-le-Grand to commemorate the 118th Infantry Regiment's seizure of that village on October 8. The last one—at the intersection of the D70 and the D960, on the south side of Prémont—honors the 117th Infantry Regiment, which liberated the village on October 8.

On the D1044 highway one kilometer north of Bellicourt is the ABMC's Bellicourt American Monument. Built atop the Saint-Quentin Canal tunnel, it commemorates the hard work of the 90,000 Americans who served under British command in northern France. Franco-American architect Paul Cret designed the memorial, dedicated in 1937. It consists of a two-stepped terrace with a large stone block in the center. On the eastern side of the monument is a relief sculpture by French artist Alfred-Alphonse Bottiau. In the center is an eagle perched atop an American flag. The seated figure on the left represents valor, while the kneeling one on the right stands for remembrance. The western face contains an engraved map showing American involvement in the fight to cross the Hindenburg Line. The names of II Corps battles appear in the frieze at the base of the monument. A semicircular terrace overlooks the fields to the west, with an orientation table in the center pointing to the locations of American battlefields in the Bellicourt area. The Knoll is 3.8 kilometers to the northwest. Mazinghien is twenty-eight kilometers to the east. Looking over the quiet green fields today, there is no obvious sign of the kilometer-wide Hindenburg Line. At the same time, the view from the terrace also gives a good sense of the commanding German defensive positions and the difficulty the Allies had in fighting their way through them. Driving across the rural roads east of the Bellicourt monument, one can drive past places like Guillemont Farm and the Knoll, though there is no signage to identify them. Indeed, it is not immediately evident that one of World War I's greatest battles raged over these fields. Only tiny fragments of bunkers and trench lines can still be found in the surrounding area today, and one must look closely to spot them.

Bellicourt American Monument, with orientation table pointing to the locations of important battle sites.

Not quite two kilometers to the northwest of Bellicourt is the Somme American Cemetery, on the D57 highway just outside of Bony. Like many U.S. war cemeteries overseas, this one began as a temporary battlefield burial ground, and grew as scattered cemeteries were consolidated and the dead were returned home. The long rectangular graves area is divided into four sections, with an American flag flying in the center. Most of the 1,837 soldiers buried here died in northern France while serving with the British, from Amiens to Mazinghien. Some fell at the Battle of Cantigny in May 1918, America's first solo offensive operation of the war (see Chapter 7). Most died within a few kilometers of the cemetery during the fight to breach the Hindenburg Line. Among those buried at Bony are three Medal of Honor recipients, four sets of brothers, and Lieutenant William Fitzsimons, a physician killed in a German air raid on his hospital on September 4, 1917—the first member of the U.S. military to die by hostile fire in World War I (see Chapter 7). A small but imposing limestone chapel occupies the southeast end of the grounds. Square and nearly windowless, *American Armies and Battlefields in Europe* compares it to "a castle guarding the graves." It might remind others of a military blockhouse. Upon entering, thin window slats in the shape of a cross, flooding the interior with light, hover above the marble altar. Narrow stained glass windows to the right and left add further illumination. On the walls are the names of 333 Americans whose bodies were never found or identified. Rosettes indicated those whose remains were later identified. Philadelphia architect George Howe designed the grounds.

Chicago Liberates a Little Piece of Picardy

Sixty kilometers to the south of Bellicourt, at a stretch of the Hindenburg Line near the village of Vauxaillon, the 370th Infantry Regiment—a part of the African American 93rd Division—was pushing the Germans back as well. Americans had fought in the fields to the south of Vauxaillon during the summer of 1918 in the Aisne-Marne and Oise-Aisne Offensives (see Chapter 8). Most American troops pulled out of the area in August to join Pershing's American First Army, but the 370th went in the opposite direction. The racially segregated U.S. Army turned most of its African American regiments over to the French (see Chapter 10). The 370th—formerly the 8th Illinois Infantry Regiment—spent the summer in training with the French in eastern France, but in September it was brought up to Picardy to beef up the depleted French 59th Division in preparation for the Grand Offensive. Charles Bradden, the regimental chaplain, remembered getting off the trucks at the village of Saint-Bandry in the Picardy countryside, and thought it "the most completely demolished place I had yet visited on the western front. Not one stone had been left standing, every house was dismantled, the streets were pitted with shell holes, the town disemboweled, the church reduced to a heap of ruins." He was particularly horrified

Somme American Cemetery, Bony, France.

to see "the poor bones of the sacred dead" in the local cemetery "thrown up by the cruel shells and thrown around the place that was known as consecrated ground." The march to Vauxaillon "brought all the man or baby within you to the fore," Bradden believed. The men were silent on the march, he recalled, "nothing but thoughts, thoughts of home that lay three thousand miles across the turbulent ocean, thoughts of deeds of commission and omission, of neglected opportunities of bringing sunshine and gladness to others' hearts and lives, just thoughts and prayers for God's protection."

They arrived at Vauxaillon on September 15, where the frontline ran roughly north to south just east of the village, perpendicular to the Oise-Aisne Canal. At first most of the Americans were held in reserve, though a few companies took part in some unsuccessful assaults at Moisy Farm and Mont des Singes east of the village. On September 24 the 370th took control of a portion of the front running from the banks of the canal, just west of the locks, southward to the Champ Vailly, near what is now the intersection of rue de Brancourt and the D551 highway. It was an active scene, and the regiment endured copious amounts of artillery and gas. On the night of September 27–28 the French got wind of a German withdrawal in front of the 59th Division to more defensible positions on the other side of the canal. The division attacked the retiring Germans at dawn. French troops swept the Germans off Mont des Singes and penetrated as far east as Pinion. The 370th found its advance much more difficult. Those Doughboys along the river advanced about

500 meters east into the woodlands along the canal. Those closer to the Champ Vailly were unable to advance at all. The attack continued on September 29, and this time the entire 370th was able to press forward. By September 30, the Americans controlled the entire south bank of the canal from the locks up to the present-day D14 highway north of Pinion. Over the next week 59th Division made several unsuccessful attempts to cross the canal, but by mid-October the pressure of Foch's offensive forced the Germans to pull back even further. On the morning of October 12 the 370th crossed the canal and advanced 500 meters into the Bois de Mortier unopposed before being relieved of frontline duty. The 59th Division pursued the Germans north and east. In the waning days of the war the Illinois men saw only scattered fighting, though there was one last tragedy for the regiment. On November 3, a German shell came down on a 370th position at Chantrud Farm near Grandlup-et-Fay, killing forty-one. When the war ended on November 11, the regiment was at Gué d'Hossus on the Belgian border.

There are no memorials to the 370th Infantry Regiment in Vauxaillon or other places it saw service. The ABMC recognized the regiment at the Château-Thierry American Monument (see Chapter 8), and in 1927 the state of Illinois likewise honored the regiment's service. Located on the south side of Chicago, the Victory Monument stands at the intersection of East 35th Street and South Martin Luther King Drive (known at the time the monument was built as Grand Boulevard) in the center of Chicago's Bronzeville district—the traditional heart of the city's African American community. The ornate circular granite shaft with four bronze relief panels is the work of sculptor Leonard Crunelle. Three panels depict figures in classical heroic poses. On one, a bare-chested African American man stands behind an eagle, symbolizing the manhood and patriotism of the regiment. Another, an African American female figure, represents motherhood. On the third is a classical female figure with a tablet in her hand listing the battles in which the 370th fought. The fourth panel lists the names of the men who died during the war. Capping the monument is a bronze statue of a Doughboy. Just two blocks away, at 3519 South Giles Street, is the 8th Illinois Infantry Regiment's armory. Constructed in 1915, it is now home to the Chicago Military Academy. Bronzeville, also known as the Black Metropolis, is one of Chicago's most important historic districts. Home to civil rights activists and cultural figures— among them Ida B. Wells, Bessie Coleman, Richard Wright, and Louis Armstrong—it has exerted an outsized influence on American history. The Bronzeville Visitor Information Center (411 East 35th Street) offers bus and walking tours of the area's rich heritage that include the First World War.

Back to Belgium

The Ypres-Lys Offensive, the portion of Foch's Grand Offensive in Belgium, began on September 28, 1918. Perhaps more than anywhere else on the Western Front, it was indeed a multinational effort. King Albert I of Belgium commanded the *Groupe d'Armées des Flandres* (GAF), which included twelve Belgian, ten British, and six French divisions. During the first few weeks the GAF made swift advances. Near Ypres, the British swiftly passed through the German trenches that had vexed them for years. But my mid-October the autumn rains, logistical problems, and stiffening German resistance slowed down King Albert's forces. Foch requested that Pershing furnish two divisions to bolster the Allied advance in Belgium. He graciously provided a pair comprising some of his best, most seasoned troops. The 37th "Buckeye" Division from Ohio and the 91st "Wild West" Division had seen a great deal of action in the first phase of the Meuse-Argonne Campaign (see Chapter 13). Withdrawn from the line on September 30, the divisions were resting and rebuilding when they got the call. The 53rd Field Artillery Brigade went north as well. Americans were once again fighting on the fields of Flanders, and the multinational force in Belgium became even more diverse.

The Americans went into the line under French command near Waregem, forty kilometers east of Ypres, on the Lys River. The 37th Division took up positions north of the city, along the railroad tracks near Olsene. The 91st Division was immediately south of town, with a wooded area known as the Spitaals Bosschen immediately to its east. At 5:30 AM on October 31, the Americans stepped off with the rest of the GAF in a drive toward the Scheldt River. On the first day the Germans put up stout resistance, but on November 1 they withdrew rapidly to the Scheldt, with the Doughboys fast on their heels. The 91st Division reached the outskirts of Oudenaarde by the end of the day, and the 37th Division reached Eine. "We rambled merrily forward," wrote Ray Johnson of the Buckeye Division, "scarcely a single burst of shrapnel hindered us, and we had to reduce only one machine gun nest." Johnson recalled that "the sun shone gloriously and we sang and whistled as we tramped on. At times we even forgot that we were in a drive!" Upon entering Eine, jubilant locals cheered the Americans and plied them with wine and beer. But the celebrations abruptly ended when the soldiers reached the banks of the Scheldt. The Germans entrenched on the opposite side hit the Americans with a volley of mortar and machine-gun fire, and then shelled the town incessantly during the night. The war was not over quite yet.

Both divisions spent several more days on the line engaged in hard fighting. The 91st Division completed the liberation of Oudenaarde before being relieved on November 4. The 37th made a heroic river crossing near Huerne on November 2. "A small body of men succeeded in swimming the river," wrote Ray Johnson, "and laboring under hot machine gun fire and shrapnel, threw a foot-bridge across by fastening tree trunks end to end." He noted that "many of our boys died or were seriously wounded in attempting to get over, but late that afternoon a total of fifty-two were on the other side and thus a foothold was established." During the night engineers built two more bridges at Heuvel and Eine, allowing the division to cross in force. By November 5, the Buckeye Division had been relieved as well. Both divisions were briefly put back on the line on November 10. The 37th Division went back to work east of Syngem, and by 11:00 AM on November 11, when the armistice took effect, they had reached the villages of Dikkele and Zwartenbroek. The 91st was in Sint-Denijs-Boekel.

At the Tacambaroplein in the center of Oudenaarde (known as Audenarde in French), the ABMC erected a small memorial to the 40,000 American soldiers who took part in the final push through Belgium. The Audenarde American Monument, designed by architect Harry Sternfeld and dedicated in 1936, is a yellow limestone stele on a raised plaza. On the front of the monument is an American shield flanked by two carved eagles. Below the shield is a dedication and above it are listed the American units that served under the King of the Belgians. The street behind the monument is Generaal Pershingstraat. Three kilometers to the north in Eine, the state of Ohio donated a bridge across the Scheldt to honor the Ohio men who crossed that river under fire during the Great War. Designed by Cleveland architectural firm of Walker and Weeks, the concrete span was completed in 1929. A year later four stone bison—symbols of courage and strength, and also of America— were added to the abutments of the bridge. The bison were the work of French sculptor Paul Moreau Vauthier, famed for his monuments marking the farthest German advance into France (see Chapter 8). Retreating British troops destroyed the bridge to halt advancing Nazi troops in 1940, and it was rebuilt after the war with new bison statues. The steel bridge crossing the Scheldt today was completed in 1980, but the four bison still guard its approaches. The name of the street crossing the bridge is "Ohiostraat." Another small but poignant memorial is located near the corner of Ter Elststraat and Vandewoestijnelaan in Waregem. Private Michele Chimienti of the 91st Division was killed in the garden of the Villa Ter Elst, an estate on the north side of town, and buried where he fell. Saddened by the death, the owner of the estate placed a small headstone on the grave. Chimenti's body was later removed and the stone lost for many years, but in 2003 it was rediscovered and placed at its current location.

Chimienti is now buried just four kilometers from where he was killed at the Flanders Field American Cemetery, along with

367 other Doughboys who died during operations in Belgium. It is located on Wortegemsweg on the south side of Waregem, on the edge of the Spitaals Bosschen through which the Wild West Division fought on October 31. The surrounding area is mainly suburban now. The cemetery's name is derived from the famous John McCrae poem, "In Flanders Fields," written by a Canadian physician at Ypres in 1915 to memorialize the dead. The poem's imagery of poppies growing on the graves of fallen soldiers gave rise to the popularity of using that flower to commemorate the war dead. The graves are divided into four rectangular plots on the edge of a large square sunken lawn. In the center of the lawn is a white limestone chapel. Above the chapel door is the building's only window, and above that the words, "Greet them ever with grateful hearts." The names of forty-three American soldiers missing or unidentified appear on the walls. Paul Cret of Philadelphia designed the chapel and cemetery. Jacques Gréber of Paris did the landscaping.

On the Italian Front

One thousand kilometers south of Belgium, a handful of Americans were on duty on the Italian front. When Americans think of the war in Italy, their thoughts usually turn to Ernest Hemingway. The son of a physician, Hemingway was born in Oak Park, Illinois in 1899. From an early age he enjoyed hunting, fishing, and other kinds of outdoor adventures, but he also discovered his talent for language. Hemingway was a reporter for the *Kansas City Star* when Congress declared war in 1917, and he wanted to be part of it. The army rejected him for poor eyesight, so he turned to the Red Cross and became an ambulance driver in Italy. Hemingway was delivering chocolates and cigarettes to Italian soldiers at Fossalta on July 8, 1918, when Austrian artillery shells came screaming in. Caught in the open on the banks of the Piave River, the eighteen-year-old ambulance driver was peppered with shrapnel. Despite his wounds, Hemingway carried a wounded Italian soldier to safety before collapsing. He was evacuated

Ernest Hemingway as an American Red Cross ambulance driver. (Courtesy of the National Archives)

to the American Red Cross Hospital in Milan to recover. There he met a nurse named Agnes von Kurowsky, and though she was seven years his senior, the two had a torrid love affair. Indeed, Hemingway hoped to marry her when they returned to the United States, but Kurowsky ended the relationship. The heartbroken young writer used the experience in his 1919 novel *A Farewell to Arms*, the first great American novel of World War I. It was the beginning of a career that made Hemingway one of the most famous and acclaimed writers on the planet.

About 100 meters from a bridge over the Piave on the SP48 highway in Fossalta stands an unassuming rectangular monument. In Italian, it notes that this was the spot where Hemingway was wounded. The hospital where he recovered, and where he got his inspiration to write *A Farewell to Arms*, is also identifiable with a plaque. It is located at 4 Via Amorari, barely a block from the great Milan Cathedral.

Like Britain and France, Italy wanted American troops, too, especially after its stinging defeat at Caporetto in 1917 (see Chapter 1). "I had opposed scattering our force in this way," Pershing later wrote of the request, but he understood the importance of the Italian front to the overall war effort. "The appeal of Italian officials and the recommendations of Americans who had visited Italy indicated that under the circumstances an exception could well be made with a small force." In July 1918, Pershing detached the 332nd Infantry Regiment from the 83rd Division, a draftee unit from Ohio, and sent it to Italy. Wildly enthusiastic crowds welcomed the *Americanos*. Upon reaching Torino, the Americans paraded "through the principal business section of the city," recalled Lieutenant August Rendigs. "Although the hour was yet early," he wrote, "we were greeted by enormous crowds that lined the streets and cheered frantically for our men and our nation." Flowers rained down from the balconies, and "young women and children darted out of the crowds to place a small bouquet with an Italian flag in some doughboy's hand or eagerly grasp a hand as our boys marched by." It was much the same in Milan, according to Rendigs. Reaching the Piazza del Duomo, "the crowd, now uncontrollable, almost bore the men from their feet in a mad frenzy to honor these first American combatant troops in Italy," he wrote. "The exultant cries continued, 'Viva l'America! Viva l'America!'"

The 332nd made its way to Verona, where the men moved into the villas, homes, and barns in the rural communities southwest of the city. "We were billeted in a large, three-story brick building which was located on the nicest street in town," recalled one member of Company K of his quarters in Villafranca. Though the village was attractive on the outside, this soldier also associated it with various pests. "Nets proved fairly efficient with mosquitos," he recalled, "but were a desperate failure with fleas and other small animals." Others—particularly officers—had better luck. Lieutenant August Rendigs remembered that while his men were quartered in "various small houses" in and around Custoza, he stayed in a hilltop villa. "The view from [the] terrace was most magnificent," he wrote, "commanding as it did miles upon miles of Italian lowlands with their myriad rows of fruit trees and grape arbors, while in the far-off distance could be seen the Alps, towering skywards, the picture being flanked on one side by the beautiful Lac de Garda and on the other by the tall spires of the cathedrals of the city of Verona." Just a few hundred meters from Rendigs's villa was a memorial ossuary holding the bones of soldiers killed in the Custoza area during Italy's wars of independence. The sight of the "skulls and bones of hundreds of men who paid the supreme price" made an impression on the American officer. Regimental headquarters was established at the Villa Boca Trezza, also known as the Villa of 1001 Roses, in the center of Sommacompagna (8 Via Cesere Battisti).

At first drill schedules were light, and the Doughboys got to play tourist. Nearby Verona saw an invasion of American soldiers on pass. Rendigs wrote that he and his friends found "many places of interest" there, including the Roman arena, "the old home of the Capulets of Shakespearean fame" and "a beautiful memorial statue to that ever-famous Italian poet, Dante." All still attract tourists today. "Some spent the day in viewing art and architecture of former ages," wrote Lettau, "while others became better acquainted with modern art—the 'Bella Signorini.'" He thought Italian women "very lovely" and "not amateurs at dressing attractively." The Doughboys found Italy charming, but there were also reminders of why they were there. "We could see airships," recalled Ferris Myricks, illuminated by searchlights, "guarding the front at night." "In the stillness of the calm summer evenings," Rendigs recalled, "the faint booming of the great guns could be heard from the Piave front."

In mid-August, the regiment centralized its activities in a large tent camp along an irrigation canal in the countryside one kilometer east of Vallegio named Camp Wallace, in honor of the regimental commander, Colonel William Wallace. Those quartered in vermin-infested homes and barns thought life at Camp Wallace an improvement. "The change from the stuffy and ofttimes crowded conditions prevalent in the villages to an open air camp was welcome," recalled Walter Hart. Others disagreed. "On some days," Lettau complained, "the heat of the sun readily penetrated the canvas and seemed to be trying to dry the blood in our bodies." At Camp Wallace, the intensity of training picked up dramatically. The regiment trained with the Italian storm troopers, known as the Arditi. Dressed in dashing green uniforms with daggers hanging from their belts, these elite soldiers "were so tough," wrote Captain Austin Story, "that it was rumored many of them had come from Italian penitentiaries." Under Arditi tutelage, the *Americanos* learned how to storm trenches, throw grenades, and operate flamethrowers. They also took hikes through the countryside as long as twenty-five kilometers to toughen them up. The Italian summer seemed a far cry from Ohio. "Shade could be found nowhere," Walter Hart discovered, "and the sun's burning rays could not be avoided." By September, segments of the regiment began rotating through the frontline trenches along the Piave near Varago to further hone their combat skills. During the first week of October, the 332nd Infantry departed Vallegio. "The command came," Hart recalled, "to destroy the gravel designs around the tents, to level the ground, and fill in the streets of the camp." Today there is no sign of the American camp.

Boarding trains at Villafranca, the regiment set out for Treviso, near the front lines along the Piave River. Here the regiment conducted one of its most bizarre missions. To boost Italian morale while simultaneously depressing that of the Austrians, the Americans conspicuously undertook long marches near the front lines along the Piave River north of the city. To make it appear as though there were more American troops at the front than there actually were, the 332nd soldiers frequently changed their clothing and equipment, then marched across ground previously covered. "Each company would start out from Treviso for a hike of 10 to 15 Kms and back by a different route," Colonel Wallace later wrote. "Each day we would change our uniform slightly—one day campaign hats, another helmets, another overseas caps, etc. For ten days the roads of this part of northern Italy were covered by marching Americans, and Austrian Air Intelligence reported over 100,000 Americans on the Italian front, when there was only one regiment of 4,000."

On October 24, Allied forces launched an offensive against the Austrians that became known as the Battle of Vittorio Veneto. At first the Doughboys of the 332nd were held in reserve, but just before midnight on October 28 they began their "Big Push" toward the front, though they could never quite seem to reach the battle area. The Americans advanced quickly, but the Austrians retreated even faster. As they advanced, they saw the destruction of war. Joseph Lettau remembered the horrific scenes on Grave di Papadopoli, an island in the Piave River that had been the scene of recent fighting:

> Several dead, bloated horses and mules halfway in the water met our eyes. Nearby were corpses lying as they had fallen two or three days before. Helmets, gas masks, rifles and shells were strewn promiscuously about, near the road. The island is a forlorn place at best, but now, battle scarred and with dead men, dead horses and implements of warfare lying about, it was one's idea of supreme desolation. Here and there were great yellow splotches, showing where the gas shells had fallen.

The Americans resumed the march the following day, but still saw no Austrians. One British supply soldier heading back to rear shouted: "Better get some aeroplanes, Sammy, if you want to catch them." The Americans reached Gaiarine by November 1 and Cimpello by the afternoon of November 2. They outran their supplies and rolling kitchens, but still saw no Austrians.

Finally, on the afternoon of November 3, advance patrols encountered some Austrians dug in on the east bank of the Tagliamento River at the crossroads hamlet of Ponte della Delizia, six kilometers east of Codroipo. The wide rocky riverbed was mainly dry, with a small stream flowing through it. A bridge spanned the river, but the retreating Austrians had set it aflame. The Americans quickly took up positions on the west bank. As the Doughboys prepared to attack, word quickly spread on both sides of the river that Austria planned to sign an armistice and stop fighting. Austrian troops tried to convince the Americans not to attack, but the Doughboys were itching for action. "The regiment could not return to America with no battles to its credit!" wrote Lettau. "Glory is always preferable to life!" At dawn on November 4, the Yanks began their advance across the rocky riverbed. After pummeling the Austrian positions with machine guns and artillery, the infantry charged. The Americans "yelled like Indians," according to Lettau, and although the Austrians returned some "hot fire," he recalled that "the boys pressed on as true brothers of the doughboys in France." Hand-to-hand fighting erupted, and as Lettau described it, the American soldiers "showed they had forgotten nothing they had learned in bayonet drills back at Camp Sherman." The Austrians pulled back, and when the armistice came at 3:00 PM that afternoon the Americans were in possession of Codroipo.

During the autumn of 1918, the Central Powers began to collapse. Bulgaria gave up as early as September 19. With the British moving up from Palestine and Syria toward the Turkish homeland, the Ottoman Empire signed an armistice on October 30. With Austria's exit from the war on November 4, the Germans stood alone. Allied victory seemed certain, but the powerful German Empire was still a formidable adversary. The American Expeditionary Force played a pivotal role in Germany's defeat.

CHAPTER 17:
FINI LA GUERRE!

By mid-October 1918, those around General Pershing noticed changes in the man. His hair had grayed. The jauntiness in his step had gone, replaced with a mien of depression. He may have even had a mild case of influenza. Allied military and political leaders had lost confidence in him. David Lloyd George described Pershing as "difficult," and Clemenceau openly called for his removal. "No more promises!" the French premier once snapped at the American commander-in-chief, "I judge only by the results." And Pershing felt the pressure. In public he maintained his ramrod straight carriage, but behind the scenes his nerves were beginning to fray. "My God," he once said, sobbing in the backseat of his car, "sometimes I don't know how I can go on." It may have been Pershing's darkest hour, but Allied fortunes had never been brighter. One by one, the nations of the Central Powers were dropping out, leaving Germany alone to face the Allies. Bowing to their inevitable defeat, the Germans entered peace negotiations. Even in the Meuse-Argonne, there was reason for Pershing to have hope. Despite their effective defense in the area, the German position between the Meuse and the Argonne was beginning to weaken. Their troops were spread thinly across the battlefield, and their reserves were exhausted. In spite of the pressures, Pershing's persistence paid off. He finally achieved victory, and his independent American army played the starring role.

Pershing scheduled another big push for October 14, but he made some significant changes to the First Army in the days beforehand. There was another reshuffling of divisions. The exhausted 1st and 80th Divisions came off the line on October 12, and the 5th "Red Diamond" and 42nd "Rainbow" Divisions came up. I Corps now consisted of the 77th and 82nd Divisions. The 32nd and 42nd Divisions made up V Corps in the center. The 5th Division assumed the 3rd Division's lines outside Cunel, but would serve as part of III Corps. The 3rd Division shifted slightly to the right, taking over line lines of the 80th Division, while the 4th Division remained in place. Even more significant were the leadership changes. Fourth Division commander General John L. Hines assumed control of III Corps. Pershing thought V Corps commander George Cameron ineffective, and replaced him with General Charles P. Summerall, who

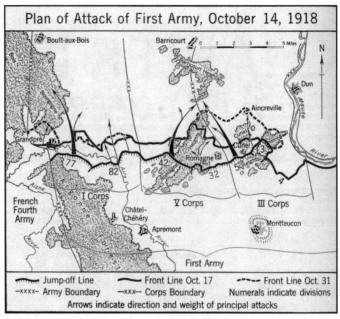

Plan of Attack of First Army, October 14, 1918

Jump-off Line — Front Line Oct. 17 ----- Front Line Oct. 31
-xxxx- Army Boundary -xxx- Corps Boundary Numerals indicate divisions
Arrows indicate direction and weight of principal attacks

had previously led the 1st Division. At I Corps, General Joseph T. Dickman, who led IV Corps in the Saint-Mihiel Offensive, replaced General Hunter Liggett, who got the biggest promotion of all—command of the whole First Army.

Anticipating a larger American combat role as the war drew to a close, Pershing created the U.S. Second Army to encompass the divisions near Saint-Mihiel, which had previously been part of the First Army. Under the command of General Robert Bullard, formerly head of III Corps, the Second Army was to hold the frontlines northeast of Saint-Mihiel and prepare for Pershing's long-anticipated drive toward Metz. It consisted mainly of divisions worn out from fighting in the Meuse-Argonne sector, like the 28th "Keystone" division from Pennsylvania, and 33rd "Prairie" Division from Illinois. Rookie units, like the 7th Division, were also one the line. The Buffalo Soldiers of the all-black 92nd Division took up a portion of the frontline under Bullard as well. The Second Army did some aggressive patrolling and trench raids, but the front had largely been static since the end of Saint-Mihiel Offensive in September. The creation of the Second Army gave the United States two armies on the Western Front rather than just one, and Pershing decided that under the circumstances he could no longer oversee day-to-day combat operations. Effective October 16, Liggett would conduct the First Army, and thus the Meuse-Argonne Offensive. With the creation of the Second Army, Pershing was—as historian Edward Lengel put it—"kicking himself upstairs."

The days leading up to the October 14 attack were hardly quiet ones. The Germans kept the Americans under constant fire, and the

Doughboys vigorously probed German positions. One such probe made Lieutenant Samuel Woodfill of the 5th Division a national hero. On the foggy morning of October 12, several companies went out on a reconnaissance patrol headed for the Bois de la Pultière, not quite a kilometer north of the American frontline. German

Dilapidated 5th Division obelisk south of Cunel, France.

machine guns opened up on them as they approached Cunel, but as the division's official history described it, Woodfill "swept the way with his own personal valor." Moving out ahead with a small party, Woodfill found a shell hole, and with several well-aimed rifle shots knocked out two German machine guns—one in the steeple of the Cunel church. Moving forward from shell hole to shell hole—one of which filled with mustard gas that burned him—Woodfill took cover behind a gravel pile and knocked out another machine gun, killing its entire crew of six with his marksmanship. With Woodfill paving the way, the Americans made it into the woods, where the young officer's heroics continued. Among other deeds, he single-handedly knocked out two more machine-gun nests, killed two Germans with a pickax, and took several prisoners. The Americans won control of the woods, but when German artillery came crashing down they fell back to their own lines. Woodfill received the Medal of Honor for his actions, presented by General Pershing himself. Indeed, Pershing heaped praise on Woodfill, whom he saw as exemplifying his open warfare tactics.

Cracking the Kreimhilde Stellung

When the First Army struck on October 14, it finally made significant breakthroughs. The critical point was the village of Romagne-sous-Montfaucon, which lay in the area assigned to the 32nd Division. The village lay astride a road leading through the Romagne Heights, and was also a major German supply depot. Just to the southwest of the village was a wooded ridgeline known as the Côte Dame Marie, along which the Germans had constructed cement pillboxes and other fortifications. "*Les Terribles*" had stood just outside Romagne-sous-Montfaucon for days. On occasion their patrols had entered the village, and they had made attacks against the Côte Dame Marie, but the Germans threw back each forward movement. But on the morning of October 14, it was different. On the right side of the 32nd Division was the 128th Infantry Regiment, made up mainly of National Guard boys from Wisconsin. When they stepped off at 5:30 am, the Germans were caught off guard. They reached Romagne-sous-Montfaucon before noon, and established a defensive line north of the village. Hundreds of Germans surrendered, and thousands more beat a hasty retreat to the north. Doughboys had been in this village before, but now they were there to stay. With the 128th Infantry in Romagne-sous-Montfaucon, the German positions on the Côte Dame Marie became vulnerable. Bitter fighting took place at the southern tip of the ridge, near the Transvaal Farm, but by 8:00 am the 126th Infantry Regiment had broken through the German lines along the eastern slope of the ridge, then pushed into the woods, outflanking the south-facing guns along the ridgeline. The 127th Infantry Regiment, working the western side, had a tougher time, but it too managed to claw its way up the slopes. The Germans withdrew, leaving the strategic ridge in the hands of the 32nd Division. By the end of the day, elements of the division had reached the present-day D123 highway across the Romagne Heights, and penetrated nearly a kilometer behind the Kreimhilde Stellung. The division boasted of being the first to pierce the vaunted German defense line, and adopted as its insignia an image of a red arrow passing through a straight line. They would forever be known as the "Red Arrow" Division.

Just to the east of the Red Arrow Division, the Red Diamond Division made important strides as well, though it paid a very heavy price for the real estate it took. Just before the 5th Division was about to jump off, German artillery hit with an unusually heavy barrage, causing many casualties and much confusion. It did not preempt the attack, though, and at 8:30 AM the survivors moved out over open ground. The Germans then hit them with abundant amounts of gas and machine-gun fire. Major John Muncaster, a battalion commander, described it as being like "a band of steel across our front." Dead American soldiers from previous assaults still lay in the fields, their bodies pulverized by artillery as the freshly dead joined them. The fields were "one huge sea of death," according to infantryman Ernest Wrentmore. Casualties were heavy, but the attack proceeded. On the left end of the division's sector, the Doughboys moved out from the Mamelle Trench toward high ground immediately east of Romagne-sous-Montfaucon. It took them an agonizing hour and half to advance roughly half a kilometer, but by 10:00 AM they had taken the crest of a hill studded with German machine guns. From there they continued north, cutting Romagne-Cunel road and moving toward the ridge above it, until their momentum slowed. On the right, the division took Cunel—like Romagne-sous-Montfaucon, a place occupied by American troops but never held—and moved into the Bois de la Pultière just to its north. The Red Diamond Division optimistically hoped to get as far as Bantheville, and though it was well short of

Doughboys entering Cunel, France, by war artist Lester G. Hornby, 1918. (Courtesy of the National Archives)

that mark, it had nevertheless taken strategically important ground behind the Kreimhilde Stellung.

To the west, the 42nd "Rainbow" Division pounded the German lines as well. Though its contribution of the October 14 attacks was comparatively modest, the Rainbow Division's exploits received much public attention due largely to the notoriety of one of its brigade commanders, Brigadier General Douglas MacArthur. His 84th Brigade drew the tough assignment of taking a high ground to the west of Romagne-sous-Montfaucon called the Côte de Châtillon. "If the Romagne Heights was the key to the Kreimhilde Stellung," wrote historian Geoffrey Perret, then "the key to the Romagne was . . . the Côte de Châtillon." The Germans knew it, and fortified the area extensively. Standing in MacArthur's way was Hill 288, a strongpoint on the Kreimhilde Stellung just northwest of the Côte Dame Marie. MacArthur reconnoitered the area in the days before the assault, and in doing so received a substantial dose of German gas that made him violently ill. On the evening before the attack, General Charles P. Summerall, the new V Corps commander, visited MacArthur at his headquarters and told him: "Give me Châtillon, or a list of five thousand casualties." It was a bold statement, but MacArthur loved the drama and did his commander one better. "If this brigade does not capture Châtillon," MacArthur assured him, "you can publish a casualty list of the entire Brigade with the Brigade Commander's name at the top." On the morning of October 14, MacArthur's men fought their way up the slopes of Hill 288. They reached the summit by noon, but took heavy casualties and were unable to proceed much farther. It took two more days of brutal combat, but by October 16 the Côte de Châtillon was in American hands. The First Army now controlled the Romagne Heights, and finally punctured the Kreimhilde Stellung.

"History records no more sustained and severe fighting than on this front during October," according to *American Armies and Battlefields in Europe*. Without question, more American blood was spilled in the area around Romagne-sous-Montfaucon than at any other spot during the Great War. Given Romagne's sacred and sanguinary place in U.S. military history, the American Battle Monuments Commission chose it to be the site of the largest World War I overseas cemetery. The Meuse-Argonne American Cemetery is located on the D123 highway between Romagne and Cunel, on land the Red Diamond Division captured on October 14. Covering more than fifty-two hectares (130.5 acres), it contains the final resting places of 14,246 Americans, from both the Meuse-Argonne Offensive and the simultaneous campaign of the Fourth French Army in the nearby Champagne region (see Chapter 16). There are

nine Medal of Honor recipients and eighteen sets of brothers buried here. Four hundred and eighty six graves hold the remains of the unknown. The New York architectural firm of York and Sawyer designed the buildings and grounds, and Alfred-Alphonse Bottiau did the sculpture works. When it was dedicated on Memorial Day 1937, General Pershing delivered the keynote address.

The machine-gun-studded ridge the 5th Division took above the Mamelle Trench on October 14 is now the location of the chapel, on the south edge

Meuse-Argonne American Cemetery, Romagne-sous-Montfaucon, France.

of the cemetery grounds. Constructed of limestone in Romanesque style, the chapel faces northward, overlooking the graves area. Inside, the stained glass windows, designed by the New York firm of Heinigke and Smith, include the corps and divisional emblems of the units that fought in the Meuse-Argonne and Champagne areas. Light colors dominate the glasswork, flooding the room in soft light in contrast with the dark marble floor. The apse, lined with the flags of the United States and Allied nations, has a small altar with a golden cross suspended above. Inlaid on the floor is the Great Seal of the United States. Two loggias with vaulted ceilings stretch out from either side of the chapel. On the walls are the names of 954 American service members whose remains were never recovered or identified. The western loggia also has a map of the Meuse-Argonne Offensive, showing the movements of American forces. The capitals of the loggia columns have military scenes in Art Deco style. On the exterior walls above the columns appear the names of important battles, and on the loggia floors arrows point to the locations of key battlegrounds. From the chapel, a tree-lined walkway leads down the hill, and the graves stretch out on either side of the walkway. They are divided into eight sections, each separated by walkways and finely clipped linden trees. The visitor building lies north of the graves area, on the hill opposite the chapel.

At first glance, the peaceful and productive farmland in the area around the Meuse-Argonne American Cemetery gives no hint of its bloody past. The fields once filled with shell holes and body parts are now filled with crops. But, looking closely, reminders of America's greatest World War I campaign are everywhere. Cunel, a tiny hamlet of just eighteen permanent residents one kilometer east of the cemetery gates, has several places of interest to the American Great War traveler. A 5th Division obelisk stands 800 meters south of Cunel on the D15 highway, marking the location of the trenches from which the division jumped off on its October 14 assault to break the Kreimhilde Stellung. Lieutenant Woodfill's superhuman actions took place along the D15 corridor, along the eastern edge of the village. The Bois de la Pultière, the target of the famous Woodfill raid, is the wooded hill just to the north of Cunel. The village church miraculously survived the war. It underwent major renovations after the war, though a pockmarked wall on its southern face still suggests its violent past. In addition to Woodfill's famous marksmanship that silenced the machine gun in its steeple, the church has one more American connection. On the southeastern exterior wall of the church, not far from Cunel's monument to its own war dead, is a curious memorial to three American fighting men killed during the war—only one of whom, Lieutenant Aaron Weld of the 3rd Division, fought in the area. Each of the three men were Harvard graduates from Massachusetts, and after the war their families got together to place the monument in Cunel. Weld is buried in the Meuse-Argonne Cemetery.

The wooded hills of the Romagne and Cunel Heights today conform remarkably well to the landscape as it was back in 1918. From the roadside these sylvan patches appear unremarkable, but walking through them one can still see evidence of the great battle that raged in them a century ago. Perhaps nowhere is this more evident than at the densely wooded areas east of Romagne-sous-Montfaucon. Logging roads and hiking trails cut through the forest along the ridgeline that eluded the Doughboys for so long. Just south of

Romagne-sous-Montfaucon off the D998 highway, a narrow country road veers off to the southwest, leading to the Côte Dame Marie, where the Red Arrow Division made its breakthrough and earned its nickname. Transvaal Farm still sits peacefully below the ridge. Along the ridgeline to the northwest is Hill 288, which MacArthur's Rainbow Division fought so hard to take. One does not have to walk far in these woods to find the remnants of zigzagging trench lines, shell holes, and even some cement bunkers. Though souvenir hunters have had a century to pick the forest floor clean of wartime artifacts like helmets, canteens, and buttons, these items may still be found in the woods. Hikers might find human remains and live ordnance too. Travelers should be respectful of history and the dead who may still lie in these woods. They should also be careful about picking things up. Great War ordnance can still kill and maim today.

Due to the dearth of interpretive signage in the area, the traveler may find it difficult to appreciate the flow of the fighting in this critically important region. The staff at the cemetery can help visitors understand the combat that took place in the vicinity. In addition, a military collector in Romagne-sous-Montfaucon named Jean-Paul de Vries has made it his business to interpret the area's Great War heritage for travelers. Since the 1970s, de Vries has scoured the woods and fields around Romagne-sous-Montfaucon and collected thousands of items once in the possession of the American, French, and German troops who fought there. In the shadow of the village church on rue de l'Andon, de Vries has put his private collection on public display. His museum, Romagne '14–'18, is jam packed with the detritus of war. The sheer volume of material left behind is impressive. Weaponry makes up a good portion of the items on display, but most evocative are the personal effects of the soldiers—including bottles, canteens, mess kits, religious items, and more than 1,500 identification tags—which give us a peek into the daily lives of men at war. The objects are often broken, twisted, and encased in a century of rust. Nevertheless, it can be a poignant experience to see a Doughboy helmet riddled with bullet holes and know that it was recovered somewhere nearby. American items make up about 35 percent of the collection. De Vries also gives guided battlefield tours.

Liggett Stands up to Pershing

By mid-October American troops had finally punched just a small hole in the Kreimhilde Stellung, and though one of the First Army's most important goals had been accomplished, the Americans were not out of the woods yet—literally. The Germans still held many key defensive positions in the Romagne and Cunel Heights, and fighting still raged from woodlot to woodlot. Frontline units were depleted and exhausted, and there were an estimated 100,000 stragglers behind the lines. Pershing demanded that the attacks continue, but he was no longer in operational command. On October 16, Hunter Liggett took command at First Army headquarters at Souilly. Unlike many World War I commanders, Liggett thought seriously about the welfare of the ordinary foot soldier. Before assuming command he made a tour of frontline units, and was not happy with what he found. "Some signs of discouragement were beginning to appear among both men and officers," Liggett recalled, likely understating the problem:

> The weather was cold, with continuous rains, the men were without adequate shelter and the difficulties of supply were disheartening. There was serious need for rest and reorganization. Such endless hammering in bad weather was a terrific strain on young troops, and a loss of cohesion and a general letting down of morale were appearing. Divisions were so reduced in strength from casualties and strays that we had to call for replacements from newly arrived divisions. It was essential, first of all, to gather up the army as a team and round up the stragglers that our full weight might be felt in one concerted blow.

Pershing was livid about the pause in offensive operations, but Liggett had enough backbone and stature to stand up to him. Exhausted divisions were pulled from the line, replaced with fresh ones. Liggett encouraged officers to visit their subordinate commands to get a real sense of conditions at the front. He also emphasized combined arms fighting, in which troops were to coordinate their rifle, machine-gun, and artillery fire on German positions, rather than the frontal assaults against machine guns that led to horrific casualties with little to show for them. Doughboys in the field were already learning to fight this way anyway, but Liggett made it First Army practice. The days of Pershing's cult of the attack were over.

Liggett's "rest and reorganization" did not mean a halt in fighting. Combat operations continued, now with the aim of gaining good ground for another major push. On the left of the First Army zone, one major goal was the capture of Grandpré, a strategic village on the Aire River near its confluence with the Aisne. Control of Grandpré would give the Americans a better foothold on the north bank of the Aire in preparation for the drive northward, but the chateau on the bluff above the river at Grandpré made it difficult to take. The 77th Division, which had been on the line continuously since September 26, entered the lower village on October 16, but the Germans, from their position in the chateau above the village, prevented the Doughboys from taking control. Relief for the Liberty Division finally came on that very same day, as the 78th "Lightning" Division, a National Army unit originating in upstate New York and northern Pennsylvania, filtered in to take over the Liberty Division positions. The Lightning Division kept up the pressure on Grandpré, but the Germans held tenaciously, especially to the chateau. Slowly, the Americans moved into the woods and farms surrounding the village, approached the chateau from the rear, and forced a German withdrawal on October 23. The chateau was largely destroyed, and most of the castle structures one sees there today have been rebuilt since the war. The Americans now controlled the entirely of the Aire Valley.

In the east, the Americans and the Germans battled furiously for control of the Cunel Heights. Every inch of mud was fiercely contested, but the Doughboys gradually gained the upper hand. By October 21, the 5th Division had cleared the Bois de Rappes north of Cunel. By October 23, the 3rd Division had cleared the Bois de Forêt and taken a wooded prominence known as Hill 299 southwest of Aincreville. The Bois de Clairs Chênes, between Hill 299 and the Bois de Rappes, was the scene of a poignant tragedy that stood out even amid the horrors of World War I. Captain Charles D. Harris, West Point Class of 1917, was just twenty years old. An engineering officer in the 3rd Division, Harris was said to be the youngest captain in the army. On October 20, the 3rd Division launched an attack into the Bois de Clairs Chênes (also known as the Grand Bois de Clery) from positions in the Bois de Forêt. The engineers were there to lay barbed wire, but when the infantry attack faltered Harris stepped into action. With a small detachment, he captured two machine guns and three German prisoners. Harris and his men turned the guns around and fired them at Germans in the Bois de Clairs Chênes, but when the Germans shot back, Harris was wounded in the chest. Stretcher-bearers reached him, but in the chaos of combat they became disoriented and fell into German hands. "I guess it's just not our day," Harris told one of his stretcher-bearers before expiring. The U.S. Army posthumously awarded him the Distinguished Service Cross, but his deeds touched many others. The Germans admired the brave young officer and gave him a dignified burial along the Andon River south of Aincreville. His body was later returned to the United States, but the citizens of Aincreville, who were finally liberated on October 31, still pay tribute to Harris. One panel on the village war memorial there reads (in French): "To our American allies and to the brave Captain Harris, liberators of Aincreville." Near the site of Harris's exploit stands another memorial. The remote marker is located about two kilometers northeast of Cunel on a narrow, nondescript, and unnamed country road that splits off from the D15 highway near the northern edge of the village.

By the end of October, the Doughboys had taken the good ground Liggett needed for his "one concerted blow." Pershing advocated making the major thrust with I Corps, on the First Army's left, against the strongest German forces that lay between Grandpré and Sedan. Liggett once again defied Pershing, and concentrated his efforts in the center. Summerall's V Corps, now composed of the 2nd and 89th Divisions, would make the main effort. I Corps, made up of the 77th, 78th, and 80th Divisions, was to hold the German forces in place, while V Corps knifed its way northward. Caught between V Corps and the Fourth French Army to their west, Liggett believed that the German troops south of Sedan would have no option but to withdraw or risk envelopment. III Corps on the right, consisting of the 5th and 90th Divisions, was to cross the Meuse, join with the French XVII Corps on that side of the river, and finally drive the Germans off the Heights of the Meuse.

The offensive resumed on November 1. A 2nd Division boulder on the D4 highway one kilometer south of Landres-Saint-Georges marks the jump-off line of that division. It was a foggy morning, much like it was when the offensive began on September 26, but the Americans had learned a lot in the intervening five weeks. Their artillery proved more accurate and deadly, and they used poison gas effectively. As the American troops pushed forward, they saw the horrible toll their arms took on the Germans. "The roads and fields were strewn with dead Germans, horses, masses of Artillery, transports, ammunition limbers, helmets, guns, and bayonets," wrote Rush Young of the 80th Division. "Small streams were flowing red with blood from the dead bodies of German soldiers and horses." By the end of the first day, V Corps had taken the Barricourt Heights, the last major obstacle to the Meuse. By November 3, the First Army had taken as much territory as it had in the preceding five weeks. German resistance began to crumble, fighting rearguard actions while withdrawing. As they drove north, the Doughboys noticed a change in scenery. No longer did they encounter the smashed ruins of abandoned villages typical of those that had endured years on the front lines. Instead, they now found villages intact. The sight of homes, shops, and cheering civilians was refreshing and novel, and told them that they were making great strides. Germany, it seemed, grew ever closer.

The Meuse remained a formidable barrier—and Germany's last hope in the region. The 5th Division made its first attempt to cross the river at 1:00 AM on November 3 at Brieulles-sur-Meuse. The task here was twofold. Not only did the river have to be crossed, but just beyond it was a barge canal. Engineers constructed a footbridge across the river in the early morning darkness and infantry got across, but the Germans on the opposite bank detected their movements and treated them to a hail of machine-gun fire before engineers could bridge the canal. Survivors found themselves trapped all that day on the narrow flat land between the river and the canal, unable to move in any direction without exposing themselves to German guns. After dark, engineers built more footbridges and more infantry crossed, but these attacks were also repulsed. After nightfall on November 4 the infantry tried once again to cross the bridges, also combined with a boat crossing. This time Americans got across the canal, pressed up toward the high ground, and established a tenuous bridgehead east of the canal. The Red Diamond Division now shifted its attention northward. In the early hours of November 5, engineers bridged the river at Cléry-le-Petit, and then the canal as well. The Germans discovered the bridges at dawn and opened fire, damaging the structures and inflicting horrific casualties, but the American momentum could not be stopped. Apparently stranded on the west bank of the canal, Captain Edward C. Allworth gathered a group of men and swam across the canal under fire. He then rallied the disorganized troops on the east side and led them up the hill toward German positions. He and his men penetrated more than a kilometer, took more than 100 prisoners, and cleared out many of the guns threatening the valley below. Allworth received the Medal of Honor for his actions. By the end of the day, a whole brigade had crossed, and entered Dun-sur-Meuse. A sturdier pontoon bridge was later constructed just south of Dun-sur-Meuse, allowing greater numbers of Doughboys across.

The crossing area is still easily visible today, especially along the D164 highway between Brieulles-sur-Meuse and Cléry-le-Petit on the west side of the river, and the D964 between Liny-devant-Dun and Dun-sur-Meuse on the east side. Travelers will note several 5th Division markers along the roads. One, located roughly one kilometer north of Liny, is in a spot that provides an excellent view of the Meuse Valley, and the November 5 crossing spot where Captain Allworth led his critically important assault. Dun-sur-Meuse pays tribute to its liberators as well. The village war memorial, located in a small park along the riverbank in the center of town, graciously recognizes "the heroes of the Fifth Division of the U.S.A. Army who fell in relief of Dun-sur-Meuse." Spanning the Meuse nearby is the Pershing Memorial Bridge, with iron railings erected by the Society of the Fifth Division. Bronze plaques—in French on the north side of the bridge and in English on the south side—indicate that the railings commemorate the division's crossing of the Meuse. In the decorative iron work above the plaques is the image of a diamond, the division's emblem.

Two days after the 5th Division crossed the Meuse, it linked up with the French XVII Corps just to the south. That corps, containing several U.S. divisions and under American command, had crossed the Meuse back on October 7 as part of Pershing's effort to silence the German guns on the Heights of the Meuse and spread out German troops (see Chapter 14). The wooded slopes gave the Germans excellent defensive positions, but the cult of the attack that dominated the thinking of Pershing and his subordinates led to assault after futile assault. In nearly a month of fighting, the XVIII Corps had taken huge casualties but precious little territory. The 29th "Blue and Grey" Division, a National Guard unit from Maryland, North Carolina, and Virginia, saw particularly bitter fighting at a place called Molleville Farm, an isolated clearing in the woodlands roughly five kilometers northeast of Consenvoye. Between October 11 and 15, the 29th Division made numerous attacks uphill across the fields. German troops, lined up along the road on northern edge of the farm (present-day

Largest of all 5th Division monuments atop the Côte Saint-Germain, near Lion-devant-Dun, France.

D19 highway), shot them to pieces repeatedly. The Blue and Grey Division eventually took the entire clearing on the 15th, and continued the attack into the woods to the north. The division was finally pulled off the line on October 30, replaced by the 79th Division, rested and refurbished after the fight at Montfaucon. After the XVIII Corps linked up with the 5th Division, the front along the Heights of the Meuse long last began to move eastward. By November 9, Franco-American forces had finally cleared the Heights of the Meuse and silenced the German artillery that had plagued the First Army for the better part of a month.

Several American monuments on the east bank of the Meuse commemorate the taking of the strategic heights. Most prominent is the memorial to the 316th Infantry Regiment of the 79th Division, on the bluff above Sivry-sur-Meuse. It stands on land taken by French troops, but is roughly equidistant between the regiment's battlefields at Montfaucon in September and its fighting east of the Meuse in October and November. Designed by French architect Marcel Delangle and completed in 1928, it is a four-sided stone tower ten meters high, with a cross decorating each side at the top. In English and French, it tells the story of the regiment and lists its most important engagements. The monument overlooks the Meuse River Valley. The view is remarkably picturesque today, with woods and fields interspersed and the Argonne Forest on the western horizon, but it also gives the Great War traveler a good idea of why German artillery from these heights was so devastating to the 79th Division and the other units of the First Army. Nearly the entire Meuse-Argonne battle area is visible.

To the north of Dun-sur-Meuse several white roadside obelisks chart the progress of the 5th Division. One, at the intersection of D964 and D102 east of Milly-sur-Bradon, marks an outpost of the division held between November 5 and 7. Another, at a crossroads on the D119 highway north of Brandeville, marks the division's progress as of November 8. Yet another obelisk on the D964 on the southern edge of Mouzay marks its progress as of November 9. On the Côte Saint-Germain—the hill where the famed pursuit pilot Frank Luke was shot down (see Chapter 11)—is the largest 5th Division obelisk of them all. This one is made of brown fieldstones rather than the white-painted cement construction of the others. It is also roughly five meters high, far taller than the others. It commemorates the division's seizure of the hill on November 6. The spot was also the division's command post at the time of the armistice. It is located on the edge of a small clearing on the northern tip of the hill. Looking to the north from the monument is the Forêt de Woëvre, through which the division attacked in the last days of the war. Several hiking trails reach the summit, but the hill can be steep. The best road access to the top of Côte Saint-Germain is from the village of Lion-devant-Dun, on the west side of the hill.

The Last Push

As the First Army drove northward, Pershing's thoughts turned to the French city of Sedan. Its capture meant more than severing an important rail line. The city had great symbolic significance for the French. In 1870, Prussian forces handed France a crushing blow at the Battle of Sedan, capturing the Emperor Napoleon III and opening the road to Paris. The nationalistic fervor of the Prussian victory led to German unification the following year, placing an even more powerful adversary of France's eastern border. For France, recapturing Sedan from the Germans smacked of some badly wanted revenge. Pershing had a little bit of revenge on his own mind—against the French. Over the years, Pershing had grown weary of what he felt were French slights and condescension against himself and his independent American army. In a candid conversation with General Robert Bullard, Pershing once asked him: "Do they patronize you?" Bullard said they did not. "They have been trying it with me," Pershing told him, "and I don't intend to stand for it." Sedan lay with the area assigned to the French Fourth Army, but that army lagged behind the American First Army. Though many historians have since doubted his veracity, Pershing claimed that French commanders told him that whoever gets to Sedan first should have the honor of taking the city. Taking Sedan from under the noses of the French "would come as the crowning vindication," wrote historian Edward Lengel, "the proof that all of his labors to create the First Army, keep it whole and independent, and guide it through the bloody battlefields of the Meuse-Argonne had not been in vain."

On November 5, Pershing issued orders to I and V Corps stating that "the honor of entering Sedan should fall to the First American Army." Uncharacteristically, he also told his commanders that divisional and corps "boundaries will not be considered binding." Unfortunately, General Liggett, the First Army commander, was not informed and what happened next was one of the most disgraceful episodes in the history of the AEF. Knowing that the war would soon be over, egotistical generals made one last corpulent grab for glory. On November 6, I Corps commander General Dickman designated the Rainbow Division, roughly five kilometers south of the city, to do the job. The 42nd Division picked up the pace, but not fast enough for Dickman. When the division halted operations for the night, Dickman issued orders that the troops "be aroused at once and sent forward," depriving them of sleep so that he could claim his prize. Dickman was not alone in his brazen desire for glory. Summerall, the V Corps commander, wanted it, too, and assigned the 1st Division to race toward Sedan. To get there before Dickman, the Big Red One had made a sharp left turn, crossing into the path of I Corps and the Rainbow Division without ever informing Dickman. During the night of November 6–7, the soldiers of the 1st and 42nd Divisions ran into one another in the darkness southeast of Sedan. Mistaking each other for Germans, they began shooting at each other until things were straightened out. MacArthur, who had a penchant for nonregulation attire, was briefly arrested on suspicion of being a German officer. The 1st Division veered so far west that on November 7 it actually encountered troops from the French Fourth Army, which threatened to open fire on the Americans if they stood between themselves and Sedan. General Liggett, learning of the confrontation, ordered the 1st Division to withdraw, and the French were able to take the city as originally planned. The last of the five 1st Division monuments stands one kilometer south of Wadelincourt on the D6, marking the farthest advance—just shy of Sedan.

The first week of November was a disaster for Germany. Not only had Germany's allies capitulated, but political chaos was brewing back home. In Kiel, German sailors mutinied over a proposed attack on the Allied navies in the North Sea, which the sailors saw as futile. Unrest quickly spread to other cities, often inspired by communists. The outcome of the World War was no longer in doubt, and Germany faced social revolution. On November 8, German representatives arrived at Foch's headquarters in the Compiègne Forest to negotiate an armistice. The Allies debated what terms to give the Germans. Pershing called for an unconditional German surrender. Most others thought the time to make peace was at hand. All agreed that increasing the pressure on the battlefield would give them better terms, and

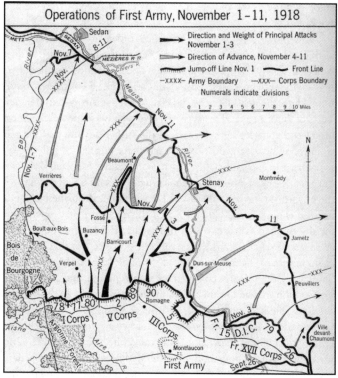

Operations of First Army, November 1–11, 1918

that through a continuation of combat operations the Allies could destroy as much of the German army as possible before the inevitable armistice came.

Foch ordered one more push across the Western Front on November 10. That morning, the 2nd and 89th Divisions crossed the Meuse River between Mouzon and Stenay. Bullard's brand-new Second Army, barely three weeks old, also stepped off on the morning of November 10 in an operation known as the Woëvre Plain Offensive. The 33rd Division, penetrating as far as five kilometers into German lines, took the villages of Saint-Hilaire-en-Woëvre and Marchéville. The 92nd Division went back into action, too, for the first time since its questionable performance at Binarville at the beginning of the Grand Offensive (see Chapter 15). It was serving on the front just east of the Moselle north of Pont-à-Mousson. This time the division fought well, advancing more than a kilometer in places and holding much of the ground it took. From its position on Xon Hill west of the village of Lesménils, for example, the 92nd advanced and occupied the Bois des Fréhaut to the north. The Bois de Viovrotte, just a few hundred meters to the east, proved more difficult. The Germans repulsed the attack into the woods on November 10, but the Americans took the woods the following morning. The successes of the Buffalo Soldiers in November were lost in the clouds of controversy swirling around its performance in the Argonne the previous September. Also forgotten were the numerous medals for valor the Buffalo Soldiers earned. This amnesia was due in part to the bitterness of General Ballou, who squashed publicity surrounding the decorations for his men and refused to let army photographers document their service.

November 10 also marked the day Kaiser Wilhelm II abdicated the German throne and fled to neutral Holland. German negotiators at Compiègne had no more cards to play. At 5:10 AM on the morning of November 11, the German delegation at Compiègne signed the armistice agreement. Fighting was to end at 11:00 AM that morning. In some places, soldiers on both sides held their arms in check and waited for the war to officially end. In most other places, combat continued right up to the very last second. For those Doughboys—and in fact for every soldier on the Western Front—the last skirmishes on that morning had an air of tragic futility. Nobody wanted to be the last man killed in the Great War. "It seemed so foolish," recalled Harold Pierce of the 28th Division, "to keep killing up to the last minute." Pierce kept low, and remembered that he was "filled with horror at the thought of being killed" hours or even minutes before the armistice took effect. "All had been willing and glad to attack the day before," wrote Adolphus Graupner of the 91st Division in Belgium, "but the prospect of an attack in the shadow of an armistice brought a change of spirit. The prospect of useless sacrifice ofAmerican lives in battle under such impending conditions had no attractions, no glory, no glamor."

At 11:00 AM on November 11, 1918, the guns of the Great War finally fell silent. A string of monuments marks the AEF's furthest line of advance that morning. There are two 2nd Division boulders on the D964 highway south of Mouzon. The first is two kilometers south of the village. The other, not quite two kilometers farther south on the border of the Departments of Meuse and Ardennes, is accompanied by a makeshift memorial to the V Corps, erected by the Doughboys right after the war. Farther to the southeast, white obelisks mark some of the final combat locations of the 5th Division. One marker stands on the D110 highway between Louppy-sur-Loison and Juvigny-sur-Loison. Another is in the northern edge of Jametz at the junction of the D69 and D905.

One memorial in the hills above the tiny town of Chaumont-devant-Damvillers tells a tale both bizarre and poignant. Company A of the 313th Infantry Regiment, 79th Division, was pushing the advance up the hill near the village on that foggy morning. It was just a few minutes before 11:00 when two American troops encountered a German checkpoint on the road. The Germans fired, though whether in anger or as a warning was unclear. The Americans hit the ground, but one of them, Private Henry Gunther of Baltimore, quickly got up and charged at the Germans. Nobody knew why he did it. Some thought perhaps that it was one last chance for battlefield glory. Others speculated that being of German ancestry he felt some need to prove his loyalty to America. His motives will forever be a mystery. His fellow Doughboys shouted at him to stop, and the Germans tried to wave him off, but Gunther kept going and

Memorial to Henry Gunther, Chaumont-devant-Damvilliers, France.

at 10:59 AM the Germans shot him dead—one minute before the armistice was to take effect. Ninety years after his death, Chaumont-devant-Damvillers erected a monument in Gunther's memory at the site of the incident. It is located on a remote, dirt road three kilometers northeast of the village. The monument is a large, rough fieldstone, embedded into which is a plaque explaining the circumstances of Gunther's death in French, English, and German. Etched into the stone below are the words: "En homage à Henry Gunther" ("In homage to Henry Gunther"). He was very likely the last soldier killed in action in all of World War I.

The Meuse-Argonne Offensive was by far the longest and bloodiest campaign in the history of the AEF. Over the course of forty-seven days, 1.2 million Americans had participated in the operation. The United States suffered 26,000 dead and 95,000 wounded. Despite all of its problems, this offensive might also have been the war's most successful. A few weeks after the armistice, Field Marshall Paul von Hindenburg sat down with an American reporter who asked him frankly: "Who won the war?" Hindenburg responded: "The American infantry." Despite the setbacks of the German offensives of 1918, Hindenburg argued that the war could have "ended in a sort of stalemate," but that "the balance was broken by the American troops." Hindenburg specifically cited the Meuse-Argonne Offensive, which he described as being "slow and difficult" and having used up "division after division" for Germany as it sought "to hold the Metz-Longuyon roads and railroads." The Meuse-Argonne Offensive, he opined, "was the climax of the war and its deciding factor. . . . The American attack won the war."

For all the criticism heaped on Pershing throughout America's participation in World War I, Hindenburg's comments must have given him some sense of vindication.

CHAPTER 18:
AFTERMATH

"Most of the artillery ceased firing when the news of the armistice was spread," wrote Adolphus Graupner of the 91st "Wild West" Division of the moment the armistice came in Belgium:

> but somewhere in the distance scattered French 75's continued to fire fitfully until the hour of eleven was near at hand, then, one by one they subsided. It seemed as tho each gun crew wanted the distinction of firing the last shot, or was reluctant to cease the hating of years. Then followed a great calm. Not the sound of a gun, the crack of a rifle, the put-put-put of a machine gun, nor the whir of an aeroplane motor could be heard.

The front lines that had just been the scene of bloody fighting often erupted in jubilant celebrations. "We were stupefied to see crowds of Boches running over to us between the mine fields," remembered Carl Stuber of the Rainbow Division, "their hands up running like mad." In some places, the Doughboys shook hands with the men who had just been their enemies, and exchanged chocolate and cigarettes for German helmets and insignia. That evening the soldiers on both sides sang songs and lit bonfires. "It seemed funny to see so many fires," recalled Anthony Cone of the 2nd Division, "when twenty-four hours before we could not even strike a match." With the end of the war, virtually every Doughboy turned his thoughts to home, but the return to civilian life often came with some bumps in the road. Some took a detour to Germany as part of the Army of Occupation. Medical and economic problems made readjustment to civilian life more problematic than many anticipated, and turbulent postwar politics sometimes pitted veteran against veteran in ugly and tragic confrontations. At first Americans went to extraordinary lengths to memorialize the War to End All Wars, but when the world did not seem to be any safer for democracy disillusion set it, and an even bloodier World War II overshadowed the intense horrors of the First. For Americans, the Great War became the Forgotten War.

Throughout their involvement in the war, America's fighting men dreamed of advancing into Germany. By the end of 1918, 200,000 made that dream a reality. Under the terms of the armistice, Allied soldiers were to occupy German territory west of the Rhine. In addition to that, they would also hold an area east of the Rhine within a thirty-kilometer radius east of three key bridgeheads—Cologne, Koblenz, and Mainz—with a neutral zone extending another ten kilometers out, giving the Allies a foothold into the German heartland. Each of the three major Allied powers took control of a bridgehead, with their occupation zone stretching westward behind it. (Belgium occupied an area around Aachen and was not responsible for a bridgehead.) The British occupied Cologne, and the French took Mainz. Koblenz came under American control. The U.S. occupation zone extended from Koblenz up the valley of the Moselle River (or Mosel, as it is known in Germany) to Trier and the Luxembourg border. To make up the Army of Occupation, Pershing created the U.S. Third Army. It was a mix of Regular Army (1st, 2nd, and 3rd), National Guard (32nd and 42nd), and National Army (89th and 90th) divisions that would serve as America's "Watch on the Rhine."

On November 17, the Third Army left the Western Front and began its march toward Germany. In a few days the Americans reached the tiny of duchy of Luxembourg, where it gathered in preparation for its advance to the Rhine. As they had done with Belgium, the Germans invaded Luxembourg in 1914 on their way to France and stayed there throughout the war. The German occupation divided Luxembourgers, whose culture is a mix of French and German and who speak both languages. Many in Luxembourg resented the invasion, though pro-German sympathies in the duchy were not uncommon. Whatever may have been in the hearts of individual Luxembourgers, they greeted the Doughboys with exuberance. The Big Red One was the first to enter the city of Luxembourg. "School children tossed flowers in their pathway," reported the *New York Times*, and "each soldier was greeted with a bouquet of chrysanthemums." The Red Arrow Division was particularly well received. "With its brigades from Wisconsin and Michigan," according to one account, "with its innumerable German-Americans from Oshkosh and Fort Atkinson and Big Rapids and Grand Rapids, to say nothing of Milwaukee, the Thirty-second just lorded it around with the natives." On November 21, Luxembourg's Grand Duchess stood on the balcony of her palace in the heart of her city and watched smiling as American troops paraded past her, General Pershing by her side.

On December 1, Americans crossed the Sauer River bridges at Wasserbillig and Echternach, and entered Germany. "What a 'grand and glorious feeling' to march into conquered territory," wrote Riley Strickland of the 90th Division, "and to know that you are a part of the victorious armies of the world of worlds." The American columns averaged fifteen to twenty kilometers a day, establishing their presence in cities and small towns along the way. "Our march was routed through a country of a most rugged and hilly nature," recalled Emil Gansser of the Red Arrow Division. "The winter rains were beginning to set in, making the roads muddy and disagreeable." "Upon entering Germany," wrote the authors of *American Armies and Battlefields in Europe*, the American troops "were regarded with a mixture of curiosity and suspicion." "We were greeted by cold stares," wrote Emil Gansser. "The inhabitants stood in their doorways, silent, furtively watching us as we passed," wrote Ernest Peixotto, though he also noticed that the children "dashed out from doorways and alley-ways, and, at the risk of their lives, boisterously greeted the honk-honk of our horn." John Barkley of the 3rd Division was surprised to see "the scared look on their faces," but he also noticed that "when we called out friendly things to them . . . their faces would light up." Barkley surmised that "they'd been told worse things about us than we'd been told about them!" though he did note that "the ex-soldiers still felt pretty bitter."

The first American troops reached the Rhine on December 9, and on the cold, gray drizzly morning of December 13 they crossed to the east bank. "After all we had heard about this famous river," wrote Emil Gansser of his crossing at Koblenz, "it appeared no different than other rivers, and was but plain water rushing on its way to join the sea." He nonetheless noted that "new history was made, for this was the first time that American soldiers ever crossed this barrier to central Germany." The Army of Occupation moved into cities and villages all across the occupation zone. The Big Red One was farthest east. They made their headquarters at Montabaur, twenty kilometers northeast of Koblenz, where—among other buildings—they took over the medieval castle on the hill overlooking the

View of Montabaur, Germany by U.S. Army war artist Jules Smith. (From Jules A. Smith, *In France with the American Expeditionary Forces*, 1919).

Montabaur, Germany today.

town. Occupation duties were light. The Doughboys patrolled the countryside armed, but it soon became evident that they had little to fear. When not on patrol, the troops endured plenty of drills and inspections. Most were anxious to go home. It was not long until the troops joked about serving in the "Army of No Occupation."

Koblenz was the center of American power in the Rhineland. The Army of Occupation made its head-quarters at the Prussian District President's Office, along the city's pleasant Rhine waterfront promenade. Most of central Koblenz was destroyed in World War II bombings, but the ornate brown limestone structure still stands on the Konrad-Adenauer-Ufer between Rheinstrasse and Stresemannstrasse. It now houses various offices of the German army. On the east bank of the Rhine, the Americans also took over the massive fortress known as Festung Ehrenbreitstein. Due to its strategic position on a cliff overlooking the Deutsches Eck (as the confluence of the Rhine and Mosel Rivers is called), the site has seen military activity since ancient times. The fortifications the Americans moved into were Prussian, built in the early nineteenth century. Ehrenbreitstein's moats and battlements

Headquarters of the U.S. Army of Occupation in Koblenz, Germany. The building now holds administrative offices for the German army.

looked impressive, but by 1919 were militarily obsolete. The massive complex gave the Third Army plenty of office space and barracks. American soldiers controlled the Pfaffendorf Bridge at Koblenz. Aside from its footings, not much remains of the structure the Doughboys patrolled. It was reconstructed in the 1930s, and then retreating Nazi troops blew it up in World War II to prevent the Allies from crossing the Rhine. Today's bridge was built in the 1950s. The YMCA followed the U.S. forces into Germany. In Koblenz, it operated a recreation hut on the grounds of the ornate Electoral Palace, which once housed the German Imperial Army Headquarters.

It was the same in other American-occupied towns. The Rainbow Division controlled the area around Ludendorff Bridge at Remagen, not quite forty kilometers downriver from Koblenz. The German

Ruins of the Ludendorff Bridge, Remagen, Germany.

military constructed this bridge during World War I to bring supplies to the Western Front, and the Doughboys of the Rainbow Division would not be the last American soldiers to take it. On March 7, 1945, American GIs seized the bridge before the Nazis could blow it up, giving the Allies a critical foothold east of the Rhine in the final days of World War II. For days after the GIs took the bridge, the Nazis tried unsuccessfully to destroy it, trying artillery barrages, air strikes, and even mines floated down the Rhine. None worked. The bridge finally collapsed on its own ten days after its capture, killing several American soldiers working to shore it up, but by that time the Allied foothold across the Rhine was well established. Today all that is left of the bridge are the distinctive black basalt towers on either bank of the river. Inside the tower on the Remagen side is the Friedensmuseum (Peace Museum), which focuses mainly on the history of bridge during World War II, though it also includes mention of the Doughboys who occupied it after World War I.

The 42nd Division's commanding officer, General Douglas MacArthur, made his living quarters at Schloss Sinzig, a castle five kilometers to the south of Remagen at Sinzig. Soldiers' quarters varied. Some Doughboys were lucky enough to stay in comfortable German army barracks. For those used to sleeping in the field, these accommodations were a godsend. "Electric lights, coal stoves, and spring beds in every room," boasted Edward Peterson of his quarters at Festung Ehrenbreitstein, whose room also came with a view. "I can see the village of Ehrenbreitstein below," he wrote, "the City of Coblenz across the stream, beyond that the Moselle River, and one of the greatest equestrian statues in the world on the triangle where the rivers meet." Most occupation troops—especially in smaller towns—stayed in the homes of ordinary Germans, an arrangement that sometimes led to tensions. "I and my section were assigned to a small house," wrote Earl Young of his time in Bad Bodendorf, near Sinzig. When the Americans arrived they found their room filled with furniture, so the soldiers promptly emptied the room. When they removed a portrait of the Kaiser "the whole family let out a howl," remembered Young, who angrily smashed the portrait and replaced it with "a photo of myself I had taken in France." He then forced the family salute it. "Within an hour's time the whole village knew of it," he later boasted, earning him the nickname the "Kaiser of Bodendorf."

The army had strict rules about fraternizing with Germans, but as time went on and the passions of war cooled, such rules were increasingly bent or even ignored. "No orders were needed to prevent fraternization with the full-grown German male of the species," stated the 32nd Division official history, "but with the 'wimmin and kids' it was different. The Yanks just couldn't get up any hate for them, and couldn't help showing their good nature." Women were the biggest temptation. "German women insisted on making friends with the American soldiers billeted in their houses," recalled William Wright of the 148th Field Artillery. John Barkley concluded that the Germans "didn't seem much different than the people I'd already known," and thought them "not as different as the French."

As the Doughboys settled into their occupation duties, world leaders gathered at Versailles, France, to hammer out a final peace settlement. President Wilson arrived at Brest on December 13, 1918—he was the first sitting U.S. president ever to visit Europe—and was greeted in Paris with great enthusiasm. Wilson believed his peace plan, the Fourteen Points, would achieve the goal of making the world "safe for democracy." It called for free trade, national self-determination, and a new global congress called the League of Nations to preserve world peace. But Wilson's idealism ran headlong into Britain and France's hard-nosed desire for security from future German aggression. Negotiations were tense and tough. The final version of the Versailles Treaty, signed in the Hall of Mirrors at the Palace of Versailles on June 28, 1919, was a series of compromises that ultimately pleased no one. Some of Wilson's idealistic goals became part of the treaty. A whole slew of new nations appeared in Eastern Europe, as the old German, Austrian, and Russian empires collapsed. Poland reappeared on the map for the first time since 1796. The League of Nations was born. But Wilson was unable to block some of the more punitive measures against Germany. Under the treaty, Germany paid monetary reparations to Britain and France. Its armed forces were limited to 100,000 men, and its navy and air forces were effectively abolished. Germany lost territory, such as Alsace and Lorraine, which returned to France. Historical debate rages about whether or not the treaty was too harsh on Germany or not harsh enough. The Germans called it the "Diktat," and it fomented angry feelings against the Allied powers.

Another stipulation of the Versailles Treaty was that the Allies were to continue their occupation of the Rhineland for fifteen years. Settling in for the long haul, the Third Army became American Forces in Germany (AFG) and was placed under the command of

General Henry T. Allen, who had led the 90th Division in France. The original occupying divisions packed up and went home, while fresh new troops replaced them. But it soon became evident that the United States did not have the resolve to spend fifteen years in Germany. Even though the United States was on the victorious side, many American began to sour on foreign affairs. In the wake of the war, some thought President Wilson's war aim of making the world "safe for democracy" a failure, if not a farce. Europe continued to squabble, and the threat of communism spreading from Russia made the world seem as dangerous and undemocratic as ever. For some, the high hopes the war spawned morphed into disillusion afterward. The end of the war brought economic recession and a wave of strikes across the United States. When the Versailles Treaty came up for a vote in the U.S. Senate, lawmakers rejected it. The United States signed a separate peace with Germany, and would not join the League of Nations its own president had worked so hard to create. The year 1920 saw the election of Wilson's successor, Warren G. Harding, who promised America a "return to normalcy"—which meant, in part, retrenchment in foreign affairs. American foreign policy would protect that nation's interests, but not go much beyond that. Disarmament was all the rage after the war, and many countries—the United States among them—began dismantling their armies and navies. In January 1923, the AFG took down the American flag over Ehrenbreitstein for the last time. Britain also tired of the occupation, and pulled out as well. France was left holding the bag.

Festung Ehrenbreitstein.

Aside from the Friedensmuseum at the Remagen, there is virtually no obvious evidence of the U.S. Rhineland occupation today. Schloss Sinzig, where MacArthur once lived, is now a local art and culture museum, the Heimat Museum (Barbarossastrasse 35). Travelers can stroll its gardens and enjoy the castle's architecture and the artworks that adorn its walls, but find no evidence of MacArthur. The medieval castle at Montabaur, with its distinctive mustard-colored turrets looming over the fairy tale town, is now a hotel and conference center. However, the very existence of Festung Ehrenbreitstein today might be considered in some respects a monument to the American occupation. Fearful of German military power, France wanted the fortress destroyed, and pressured the American forces to place it under French control. "I was determined that it should not be destroyed," General Allen wrote in his memoirs. Arguing for its historical significance and military obsolescence, Allen deftly fended off the French. Festung Ehrenbreitstein exists today, arguably, thanks to General Allen and the American Army of Occupation. Ehrenbreitstein is now one of Koblenz's most popular tourist destinations. A cable car connects it to the Koblenz riverfront, and one can still walk its impressive walls and enjoy magnificent views of the Rhine. Ehrenbreitstein's military career came to an end after World War II. It now hosts several museums, gardens, a restaurant, a youth hostel, and a German war memorial. Allen is not commemorated among the ramparts and casements, though a street just to the northeast of the fortress is named General-Allen-Strasse in his honor.

Most of the two million Doughboys overseas at the time of the armistice remained in France, and they wanted nothing more than to go home. "Since the guns have ceased their angry roar, I've been so confounded homesick I can hardly bear it," wrote Edwin Tippett shortly after the armistice. "While the noise of war was in my ears, and there was work to do, I did not have time to get homesick, but since then I have been crazy." But until transportation could be arranged and the final peace treaty hammered out, most would have to wait. Officials found ways to keep the boys busy. The YMCA stepped up its efforts to entertain them and keep them out of trouble. U.S. Army leave areas (see Chapter 9) saw a great uptick in business. Leave trains streamed toward the south of France in ever-increasing numbers, and Paris was flooded with uniformed Americans longing to see the city before going home. Victory brought still more tourist opportunities. Rhine River cruises proved to be particularly popular. "Every doughboy in the A.E.F. felt that his foreign service was incomplete until he had seen the Rhine," wrote one Sergeant Scott of the 89th Division, who joined a group of American soldiers at Koblenz for a cruise. "Our boat was a fine excursion schooner flying the Stars and Stripes," he recalled:

> A "Y" man lectured at intervals and pointed out places of interest. The weather was fine. We had abundant opportunity to take pictures. Here it was—all that we had read about and dreamed about and more. Little villages with their backgrounds of vineyards clustered along the water's edge so close together that it was almost impossible to tell where one left off and the next began. The castles were built high up on steep cliffs; each had a history of its own and held itself, even in its ruins, aloft from the present commercial life below.

The next day Scott took an excursion to the Stolzenfels castle, one of the Rhine's most magnificent. "This trip made us feel pretty good to be in the Army of Occupation."

At the French city of Beaune, the army created the AEF University on the grounds of a wartime hospital complex. Classes ran the gamut from agriculture to fine arts, and as more and more soldiers matriculated the complex expanded further. Many Doughboys jumped at the chance to go to college. "Nine were given permission to go as students," recalled Frederick Pottle, though he found the experience somewhat disappointing, since "being a student at Beaune in the early days meant constructing concrete barracks in the rain." In addition to the Beaune facility, there were branch schools all across France, from Brest to Marseilles. As many as 15,000 soldier-students studied at Beaune, taught by more than 500 professors, many of whom were imported from the United States and some of whom came from Ivy League schools. Thousands more were permitted to enroll in British and French universities. Today a plaque on an unremarkable stone wall in Beaune marks the spot of the hospital and the university. It is located at the intersection of rue du Docteur Tassin and route de Vignolles. The latter street is also known—appropriately enough—as rue de l'Universitè Amèricain. Athletics was another way to keep the troops busy. In June and July of 1919, the AEF and the YMCA sponsored an athletic competition called the Inter-Allied Games. U.S. Army engineers built a venue for the games called Pershing Stadium, in the Bois de Vincennes on the southeastern edge of Paris. Eighteen different nations competed, and among the participants was the AEF boxing champion, Gene Tunney, who later gained fame as a champion professional boxer. When Paris hosted the 1924 Olympics, the *Stade Pershing* was one of its venues. The stadium seating has long since been torn down, but the old athletic field remains in a sports complex still called *Stade Pershing* on the route du Bousquet Mortemart.

To perpetuate the friendships and the spirit of patriotism forged in wartime, a group of officers in Paris, led by Theodore Roosevelt Jr., began laying plans for an association of AEF veterans. In March 1919, a group of officers and enlisted men held a convention at the Cirque de Paris and formed an organization they called the American Legion. The Cirque de Paris no longer exists, but a plaque on the wall at 14 rue Ernest Psichari, where the convention hall once stood, commemorates the founding of the organization. In May, the American Legion held its first caucus at the Shubert Theater in Saint Louis, and its first national convention at the Minneapolis Auditorium (11th and Nicolet Avenue) that November. The American Legion quickly became the largest veterans' organization in the United States. By 1940, one out of every four ex-Doughboys was a member. The American Legion now accepts members from numerous conflicts and remains the largest veterans organization in the United States. Great War veterans would go on to found other groups, like the Disabled American Veterans, or join existing ones, like the Veterans of Foreign Wars.

Homeward Bound at Last

Before long, the American soldiers began to make the long trek home. Camp Pontanézen near Brest, the largest of the rest camps taking in arrivals to France, now prepared them for the return trip. It was the same at Knotty Ash in Liverpool and the various camps near Saint-Nazaire. From the camps, they marched to the docks, boarded the ships, and sailed west into the Atlantic toward America. Not all Americans went home, of course. France had long been home to an American expatriate community, and in the wake of the war it found itself irrevocably changed by the Doughboy presence. Books left over from AEF libraries, for example, formed the core of the collection of the American Library in Paris at 10 rue de l'Elysée. Founded in 1920 with money from the family of Alan Seeger, an American in the French army killed in 1916 (see Chapter 1), it counted American "Lost Generation" writers like Ernest Hemingway and F. Scott Fitzgerald as patrons during the 1920s. The American Library in Paris is now at 10 rue di Général Camou. American Episcopal Protestants had consecrated the Holy Trinity Church in Paris on avenue George V in 1886. Now known as the American Cathedral in Paris, Doughboys crowded its pews during the war, and afterward the cathedral created a memorial to those Americans killed in the war. The walls of the cathedral's cloister are embossed with the emblems of AEF divisions and other units, along with a list of the campaigns in which they fought. Several plaques in the interior of the church have a Great War connection, too. One is dedicated to Ronald Wood Hoskier, a Lafayette Escadrille pilot killed in April 1918, who has several monuments dedicated to him in Picardy (see Chapter 1). Another is dedicated to Margaret Beekman, church member and director of the American Soldiers and Sailors Club, which was located at 11 rue Royale during the war.

Indeed, postwar Paris was crawling with more Americans than ever before. The famous Lost Generation writers joined the scores of other Americans involved in business and diplomatic pursuits, many of whom were veterans. The wealthy and well-connected members of the American Legion built a clubhouse for themselves called Pershing Hall at 49 rue Pierre Charron. Paul Doumer, the French president, was even on hand for the dedication ceremony in 1929. The Legionnaires no longer use the building. It is now a five-star luxury hotel called the Hotel Pershing Hall, which keeps alive its American connections. The American Legion emblem still appears above the hotel entrance. On the façade of the building above the first-floor windows are sculptures of an American eagle and a helmeted American soldier, a sailor, and an aviator. Once inside, the American connections are even more evident. A plaque on the building's keystone notes that it was once part of the destroyed bridge at Château-Thierry (see Chapter 8). Each floor of the hotel has an alcove with some remembrance of the American contribution to the Great War. One has a bust of General Pershing. Another has a memorial brass plaque to the Yale University alumni killed in the war. Still another lists the dead from Princeton. The Hotel Pershing Hall remains a gathering place for Americans in Paris today. Elections, the Super Bowl, and other such U.S. national events are likely to draw an American expatriate crowd to the hotel. An American Legion post still operates in Paris today, though at a different location.

Most returning soldiers landed at Hoboken, passing through the same port buildings from which they departed, and spent their first night in America at Camp Merritt, New Jersey, in the same barracks they had slept in months before. Then they boarded trains to an army camp close to their home of record—often the training camp that introduced them to the army—for their discharge. To see them to their homes, the government gave soldiers a $60 discharge bonus and a three-and-a-half-cent-per-mile travel allowance. Once back in their homes or on their farms, many ex-soldiers took off their uniforms, got on with their lives, and never looked back. For others, the return to civilian life was more complicated. Discharged soldiers often had trouble finding work in the postwar recession. Medical problems plagued thousands of veterans. The federal government offered pensions and job training to disabled veterans, and spent million on hospitals, but some veterans found it insufficient. Not all wounds were physical. What medical science now knows as Post Traumatic Stress Disorder was then called "shell shock," and it was poorly understood. For large numbers of veterans, the war changed their entire outlook on life. "How can you tell them 'As You Were,'" wrote one ex-soldier, "after they have lived with Death?"

Tensions Back Home

Once back home, World War I veterans were at the center of some of America's most important and divisive political debates of the 1920s and 1930s. One was the crusade against communism. In the uncertain postwar years, fear that communism might spread from Russia to other parts of the world ran high. War-ravaged countries like Germany and Italy saw particularly strong communist movements, and there were even concerns in the United States. In 1919 and 1920, a series of terrorist bombings tied to communists rocked the country. The number of actual communists in the United States was small, but the atmosphere of uncertainty, combined with the lingering hyperpatriotism of the war years, led to exaggerated fears of communism in America. The result was the first Red Scare. In response to the bombings, President Wilson's attorney General, A.

Mitchell Palmer, led a series of "Red Raids." Casting his net wide, Mitchell rounded up known communists, suspected ones, or anyone he felt posed a threat to the nation. He often played fast and loose with the Constitution, jailing people or deporting them on flimsy pretexts. Civil libertarians cried foul, but many patriotic societies supported Mitchell's campaign against communism. Among the loudest anticommunist voices in America during the Red Scare was the American Legion.

In some places, Red Scare tensions led to violence, perhaps most notably in the small lumber town of Centralia, Washington. The International Workers of the World (IWW) was a radical labor union popular with many Northwestern lumbermen. Indeed, the army took over the Northwest logging industry during the war due the frequency of IWW strikes (see Chapter 11). At the same time, many returning World War I veterans in Centralia joined the American Legion. Tensions between the two groups quickly emerged. Legionnaires tended to see the IWW as a communist front. IWW members, known as "Wobblies," saw the American Legion as dangerously reactionary. Over the course of 1919 tensions had grown so high that there were scattered acts of violence between the groups. Both began to arm themselves for protection.

On November 11, 1919, local Legionnaires marched in Centralia's first Armistice Day parade to celebrate the one-year anniversary of the Great War's end. The parade wound its way through town, but paused in front of the local IWW union hall at 807 North Tower Street. What happened next remains the subject of fierce debate. Legionnaires claimed that Wobblies opened fire on them. Wobblies claimed that the Legionnaires stormed their offices, and that they only shot back in self-defense. Whatever the case, three Legionnaires lay dead along Tower Street. A fourth, Ernest Hubbard, joined a posse of Legionnaires in pursuit of one Wobbly who fled the scene. His name was Wesley Everest, and he was also a World War I veteran. Everest's personal story is murky. A logger and an IWW member, Everest spent the war at the army lumber mill at Fort Vancouver, Washington. Far from an ideal soldier, he often landed in the brig for refusing to salute the flag and, as one of his comrades remembered, Everest was "constantly trying to organize the soldiers." The posse caught up with Everest at the banks of the Skookumchuck River. In the shootout that followed, Hubbard was killed. Everest was arrested and hauled into the local jail, where an angry mob soon gathered. That evening, someone cut the power to downtown Centralia, and in the darkness, Everest was hauled out of jail and hung from a bridge over the Chehalis River. Eleven IWW members were put on trial for the murder of the four Legionnaires, eight of whom were convicted and given long prison sentences. Nobody was ever tried for Everest's murder.

Dubbed the Armistice Day Riot or the Centralia Massacre, the episode still divides the town. In the center of Centralia's George Washington Park is a World War I monument. At first glance it seems like an unremarkable bronze Doughboy, but a closer look shows that it is not. The faces of the four Legionnaires killed on Armistice Day 1919 look out from bronze plaques affixed to the pedestal. The names of the four are also engraved on the front, as is a dedication that explains that the four men were "slain in the streets of Centralia . . . while on peaceful parade wearing the uniform of the country they loyally and faithfully served." Wesley Everest is not forgotten either. A colorful mural on the side of a building just across the street from the Doughboy monument, entitled "The Resurrection of Wesley Everest," depicts him with arms raised and fists clenched, rising from his grave. The right half of his body is clad in workman's overhauls, his left in a World War I uniform. The mural, the work of a local labor activist, overlooks the World War I monument in the park; only a stand of trees separates them. The IWW union hall on North Tower Street has long since been replaced. Everest's grave is located in Greenwood

Wesley Everest mural, Centralia, Washington.

Memorial Park, at 1905 Johnson Road on the northwest side of town. After his murder Everest was buried in secret in an unmarked grave, but today he has two headstones. One has the IWW emblem. The other is a U.S. government headstone for veterans. It lists his unit as the 91st Division, though Everest is not known to have ever left the United States. Three of the four Legionnaires are also buried in Centralia, though in different cemeteries.

Government programs for veterans comprised another hot topic in the postwar years. Veterans' groups like the American Legion kept an eagle-eyed watch on agencies like the Veterans' Bureau—the forerunner of today's Department of Veterans Affairs—to ensure that those who fought in the Great War would be cared for properly afterward. One of the veterans' most frequent complaints was that their military service left them economically disadvantaged. While the ordinary private soldier in the army made a dollar a day, they pointed out, war workers back home made three to four times that amount. While they were making the world "safe for democracy," those who stayed behind got the raises and promotions they did not. In the early 1920s, veterans' organizations pressed for Congress for a "bonus"—a cash payment to compensate for the economic disadvantages their wartime service engendered. Critics charged that the proposal was too expensive, but after World War I politicians found it hard to resist the veterans. In 1924 Congress passed the Adjusted Compensation Act, overriding the veto of President Calvin Coolidge. The law gave the veterans the bonus they sought, but there was a catch—it was not payable until 1945.

In the prosperous days of the 1920s most veterans were willing to wait for their bonus, but with the onset of the Great Depression in 1929 many called for an early payment. In 1932, an ex-Doughboy in Portland, Oregon, named Walter W. Waters led a group of veterans to Washington, DC, hopping freight cars and sometimes traveling in motorcades provided by sympathetic local politicians. They dubbed themselves the Bonus Expeditionary Force (BEF), and attracted headlines around the nation. Learning of Waters's movement, other veterans made their way to the nation's capital. In all, more than 20,000 converged on Washington, camping out in various places across the city. Most stayed at an improvised shantytown on the flats of the Anacostia River across from the Washington Navy Yard. They called it Camp Marks, in honor of the sympathetic police district captain who allowed them to stay there. The Washington police chief Pelham Glassford arranged for others to stay in abandoned Treasury Department buildings on the 400 block of Constitution Avenue that were about to be demolished, and the veterans gratefully called this place Camp Glassford. From the camps, the veterans went to Capitol Hill each day, hoping to persuade Congress to approve an early bonus payment. The presence of BEF alarmed official Washington. Communists had staged a "Hunger March" the previous year, and fears of radicalism permeated the city. Some reports suggested that the BEF was riddled with communists, though such fears were grossly exaggerated, President Herbert Hoover asked army chief of staff General Douglas MacArthur to be on alert in case the "Bonus March" spun out of control.

The House of Representatives passed a bonus bill on June 15, but the Senate rejected it two days later, leaving the veterans without an early payment. For the next month many veterans lingered in the capital, and President Hoover grew concerned. On July 21, Hoover ordered the police to clear the BEF camps, and alerted the army to be ready to step in if necessary. When the police showed up at Camp Glassford on the hot, sticky day of July 28, the situation turned violent. Veterans began throwing bricks. In one incident in the early afternoon, a group of marchers rushed at police. One officer fired, shooting two veterans dead. News of the bloodshed prompted Hoover to call in the army. He ordered MacArthur to use restraint and confine his activities to the downtown area, but it soon became clear that the general had other plans. MacArthur gathered a force on the Ellipse behind the White House that included tanks, mounted cavalry, and trucks carrying machine guns. At 4:30 PM, MacArthur's troops proceeded east down Pennsylvania Avenue toward Camp Glassford. Confronted with rock-throwing veterans, the soldiers used bayonets and copious amounts of tear gas to clear the ex-soldiers from the buildings. "The blue haze of gas that hung like an ominous pall over the section of shanties and condemned Federal buildings," read one press account, was "reminiscent of scenes in war-town France." That evening, in further defiance of Hoover's orders, MacArthur marched his men across the 11th Street Bridge over the Anacoastia River to Camp Marks and burned it to the ground.

The images of Bonus March—tanks and trucks rolling down Pennsylvania Avenue, smoke and tear gas obscuring the views of the Capitol Building—reminded many of war or revolution, and deeply disturbed an already Depression-addled nation. Perhaps most heart-wrenching of all was the sight of men who had once served together now fighting each other in the nation's capitol. Washington

World War I veterans confront Washington, DC police during the Bonus March of 1932. (Courtesy of the National Archives)

police chief Pelham Glassford had commanded an artillery unit in France, and many of his policemen were veterans. Among the army officers participating in the operation was Dwight D. Eisenhower, who served as MacArthur's aid, and George S. Patton Jr., who led the troops to the Anacostia Flats. As the remnants of Camp Marks smoldered on the morning of July 29, one of the Bonus Marchers came to see Patton. It was Joseph T. Angelo, the man who had saved his life in battle at Cheppy during the Meuse-Argonne Offensive (see Chapter 13). Patton claimed not to know the man and gruffly sent him away. He later confided to a group of officers that he did indeed know Angelo, and in fact had been helping him financially. "Can you imagine the headlines if the papers got wind of our meeting here this morning?" Patton asked, and added that he would "continue to take care of him." The abandoned buildings of Camp Glassford were demolished soon after the Bonus March as planned. The National Gallery of Art and the Federal Trade Commission now occupy the sites. Camp Marks is now part of Anacostia Park, a unit of the National Park Service. There are no historical markers or monuments identifying the locations of the tragic events.

The story of the Bonus Army did not end at the Anacostia Flats. Hoover's successor, Franklin D. Roosevelt, also opposed an early bonus, and in fact slashed veterans' programs as an economy measure. However, Roosevelt carved out room for veterans in many of his Depression-fighting New Deal programs, such as the work camps of the Civilian Conservation Corps (CCC) and the Federal Emergency Relief Agency (FERA). Veterans were usually glad for the work, though some viewed them with a suspicious eye. CCC and FERA often undertook construction projects in remote areas like national parks, leading critics to charge that Roosevelt was simply trying to remove potential agitators from society to avoid another Bonus March. Such criticism increased after the Labor Day 1935 tragedy in the Florida Keys. That summer, FERA put veterans to work on improving the Overseas Highway connecting the Key West with the mainland. The veterans worked from camps strung out from Windley Key to Lower Matecumbe, quarrying stone and pounding pilings for the highway. Work continued over Labor Day weekend, and though there were signs of an approaching storm, FERA managers took few precautions until it was too late. The hurricane that hit the Florida Keys on September 2, 1935, was one of the most powerful on record, and the veterans were stranded on the Keys to face it with nowhere to go. Winds whipped the veterans' camps, and the storm surge washed over them. By the time it was over 257 veterans had been killed, as were 259 local residents. An outraged Key West resident named Ernest Hemingway was quoted as claiming that "the hurricane did the job as well as Herbie Hoover did at Anacostia Flats." At the intersection of U.S. Highway 1 and Johnston Street on Upper Matecumbe Key is a memorial to those killed in the tragedy. Made of locally quarried stone, the twenty-foot-high monument resembles a Mayan temple. On its face is a relief sculpture of windblown palm trees and a rough seascape. Below the monument is a crypt holding the remains of veterans and civilians who died in the tragedy.

In 1936 the veterans finally got their early bonus payment, and the lessons of the bonus fight were not lost on America's political leaders as the nation entered World War II. In that conflict, sixteen million Americans wore the uniform—three times as many as served in World War I—comprising 10 percent of the entire U.S. population. World War II promised an even bigger wave of veterans, and political leaders feared that maladjusted ex-soldiers might pose an even bigger social problem for the nation than was the case after the First World War. There were plenty of ideas floating around wartime Washington about how to help World War II veterans return to civilian life more smoothly, but it was the American Legion—drawing upon the experiences of Great War veterans—that put the ideas all together into a single package. In Room 507 of the Mayflower Hotel (1127 Connecticut Avenue NW) in Washington, Harry W. Colmery, a former American Legion national commander and member of its legislative committee, wrote out a draft on hotel stationery of a comprehensive package of benefits for World War II veterans. Among his proposals were unemployment compensation for veterans who could not find work, home and business loans, and educational assistance. The American Legion called it the "G.I. Bill of Rights," and sent it to Congress, where it got a very warm reception. In June 1944, President Roosevelt signed the Serviceman's Readjustment Act, better known as the G.I. Bill of Rights, into law. The law was remarkably successful, and nearly every major piece of veterans' legislation since World War II has been patterned on the G.I. Bill—another legacy of the Great War that still reverberates through American society today.

Communities across America Memorialize the Doughboy

Almost immediately after the war ended on November 11, 1918, the commemorations began. Doughboy statues went up in parks and town squares all across the United States, joining Billy Yank or Johnny Reb from the Civil War. Scores of communities purchased a mass-produced sculpture by artist E. M. Viquesney called *Spirit of the American Doughboy*. Viquesney's Doughboy was in full combat gear, holding his rifle in his left hand and a grenade high in his right. Viquesney also offered a work entitled *Spirit of the American Navy*, but that one did not sell nearly as well. By one estimate, 10 percent of all World War I memorials in the United States were his creations. More than 150 of them still stand in public places across the country, from Aberdeen, Washington, to Sinton, Texas, to Lincoln, Maine. Most people today walk past them and barely notice. There were other kinds of memorials. Some communities displayed weaponry, like big artillery guns. Edward M. Coffman, America's foremost scholar of World War I, remembered of growing up in small-town Kentucky in the 1930s that "the captured German field piece that graced the courthouse yard was a magnate for small boys. I know I sent a few imaginary rounds downrange myself." Coffman also recalled that his church had "a large panel with the names of all the members who had served" with "the two who had died lettered in gold." Parks and playgrounds, highways, and many other places were named in honor of the Great War veterans.

Larger communities erected more elaborate monuments. As early as 1919, a group of prominent citizens in Kansas City, Missouri, began a campaign to build a Great War memorial in their city. They raised $2.5 million in just two weeks, and selected a spot on a hill above Union Station, overlooking downtown Kansas City. Construction began in 1921, and among those on hand for the groundbreaking ceremony were General Pershing and Marshal

Foch. They called it the Liberty Memorial. It was dedicated on Armistice Day 1926, and President Calvin Coolidge gave the dedicatory address. Architect Harold Van Buren Magonigle designed it in an Egyptian Revival style. Dominating the memorial terrace is a 217-foot cylindrical tower. Four forty-foot-tall guardian spirits by sculptor Robert Aitken decorate its sides. Atop the tower is an observation deck, and at night, lights and steam simulate a torch called the Flame of Inspiration. Flanking the tower are two buildings guarded by Assyrian Sphinxes. For many years these buildings hosted a Great War museum. Over the years the Liberty Memorial fell into disrepair. Restoration efforts began in the 1990s, and among the results was a greatly expanded museum. Beneath the Liberty Memorial today is the National World War I Museum, which opened in 2006. This is not just the largest museum in the United States dedicated to the Great War, but Congress has granted it the status of being America's "official" World War I museum. The museum looks at the Great War in its totality, not just the American involvement. The vast collection of items on display is mindboggling, and ranges from tanks and artillery pieces to postcards and shaving kits. Life-size dioramas and interactive tables add further to the sensory experience of the museum. It is one of the most impressive war museums anywhere in the world.

Indianapolis also began planning a memorial in 1919. Its memorial project was in part an effort to convince the American Legion to locate its national headquarters in that city. It took several years to get the project off and running, but General Pershing laid the cornerstone for the Indiana World War Memorial on July 4, 1927, and it was completed in 1933. The Cleveland architectural firm of Walker and Weeks designed it in the classical Greek style, inspired by the ancient Greek Mausoleum of Halicarnassus. The Indiana World War Memorial is a square structure with a pyramidal top, rising 210 feet high. The exterior of Indiana limestone, with its graceful classical columns and Art Deco relief sculptures, is impressive enough, but the main highlights are inside. The heart of the memorial is the Shrine Room, built of materials from all over the world to symbolize the global nature of the Great War. Red Vermont marble columns, forty feet high, represent the blood spilled during the war. A marble altar occupies the center of the room, and suspended from the ceiling is a large star made of Swedish crystal. Below the star hangs a huge American flag. A marble frieze with Great War imagery encircles the room. In addition to the Shrine Room, the memorial building also holds a meeting space called the Pershing Auditorium, and the Indiana War Museum, which preserves Hoosier State military history. Outside of the building, a grassy memorial mall stretches north for three blocks. Now known simply as the Indiana War Memorial, the building and grounds are among the dominant

Indiana World War Memorial, Indianapolis, Indiana.

and impressive features of downtown Indianapolis.

And the plan to lure the American Legion worked. At its 1919 Minneapolis convention, the Legionnaires voted to locate its national headquarters in Indianapolis—long before construction on the memorial even began. Today American Legion headquarters is located on the mall north of the Indiana War Memorial at 700 North Pennsylvania Street. Visitors are welcome to stop in and see the Emil A. Blackmore Museum, on the fourth floor of the building. This museum contains a wide range of war trophies that members brought home over the years (including a good number from the First World War), but what makes it special is its collection of American Legion memorabilia, which few military museums ever exhibit. There are uniforms, badges, and ceremonial accoutrements, like the gavel from the first Legion convention in Minneapolis. The Legion's political connections are also evident. On display is a pair of beautiful blue vases with the American Legion emblem embossed on them, presented by French President Albert Lebrun in 1937, as well as a painting of President (and American Legion member) Harry S. Truman. Just steps away from the Legion headquarters, at the head of the memorial mall along East St. Clair Street, is one more Hoosier tribute to the Great War. The red marble cenotaph there, guarded by four gilded eagles on red marble columns, was intended to be the final resting place of James B. Gresham of Evansville, Indiana—one of the first three American soldiers killed in ground combat at Bathelémont-lès-Bauzemont, France, in November 1917 (see Chapter 7). The Gresham family ultimately decided to leave the soldier where he lay at Locust Hill Cemetery in Evansville, but the cenotaph is still there, now dedicated to all of Indiana's Great War dead.

The American Battle Monuments Commission concentrated its memorialization efforts overseas (see Introduction), but it maintains one Great War memorial in the nation's capital, just a few blocks from the White House. The American Expeditionary Forces Memorial is in Pershing Park, on Pennsylvania Avenue between 14th and 15th Streets. This memorial consists of two red granite walls at a right angle, accompanied by a life-size statue of General Pershing. Etched into the walls is plenty of text describing the course of American involvement in World War I, along with a map of American battlefields. Central Washington has a few more Great War memorials, though they are scattered. The Society of the

1st Infantry Division veterans erected a memorial on 17th Street NW, in front of the Old Executive Building. Architects Cass Gilbert and Daniel Chester French designed a seventy-eight-foot marble shaft, capped with a gilded victory statue, which was dedicated in 1924. In 1936, the 2nd Division veterans also erected a memorial not far away, on Constitution Avenue on the Ellipse. It features a gilded flaming sword, symbolizing the division's defense of Paris in the summer of 1918. In both cases, additions commemorate later wars. The District of Columbia memorial to its Great War dead lies south of the reflecting pool on the Mall, just a few hundred yards east of the Lincoln Memorial. A marble temple, it was dedicated in 1931 and was the first war memorial on the Mall, which is now strewn with memorials to twentieth-century wars. The Korean and Vietnam War memorials are just to the west. The World War II memorial is just steps away to the east. Sadly, perhaps, the gallery of war memorials on the west end of the Mall does not include a national memorial dedicated specifically to the Great War, the first of America's twentieth-century conflicts.

The most sacred of all American war memorials, the Tomb of the Unknown Soldier in Arlington National Cemetery outside Washington, also has its origins in the First World War. On Armistice Day 1920, France interred the remains of an unidentified soldier beneath the Arch de Triomphe in Paris. Congressman Hamilton Fish of New York, who had served as a white officer in the Harlem Hell Fighters regiment, thought the gesture moving. "I wanted America," he explained in his memoirs, "as a beacon of freedom and democracy, to have her own memorial to honor the Unknown Soldier." In December 1920, Fish introduced a resolution in Congress for the interment of an unknown American service member from the Great War in Arlington National Cemetery, at a spot overlooking the city below the Memorial Amphitheater. Congress heartily approved. In October 1921, coffins containing the unidentified remains of four Doughboys from four U.S. cemeteries in France (Aisne-Marne, Meuse-Argonne, Saint-Mihiel, and the Somme) were brought to the city hall of Châlons-sur-Marne (now Châlons-en-Champagne). In an elaborate ceremony on October 24, Sergeant Edward F. Younger picked one of them to return home. As an army band played a hymn, Younger walked around the coffins with a white rose in his hand. He circled them three times and then suddenly stopped. "It was as though something pulled me," he later said. "A voice seemed to say, 'this is a pal of yours.'" By placing the rose on the coffin before him, Younger selected America's Unknown Soldier. The chosen soldier was then transported through Paris to Le Havre and transferred to the U.S.S. *Olympia* for the voyage back to America. The French navy fired a 17-gun salute as the *Olympia* headed out to sea.

The *Olympia* arrived in at the Washington Navy Yard on November 9. The Unknown Soldier lay in state in the Capitol, where 90,000 filed past to pay their respects. Then, on the morning of November 11, he was brought to Arlington National Cemetery in an elaborate funeral cortege that included President Harding and former president Woodrow Wilson, who, having suffered a stroke two years earlier, rode in a horse-drawn carriage. The eight pall-bearers came from every branch of service, and among them were three Medal of Honor recipients: Alvin York, Samuel Woodfill, and Charles Whittlesey. (Tragically, Whittlesey took his own life just weeks later, jumping off a cruise ship bound for Havana.) The interment ceremony began at midday. The Unknown Soldier was placed in the apse of the amphitheater, and after a two-minute silence President Harding spoke. "He might have come from any one of millions of American homes," he said, speculating that per-haps "hundreds of mothers are wondering today, finding a touch of solace in the possibility that the nation bows in grief over the body of one she bore." The president told the crowd that he could "sense the prayers of our people, of all people, that this Armistice Day shall mark the beginning of a new and lasting era of peace on earth." A slew of military decorations were then placed on the casket, includ-ing the Congressional Medal of Honor. The Unknown Soldier was then carried to the grave. Reverend Charles Brent, who had served as chief chaplain of the AEF, conducted the graveside ceremony. Congressman Fish laid a wreath on the casket, and Chief Plenty Coups of the Crow Nation, representing all Native American tribes, briefly lay a war bonnet and coup stick on the coffin. Then an honor guard fired a 21-gun salute as the casket was lowered into the grave. It came to rest on a layer of soil brought from France.

The 3rd Infantry Regiment of the U.S. Army keeps constant watch over the tomb, and conducts an elaborate changing of the guard ceremony every day on the hour—and every half hour in the summer. The Tomb of the Unknown Soldier has been expanded over the years. The marble sarcophagus above the tomb was added in 1926. Etched into the stone are the words, "Here rests in honored glory an American soldier known but to God." Unknowns from World War II and Korea were added in later years. So was a Vietnam unknown but, thanks to DNA testing, his remains were later iden-tified. The amphitheater above the tomb includes an exhibit hall dedicated to what is now called the Tomb of the Unknowns. Among the items on display is the war bonnet and coup stick Chief Plenty Coups placed on the casket at the 1921 interment ceremony.

After the war, more than 2,000 of America's Great War dead were brought to Arlington from the battlefield cemeteries of France and reinterred in Section 18, in the southwestern corner of the grounds. In their honor, a patriotic society called the American

Women's Legion erected a thirteen-foot-high cross made of Vermont marble. Known as the Argonne Cross, it was originally encircled with pine trees from the Argonne forest, but they have since died. Over the years, as the Great War generation passed on, more and more World War I veterans joined their old comrades in Section 18. Among those buried there is Frank Buckles, America's last surviving World War I veteran, who passed away on February 27, 2011. Just to the east of Section 18 is Section 34, and atop a knoll in that portion of the cemetery is a solitary, ordinary government tombstone. It marks the final resting place of General John J. Pershing, who died in 1948. In death as in life, Pershing is near, but yet somewhat distant from, the men he commanded.

Grave of General John J. Pershing, Arlington National Cemetery. In the background is Section 18, where World War I veteran burials are concentrated.

The War to End All Wars did not live up to its name, of course, and in fact Americans soon forgot about it. Its unfulfilled promises led to disillusion. The rise of totalitarian communism and fascism in the 1920s and 1930s, which the war had spawned, seemed to only make the world *less* safe for democracy, and the war's utter savagery shook the confidence of millions around the world in the progress of civilization. America's Lost Generation writers were not alone in their criticism of the war. Artists on both sides of the Atlantic—many of whom were Great War veterans themselves—began to portray the world in far more skeptical terms. Certainly African Americans felt disappointment. Despite serving and fighting to make the world "safe for democracy," black America found that freedom would still be denied them at home. By the 1930s, with the nation suffering through Great Depression and another war looming in Europe, isolationist sentiment in the U.S. was on the rise. Many Americans came to believe that Britain and France had tricked the United States into going to war in 1917, or that arms manufacturers, in conjunction with bankers and other so-called "merchants of death," had led the nation to the war for profit. According to a 1937 Gallup public opinion poll, 70 percent of Americans believed that U.S. entry into World War I had been a mistake.

When World War II finally came, it was vastly greater in scope—something that seemed impossible in 1918—and consumed every ounce of the nation's attention. Edward M. Coffman noted the erosion of the Great War's memory in his small Kentucky town during the 1940s. "The German gun went into the scrap drive," he recalled. "There was no longer in the schools a minute of silence on November 11; and the panel in my church disappeared into storage while virtually everyone we knew of military age went into the service." Even beyond its mindboggling scale, World War II gave us bad guys that were fascinatingly bad, and it ended in an unambiguous unconditional surrender. The First World War has never been able to escape the shadow of World War II. In the decades since, Hollywood and historians alike turned their attention to World War II, portraying the First World War (if at all) as little more than the warm-up act. As the years went on, the Great War receded even further back into America's national memory. The 50th Anniversary of American involvement in the Great War came in 1967 and 1968, as the United States was mired in the divisive days of the Vietnam War. "The United States was caught up in an unpopular war," wrote Professor Coffman, "and had little sympathy for much less knowledge of the events and the veterans of World War I." Unlike the well-deserved tributes that "Greatest Generation" received during the 50th anniversary of World War II in the 1990s, the golden anniversary of the Great War in the United States went unnoticed and uncommemorated.

It has now been a century since the Great War, and Americans have another opportunity to reflect upon its immense impact on their nation. The questions it raised about issues like America's place in the world, the balance between security and civil liberties, and the impact of technological change of the battlefield all have relevance to the nation today. Most importantly of all, the Great War centennial gives America another chance to rediscover the Doughboys. Most were unwilling warriors who, when called to duty, threw themselves into the task with energy and enthusiasm. They were the first Americans to experience the unspeakable horrors of industrialized warfare full force. They helped bring the United States into the modern world, and may well have won the war. Reminders of the Doughboys are all around us, if we only bother to look.

APPENDIX A:
AMERICAN BATTLE MONUMENTS COMMISSION

The American Battle Monuments Commission maintains eight overseas cemeteries for the Great War dead. Each has a visitor reception center, where travelers can get more information about ABMC monuments in the area and other sites of interest. Below is a list of the cemeteries with contact information:

Aisne-Marne American Cemetery
02400 Belleau, France
www.abmc.gov/cemeteries/cemeteries/am.php

Brookwood American Cemetery
Brookwood, Surrey
GU 240 BL England
www.abmc.gov/cemeteries/cemeteries/bk.php

Flanders Field American Cemetery
Wortegemseweg 117
B-8790 Waregem, Belgium
www.abmc.gov/cemeteries/cemeteries/ff.php

Meuse-Argonne American Cemetery
55110 Romagne-sous-Montfaucon, France
www.abmc.gov/cemeteries/cemeteries/ma.php

Oise-Aisne American Cemetery
02130 Fère-en-Tardenois, France
www.abmc.gov/cemeteries/cemeteries/oa.php

Somme American Cemetery
rue de Macquincourt
02420 Bony France
www.abmc.gov/cemeteries/cemeteries/so.php

Saint-Mihiel American Cemetery
route de Verdun
54470 Thiaucourt, France
www.abmc.gov/cemeteries/cemeteries/sm.php

Suresnes American Cemetery
323 boulevard Washington
920150 Suresnes, France
www.abmc.gov/cemeteries/cemeteries/su.php

ABMC Main Office:

Courthouse Plaza II, Suite 500
2300 Clarendon Boulevard
Arlington, VA 22201
www.abmc.gov

APPENDIX B:
BOOKS

Hundreds of Doughboy memoirs and unit histories, as well as thousands of pages of wartime government publications, have been digitized and are available free of charge on the following websites:

Google Books
books.google.com

Hathitrust Digital Library
www.hathitrust.org

Internet Archive
www.archive.org

Project Gutenberg
www.gutenberg.org

Below are some selected historical studies on the American military experience in the Great War for further reading:

American Battle Monuments Commission. *American Armies and Battlefields in Europe: A History, Guide, and Reference Book.* Washington: Government Printing Office, 1938.

Badger, Reid. *A Life in Ragtime: A Biography of James Reese Europe.* New York: Oxford University Press, 1995.

Barnes, Alexander. *In A Strange Land: The American Occupation of Germany, 1918–1923.* Altglen, PA: Schiffer, 2011.

Braim, Paul. *The Test of Battle: The American Expeditionary Forces in the Meuse-Argonne Campaign.* Newark, DE: University of Delaware Press, 1987.

Bruce, Robert. *A Fraternity of Arms: America and France in the Great War.* Lawrence, KS: University of Kansas Press, 2003.

Budreau, Lisa M. *Bodies of War: World War I and the Politics of Commemoration in America, 1919–1933.* New York: New York University Press, 2010.

Byerly, Carol R. *Fever of War: The Influenza Epidemic in the U.S. Army during World War I.* New York: New York University Press, 2005.

Clark, George. *Devil Dogs: Fighting Marines of World War I*. Novato, CA: Presidio, 1999.

Coffman, Edward M. *The War to End All Wars: The American Military Experience in World War I*. Madison: University of Wisconsin Press, 1986.

Dickon, Chris. *The Foreign Burial of American War Dead*. Jefferson, NC: McFarland, 2011.

Eisenhower, John S.D. *Yanks: The Epic Story of the American Army in World War I*. New York: Free Press, 2001.

Ellis, John. *Eye Deep in Hell: Trench Warfare in World War I*. Baltimore: Johns Hopkins University Press, 1976.

Farwell, Byron. *Over There: The United States in the Great War, 1917–1918*. New York: Norton, 1999.

Faulkner, Richard S. *The School of Hard Knocks: Combat Leadership in the American Expeditionary Forces*. College Station: Texas A&M University Press, 2012.

Ferrell, Robert. *Unjustly Dishonored: An African American Division in World War I*. Columbia: University of Missouri Press, 2011.

Feuer, A.B. *The U.S. Navy in World War I: Combat at Sea and in the Air*. Westport, CT: Praeger, 1999.

Ford, Nancy Gentile. *Americans All!: Foreign-born Soldiers in World War I*. College Station: Texas A&M University Press, 2001. Gavin, Lettie. *American Women in World War I: They Also Served*. Niwot: University of Colorado Press, 1997.

Grotelueschen, Mark E. *The AEF Way of War: The American Army and Combat in World War I*. New York: Cambridge University Press, 2007.

Gutiérrez, Edward. Doughboys on the Great War: How American Soldiers Viewed Their Military Experience. Lawrence: University Press of Kansas, 2014.

Hallas, James H., ed. *Doughboy War: The American Expeditionary Force in WWI*. Mechanicsburg, PA: Stackpole Books, 2000.

Harris, Stephen L. *Harlem's Hell Fighters: The African-American 369th Infantry in World War I*. Washington: Brassey's, 2003.

Hudson, James J. *Hostile Skies: A Combat History of the American Air Service in World War I*. Syracuse, NY: Syracuse University Press, 1968.

Keene, Jennifer D. *Doughboys, the Great War, and the Remaking of America*. Baltimore: Johns Hopkins University Press, 2001.

Keene, Jennifer D. *World War I: The American Soldier Experience*. Lincoln: University of Nebraska Press, 2011.

Kennett, Lee. *The First Air War, 1914–1918*. New York: Free Press, 1991.

Klim, Jake. *Attack on Orleans: The World War I Submarine Raid on Cape Cod*. Charleston, SC: History Press, 2014.

Lacey, Jim. *Pershing*. New York: Palgrave Macmillan, 2008.

Lee, David D. *Sergeant York: An American Hero*. Lexington: University of Kentucky Press, 1985.

Lengel, Edward G. *To Conquer Hell: The Meuse-Argonne, 1918*. New York: Holt, 2008.

Mastriano, Douglas. *Alvin York: A New Biography of the Hero of the Argonne*. Lexington: University Press of Kentucky, 2014.

Mead, Gary. Doughboys: *America and the First World War*. New York: Overlook, 2000.

Meigs, Mark. *Optimism at Armageddon: Voices of American Participants in the First World War*. New York: New York University Press, 1997.

Nouailhat, Yves Henri. *Les Américains à Nantes et Saint-Nazaire, 1917–1919*. Paris: Les Belles Lettres, 1972.

Rubin, Richard. *The Last of the Doughboys: The Forgotten Generation and Their Forgotten World War*. Boston: Houghton Mifflin Harcourt, 2013.

Shellum, Brian G. *Black Officer in a Buffalo Soldier Regiment: The Military Career of Charles Young*. Lincoln: University of Nebraska Press, 2010.

Slotkin, Richard. *Lost Battalions: The Great War and the Crisis of American Nationality*. New York: Holt, 2005.

Smythe, Donald. *Pershing: General of the Armies*. Bloomington: Indiana University Press, 1986.

Snell, Mark. Unknown Soldiers: The American Expeditionary Forces in Memory and Remembrance. Kent, OH: Kent State University Press, 2008.

Stallings, Laurence. *The Doughboys: The Story of the AEF, 1917-1918*. New York: Harper & Row, 1963.

Zieger, Robert H. *America's Great War: World War I and the American Experience*. Lanham, MD: Rowman and Littlefield, 2000.

APPENDIX C:
MEMORIALS, MUSEUMS, AND HISTORICAL SITES

There are thousands of Great War memorials around the world. Those dedicated to the American Doughboy have been erected by federal, state, and local governments, as well as private individuals and veterans organizations. There is no comprehensive listing of them, but there are several valuable websites that can help travelers locate U.S.-related Great War monuments big and small:

American War Memorials Overseas
www.uswarmemorials.org

E. M. Viquesnay Doughboy Database
doughboysearcher.weebly.com

Monuments, Memorials, and Cemeteries of the AEF (The Doughboy Center)
www.worldwar1.com/dbc/monument.htm

World War I Memorial Inventory Project
wwi-inventory.org

Hundreds of museums and historic sites around the world preserve the physical remnants of the U.S. Great War experience. These places frequently change their exhibits, hours, and admission prices, so travelers would be wise to plan ahead before visiting. Many are located on active military installations, and visitors will have to meet security requirements before gaining admission. Below is a list of museums and historic sites mentioned in this text or that have substantial exhibits on the U.S. participation in the First World War.

Canada

Shearwater Aviation Museum
12 Wing
PO Box 5000 Station Main
Shearwater, Nova Scotia B0J 3A0
www.shearwateraviationmuseum.ns.ca

France

14-18 Nantillois
7 Grande rue
55270 Nantillois
www.14-18nantillois.com

American Cathedral in Paris
23 avenue George V
75008 Paris
www.americancathedral.org

Caverne du Dragon
Chemin des Dames
02160 Oulches-la-Vallée-Foulon
www.caverne-du-dragon.com

Centre d'interprétation de Suippes
4 Ruelle Bayard
51600 Suippes
www.marne14-18.fr

Historial de la Grande Guerre
Château de Péronne BP 20063
80201 Péronne
en.historial.org

Musée de l'Argonne
9 rue Louis XVI
55270 Varennes-en-Argonne

Musée de la Grande Guerre
rue Lazare Ponticelli
77110 Meaux
www.museedelagrandeguerre.eu

Musée de la Mémoire de Belleau 1914-1918
place du Général Pershing
02400 Belleau
www.musee-memoire-souvenir-belleau.com

Musée de Sologne
Moulin du Chapitre
41200 Romorantin-Lanthenay
www.museedesologne.com

Musée du Costume Militaire
4 rue Neuve
54470 Thiaucourt-Regniéville

Musée Franco-Américain du Château de Blérancourt
Château de Blérancourt
02300 Blérancourt
www.museefrancoamericain.fr

Musée Mémorial de Sommepy
Mairie-20 rue Foch
51600 Sommepy-Tahure
champagne1418.pagesperso-orange.fr/circuit/circuitsouain/museesom-
mepy/musee.htm

Musée National de la Marine-Brest
Château de Brest
29200 Brest
www.musee-marine.fr/brest

Romagne '14-'18
2 rue de l'Andon
55110 Romagne-sous-Montfaucon
www.romagne14-18.com

Germany

Festung Ehrenbreitstein
56077 Koblenz
www.diefestungehrenbreitstein.de

Friedensmuseum Brücke von Remagen
An der Alten Rheinbrücke 11/Rheinpromenade
53424 Remagen
www.bruecke-remagen.de

Great Britain

Brookwood Cemetery
Glades House
Cemetery Pales
Brookwood, Woking, Surrey GU24 0BL
www.brookwoodcemetery.com

Merseyside Maritime Museum
Albert Dock
Liverpool L3 4AQ
www.liverpoolmuseums.org.uk/maritime

Museum of Islay Life
Port Charlotte
Isle of Islay PA48 7UA
www.islaymuseum.org

Ireland

Cobh Heritage Center
Deep Water Quay
Cobh, County Cork
www.cobhheritage.com

Cobh Museum
Scots Church, High Road
Cobh, County Cork
www.cobhmuseum.com

The *Titanic* Trail
Melleiha Carrignafoy
Cobh, County Cork
www.titanic.ie

United States

NORTHEAST
Army Reserve Mobilization Museum
Fort Dix, NJ 08640
www.dix.army.mil/Army_Reserve_Museum/default.html

Boston National Historic Park
Charlestown Navy Yard
Boston, MA 02129
www.nps.gov/bost/contacts.htm

Brookhaven National Laboratory
PO Box 5000
Upton, NY 11973
www.bnl.gov

Camp Hero State Park
1898 Old Montauk Highway
Montauk, NY 11954
nysparks.com/parks/97/details.aspx

Cape Cod National Seashore
99 Marconi Site Road
Wellfleet, MA 02667
www.nps.gov/caco/index.htm

Cape Henlopen State Park
15099 Cape Henlopen Drive
Lewes, DE 19958
www.destateparks.com/park/cape-henlopen/

Clinton County Historical Association and Museum
98 Ohio Avenue
Plattsburgh, NY 12901
www.clintoncountyhistorical.org

Cradle of Aviation Museum
Charles Lindbergh Boulevard
Garden City, NY 11530
www.cradleofaviation.org

Eisenhower National Historic Site
1195 Baltimore Pike
Gettysburg, PA 17325
www.nps.gov/eise/index.htm

Fort Devens Museum
94 Jackson Road
Devens, MA 01434-4011
www.fortdevensmuseum.org

Fort George G. Meade Museum
4674 Griffin Avenue
Fort Meade, MD 20755
www.ftmeade.army.mil/Museum/Index.htm

Gateway National Recreation Area
210 New York Avenue
Staten Island, NY 10305
www.nps.gov/gate/index.htm

Gettysburg National Military Park
1195 Baltimore Pike, Suite 100
Gettysburg, PA 17325
www.nps.gov/gett/index.htm

Independence Seaport Museum
211 S. Christopher Columbus Boulevard
Philadelphia, PA 19106
www.phillyseaport.org

Liberty State Park
Morris Pesin Drive
Jersey City, NJ 07305
www.libertystatepark.org

National Air and Space Museum
600 Independence Avenue SW
Washington, DC 20560
airandspace.si.edu

National Guard Memorial Museum
One Massachusetts Avenue NW
Washington, D.C. 20001
www.ngaus.org/national-guard-memorial-museum

National Museum of American History
14th St and Constitution Avenue NW
Washington, DC 20001
americanhistory.si.edu

National Museum of the United States Navy
736 Sicard Street SE
Washington, DC 20374
www.history.navy.mil/branches/org8-1.htm

Old Croton Aqueduct State Historic Park
15 Walnut Street
Dobbs Ferry, NY 10522
nysparks.com/parks/96/details.aspx

Old Rhinebeck Aerodrome
9 Norton Road
Red Hook, NY 12571
www.oldrhinebeck.org

Palisades Interstate Park
PO Box 155
Alpine, NJ 07620
www.njpalisades.org

Sleepy Hollow Cemetery
540 N. Broadway
Sleepy Hollow, NY 10591
www.sleepyhollowcemetery.org

United States Naval Academy Museum
Preble Hall, 118 Maryland Avenue
Annapolis, MD 21402
www.usna.edu/Museum

West Point Museum
2110 New South Post Road
West Point, NY 10996
www.usma.edu/museum

MIDWEST
Bronzeville Visitor Information Center
3501 South Martin Luther King Drive
Suite One East
Chicago, IL 60653
http://www.bviconline.info

Camp Grant Museum
1004 Samuelson Road
Rockford, IL 61109
campgrantmuseum.weebly.com

Charles Young Buffalo Soldiers National Monument
1120 U.S. Route 42 East, U.S. 42
Wilberforce, OH 45385
www.nps.gov/chyo/index.htm

Dayton Aviation Heritage National Historical Park
16 S. Williams Street
Dayton, OH 45402
www.nps.gov/daav/index.htm

EAA AirVenture Museum
3000 Poberezny Road
Oshkosh, WI 54901
www.airventuremuseum.org

Emil A. Blackmore Museum
American Legion National Headquarters
700 N. Pennsylvania Avenue
Indianapolis, IN 46204
www.legion.org/library/museum

First Division Museum at Cantigny
1s151 Winfield Road
Wheaton, IL 60189-3353
www.firstdivisionmuseum.org

Fort Des Moines Museum and Education Center
75 E. Army Post Road
Des Moines, IA 50315

Great Lakes Naval Museum
610 Farragut Avenue
Great Lakes, IL 60088
www.history.navy.mil/museums/greatlakes/index.htm

Harry Truman Presidential Library and Museum
500 W. U.S. Highway 24
Independence, MO 64050
www.trumanlibrary.org

Hopewell Culture National Historical Park
16062 Ohio 104
Chillicothe, OH 45601
www.nps.gov/hocu

Indiana War Memorial
431 N. Meridian Street
Indianapolis, IN 46204
www.in.gov/iwm/

Iowa Gold Star Military Museum
7105 Northwest 70th Avenue
Johnston, IA 50131-1824
www.iowanationalguard.com/History/Museum/Pages/home.aspx

Mitchell Gallery of Flight
General Mitchell International Airport
5300 S. Howell Avenue
Milwaukee, WI 53207
www.mitchellgallery.org

Mott's Military Museum
5075 S. Hamilton Road
Groveport, OH 43125
www.mottsmilitarymuseum.org

National World War I Museum
100 W. 26 Street
Kansas City, MO 64108
theworldwar.org

National Museum of the U.S. Air Force
1100 Spaatz Street
Wright-Patterson AFB OH 45433
www.nationalmuseum.af.mil

Pershing Boyhood Home State Historic Park
1100 Pershing Drive
Laclede, MO 64651-0141
www.mostateparks.com/park/gen-john-j-pershing-boyhood-home-state-
historic-site

Seth Atwood Park
2685 New Milford School Road
Rockford, IL 61109
www.rockfordparkdistrict.org/atwood

Wisconsin Veterans Museum
30 West Mifflin Street
Madison, WI 53703
www.wisvetsmuseum.com

South

82nd Airborne Division Museum
5108 Ardennes Road
Fort Bragg, NC 28301
82ndairbornedivisionmuseum.com

African American Military History Museum
305 E. 6th Street
Hattiesburg, MS 39401
www.hattiesburguso.com

Alvin C. York State Historic Park
Pall Mall, TN 38577
tnstateparks.com/parks/about/sgt-alvin-c-york

Anderson County Museum
202 E. Greenville Street
Anderson, SC 29624
andersoncountymuseum.org

Arkansas National Guard Museum
6th & Missouri, Camp Robinson
North Little Rock, AR 72199
www.arngmuseum.com

Big Bend National Park
PO Box 129
Big Bend National Park, TX 79834
www.nps.gov/bibe/contacts.htm

Buffalo Soldiers National Museum
3816 Caroline Street
Houston, TX 77004
buffalosoldiersmuseum.com/cms/

Battleship *Texas* State Historic Site
3523 Independence Pkwy.
La Porte, TX 77571
www.tpwd.state.tx.us/state-parks/battleship-texas

Call Field Museum
Wichita Falls Municipal Airport
4000 Armstrong Drive
Wichita Falls, TX 76305
www.museumofnorthtexashistory.org/call-field-exhibit.html

Fort Sam Houston Museum
1210 Stanley Road, Building 123
Fort Sam Houston, TX 78234

Fort Sill Museum
435 Quanah Road
Fort Sill, OK 73503
sill-www.army.mil/museum/FSNHLM/aboutus.html

Frontiers of Flight Museum
6911 Lemmon Avenue
Dallas, TX 75209
www.flightmuseum.com

General George S. Patton Museum of Leadership
4554 Fayette Avenue
Fort Knox, KY 40121
www.generalpatton.org

Hampton Roads Naval Museum
One Waterside Drive
Norfolk, VA 23510-1607
www.hrnm.navy.mil

MacArthur Memorial
MacArthur Square
Norfolk, VA 23510
www.macarthurmemorial.org

Mariners' Museum
100 Museum Drive
Newport News, VA 23601
www.marinersmuseum.org

Mountain Longleaf National Wildlife Refuge
PO Box 5087
Fort McClellan, AL 36205
www.fws.gov/southeast/mountainlongleaf/

Mississippi Armed Forces Museum
Building 850
Camp Shelby, MS
www.armedforcesmuseum.us/Pages/Home.html

National Infantry Museum
1775 Legacy Way #220
Columbus, GA 31903
www.nationalinfantrymuseum.org

National Naval Aviation Museum
1750 Radford Boulevard
NAS Pensacola, FL 32508
www.navalaviationmuseum.org

National Museum of the Marine Corps
18900 Jefferson Davis Highway
Triangle, VA 22134
www.usmcmuseum.org

Parris Island Museum
Bldg. #111, Marine Corps Recruit Depot
Parris Island, SC 29905
parrisislandmuseum.com

Signal Corps Museum
504 Chamberlain Avenue
Fort Gordon, GA 30905
www.signal.army.mil/ocos/museum

South Carolina Confederate Relic Room and Military Museum
301 Gervais Street
Columbia, SC 29201
www.crr.sc.gov/Pages/default.aspx

Tennessee State Museum
505 Deaderick Street
Nashville, TN 37243
www.tnmuseum.org

U.S. Army Basic Combat Training Museum
Building 4442, Jackson Boulevard
Ft Jackson, SC 29207
www.jackson.army.mil/sites/garrison/pages/673

U.S. Army Quartermaster Museum
2220 Adams Avenue, Building 5218
Fort Lee, VA 23801-1601
www.qmmuseum.lee.army.mil

U.S. Army Women's Museum
2100 A Avenue
Fort Lee, VA 23801
www.awm.lee.army.mil

USAF Airman Heritage Center
PO Box 761422
San Antonio TX 78245-6422
www.myairmanmuseum.org

Virginia War Museum
9285 Warwick Boulevard
Newport News, VA 23607
www.warmuseum.org

Woodrow Wilson Presidential Library and Museum
20 N. Coalter Street
Staunton, VA 24401
www.woodrowwilson.org

WEST
Columbus Historical Museum
New Mexico 9
Columbus, NM 88029
www.columbushistoricalsociety.org

Fort Assiniboine
c/o Havre Area Chamber of Commerce
130 5th Avenue
Havre, MT 59501
www.havremt.com/attractions/fort_assinniboine.htm

Fort Bayard Historical Preservation Society
PO Box 14
Silver City, NM 88062
www.fortbayard.org/index.html

Fort Huachuca Museum
41401 Grierson Avenue
Fort Huachuca, AZ 85613
huachucamuseum.com

Fort Lewis Museum
PO Box 331001
Fort Lewis, WA 98433-1001
www.fortlewismuseum.com

Fort Stanton State Historic Site
PO Box 1
104 Kit Carson Rd
Fort Stanton, NM 88323
fortstanton.org

Fort Vancouver National Historic Site
612 E. Reserve Street
Vancouver, WA 98661
www.nps.gov/fova

March Field Air Museum
22550 Van Buren Boulevard
March Air Reserve Base, CA 92518
www.marchfield.org

Museum of Flight
9404 East Marginal Way South
Seattle, WA 98108
www.museumofflight.org

Olympic National Park
3002 Mount Angeles Road
Port Angeles, WA 98362
www.nps.gov/olym/index.htm

Pancho Villa State Park
400 West Highway 9
Columbus, NM 88029
www.emnrd.state.nm.us/SPD/panchovillastatepark.html

Pimeria Alta Historical Museum
136 North Grand Avenue
Nogales, AZ 85621
www.pimeriaaltamuseum.com

Presidio of San Francisco National Historic Site
Golden Gate National Recreation Area
Fort Mason, Building 201
San Francisco, CA 94123
www.nps.gov/prsf/index.htm

Vintage Aero Flying Museum
7125 Parks Lane
Fort Lupton, CO 80621
www.vafm.org

APPENDIX D:
HISTORICAL SOCIETIES AND TOURISM AUTHORITIES

Below is a list of historical societies and tourism authorities mentioned in the text, as well as others that can also provide guidance to travelers seeking out the American Great War experience. Several regional tourist authorities in Europe have developed special programs and tours for the Great War Centennial.

369th Historical Society
www.369historicalsociety.org

Aisne Tourism
www.evasion-aisne.com

Brittany Tourism
www.brittanytourism.com

Camp Taylor Historical Society
camptaylorhistorical.org

Champagne-Ardenne Tourism
www.champagne-ardenne-tourism.co.uk

Cobh Tourism
visitcobh.com

First Aero Squadron Foundation
firstaerosquadron.com

Gibraltar Tourism
www.visitgibraltar.gi

Houston Archeological Society
www.txhas.org

Islay Ultimate Online Guide
www.islayinfo.com

Koblenz Tourism
www.koblenz-touristik.de

Lafayette Escadrille Memorial Foundation
rdisa.pagesperso-orange.fr

Langres Regional Tourism
www.tourisme-langres.com

Liverpool History Society
www.liverpoolhistorysociety.org.uk

Loire Valley Tourism
www.loirevalleytourism.com

London Tourism
www.visitlondon.com

Lorraine Tourism
www.tourism-lorraine.com

Meurthe and Moselle Tourism
www.tourisme-meurtheetmoselle.fr

Meuse Tourism
www.meusetourism.com/

Paris Tourism
en.parisinfo.com

Picardy Tourism
www.picardietourisme.com

Royal Society for the Protection of Birds—The Oa
www.rspb.org.uk/reserves/guide/t/theoa/

Reims Tourism
www.reims-tourisme.com

Saint-Nazaire Tourism
visit-saint-nazaire.com

Sergeant York Discovery Expedition
sgtyorkdiscovery.com

Sergeant York Patriotic Foundation
www.sgtyork.org

APPENDIX D: HISTORICAL SOCIETIES AND TOURISM AUTHORITIES

Sergeant York Project
www.sergeantyorkproject.com

Somme Tourism
www.visit-somme.com

To Honour A Promise
www.tohonourapromise.co.uk

Verdun Tourism
www.en.verdun-tourisme.com

Ypres Tourism
www.toerismeieper.be

INDEX
OF PLACE NAMES